Complete German Course for First Examinations

L. J. RUSSON M.A.

LONGMAN

by A. Russon and L.J. Russon
Advanced German Course
Key to Advanced German Course

LONGMAN GROUP UK LIMITED
Longman House
Burnt Mill, Harlow, Essex CM20 2JE, England
and Associated Companies throughout the world

© Longman Group UK Ltd 1948

Second edition 1967
Thirteenth impression 1988

ISBN 0-582-36160-5

Produced by Longman Singapore Publishers Pte Ltd
Printed in Singapore

Preface to the Second Edition

This new edition has made it possible to make a number of changes without, however, affecting to any serious extent the pagination of the book.

The major change has been the substitution of Roman for Gothic throughout. As no books or newspapers are now printed in Gothic it seemed pointless to preserve this feature of the earlier edition. However, since quite a number of books in libraries are in Gothic it will still be necessary for many years to come for some of our students to be able to read it; and to help them to do this a passage in Gothic is printed in this edition with a line-by-line equivalent in Roman on the page opposite.

Most of the changes have been made in the section on grammar. Within the limits imposed by the necessity to make it possible to use this new edition alongside the earlier one the opportunity has been seized (i) to take into account the changes in the German language, and in the attitude towards it, that have taken place in the last few decades; (ii) to formulate more accurate statements about the German language, eliminating ambiguities and rephrasing examples; and (iii) to indicate where necessary the differences between the spoken and the written language.

I am very much indebted to our former German Assistant, Herr Schwöbel, for reading through the grammar section with a very critical eye and pointing out everything that struck him as in the least old-fashioned or incorrect; to my colleague, Mr J. R. Surry, for his very careful scrutiny of the grammar section in particular and for his many valuable suggestions; and above all to my wife for her unlimited patience and sound judgement.

In conclusion I should say that among the many books of reference I have consulted I have found the publications of the Dudenredaktion, particularly the *Duden-Grammatik* and *Hauptschwierigkeiten der deutschen Sprache*, outstandingly useful. I have also consulted the Dudenredaktion on several points not dealt with in their publications, and should like to thank them for their detailed and helpful answers.

L. J. R.

Winchester, 1967

Acknowledgements

We are grateful to the following for permission to include copyright material:

S. Fisher Verlag for an extract from 'Der blinde Geronimo und sein Bruder' by Arthur Schnitzler from *Arthur Schnitzler Gesammelte Werke, Die erzählenden Schriften, Erster Band,* © S. Fischer Verlag, Frankfurt am Main, 1961, and for the poem 'Elternlied' from Franz Werfel *Das lyrische Werk* (containing formerly published and posthumous poems), © S. Fischer Verlag GmbH, Frankfurt am Main, 1967; Insel Verlag, Frankfurt am Main, for two extracts by Hans Carossa, the poem 'Die Beiden' by Hugo von Hofmannsthal, three poems – 'Herbsttag', 'Der König' and 'Die Erblindende' by R. M. Rilke, and the poem 'Der alte Gärtner' by Richard Schaukal; Insel-Verlag Anton Kippenberg, Leipzig, for the poem 'Frieden' by R. Huch; Verlag Helmut Kupper (Georg Bondi) for the poem 'Jahrestag' by Stefan George from *Stefan George: Werke*; Longmans Green & Co. Ltd for extracts from the simplified versions of *Robinson Crusoe, Quentin Durward, Gulliver's Travels,* simplified for New Method Supplementary Reader Series by Dr M. West; Dr Wilhelm von Scholz for an extract from *Der wilde Ritt*; Mrs Sondheimer-Herrmann for the poem 'Ein deutscher Dichter bin ich einst gewesen' by her late husband, Max Herrmann-Neisse; Suhrkamp Verlag for short passages (re-titled) from *Weg nach Innen* by Hermann Hesse; Vera Tugel-Dehmel for the poem 'Manche Nacht' by Richard Dehmel; and Paul Zsolnay Verlag for two extracts from *Die Verdammten* by Frank Thieß.

Contents

Abbreviations and Signs used

A	accusative; governs accusative
AD	governs accusative and/or dative
adj.	adjective
adv.	adverb
AG	governs accusative and genitive
cf.	compare
cond.	conditional
conj.	conjunction
D	dative; governs dative
e.g.	for example
etc.	etcetera
f.	feminine
fut.	future
G	genitive; governs genitive
i.e.	that is
imper.	imperative
impf.	imperfect
ind.	indicative
intr.	intransitive
irr.	irregular
lit.	literally
m.	masculine
N	nominative
n.	neuter
Nr.	*Nummer* (= number)
o.s.	oneself
P	followed by prepositional object
p.	page
part.	participle
pers.	person
pf.	perfect
pl.	plural
plpf.	pluperfect
prep.	preposition

pres.	present
pron.	pronoun
S	*Seite* (= page)
s.	strong verb
s.b.	somebody
s.th.	something
subj.	subjunctive
tr.	transitive
viz.	namely

*	conjugated with *sein*
(*)	conjugated with *sein* or *haben* according to meaning
>	becomes
+	plus
-	inserted between prefix and verb indicates that the verb is separable

Section One

Grammar

Word Order[1]

1 Main Clauses

In a sentence consisting of one **main** clause the FINITE VERB is always the **second** idea except:

(a) In questions **not** introduced by an interrogative adverb, adjective or pronoun (e.g. *wann? wer?* – see *44, 60–62*).

(b) In commands.

1	2			
Er	**liest**	mir	die Zeitung	vor.
He	*reads*	*to me*	*the paper*	*aloud.*
Jeden Tag	**hat**	er	die Zeitung	vorgelesen.
Every day	*has*	*he*	*the paper*	*aloud read.*
Die Zeitung	**wird**	er	gelesen	haben.
The paper	*will*	*he*	*read*	*have.*
Wann	**hat**	er	die Zeitung	gelesen?
When	*has*	*he*	*the paper*	*read?*

BUT				
(a) **Hat**	er	sie	schon	gelesen?
Has	*he*	*it*	*already*	*read?*
(b) **Lesen**	Sie	sie	jeden Tag	vor!
Read		*it*	*every day*	*aloud.*

NOTE: **All** infinitives, past participles and separable prefixes stand **last** in main clauses.

2 Compound Sentences

In a sentence consisting of two or more **main** clauses (i.e., in a **compound** sentence) the FINITE VERB is the **second** idea in each clause, except after direct speech, when there is inversion of subject and verb.

---

[1] The 'English' renderings of the German examples in *1–4* are given in the word order of the original in order to show more strikingly the difference between English and German in this respect.

I	2			I	2	
Er	**stand**	auf	und	(er)	**ging**	aus.
He	*got*	*up*	*and*	*(he)*	*went*	*out.*
Er	**setzte**	sich,	aber	(er)	**sagte**	nichts.
He	*seated*	*himself*	*but*	*(he)*	*said*	*nothing.*
Er	**setzte**	sich,		(er)	**sagte**	aber nichts.
He	*seated*	*himself*		*(he)*	*said*	*however nothing*
Er	**las**	ein Buch,	und	ich	**schrieb**	Briefe.
He	*read*	*a book*	*and*	*I*	*wrote*	*letters.*
Er	**setzte**	sich,	und	dann	**las**	er Briefe.
He	*seated*	*himself*	*and*	*then*	*read*	*he letters.*
Er	**setzte**	sich,	denn	er	**war**	müde.
He	*seated*	*himself,*	*for*	*he*	*was*	*tired.*

BUT

„Ich **bin** müde", **sagte** · er.
'I am tired,' said he.

NOTE 1: In a compound sentence the main clauses are usually joined by a co-ordinating conjunction. (See 6.)

NOTE 2: The subject, if it is the same as in the first clause, may be omitted after *und*, *aber* and *sondern* in the second clause provided no other word precedes the verb.

NOTE 3: For explanation of the use of the comma, see *125(a)iii.*

3 Subordinate Clauses

In a **subordinate** clause the FINITE VERB is always the **last** word except:

(a) When there are two infinitives in the clause.
(b) When *wenn* is omitted in conditional clauses. (See *113(e).*)
(c) When *ob* or *wenn* are omitted in *als ob* or *als wenn* clauses. (See *114(b)iii.*)

Wenn	er	die Zeitung	**vorliest,** ...
When	*he*	*the paper*	*aloud reads* ...
(Der Mann),	der	sie	vorgelesen **hat,** ...
(The man)	*who*	*it*	*aloud read has* ...
(Ich fragte), wann	ich	sie	haben **könnte.**
I asked when	*I*	*it*	*have could.*

BUT

(a) Wenn	er	sie	**hätte**	lesen können, ...
If	*he*	*it*	*had*	*read been able to ...*

(b) **Hätte**   er   sie   gelesen, ...
     Had   *he*   *it*   *read* ...

(c) Als   **hätte**   er   sie   gelesen ...
     As though   *had*   *he*   *it*   *read* ...

NOTE: A subordinate clause is introduced by any one of the following:
    (a) A subordinating conjunction. (See 7(*a*).)
    (b) An interrogative pronoun or adverb in indirect questions. (See 7(*b*).)
    (c) A relative pronoun or adverb. (See 63–6.)

4 Complex Sentences

(a) When the main clause precedes the subordinate clause the FINITE VERB stands **second** in the **main** clause and **last** in the **subordinate** clause:

Er   **liest**   die Zeitung,   wenn   er   nach Hause   **kommt.**
He   *reads*   *the paper*   *when*   *he*   *home*   *comes.*

NOTE 1: If a subordinate clause is inserted in another the FINITE VERB goes to the **end** of **each subordinate** clause:

Er   sagte,   daß,   wenn   er   Zeit   **hätte,**   er   es   tun   **würde.**
He   *said*   *that*   *if*   *he*   *time*   *had*   *he*   *it*   *do*   *would.*

NOTE 2: When *daß* is omitted in indirect speech the FINITE VERB stands **second** in the **subordinate** clause:

Er   sagte,   er   **hätte**   keine   Zeit.
He   *said*   *he*   *had*   *no*   *time.*

(b) When the subordinate clause precedes the main clause the FINITE VERB stands **first** in the **main** clause, i.e. there is inversion of subject and verb:

		I	2		
Als er		**zurückkam,**	**war**	er sehr	müde.
When *he*		*back came*	*was*	*he very*	*tired.*
Nachdem er gegessen		**hatte,**	**las**	er die	Zeitung.
After *he* *eaten*		*had*	*read*	*he the*	*paper.*
Da er faul **ist** und nicht	**arbeitet,**		**macht**	er keine	Fort-schritte.
Since he lazy is and not	*works*		*makes*	*he no*	*progress.*
Wenn er es **hätte** tun	**können,**		**hätte**	er es	getan.
If *he* *it* *had* *do*	*been able to*		*would*	*have* *he it*	*done.*

(c) After a concessive clause introduced by the conjunctions *was* ...
auch, wie ... auch, wo ... auch, etc., where *auch* = 'ever' (therefore not after *wenn ... auch* = even if), there is **no inversion** of subject and verb in the **main** clause:

			1	2		
Was	er	auch	**sagt,**	ich	**glaube**	ihm nicht.
What	*he*	*ever*	*says,*	*I*	*believe*	*him not.*

5 Order of Words within the Clause

(a) DIRECT AND INDIRECT OBJECTS

i. If both objects are **nouns** the **indirect** (=dative) precedes the **direct** (=accusative):

1 2
Er gab dem Mann das Buch. *He gave the book to the man.*

ii. If both objects are **personal pronouns** the **direct** precedes the **indirect** (though *das* tends to follow):

1 2
Er gab es ihm. *He gave it to him.*

iii. If one object is a personal pronoun and the other a noun, the **pronoun,** whether accusative or dative, comes **first:**

1 2
Er gab es dem Mann. *He gave it to the man.*
Er gab ihm das Buch. *He gave the book to him.*

(b) ADVERBS AND ADVERBIAL PHRASES

i. The normal order of precedence is:

1. Adverbs of **Time.** 2. Adverbs of **Manner.** 3. Adverbs of **Place.**

1	2	3
TIME	MANNER	PLACE
Er fährt jeden Tag	mit dem Zug	zur Schule.

He goes to school every day by train.

ii. If there are several adverbial expressions of time or of place the more general usually comes first:

1	2	3
Er kommt jeden Tag	morgens	um 9 Uhr.

He comes at 9 o'clock in the morning every day.

Er ist draußen im Garten
He is outside in the garden.

Er bleibt jedes Jahr 4 Wochen bei uns.
He stays four weeks with us every year.

iii. Note that the adverb, unless it is the first word in the sentence, is preceded by all pronouns:

Gestern hat er sich sehr amüsiert. ⎫
Er hat **sich** gestern sehr amüsiert. ⎬ *He enjoyed himself yesterday.*

Ich gab **ihm** gestern das Buch.   *I gave him the book yesterday.*
Ich gab **es** gestern dem Mann.   *I gave it to the man yesterday.*
Ich gab **es ihm** gestern.   *I gave it to him yesterday.*

iv. In a subordinate clause the adverb usually precedes the predicative adjective or complement of the verb:

Da es **draußen** schön ist, ...   *Since it is fine outside ...*
Da **heute** schlechtes Wetter ist ...   *Since the weather is bad today ...*

(c) POSITION OF NICHT

i. In a negative **main** clause *nicht* immediately precedes the past participle, infinitive(s), separable prefix, predicative adjective or adverb or adverbial phrase of place, manner or degree. If none of these is present *nicht* is the last word.

Ich habe ihn **nicht** gesehen.   *I have not seen him.*
Hast du ihn **nicht** gesehen?   *Haven't you seen him?*
Ich kann heute **nicht** kommen.   *I can't come today.*
Ich hätte ihn **nicht** sehen sollen.   *I should not have seen him.*
Sehen Sie sich jetzt **nicht** um!   *Don't look round now.*
Es ist heute **nicht** kalt.   *It is not cold today.*
Er kam heute **nicht** zu Fuß.   *He didn't come on foot today.*
Ich sehe den Mann **nicht**.   *I don't see the man.*
Vergessen Sie mich **nicht**!   *Don't forget me.*

ii. In a negative **subordinate** clause *nicht* precedes the finite verb. If there is a past participle, infinitive(s) or predicative adjective, *nicht* precedes these:

Wenn ich es **nicht** tue, ...   *If I do not do it ...*
Wenn ich es **nicht** getan hätte, ...   *If I had not done it ...*
Wenn Sie **nicht** kommen kön-
nen, ...   *If you cannot come ...*

Wenn Sie **nicht** hätten kommen können, . . .	*If you had not been able to come . . .*
Wenn es **nicht** kalt wäre, . . .	*If it were not cold . . .*

iii. If a particular word in the sentence is to be negatived *nicht* immediately precedes that word:

Ich habe **nicht viel** gelesen.	*I haven't read **much**.*
Das ist **nicht mein** Buch.	*That is not **my** book.*
Kann ich **nicht heute** kommen?	*Can't I come **today**?*

(d) POSITION OF REFLEXIVE PRONOUN

i. In a **main** clause *sich*, etc., immediately follows the finite verb in statements; in questions the noun subject may come between the verb and *sich*:

Er setzt **sich** auf den Stuhl.	*He sits down on the chair.*
Hat er **sich** hingesetzt?	*Did he sit down?*
Hat **sich** der Mann (*or* der Mann **sich**) hingesetzt?	*Did the man sit down?*

ii. In a **subordinate** clause *sich*, etc., usually immediately follows the subject of the clause:

Da er (*or* der Mann) **sich** nicht amüsiert hat, . . .	*Since he (or the man) didn't enjoy himself . . .*

(e) After interjections separated by punctuation from the beginning of German sentences there is **no** inversion of subject and verb:

Ja, das ist wahr.	*Yes, that is true.*
Im Gegenteil, ich bin gelaufen.	*On the contrary, I ran.*
Ach! das wußte ich nicht.	*Oh! I didn't know that.*

(f) For word order with separable verbs, see *102(b)*.

Conjunctions

6 Co-ordinating Conjunctions

und	*and*	aber	*but, however*
denn	*for*	allein	*but, only (literary)*
oder	*or*	sondern	*but, on the contrary*

NOTE: Co-ordinating conjunctions do not alter the construction:

Du kannst es tun, **denn** es **ist** ganz einfach.	*You can do it, for it is quite simple.*
Da er gearbeitet hat **und** müde geworden **ist**, ist er schlafen gegangen.	*Since he has worked and has got tired he has gone to bed.*

7 Subordinating Conjunctions and Interrogatives

(a) SUBORDINATING CONJUNCTIONS

als	*when, as, than*	sobald⎫ sowie⎭	*as soon as*
als ob/wenn	*as if/though*	so daß	*so that (result)*
(an)statt daß	*instead of (+ gerund)*	sofern⎫ soweit⎭	*as far as*
ausgenom- men, wenn	*unless*	solange	*as long as*
bevor⎫ ehe⎭	*before*	sooft	*whenever*
		trotzdem	*despite the fact that*
bis	*till, until*	vorausgesetzt, daß	*provided that*
da	*since, as (causal)*	während	*while, whereas*
damit	*so that (purpose)*	was . . . auch	*whatever*
damit . . . nicht	*lest*	weil	*because*
daß	*that, so that*	wenn	*if, when, whenever*
erst, als/wenn	*not until*	wenn . . . auch	*even if*
falls	*in case, if*	wenn. . . nicht	*unless*
indem	*while, as*	wer . . . auch	*whoever*
nachdem	*after*	wie	*as (manner, time), when*
ob	*whether, if*		
obgleich⎫ obschon⎬ obwohl⎭	*although*	wie . . . auch	*however*
		wie sehr . . . auch	*however much*
ohne daß	*without (+gerund)*	wo . . . auch	*wherever*
seit⎫ seitdem⎭	*since (temporal)*	zumal	*especially as*

(b) INTERROGATIVE ADVERBS AND PRONOUNS INTRODUCING INDIRECT QUESTIONS

wann	*when*	was	*what*
warum⎫ weshalb⎭	*why*	wer	*who*
		wo	*where*
wie	*how*	woher	*where from*
wieviel	*how much/many*	wohin	*where to*
wie viele	*how many*	worin	*in what*
wie lange	*how long*	womit	*with what*
	etc.		etc.

NOTE: Subordinating conjunctions and interrogatives introducing indirect questions send the finite verb to the end of the clause:

Nachdem er gegessen **hatte**, ging er aus. *After he had eaten he went out.*

Er fragte ihn, **wann** er ausgehen **wollte**. *He asked him when he intended to go out.*

8 Some Difficult Conjunctions

AS

Da er große Eile hatte, blieb er nur kurze Zeit.
As (=since) he was in a great hurry he only stayed a short time.

Indem er das sagte, lächelte er.
As he said (=saying) that he smiled.

Als er ins Zimmer kam, schaltete er das Licht an.
As (=when) he came into the room he switched on the light.

Wie du siehst, habe ich geschlafen.
As (=in the way that) you see, I have been asleep.

BUT

Es ist nicht kalt, **aber** ich friere.
It is not cold but I am freezing. (=I, however, am freezing.)

Ich hoffte auf ihn, **allein** er kam nicht.
I counted on him but (=only, nevertheless) he did not come.

Ich fahre **nicht** mit dem Wagen, **sondern** gehe zu Fuß.
I do not go by car but (=on the contrary) walk.

Sie ist **nicht** schön, **sondern** häßlich.
She is not beautiful, but (=on the contrary) ugly.

Das sind nichts **als** leere Worte.
Those are nothing but empty words.

NOTE: *Sondern* is to be used when **all** the following conditions are fulfilled:

   (a) The first statement must be in the negative or imply a negative.
   (b) The second statement must contradict the first.
   (c) Each statement must have the same subject.

IF

Wenn du Lust hast, kannst du mitkommen.
If you care to you can come with us.

Ich weiß nicht, **ob** ich Zeit habe.
I do not know if (=whether) I have time.

SINCE

Da er klug ist, lernt er schnell.
Since (=as) he is clever he learns quickly.

Seitdem er die Schule verlassen hat, hat er keine Stelle gehabt.
Since (=since the time) he left school he has not had a job.

Es sind zwei Jahre, **daß** ich ihn nicht gesehen habe.
It is two years since I've seen him.

SO THAT

Gib mir einen Bleistift, **damit** ich schreiben kann.
Give me a pencil so that (=in order that) I can write.

Es hörte auf zu regnen, **so daß** wir ausgehen konnten.
It stopped raining, so that (=with the result that) we could go out.

WHEN

Wenn ich ihn sehe, werde ich mich freuen.
When I see him I shall be glad. (A future event.)

Wenn ich ihn sehe, freue ich mich.
When (=whenever) I see him I am glad.

Wenn ich ihn sah, freute ich mich.
When (=whenever) I saw him I used to be glad.

Als ich ihn sah, freute ich mich.
When I saw him, I was glad. (**One** occasion in the **past**.)

Sobald (*or* **nachdem**) Sie ihn gesehen haben, kommen Sie zurück!
When (=as soon as) you have seen him, come back.

Ich weiß nicht, **wann** er kommt.
I don't know when he's coming. (Indirect question.)

Kaum hatte er begonnen, {**da** (*or* **so**) wurde er unterbrochen.
{**als** er unterbrochen wurde.
Scarcely had he begun when he was interrupted.

Es gibt Augenblicke, **in denen** (*or* **wo** *or* **da**) man schweigen muß.
There are moments when one has to hold one's tongue.

WHILE

Indem er das sagte, sah er mich an.
(While) saying that he looked at me.
(Same subject in each clause; simultaneous actions of **short** duration.)

Während er sprach, sah er mich immerfort an.
Whilst he spoke he kept looking at me. (Simultaneous actions of some
duration.)

Während er das sagte, sah ich ihn ungläubig an.
Whilst he said that I looked at him incredulously. (Different subjects in
the two clauses.)

9

9 Adverbial Conjunctions

also	⎱		dennoch ⎱	
daher	⎰		(je)doch ⎰	*yet, nevertheless*
darum	⎱	*therefore, and so*	indes(sen) ⎱	
deshalb	⎰		unterdessen ⎰	*meanwhile*
so			kaum	*hardly*
auch		*also, and (too)*	sonst	*otherwise, or else*
auch . . . nicht	*nor, not . . . either*		trotzdem	*in spite of that*
außerdem	*besides*		übrigens	*moreover, besides, anyhow*
da		*then, so*	zwar	*to be sure, it is true*

NOTE: When adverbial conjunctions begin a sentence, **inversion** of subject and verb usually takes place:

Auch arbeitet er **nicht**.	*Nor does he work.*
Da wußte ich, daß . . .	*So (then) I knew that . . .*
Daher hat er nichts getan.	*And so he did nothing.*
Zwar weiß ich viel, **doch** möcht' ich alles wissen.	*To be sure I know much, yet I would like to know everything.*
Kaum hatte er begonnen, da . . .	*Scarcely had he begun, when . . .*

10 Correlative Conjunctions

bald . . ., bald	*now . . . now*
entweder . . ., oder	*either . . . or*
je . . ., desto	*the (more) . . . the (more)*
nicht nur . . ., sondern auch	*not only . . . but also*
sowohl . . . als/wie auch	*both . . . and*
teils . . ., teils	*partly . . . partly; some . . . others*
weder . . . noch	*neither . . . nor*

(a) Connecting two clauses:

Bald regnet es, **bald** schneit **es**.
Now it rains, now it snows.

Teils kamen sie zu Fuß, **teils** kamen sie zu Pferde.
Some came on foot, others came on horseback.

Weder hat er uns geschrieben, **noch** ist er zu uns gekommen.
He has neither written to us nor visited us. (Same subject in each clause.)

Weder er hat geschrieben, **noch** sie hat von sich hören lassen.
Neither he has written nor has she given any news of herself. (Different subjects in the two clauses.)

Entweder du sagst (*or* sagst du) es ihm, **oder** ich tue es.
Either you tell him or I shall.

Je älter man wird, **desto** klüger wird man.
The older one gets the shrewder one becomes.

(b) Connecting two subjects, objects or predicative adjectives with one verb, or two verbs with one subject:

Sowohl Kohle **als/wie auch** Eisen sind dort vorhanden.
Both coal and iron are to be found there.

Mit Kohle kann man **sowohl** heizen **als/wie auch** kochen.
With coal you can heat as well as cook.

Weder er **noch** ich **können** es tun.
Neither he nor I can do it.

Er hat **weder** geschrieben **noch** angerufen.
He neither wrote nor rang up.

Es gibt **entweder** Tee **oder** Kaffee.
There is either tea or coffee.

Er hat es **entweder** gekauft **oder** gemietet.
He has either bought it or rented it.

Sie besitzt **nicht nur** Schönheit, **sondern auch** Mut.
She has not only beauty but also courage.

Sie ist **nicht nur** schön, **sondern auch** mutig.
She is not only beautiful but also brave.

Er zahlte **teils** mit Geld, **teils** mit Gut.
He paid partly in cash, partly in kind.

The Articles

11 Declension of the Definite Article

	sing.			pl.
	m.	f.	n.	m.f.n.
N.	der	die	das	die
A.	den	die	das	die
G.	des	der	des	der
D.	dem	der	dem	den

12 Declension of the Indefinite Article and its Negative

| | sing. | | | sing. | | | pl. |
	m.	*f.*	*n.*	*m.*	*f.*	*n.*	*m.f.n.*
N.	ein	eine	ein	kein	keine	kein	keine
A.	einen	eine	ein	keinen	keine	kein	keine
G.	eines	einer	eines	keines	keiner	keines	keiner
D.	einem	einer	einem	keinem	keiner	keinem	keinen

13 Use of the Definite Article

The **definite article** is normally required:

(a) In definitions:

Der Baum ist eine Pflanze.   *A tree is a plant.*

(b) Before abstract nouns in generalising statements:

Die Zeit vergeht schnell.   *Time passes quickly.*

(c) When a proper noun is preceded by an adjective:

der kleine Paul   *little Paul*
das moderne Deutschland   *modern Germany*

(d) In quotations of prices:

2 Mark **das** Kilo; 3 Mark **das** Stück   *2 marks a kilo; 3 marks each (apiece)*

(e) Before names of rivers, mountains, lakes, streets, squares and buildings:

der Rhein; **die** Themse   *the Rhine; the Thames*
die Zugspitze; **der** Bodensee   *the Zugspitze; Lake Constance*
die Schloßstraße; **die** Paulskirche; **der** Alexanderplatz   *Castle Street; St Paul's Church; Alexander Square*

(f) Before names denoting periods of time and meals, especially when governed by a preposition:

der Herbst; **der** August   *Autumn; August*
im Herbst; **im** August; **am** Montag   *in autumn; in August; on Monday*
am Morgen; nach **dem** Frühstück   *in (on) the morning; after breakfast*

NOTE: The contracted form of preposition and definite article (cf. *84*, note 1; *86(a)*, note 1; *87(a)*, note) is obligatory in such time expressions.

(g) Before names of parts of the body and of clothing when these refer to the subject of the sentence and are **not** qualified by an adjective:

Ich hob **die** Hand.	*I raised my hand.*
Er kam ins Zimmer, **die** Hände in **den** Taschen.	*He came into the room with his hands in his pockets.*

BUT Er öffnete seine müden Augen.   *He opened his tired eyes.*

(h) As in (g) above, the possessor being indicated by the dative pronoun (cf. *103*):

Er hat **mir das** Leben gerettet.	*He saved my life.*
Ich wusch **mir die** Hände.	*I washed my hands.*

(i) Before names of countries and provinces which are feminine or plural:

die Schweiz; **die** Niederlande   *Switzerland; Holland*

BUT Deutschland; Preußen   *Germany; Prussia*

NOTE: **das** Elsaß (*Alsace*).

(j) In certain stock phrases (cf. also *86, 87*):

in **der** Schule; in **der** Stadt	*in school; in town*
im Bett; aus **dem** Bett	*in bed; out of bed*
in **der** Tat; **den** Mut verlieren	*indeed; lose courage*
im allgemeinen	*in general, as a rule*
zur Schule; **zur** Kirche	*to school; to church*
mit **der** Bahn; mit **dem** Schiff	*by rail; by boat*

14 Omission of the Article

(a) After *sein, werden* and *bleiben* the article may be omitted before nouns denoting a person's profession or nationality:

Er ist Deutscher.	*He is a German.*
Er will Arzt werden.	*He wants to be(come) a doctor.*
Er blieb Soldat.	*He remained a soldier.*

NOTE: If such nouns are qualified by an adjective the article is required:
Er ist ein berühmter Arzt.   *He is a famous doctor.*

(14)

(b) The article is usually omitted in proverbs:

Gewalt geht vor Recht.   *Might is right.*

(c) The partitive article (**some, any**) is usually not translated except by *kein* when this is the only word showing that the sentence is negative:

Ich habe Brot.	*I have **some** bread.*
Er hat vom Brot gegessen.	*He ate **some** of the bread.*
Haben Sie Eier gekauft?	*Did you buy **any** eggs?*
Ich trinke nie Milch.	*I never drink **any** milk.*
BUT Ich habe keine Milch.	*I haven't **any** milk.*

NOTE: *Some* when stressed may be rendered by *etwas* (sing.) or *einige* (pl.):
Ich habe etwas Brot.   *I have **some** bread (= a bit of bread).*
Ich habe einige Freunde.   *I have **some** friends (= a few friends).*

(d) Common expressions which do not contain the article:

Er hat Angst (Furcht) vor (D) . . .	*He is afraid of . . .*
Er hat guten Appetit.	*He has a good appetite.*
Wir haben Besuch.	*We have a visitor (or visitors).*
Er ist auf/zu Besuch bei . . .	*He is on a visit at . . .*
Er geht auf/zu Besuch zu . . .	*He goes on a visit to . . .*
Er hat (großen) Durst.	*He is (very) thirsty.*
Er hat keinen Durst.	*He is not thirsty.*
Er hat keine/große Eile.	*He is in no/a great hurry.*
Er ist immer in Eile.	*He is always in a hurry.*
Er kam zu Ende.	*He came to an/the end.*
Sie haben Fieber.	*You have a temperature.*
Er hat (großen) Hunger.	*He is (very) hungry.*
Er hat Kopfschmerzen.	*He has a headache.*
Ich habe (keine) Lust.	*I (don't) feel inclined to.*
Du hast recht/unrecht.[1]	*You are right/wrong.*
(Es ist) schade.[1]	*It is a pity.*
Er hat Schmerzen.	*He is in pain.*
Er sprach mit lauter Stimme.	*He spoke in a loud voice.*
Er ist in guter (schlechter) Stim-mung.	*He is in a good (bad) mood.*

[1] These nouns are now written with small letters.

Nouns

15 The Gender of Nouns [1]

It is very often not possible to tell the gender of a German noun from its meaning or form. The following rules, however, will help in many cases.

(a) MASCULINE

i. Names of seasons, months and days (*52*) and of points of the compass, e.g. *der Herbst, Mai, Montag, Norden.*

ii. The suffixes *-ig* and *-ling* (Group Ia), and *-er*, denoting persons (Group Ic), e.g. *der König, Frühling, Dichter.*

iii. Most nouns ending in *-en*, e.g. *der Morgen.* (Exceptions: *das Eisen, das Zeichen*; all infinitives used as nouns; and all diminutives in *-chen.*) These belong to Group Ic.

(b) FEMININE

i. Names of most fruits and trees, e.g. *die Birne, die Eiche.* (Exceptions: *der Apfel* and nouns ending in *-baum.*)

ii. All nouns ending in the suffixes *-ei, -ie, -ik, -in, -ion, -heit, -keit, -schaft, -tät,* and *-ung,* e.g. *die Chemie, Musik, Königin, Schönheit, Universität, Zeitung.*

iii. Most nouns ending in *-e*, especially abstract nouns, e.g. *die Farbe, Brücke.* (Exceptions: masculine nouns in Groups II and IIIb; neuter nouns in Group IIIa.)

NOTE: The suffix *-in* added to certain masculine nouns (particularly to those ending in *-er*) gives the feminine equivalent of them, e.g. *Lehrer > Lehrerin*; *Bauer > Bäuerin.* Such nouns usually modify the vowel if possible. (See *19(b)(ii)*.)

(c) NEUTER

i. Names of continents and of most towns and countries (see *25*), e.g. *das alte Berlin, das moderne Frankreich.*

ii. Names of most metals, e.g. *das Eisen, das Gold.* (Exceptions: *der Stahl, die Bronze.*)

iii. All infinitives used as nouns (see *20(c)i*), e.g. *das Lesen.* (Exceptions: *der Gefallen,* favour; *der Braten,* roast joint.)

iv. The suffixes *-ment, -tum* and *-chen, -lein,* e.g. *das Parlament, Bistum* (bishopric), *Brötchen, Fräulein.* (Exceptions: *der Moment* (moment), *Irrtum, Reichtum.*)

NOTE: The suffixes *-chen* and *-lein* form diminutives, e.g. *Brot > Brötchen*, *Frau > Fräulein.* Such diminutives usually modify the vowel if possible.

[1] The groups refer to *16*.

16 The Declension of Nouns

	STRONG						WEAK	MIXED	
	Ia		**Ib**		**Ic**		**II**	**IIIa**	**IIIb**
	Pl. not modified	*Pl. modified*	*Pl. not modified*	*Pl. modified*	*Pl. not modified*	*Pl. modified*			
Masc. Sing.			(3)	(10)			(20)	(20)	(10)
N.	Tag	Sohn	Geist	Wald	Onkel	Apfel	Mensch	Staat	Name
A.	Tag	Sohn	Geist	Wald	Onkel	Apfel	Menschen	Staat	Namen
G.	Tag(e)s	Sohn(e)s	Geistes	Wald(e)s	Onkels	Apfels	Menschen	Staat(e)s	Namens
D.	Tag(e)	Sohn(e)	Geist(e)	Wald(e)	Onkel	Apfel	Menschen	Staat(e)	Namen
Pl.									
N.	Tage	Söhne	Geister	Wälder	Onkel	Äpfel	Menschen	Staaten	Namen
A.	Tage	Söhne	Geister	Wälder	Onkel	Äpfel	Menschen	Staaten	Namen
G.	Tage	Söhne	Geister	Wälder	Onkel	Äpfel	Menschen	Staaten	Namen
D.	Tagen	Söhnen	Geistern	Wäldern	Onkeln	Äpfeln	Menschen	Staaten	Namen
Fem. Sing.	(10)	(30)				(2)		(20)	
N.	Trübsal	Stadt	None	None	None	Mutter	Frau	Frau	None
A.	Trübsal	Stadt				Mutter	Frau	Frau	
G.	Trübsal	Stadt				Mutter	Frau	Frau	
D.	Trübsal	Stadt				Mutter	Frau	Frau	
Pl.									
N.	Trübsale	Städte	None		None	Mütter	Frauen	Frauen	None
A.	Trübsale	Städte				Mütter	Frauen	Frauen	
G.	Trübsale	Städte				Mütter	Frauen	Frauen	
D.	Trübsalen	Städten				Müttern	Frauen	Frauen	
Neut. Sing.		(1)	(10)		(1)	(1)		(7)	(1)
N.	Tier	Floß	Kind	Haus	Fenster	Kloster	None	Bett	Herz
A.	Tier	Floß	Kind	Haus	Fenster	Kloster		Bett	Herz
G.	Tier(e)s	Floßes	Kind(e)s	Hauses	Fensters	Klosters		Bett(e)s	Herzens
D.	Tier(e)	Floß(e)	Kind(e)	Haus(e)	Fenster	Kloster		Bett(e)	Herzen
Pl.									
N.	Tiere	Flöße	Kinder	Häuser	Fenster	Klöster	None	Betten	Herzen
A.	Tiere	Flöße	Kinder	Häuser	Fenster	Klöster		Betten	Herzen
G.	Tiere	Flöße	Kinder	Häuser	Fenster	Klöster		Betten	Herzen
D.	Tieren	Flößen	Kindern	Häusern	Fenstern	Klöstern		Betten	Herzen

NOTE: The approximate number of nouns, excluding compound nouns, in the various groups is given where this is not large.

17 Notes on the Declension of Nouns

(a) There are three types of declension:

i.   **Strong** masculine and neuter nouns are characterized by the termination -(e)s in the genitive singular. No feminine nouns inflect in the singular.

ii. **Weak** nouns are all masculine. They end in -(e)n in all the cases except the nominative singular.

iii. **Mixed** nouns resemble strong nouns in the singular and weak nouns in the plural.

(b) Masculine and neuter nouns ending in a sibilant, i.e. -s, ß, -z, -tz, -x and -sch, add **-es** in the genitive singular; those ending in -el, -en, -er and -lein (i.e. Groups Ic and IIIb) add **-s** only. The rest take either form, in conversation usually the shorter.

(c) The **-e** in the dative singular of masculine and neuter nouns of strong and mixed declension is optional except with nouns ending in -el, -en, -er and -lein (i.e. in Groups Ic and IIIb) when it **must** be omitted. It is usually omitted in conversation.

(d) Nouns ending in -chen and -lein (diminutives, all neuter) belong to Group Ic.

(e) Nouns ending in -nis (f. and n.) and in -in (f. only) double the final consonant before adding the plural endings.

(f) The accusative singular of all feminine and neuter nouns is the same as the nominative singular.

(g) The accusative and genitive plural of all nouns are the same as the nominative plural.

(h) In the dative plural **-n** is added to all nouns ending in -el and -er, and **-en** is added to all other nouns except those which end in -en or -lein like *Wagen* and *Fräulein*.

(i) No nouns in Groups II and III modify in the plural.

(j) A number of nouns of foreign derivation add -s to form the plural. There are other anomalous plurals. Cf. *21*.

18 Masculine Nouns

(a) GROUP IA (STRONG)

i. Declined like **Tag(-e)**, i.e. plural not modified:

Abend, *evening*	Gewinn, *profit, gain*	Schritt, *pace, step,*
Apparat, *set*	Griff, *grip, handle*	*yard*
Arm, *arm*	Halt, *halt, hold*	Schuh, *shoe, boot*
Aufenthalt, *stay*	Herbst, *autumn*	Sieg, *victory*
Aufstieg, *climb, rise*	Hund, *dog*	Sinn, *sense*
Bahnsteig, *platform*	Ingenieur, *engineer*	Stein, *stone*
Befehl, *command*	Jüngling, *youth*	Stern, *star*
Beginn, *beginning*	Kerl, *fellow, chap*	Stoff, *stuff, material*
Berg, *mountain, hill*	König, *king*	Streit, *quarrel, dispute*
Bericht, *report*	Kreis, *circle*	Tag, *day*
Besitz, *possession*	Krieg, *war*	Teich, *pond*
Besuch, *visit*	Laut, *sound*	Teil, *part, share*
Beweis, *proof*	Monat, *month*	Tisch, *table*
Bleistift, *pencil*	Mond, *moon*	Unterschied, *difference*
Blick, *glance, view*	(Omni)Bus,[1] *omnibus*	Vergleich, *comparison;*
Blitz, *lightning*	Ort, *place*	*agreement*
Brief, *letter*	Pfennig, *pfennig*	Verlust, *loss*
Dieb, *thief*	Preis, *price; prize*	Versuch, *attempt;*
Dienst, *service*	Punkt, *point, full stop*	*experiment*
Dom, *cathedral*	Reiz, *charm*	Weg, *way, road*
Druck, *print(ing)*	Ring, *ring*	Wein, *wine*
Erfolg, *success*	Roman, *novel*	Wert, *value, worth*
Feind, *enemy*	Ruf, *shout; repute*	Wind, *wind*
Film, *film*	Schein, *light; ticket;*	Wirt, *landlord, host*
Fisch, *fish*	*banknote*	Zweck, *purpose, point*
Freund, *friend*	Schirm, *screen, shade*	Zweig, *branch*
Frühling, *spring*	Schrei, *shout, scream*	Zwerg, *dwarf*

ii. Declined like **Sohn(-̈e)**, i.e. plural modified:

Arzt, *doctor*	Entschluß,[2] *decision*	Gebrauch, *use*
Ast, *branch, bough*	Fall, *case; fall*	Grund, *reason;*
Bach, *stream*	Fang, *capture, catch*	*ground, bottom*
Ball, *ball*	Flug, *flight*	Gruß, *greeting*
Baum, *tree*	Fluß,[2] *river*	Hals, *neck*
Beitrag, *contribution*	Fuß, *foot*	Hang, *slope; tendency*
Brauch, *custom*	Gang, *gait; passage*	Herzog, *duke*
Druck, *pressure*	Gast, *guest, visitor*	Hof, *court, yard; farm*

[1] Plural: (-se)   [2] Plural (-̈(ss)e)

Hut, *hat*	Rat, *councillor*	Strom, *wide river*
Kahn, *boat*	Raum, *space, room*	Strumpf, *stocking*
Kamm, *comb*	Rock, *coat; skirt*	Stuhl, *chair*
Kampf, *fight, struggle*	Saal,[1] *(big) room, hall*	Sturm, *storm, gale*
Kauf, *purchase*	Satz, *sentence; jump*	Sturz, *crash, overthrow*
Koch, *cook*	Schatz, *treasure*	Tanz, *dance*
Kopf, *head*	Schlag, *blow, stroke*	Ton, *tone, sound, note*
Korb, *basket*	Schluß,[2] *end, conclusion*	Traum, *dream*
Kuß,[2] *kiss*	Schrank, *cupboard*	Turm, *tower*
Lauf, *run, course*	Sohn, *son*	Verkauf, *sale*
Lohn, *wage, reward*	Spruch, *maxim; verdict*	Vorwand, *pretext*
Markt, *market*	Stab, *staff, stick*	Wunsch, *wish*
Plan, *plan*	Stall, *stable*	Zahn, *tooth*
Platz, *place, seat;*	Stand, *state; class;*	Zaun, *fence*
square	*profession*	Zug, *train; feature;*
Rang, *rank; balcony*	Stock, *stick; storey*[3]	*procession*

(b) GROUP IB (STRONG)

i. Declined like **Geist(-er)**, i.e. plural not modified:

Bösewicht, *villain*	Geist, *mind, spirit*	Leib, *body*

ii. Declined like **Wald(-er)**, i.e. plural modified:

Gott, *god*	Rand, *edge*	Vormund, *guardian*
Irrtum, *error*	Reichtum, *riches,*	Wald, *wood, forest*
Mann, *man, husband*	*wealth*	Wurm, *worm*
Mund, *mouth*	Strauch, *shrub, bush*	

(c) GROUP IC (STRONG)

i. Declined like **Onkel(-)**, i.e. plural not modified:

Apotheker, *chemist*	Fehler, *mistake; flaw*	Hügel, *hill*
Arbeiter, *workman*	Felsen, *rock*	Jäger, *huntsman*
Ausländer, *foreigner*	Finger, *finger*	Kaiser, *emperor*
Bäcker, *baker*	Fleischer, *butcher*	Käse, *cheese*
Besucher, *visitor*	Flügel, *wing; grand*	Keller, *cellar*
Bürger, *citizen*	*piano*	Kellner, *waiter*
Dampfer, *liner*	Führer, *leader, guide*	Koffer, *suitcase*
Dichter, *poet*	Füller, *fountain pen*	Körper, *body*
Diener, *servant*	Gegner, *opponent*	Kragen, *collar*
Einwohner, *inhabitant*	Gipfel, *mountain-top*	Kuchen, *cake*
Enkel, *grandson*	Händler, *dealer, trader*	Lehrer, *teacher*
Esel, *ass*	Haufen, *heap, crowd*	Löffel, *spoon*
Fahrer, *driver*	Himmel, *sky, heaven*	(-)macher, (-)*maker*

[1] Plural: *Säle*   [2] Plural: *(-(ss)e)*   [3] Plural: *Stockwerke*

(18)

Maler, *painter*
Meister, *master* (*123*)
Minister, *minister*
Morgen, *morning*
Nebel, *mist, fog*
Onkel, *uncle*
Pfarrer, *clergyman*
Räuber, *robber*
Redner, *speaker*
Reiter, *rider, horseman*
Richter, *judge*

Ritter, *knight*
Rücken, *back*
Schatten, *shadow,*
  shade
Schlüssel, *key*
Schneider, *tailor*
Schriftsteller, *writer*
Schüler, *schoolboy*
Sommer, *summer*
Spiegel, *mirror*

Spieler, *player,*
  gambler
Teller, *plate*
Titel, *title*
Träger, *porter; girder*
Wagen, *cart, car*
Wechsel, (*ex*)*change*
Winter, *winter*
Zuschauer, *spectator*
Zweifel, *doubt*

ii. Declined like **Apfel**(⸚), i.e. plural modified:

Apfel, *apple*
Boden, *ground; attic*
Bruder, *brother*
Garten, *garden*
Hafen, *harbour*
Hammer, *hammer*

Kasten, *box*
Laden, *shop; shutter*
Mangel, *lack, defect*
Mantel, *coat, cloak*
Nagel, *nail*
Ofen, *stove*

Sattel, *saddle*
Schaden, *damage,*
  injury
Vater, *father*
Vogel, *bird*

(d) **Group II (Weak)**, declined like **Mensch**(-en, -en) or **Junge**(-n, -n)

Affe, *monkey, ape*
Bär, *bear*
Bauer,[1,2] *peasant,*
  farmer
Bote, *messenger*
Buchstabe, *letter* (*of*
  alphabet)
Christ, *Christian*
Elefant, *elephant*
Erbe, *heir*
Fürst, *prince*
Gesell(e), *companion;*
  journeyman

Graf, *count*
Held, *hero*
Herr,[3] *gentleman,*
  master, lord, Mr.
Jude, *Jew*
Junge, *boy, lad*
Kamerad, *comrade,*
  chum
Knabe, *boy, lad*
Kunde, *customer*
Löwe, *lion*
Matrose, *sailor*
Mensch, *man, person*

Nachbar,[1,2] *neighbour*
Narr, *fool*
Neffe, *nephew*
Ochse, *ox*
Präsident, *president*
Prinz, (*royal*) *prince*
Riese, *giant*
Schurke, *scoundrel*
Sklave, *slave*
Soldat, *soldier*
Student, *student*
Zeuge, *witness*

(e) **Group IIIa (Mixed)**, declined like **Staat**(-(e)s, -en)

Schmerz, *pain, ache*
See,[4] *lake*

Staat, *state*
Strahl, *ray*

Vetter,[4] *cousin*

(f) **Group IIIb (Mixed)**, declined like **Name**(-ns, -n)

Friede,[5] *peace*
Gedanke, *thought, idea*

Glaube,[5] *belief*
Name, *name*

Wille,[5] *will*

---

[1] Also, more rarely, declined strong in the singular   [2] Declension: (-n, -n)
[3] Declension: (-n, -en)   [4] Plural: (-n)   [5] Rarely used in the plural

(g) Masculine Nouns normally used only in the Singular

Appetit, *appetite*	Kaffee, *coffee*	Stolz, *pride*
Atem, *breath*	Lärm, *noise, din*	Strand, *shore, beach*
Dank, *thanks*	Mut, *courage*	Süden, *south*
Donner, *thunder*	Norden, *north*	Tabak, *tobacco*
Durst, *thirst*	Osten, *east*	Tee, *tea*
Ernst, *seriousness*	Rauch, *smoke*	Trost, *consolation*
Fleiß, *diligence*	Regen, *rain*	Trotz, *defiance*
Hagel, *hail*	Schlaf, *sleep*	Unterricht, *instruction*
Handel, *trade,*	Schmutz, *dirt*	Verkehr, *traffic, inter-*
commerce	Schnee, *snow*	*course*
Haß, *hatred*	Schutz, *protection*	Westen, *west*
Hunger, *hunger*	Sport, *sport*	Zorn, *anger*
Inhalt, *contents*	Staub, *dust*	Zucker, *sugar*

19 Feminine Nouns

(a) GROUP IA (STRONG)

i. Declined like **Trübsal(-e)**, i.e. plural not modified:

Erlaubnis,[1] *permission*   Kenntnis,[1] *knowledge*   Trübsal, *affliction*
Finsternis,[1] *darkness*

ii. Declined like **Stadt(ِ-e)**, i.e. plural modified:

Angst, *fear*	Hand, *hand*	Maus, *mouse*
Ankunft, *arrival*	Haut, *skin*	Nacht, *night*
Axt, *axe*	Kraft, *strength*	Naht, *seam*
Bank, *bench*	Kuh, *cow*	Not, *need, distress*
Braut, *fiancée*	Kunst, *art*	Nuß,[2] *nut*
Brust, *breast, chest*	Luft, *air*	Schnur, *lace, string*
Faust, *fist*	Lust, *desire*	Stadt, *town, city*
Frucht, *fruit*	Macht, *power*	Wand, *(inner) wall*
Gans, *goose*	Magd, *serving-girl*	Wurst, *sausage*

(b) Group Ic (Strong), declined like **Mutter** (ِ-), i.e. plural modified:

Großmutter, *grand-*	Mutter, *mother*	Tochter, *daughter*
mother		

(c) Group III (Mixed), declined like **Frau(-en)** or **Ecke(-n)**:

NOTE 1: Nouns of this group ending in *-e, -er* and *-el* only add *-n* to form the plural.

NOTE 2: Many nouns of this group can, because of their meaning, only be used in the singular.

[1] Plural: (*-se*)   [2] Plural: (ِ-(*ss*)*e*)

i(α)

Antwort, *answer*
Apotheke, *chemist's shop*
Arbeit, *work*
Armut,[1] *poverty*
Art, *kind*
Bahn, *rail, track, path*
Bank, (*money*) *bank*
Bedingung, *condition* (*stipulation*)
Bibliothek, *library*
Birne, *pear; light-bulb*
Blume, *flower*
Brücke, *bridge*
Butter,[1] *butter*
Dame, *lady*
Ecke, *corner*
Eiche, *oak*
Erde, *earth, ground*
Fahrt, *ride, journey*
Familie, *family*
Farbe, *colour, paint*
Feder, *feather; pen*
Flasche, *bottle*

Frau, *woman, wife, Mrs*
Freude, *joy*
Furcht,[1] *fear*
Gabe, *gift*
Gabel, *fork*
Geburt, *birth*
Gefahr, *danger*
Gegend, *district*
Gegenwart,[1] *present* (*time*), *presence*
Gelegenheit, *opportunity*
Geschichte, (*hi*)*story*
Gestalt, *shape, figure*
Gewalt, *force, violence*
Grenze, *frontier*
Hälfte, *half*
Heimat,[1] *home*
Heirat, *marriage*
Hilfe, *help*
Hitze,[1] *heat*
Hütte, *cottage, hut*
Insel, *island*

Jacke, *jacket*
Jugend,[1] *youth*
Karte, *card, map*
Kartoffel, *potato*
Katze, *cat*
Kirche, *church*
Klasse, *class*
Kohle, *coal*
Kost,[1] *fare* (=*food*)
Kreide, *chalk*
Krone, *crown*
Küche, *kitchen*
Lage, *situation*
Lampe, *lamp*
Mahlzeit, *meal*
Mark,[1] *mark* (*coin*)
Marke, *brand; stamp*
Masse, *mass*
Mauer, (*outer*) *wall*
Medizin, *medicine*
Meile, *mile*
Menge, *crowd, lot*
Milch,[1] *milk*
Mitte, *middle*

i(β)

Mühe, *trouble*
Musik,[1] *music*
Mütze, *cap*
Nachricht, *news*
Nase, *nose*
Natur, *nature*
Nichte, *niece*
Nummer, *number* (*123*)
Person, *person*
Pflicht, *duty*
Polizei,[1] *police*
Post,[1] *post, mail*

Quelle, *source, spring*
Rolle, *role, part*
Rose, *rose*
Runde, *round*
Sache, *thing*
Scham,[1] *shame*
Schlacht, *battle*
Schrift, *writing*
Schublade, *drawer*
Schuld, *guilt; debt*
Schule, *school*
Schulter, *shoulder*
Schwester, *sister*

See, *sea*
Seele, *soul*
Seite, *side; page*
Sicht,[1] *sight* (*123*)
Sonne, *sun*
Sorte, *sort*
Sprache, *language*
Spur, *trace, sign*
Straße, *street*
Stufe, *step, stair*
Stunde, *hour; lesson*
Summe, *sum* (*of money*)

[1] Used only in the singular.

Suppe, *soup*	Tugend, *virtue*	Wiese, *meadow*
Tafel, (*black-*)*board*	Tür, *door*	Woche, *week*
Tanne, *fir*	Uhr, (*o'*)*clock, watch*	Wolke, *cloud*
Tante, *aunt*	Vergangenheit,[1] *past*	Zahl, *number, figure*
Tasche, *pocket*	Wahl, *choice, election*	(*123*)
Tasse, *cup*	Wange, *cheek*	Zeile, *line* (*of print*)
Tat, *deed*	Ware, *goods, wares*	Zeit, *time* (*123*)
Tinte, *ink*	Weile,[1] *while*	Zeitung, *newspaper*
Träne, *tear*	Weise, *manner; melody*	Zigarette, *cigarette*
Treppe, *staircase,*	Welle, *wave*	Zigarre, *cigar*
stairs	Welt, *world*	Zukunft,[1] *future*

ii. **Derivatives** from **masculine nouns** by the addition of **-in** (pl., **-innen**) and modification of vowel usually, if possible, e.g. **Arzt > Ärztin, Lehrer > Lehrerin**:

Arbeiterin, *work-*	Feindin, *enemy*	Kundin,[2] *customer*
woman	Freundin, (*girl*) *friend*	Lehrerin, *school-*
Ärztin, *lady-doctor*	Fürstin, *princess*	mistress
Ausländerin,	Gräfin, *countess*	Malerin,[2] *painter*
foreigner	Heldin, *heroine*	Nachbarin,[2] *neighbour*
Bäuerin, *peasant-*	Herrin, *mistress*	Prinzessin,[3] *princess*
woman	Herzogin,[2] *duchess*	Reiterin, *rider*
Bürgerin, *citizeness*	Jüdin, *Jewess*	Schülerin, *schoolgirl*
Dichterin, *poetess*	Kaiserin, *empress*	Sklavin,[2] *slave*
Enkelin, *grand-*	Kellnerin, *waitress*	Studentin, *girl-student*
daughter	Köchin, *cook*	Wirtin, *hostess*
Erbin, *heiress*	Königin, *queen*	Zeugin, *witness*

iii. **Derivatives** from **adjectives**:

(α) By the addition of **umlaut** (if possible) and **-e** (see *33(b)i*):

Blässe,[1] *pallor*	Größe, *size*	Nähe,[1] *vicinity*
Bläue,[1] *blueness*	Güte,[1] *goodness*	Schwäche, *weakness*
Breite, *width, latitude*	Höhe, *height*	Spitze, *point*
Ebene, *plain*	Höhle, *cavity, hollow,*	Stärke, *strength*
Ferne, *distance*	cave	Stille, *stillness*
Fläche, *flatness, plane*	Kälte,[1] *cold(ness)*	Strenge,[1] *severity*
Fremde,[1] *foreign parts*	Länge, *length, longi-*	Tiefe, *depth*
Frische,[1] *freshness*	tude	Treue,[1] *loyalty, troth*
Frühe,[1] *early morning*	Leere,[1] *emptiness*	Wärme,[1] *warmth*

[1] Used only in the singular   [2] Note no modification of vowel
[3] Note irregularity

(β) By the addition of **-heit** (see *33(b)ii*):

Dunkelheit,[1] *darkness*	Krankheit, *illness*	Vollkommenheit,
Einzelheit,[2] *detail*	Schönheit, *beauty*	*perfection*
Freiheit, *freedom*	Sicherheit, *certainty*	Wahrheit, *truth*
Gesundheit,[1] *health*		

(γ) By the addition of **-keit** (see *33(b)iii*):

Aufmerksamkeit,	Höflichkeit, *politeness*	Schwierigkeit,
attention	Möglichkeit, *possi-*	*difficulty*
Dankbarkeit,[1]	*bility*	Wahrscheinlichkeit,
gratitude	Notwendigkeit,	*probability*
Fähigkeit, *ability*	*necessity*	Wichtigkeit,[1]
Grausamkeit, *cruelty*	Pünktlichkeit,[1]	*importance*
Gründlichkeit,[1]	*punctuality*	Wirklichkeit, *reality*
thoroughness		

iv. **Derivatives** from **nouns, adjectives** or **verbal nouns** by the addition **-schaft**:

Bekanntschaft,	Gesellschaft, *company,*	Nachbarschaft,
acquaintance	*society, party*	*neighbourhood*
Eigenschaft, *quality*	Grafschaft, *county*	Wirtschaft, *household;*
Feindschaft, *hostility*	Landschaft, *landscape*	*housekeeping; inn*
Freundschaft,	Leidenschaft, *passion*	Wissenschaft, *science,*
friendship		*learning*

v. **Derivatives** from **verbs:**

(α) By the omission of the last letter of the infinitive, e.g. **eilen > Eile** (see *92(b)*, weak verbs):

Bitte,[3] *request*	Fülle,[1] *abundance*	Reise, *journey*
Bürste, *brush*	Klage, *complaint,*	Ruhe,[1] *rest*
Dauer,[1] *duration*	*grievance*	Sage, *legend*
Decke, *cover, blanket;*	Klingel, *doorbell*	Sorge, *care (=concern)*
ceiling	Liebe, *love*	Spitze, *point*
Ehre, *honour*	Pfeife,[2] *pipe, whistle*	Stelle, *place, spot*
Eile,[1] *haste, hurry*	Pflanze, *plant*	Stimme, *voice; vote*
Ernte, *harvest*	Pflege, *care (nurture)*	Strafe, *punishment*
Feier, *celebration*	Probe, *test, sample*	Strecke, *stretch*
Fliege,[3] *fly*	Rede, *speech*	Suche, *search*
Folge, *consequence*	Regel, *rule* [turn	Wache, *sentry*
Frage, *question*	Reihe, *row, series;*	

[1] Used only in the singular   [2] Note irregularity
[3] Derived from strong verb

(β) By adding **-ung** to the stem of the infinitive, e.g. **achten** > **acht-** > **Achtung:**

(Cf. *92(c)*, weak verbs.)

Achtung,[1] *esteem, attention*
Ahnung, *idea*
Änderung, *alteration*
Bildung, *formation, culture*
Dämmerung,[2] *dusk, [dawn*
Dichtung, *poetry*
Drohung, *threat*
Fassung, *setting (of jewel); composure*
Forderung, *demand*
Füllung, *filling*
Haltung,[3] *bearing*
Handlung,[4] *action, plot (of play), business*
Heizung, *heating*
Hoffnung,[4] *hope*

Kleidung, *clothing*
Lösung, *solution*
Meinung, *opinion*
Mischung, *mixture*
Neigung, *inclination*
Öffnung, *opening*
Ordnung, *order (123)*
Prüfung, *examination*
Rechnung, *calculation, bill*
Regierung, *government*
Rettung, *rescue*
Richtung, *direction*
Rührung,[1] *emotion*
Sammlung,[4] *collection*
Sitzung,[3] *sitting*
Stärkung, *strengthening*

Stellung, *situation, job*
Stimmung, *mood*
Störung, *disturbance*
Teilung, *division*
Trennung, *separation*
Übung, *practice*
Wanderung, *walk, hike*
Warnung, *warning*
Wendung, *turn(ing)*
Wirkung, *effect*
Wohnung, *dwelling, flat*
Zahlung, *payment*
Zeichnung, *drawing, design*
Zögerung, *hesitation*

(Cf. *102(a)* and *(c)* and *104*, weak inseparable verbs.)

Bedeutung, *meaning*
Begegnung, *meeting*
Begleitung, *accompaniment*
Behandlung,[4] *treatment*
Behauptung, *assertion*
Bemerkung, *remark*
Beobachtung, *observation*
Beschäftigung, *occupation*
Bestellung, *order (123)*
Bestimmung, *destination*
Bewegung, *movement*
Entdeckung, *discovery*
Entfernung, *distance*

Entschuldigung, *excuse*
Entwicklung,[4] *development*
Erfüllung, *fulfilment*
Erholung, *recovery*
Erinnerung, *remembrance*
Erkältung, *cold (illness)*
Erklärung, *declaration, explanation*
Eroberung, *conquest*
Erwartung, *expectation*
Erwiderung, *reply*
Erzählung, *tale*

Überraschung, *surprise*
Übersetzung, *translation*
Überzeugung, *conviction*
Untersuchung, *investigation*
Verbesserung, *improvement*
Verfassung, *constitution [hurt*
Verletzung, *injury,*
Versammlung,[4] *gathering*
Versuchung, *temptation*

[1] Used only in the singular
[2] Derived from impersonal verb (*105*)
[3] Derived from strong verb
[4] Note irregularity

Verteidigung, *defence*
Verwandlung,[2] *trans-*
　formation
Verweigerung, *refusal*

Vollendung,[1]
　completion
Widerlegung,
　refutation

Wiederholung,
　repetition
Zerstörung,
　destruction

(Cf. *102(b)* and *(c)*, strong inseparable verbs.)

Beschreibung,
　description
Besprechung,
　discussion
Beziehung, *relation*
　(-ship), reference
Empfehlung,
　recommendation
Entlassung, *dismissal*
Entscheidung,
　decision
Erfahrung, *experience*
Erfindung, *invention*

Erhebung, *rising*
Erscheinung,
　appearance, pheno-
　menon
Erwerbung,
　acquisition
Erziehung,[1] *education*
Übertreibung,
　exaggeration
Überwindung,
　overcoming
Umgebung,
　surrounding(s)

Unterbrechung,
　interruption
Unterhaltung, *con-*
　versation; enter-
　tainment
Unternehmung,
　undertaking
Verbindung, *connec-*
　tion
Vergebung,[1] *forgive-*
　ness
Verzeihung, *pardon*

(Cf. *102(b)* and *(c)* and *104*, weak and strong separable verbs.)

Ablehnung, *refusal*
Anstrengung, *effort*
Auffassung, *conception*
Aufregung, *excitement*
Ausführung, *execution*
Darstellung,
　representation
Einladung, *invitation*

Fortsetzung, *con-*
　tinuation
Herstellung,
　production
Hinzufügung,
　addition
Mitteilung, *informa-*
　tion

Vorbereitung,
　preparation
Vorlesung, *lecture*
Vorstellung,
　performance
Zusammensetzung,
　combination

20 Neuter Nouns

(a) GROUP IA (STRONG)

i. Declined like **Tier(-e)**, i.e. plural not modified.

Bein, *leg*
Bier, *beer*
Boot, *boat*
Brot, *bread, loaf*
Ding, *thing*
Dutzend, *dozen*

Ereignis,[3] *event*
Fell, *skin, hide*
Gebet, *prayer*
Gedicht, *poem*
Gefängnis,[3] *(im)prison*
　(-ment)

Gefühl, *feeling*
Geheimnis,[3] *secret,*
　mystery
Geräusch, *noise, sound*
Gericht, *lawcourt; dish*
　(=course)

[1] Used only in the singular　　　[2] Note irregularity　　　[3] Plural: (*-se*)

Geschäft, *business, shop*
Geschenk, *gift, present*
Gesetz, *law*
Gespräch, *conversation*
Gewehr, *gun, rifle*
Gewicht, *weight*
Grammophon, *gramophone*
Haar, *hair*
Heer, *army*
Heft, *exercise book*
Heim, *home*
Hundert, *hundred*
Jahr, *year*
Kinn, *chin*
Knie,[2] *knee*

Konzert, *concert*
Mal, *time, occasion*
Maß, *measure*
Meer, *sea, ocean*
Netz, *net; luggage rack*
Öl, *oil*
Paar, *pair, couple*
Paket, *parcel, packet*
Papier, *paper*
Pferd, *horse*
Problem, *problem*
Pult, (*school*) *desk*
Recht, *right, law*
Reich, *realm*
Resultat, *result*
Salz, *salt*
Schaf, *sheep*
Schicksal, *fate*

Schiff, *ship*
Schwein, *pig*
Seil, *rope*
Spiel, *game, match, play*
Stück, *piece; play*
System, *system*
Tier, *animal*
Tor, *gate*
Verhältnis,[1] *relation (-ship)*
Werk, *work (123)*
Wort, *word (related)*
Zelt, *tent*
Zeug, *stuff, substance*
Ziel, *aim, destination*

ii. Declined like **Floß(-̈e)**, i.e. plural modified:

Floß, *raft*

(b) GROUP IB (STRONG)

i. Declined like **Kind(-er)**, i.e. plural not modified:

Bild, *picture*
Ei, *egg*
Feld, *field*
Geld, *money*
Geschlecht, *sex, gender, dynasty*

Gesicht, *face*
Gespenst, *ghost*
Glied, *limb*
Kind, *child*
Kleid, *dress, frock*
Licht, *light*

Lied, *song*
Nest, *nest*
Rind, *ox, cow, cattle*
Schild, *nameplate*
Schwert, *sword*
Weib, *woman*

ii. Declined like **Haus(-̈er)**, i.e. plural modified:

Amt, *office* (=*position*)
Bad, *bath*
Blatt, *leaf*
Buch, *book*
Dach, *roof*
Dorf, *village*
Fach, (*school*) *subject*

Glas, *glass*
Gras, *grass*
Gut, *estate; goods*
Haupt, *head*
Haus, *house*
Holz, *wood*
Huhn, *chicken*

Land, *land, country*
Rad, *wheel; bicycle*
Schloß,[3] *castle, palace*
Tal, *valley*
Tuch, *cloth*
Volk, *people, nation*
Wort, *word* (*unrelated*)

[1] Plural: (-*se*)   [2] Plural: *Knie* (pronounced: *kniə*)   [3] Plural: (-̈(*ss*)*er*)

(c) GROUP IC (STRONG)

i. Declined like **Fenster(-)**, i.e. plural not modified:

(α)

Fenster, *window*	Messer, *knife*	Ufer, *bank, shore*
Feuer, *fire*	Mittel, *means*	Viertel, *quarter*
Fieber, *fever*	Möbel, *piece of*	Wasser, *water*
Fräulein,[1] *Miss*	*furniture*	Wesen, *being, essence*
Gebäude, *building*	Muster, *pattern, model*	Wunder, *wonder,*
Gemüse, *vegetable*	Opfer, *victim, sacrifice*	*miracle*
Mädchen, *girl; maid*	Segel, *sail*	Zeichen, *sign*
Märchen, *fairy-tale*	Theater, *theatre*	Zimmer, *room*

(β) **Infinitives** used as **nouns**

Aussehen,[2] *appearance*	Laufen,[2] *running*	Schwimmen,[2]
Benehmen,[2] *behaviour*	Leben, *life, living*	*swimming*
Erstaunen,[2] *astonish-*	Leiden, *suffering,*	Trinken,[2] *drinking*
ment	*illness*	Vermögen, *ability;*
Essen, *eating, meal*	Lernen,[2] *learning*	*fortune*
Fahren,[2] *driving*	Lesen,[2] *reading*	Verschwinden,[2]
Gehen,[2] *walking*	Mißtrauen,[2] *mistrust*	*disappearance*
Klingeln,[2] *ringing*	Rauchen,[2] *smoking*	Versprechen, *promise*
Klopfen,[2] *knocking*	Rechnen,[2] *arithmetic*	Vertrauen, *confidence*
Kochen,[2] *cooking*	Reisen,[2] *travelling*	Wandern,[2] *hiking*
Lächeln,[2] *smile, smiling*	Schreiben, *letter,*	Weinen,[2] *weeping*
Lachen,[2] *laugh(ing),*	*writing*	Wissen,[2] *knowledge*
laughter	Schweigen,[2] *silence*	Zeichnen,[2] *drawing*

ii. Declined like **Kloster(⁻)**, i.e. plural modified:

Kloster, *monastery.*

(d) GROUP IIIA (MIXED), declined like **Bett(-(e)s, -en)**

Auge,[3] *eye*	Hemd, *shirt*	Interesse,[3] *interest*
Bett, *bed*	Insekt, *insect*	Ohr, *ear*
Ende,[3] *end*		

(e) GROUP IIIB (MIXED), declined like **Herz(-ens, -en)**

Herz, *heart.*

---

[1] Colloquial plural: (-s) [2] Used only in the singular
[3] Declension: (-s, -n)

(f) NEUTER NOUNS NORMALLY USED ONLY IN THE SINGULAR

Alter, *age*	Gold, *gold*	Pfund, *pound*
Blut, *blood*	Kilo, *kilo*	Radio, *radio*
Eis, *ice*	Leder, *leather*	Silber, *silver*
Eisen, *iron*	Leid, *harm, sorrow*	Stroh, *straw*
Fleisch, *meat, flesh*	Liter,[1] *litre*	Vergnügen, *pleasure*
Gepäck, *luggage*	Lob, *praise*	Vieh, *cattle*
Glück, *happiness,*	Meter,[1] *metre, yard*	Wachs, *wax*
luck	Obst, *fruit*	Wetter, *weather*

21 Irregular Plurals

(a) das Auto(-s), *car*   das Hotel(-s), *hotel*   das Restaurant(-s),
   das Büro(-s), *office*   das Kino(-s), *cinema*   *restaurant*
   das Café(-s), *café*   das Sofa(-s), *sofa*

(b) das Examen (— *or* Examina), *examination.*

(c) der Rat (Ratschläge), *advice.*

(d) der Tod (Todesfälle), *death, casualty.*

22 Nouns used normally only in the Plural

Eltern, *parents*	Kosten, *costs*	Pfingsten,[2] *Whitsun*
Ferien, *holidays*	Leute, *people*	Weihnachten,[2]
Kleider, *clothes*	Ostern,[2] *Easter*	*Christmas*

23 Compound Nouns

The gender and declension of a compound noun are always those of its last component:

   der Welt**krieg**(-e); **die** Haus**frau**(-en); **das** Rat**haus**(-̈er)

(a) Compounds made up of **two nouns** without any change:

m.	*f.*	*n.*
Apfelbaum, *apple*	Abendzeitung,	Abendessen, *supper*
tree	*evening paper*	Dienstmädchen,
Autofahrer, *car-driver*	Briefmarke, *stamp*	*servant, maid*
Birnbaum,[3] *pear tree*	Brieftasche, *wallet*	Flugzeug, *aeroplane*
Bahnhof, *station*	Buchhandlung,	Geldstück, *coin*
Briefkasten, *letterbox*	*bookshop*	Handgepäck,[4] *hand*
Briefträger, *postman*	Eisenbahn, *railway*	*luggage*

---

[1] Colloquially: *der Liter, der Meter*

[2] Also neuter sing., and always sing. when followed by a verb:
   Fröhliche (*merry*) Weihnachten! Diese(s) Ostern.
   BUT Weihnachten *kommt* bald

[3] The *-e* of the first noun of the compound is omitted

[4] Used only in the singular

m.	*f.*	*n.*

m.

Buchhändler, *book-
seller*

Eckplatz,[1] *corner seat*

Flughafen, *airport*

Fußboden, *floor*

Gepäckträger, *porter*

Handschuh, *glove*

Hauptbahnhof, *main
station*

Hauptmann,[2] *captain
(infantry)*

Hundertmarkschein,
100 mark note

Marktplatz, *market
place*

Milchmann, *milkman*

Mondschein,[3]
moonlight

Papierkorb, *paper
basket*

Regenmantel, *rain-
coat*

Regenschirm,
umbrella

Schuhmacher, *shoe-
maker*

Schutzmann,[2]
policeman

Sommertag, *summer
day*

Teelöffel, *teaspoon*

Tiergarten, *zoo*

Uhrmacher, *watch-
maker*

Wasserstoff,[3] *hydrogen*

Weinberg, *vineyard*

Weltkrieg, *world war*

Zahnarzt, *dentist*

Zimmermann,[2] *carpenter*

f.

Geldstrafe, *fine*

Haarbürste, *hairbrush*

Handarbeit, *manual
labour; needlework*

Handschrift, *hand-
writing; manuscript*

Handtasche, *handbag*

Hauptsache, *chief
thing*

Hauptstadt, *capital*

Hauptstraße, *high
street*

Hausfrau, *housewife*

Haustür, *front door*

Landstraße, *main road*

Luftpost,[3] *air-mail*

Nordsee,[3] *North Sea*

Ostsee,[3] *Baltic*

Postkarte, *postcard*

Schularbeit,[1] *home-
work*

Seereise, *voyage*

Sommerfrische,
*summer holiday-
resort*

Tatsache, *fact*

Teetasse, *teacup*

Viertelstunde, *quarter
of an hour*

Zahnbürste, *tooth-
brush*

Zeitschrift, *journal,
periodical*

n.

Handtuch, *towel*

Handwerk, *handicraft,
trade*

Jahrhundert, *century*

Luftschiff, *airship*

Mundtuch, *table-
napkin*

Mittagessen, *dinner*

Mittelalter,[3] *Middle
Ages*

Nordamerika,[3]
N. America

Ostpreußen,[3]
E. Prussia

Postamt, *post office*

Rathaus, *town hall*

Rindfleisch,[3] *beef*

Schweinefleisch,[3, 4]
pork

Seebad, *sea-side resort*

Spielzeug,[3] *toy(s)*

Südengland,[3]
S. England

Tischtuch, *tablecloth*

Weinglas, *wineglass*

Weltreich, *empire*

Werkzeug, *tool*

Westafrika,[3] *W. Africa*

Zeitalter, *age, era*

Zeitwort,[5] *verb*

pl.

Kopfschmerzen, *headache*

Halsschmerzen, *sore throat*

Naturwissenschaften, *natural sciences*

Sommerferien, *summer holidays*

---

[1] The *-e* of the first noun of the compound is omitted
[2] Plural of *-mann* = *-leute* in these compounds   [3] Used only in the singular
[4] Note the addition of *-e* in this compound   [5] Plural: *-wörter*

(b) Compounds made up of **two nouns**, the first with the ending -(e)s, -n or with plural ending:

i.

m.	*f.*	*n.*
Geburtstag, *birthday*	Ansichtspostkarte, *picture postcard*	Geburtstagsgeschenk, *birthday present*
Landsmann,[1] *fellow countryman*	Auffassungsgabe,[2] *intelligence*	Geschichtsbuch, *history book*
Staatsmann, *statesman*	Geistesgegenwart,[2] *presence of mind*	Tageslicht,[2] *daylight*
Weihnachtsbaum, *Christmas tree*	Jahreszeit, *season*	Weihnachtslied, *Christmas carol*
	Tageszeit, *time of day*	Wirsthaus, *inn*
	Tageszeitung, *daily paper*	

ii.

m.	*f.*	*n.*
Augenblick, *moment*	Bauernfrau, *peasant woman*	Bauernhaus, *farmhouse*
Bauernhof, *farm*	Tintenflasche, *ink bottle*	Klassenzimmer, *classroom*
Familienname, *surname*	Straßenbahn, *tram*	Taschenmesser, *pocket knife*
Lampenschirm, *lampshade*	Wochenzeitung, *weekly newspaper*	Taschentuch, *handkerchief*
Sonnenschein,[2] *sunshine*		

iii.

m.	*f.*	*n.*
Bücherschrank, *book-case*	Briefmarkensammlung, *stamp collection*	Bilderbuch, *picture book*
Personenzug, *slow train*	Kleiderbürste, *clothes brush*	Geschichtenbuch, *story book*
Stundenplan, *timetable (school)*	Schülermütze, *school cap*	Kinderbuch, *children's book*
		Wörterbuch, *dictionary*

(c) Compounds made up of **verb** and **noun**:

m.	*f*	*n.*
Backofen, *oven*	Fahrkarte, *ticket*	Badezimmer, *bathroom*
Fahrplan, *timetable (railway)*	Fahrschule, *driving school*	Eßzimmer, *dining-room*
Fallschirm, *parachute*	Haltestelle, *bus stop*	

[1] Plural: *Landsleute*   [2] Used only in the singular

m.	*f.*	*n.*
Heizkörper, *radiator*	Laufbahn, *career*	Fahrgeld, *fare*
Kaufmann,[1] *merchant*	Leihbibliothek,	Fahrrad, *bicycle*
Liegestuhl, *deckchair*	*lending-library*	Lesebuch, *reader*
Schauspieler, *actor*	Schauspielerin,[2]	*(=book)*
Schreibtisch, *desk*	*actress*	Schauspiel, *play,*
Spaziergang, *stroll*	Spazierfahrt, *drive*	*drama*
Wartesaal,[3] *waiting-*	Sprechstunde,	Schlafzimmer,
room	*consulting-hour*	*bedroom*
	Stehlampe, *standard*	Streichholz, *match*
	lamp	Studierzimmer, *study*
		Trinkgeld, *tip*
pl.		Wohnzimmer,
Eßwaren, *edibles, provisions.*		*sitting-room*

(d) Compounds made up of **adjective** and **noun**:

m.	*f.*	*n.*
Dummkopf, *blockhead*	Fremdsprache,	Festland, *continent*
Edelmann,[1] *nobleman*	*foreign language*	Frühstück, *breakfast*
Edelstein, *precious stone*	Großmacht, *Great*	Kleingeld,[4] *change*
Großvater, *grand-*	*Power*	*(123)*
father	Großmutter, *grand-*	Schwarzbrot,[4] *rye-*
Halbkreis, *semicircle*	*mother*	*bread*
Rotwein, *red wine*	Großstadt, *great city,*	Weißbrot,[4] *wheatbread*
Sauerstoff,[4] *oxygen*	*metropolis*	
Schnellzug, *fast train*	Hochzeit, *wedding*	
Vollmond,[4] *full moon*	Kleinstadt, *small town*	

pl.
Großeltern, *grandparents*

(e) Compounds made up of **prefix** (preposition or adverb) and **noun**:

m.	*f.*	*n.*
Anblick, *sight (123)*	Abfahrt, *departure*	Abteil, *compartment*
Anfall, *attack*	Abneigung, *dislike*	Ausland,[4] *foreign parts*
Anfang, *beginning*	Abreise, *departure*	Beispiel, *example*
Angriff, *attack*	*(persons)*	Gegenteil, *opposite*
Anteil, *share*	Abschrift, *copy*	Hinterbein, *hind leg*
Anzug, *suit*	Absicht, *intention*	Mitglied, *member*
Aufsatz, *essay*	Anfrage, *inquiry*	Mitleid,[4] *sympathy*

[1] Plural: *-leute*   [2] Plural: *(-nen)*   [3] Plural: *-säle*   [4] Used only in the singular

m.	*f.*	*n.*
Aufstand, *insurrection*	Anklage, *accusation*	Nachspiel, *epilogue*
Ausdruck,[1] *expression*	Anlage, *park; works;*	*(in play)*
Ausflug, *excursion*	*talent*	Nachwort,[2] *epilogue*
Beifall,[3] *applause*	Ansicht, *opinion, view*	*(in book)*
Eindruck,[1] *impression*	Anzahl,[3] *number (123)*	Nebenfach, *sub-*
Einfall, *idea*	Aufgabe, *task, exercise*	*sidiary subject*
Fortschritt, *progress*	Ausdauer,[3] *persever-*	Nebengebäude,
Gegenstand, *object,*	*ance; endurance*	*annex*
subject	Ausrede, *excuse*	Nebengeräusch,
Hintergrund, *back-*	Aussicht, *prospect,*	*atmospherics*
ground	*view*	Nebenzimmer, *next*
Mittag, *midday, noon*	Auswahl, *selection*	*room*
Nachdruck,[3] *emphasis*	Einwendung, *objection*	Unglück, *misfortune*
Nachmittag, *afternoon*	Nachfrage,[3] *demand*	Unterhaus,[3] *House of*
Nachteil, *disadvantage*	*(for goods)*	*Commons*
Nebenfluß, *tributary*	Nachsicht,[3] *indulgence*	Unterhemd,[3] *vest*
Umfang, *size, extent*	Nachwelt,[3] *posterity*	Unterseeboot,
Umschlag, *envelope*	Niederlage, *defeat*	*submarine*
Umstand, *circumstance*	Oberfläche, *surface*	Unwetter, *storm*
Umweg, *detour*	Überfahrt, *crossing*	Urteil, *judgment,*
Unfall, *accident*	Übermacht,[3] *superior*	*verdict*
Unsinn,[3] *nonsense*	*force*	Vorbild, *model,*
Unterrock, *petticoat*	Überschrift, *title (of*	*pattern*
Vordergrund, *fore-*	*book)*	Vorderbein, *foreleg*
ground	Übersicht, *synopsis*	Vorrecht, *privilege*
Vorfall, *incident*	Umgegend, *vicinity,*	Vorspiel, *prelude;*
Vorhang, *curtain*	*environs*	*curtain-raiser*
Vormittag, *forenoon*	Unschuld,[3] *innocence*	Vorurteil, *prejudice*
Vorname, *Christian*	Untergrundbahn,	Vorwort,[2] *preface*
name	*underground railway*	Vorzeichen, *omen*
Vorsatz, *intention*	Unterschrift, *signature*	
Vorschlag, *suggestion*	Ursache, *cause*	
Vorteil, *advantage*	Vorliebe,[3] *preference,*	
Widerspruch, *contra-*	*special liking (for)*	
diction	Vorrede, *introduction*	
Widerstand, *resistance*	*(in book)*	
Zufall, *chance (event)*	Vorschrift, *regulation;*	
Zustand, *condition*	*prescription*	
(=state)	Vorsicht,[3] *caution*	

[1] Plural: *-drücke*   [2] Plural: *-worte*   [3] Used only in the singular

24 Declension of Proper Nouns

(a) Christian names both male and female normally take **-s** in the genitive:

> Wilhelms Bruder; Marias Schwester; Julies Buch.

(b) Male Christian names ending in a sibilant (s, z, x) take in the genitive either an apostrophe or (in the spoken language particularly) the construction with *von* is substituted:

> Franz' Mutter/die Mutter von Franz
> Max' Vater/der Vater von Max

(c) Surnames ending in **-s** show the genitive case either by the definite article or by an apostrophe or the construction with *von* is substituted:

> Der Tod des Sokrates; Brahms' Werke; die Operetten von Strauß.

(d) Surnames or Christian names preceded by adjectives or articles are not declined:

> Die Siege (*victories*) des Alten Fritz.

(e) The article is normally omitted with names not ending in a sibilant:

> Goethes Werke *or* die Werke Goethes (*not* Die Werke des Goethes).

(f) In a compound name only the last element is declined:

> Die Erzählungen Johann Peter Hebels *or* Johann Peter Hebels Erzählungen.

(g) If *von* is part of the name only the last element is declined; but if the name following *von* clearly refers to a place, only the name preceding *von* is declined:

> Die Werke Friedrich von Schillers.
> BUT Das Leben Gustav Adolfs von Schweden.

(h) When a name is followed by one in apposition (cf. *37*) both are declined:

> *N.* Heinrich der Löwe.
> *A.* Heinrich den Löwen.
> *G.* Heinrichs des Löwen.
> *D.* Heinrich dem Löwen.

(i) If a title without article precedes a name, the name is declined; if the title has the article, the title is declined:

Onkel Richards Haus; das Haus des Onkels Richard.
Die Siege Kaiser Karls/des (mächtigen) Kaisers Karl.

NOTE: *Herr* is always declined:
Herrn Müllers Haus; das Haus des Herrn Müller.
Herrn Professor Schmidts Wohnung; die Wohnung des Herrn Professor Schmidt.
An Herrn Müller (*in addressing envelopes*).

(j) With place-names the masculine and neuter genitive inflexion **-s** is usually shown as well as the article except after an adjective, when it is often omitted:

Die Ufer des Rheins; des heutigen Frankreich(s).

(k) With place-names ending in a sibilant the genitive cannot be formed. One writes therefore:

Die breiten Straßen von Paris; die breiten Straßen der Stadt Paris.

BUT Die breiten Straßen Berlins (*or* von Berlin).

(l) The months of the year are usually left uninflected:

Anfang Januar; Ende Oktober; Mitte April.

(m) The plural of surnames is usually shown by the addition of **-s**; those ending in a sibilant add **-ens**:

Die Meyers; die Buddenbrooks; die Schulzens.

25 Geographical Names

Continent, Country	Meaning	Inhabitant (fem. form given in brackets)	Adjective
Afrika	*Africa*	Afrikaner[1](-in)	afrikanisch
Amerika	*America*	Amerikaner[1](-in)	amerikanisch
Asien	*Asia*	Asiat[2](-in)	asiatisch
Australien	*Australia*	Australier[1](-in)	australisch
Europa	*Europe*	Europäer[1](-in)	europäisch
Ägypten	*Egypt*	Ägypter[1](-in)	ägyptisch
Bayern	*Bavaria*	Bayer[3](-in)	bayrisch
Belgien	*Belgium*	Belgier[1](-in)	belgisch
China	*China*	Chines-e[3](-in)	chinesisch
Dänemark	*Denmark*	Dän-e[3](-in)	dänisch

[1] Declined like *Onkel* (*16*, Group Ic) [2] Declined like *Mensch* (*16*, Group II)
[3] Declined like *Junge* (*18(d)*, Group II)

(25)

Continent, Country	Meaning	Inhabitant (fem. form given in brackets).	Adjective
Deutschland	*Germany*	der Deutsche[1]	deutsch
England	*England*	Engländer[2](-in)	englisch
Frankreich	*France*	Franz-ose[3](-ösin)	französisch
Griechenland	*Greece*	Griech-e[3](-in)	griechisch
Indien	*India*	Inder[2](-in)	indisch
Irland	*Ireland*	Irländer[2](-in)	irisch
Italien	*Italy*	Italiener[2](-in)	italienisch
Japan	*Japan*	Japaner[2](-in)	japanisch
Kanada	*Canada*	Kanadier[2](-in)	kanadisch
Neuseeland	*New Zealand*	Neuseeländer[2](-in)	neuseeländisch
die Niederlande[4] (pl.)	*the Netherlands*	Niederländer[2](in)	niederländisch
Norwegen	*Norway*	Norweger[2](-in)	norwegisch
Österreich	*Austria*	Österreicher[2](-in)	österreichisch
Polen	*Poland*	Pol-e[3](-in)	polnisch
Portugal	*Portugal*	Portugies-e[3](-in)	portugiesisch
Preußen	*Prussia*	Preuß-e[3](-in)	preußisch
Rußland	*Russia*	Russ-e[3](-in)	russisch
Sachsen	*Saxony*	Sachs-e[3](-in)	sächsisch
Schottland	*Scotland*	Schott-e[3](-in)	schottisch
Schweden	*Sweden*	Schwed-e[3](-in)	schwedisch
die Schweiz[4]	*Switzerland*	Schweizer[2](-in)	schweizerisch
Spanien	*Spain*	Spanier[2](-in)	spanisch
Südafrika	*S. Africa*	Südafrikaner[2](-in)	südafrikanisch
die Tschecho-slowakei[4]	*Czecho-slovakia*	Tschech-e[3](-in)	tschechisch
die Türkei[4]	*Turkey*	Türk-e[3](in)	türkisch
Ungarn	*Hungary*	Ungar[5](-in)	ungarisch
die Vereinigten Staaten[4] (m. pl.)	*U.S.A.*	Amerikaner[2](-in)	amerikanisch
Wales	*Wales*	Waliser[2](-in)	walisisch

NOTE 1: Names of continents and countries, unless otherwise indicated, are neuter.

NOTE 2: Die BRD (= Bundesrepublik Deutschland), *German Federal Republic/West Germany*; die DDR (= Deutsche Demokratische Republik), *German Democratic Republic/ East Germany*.

[1] Declined like an adjective, see *34*
[2] Declined like *Onkel* (*16*, Group Ic)
[3] Declined like *Junge* (*18(d)*, Group II)
[4] Cf. *13(i)*   [5] Declined like *Mensch* (*16*, Group II)

The Cases

26 The Nominative

The nominative is used to denote:

(a) The **subject** of the sentence:

Der König wurde krank.	*The king fell ill.*

(b) **The complement** of the verbs *sein, werden* and *bleiben*:

Er ist **ein berühmter Arzt.**	*He is a famous doctor.*
Er ist **ein Mann** geworden.	*He has become a man.*
Ich bleibe **dein Freund.**	*I remain your friend.*

27 The Accusative

The accusative is used:

(a) To denote the **direct object** of a transitive verb:

Ich gab ihm **den Bleistift.**	*I gave him the pencil.*

(b) To denote **duration of time** and **distance covered.**

Sie blieb **einen Monat** (lang).	*She stayed for a month.*
Den ganzen Tag arbeitete er.	*He worked all day long.*
Er ging **einen Schritt** weiter.	*He went one step farther.*

(c) To denote **definite time when** unless *am* is used:

Er kam **jeden Tag** (**vorigen** *or* **letzten Freitag**).	*He came every day (last Friday).*

(d) To denote **direction**:

Er stieg **den Berg** hinauf.	*He climbed up the mountain.*

(e) In **absolute** constructions:

Er stand da, **den Hut** auf dem Kopf.	*He stood there with his hat on his head.*

(f) With certain adjectives:

Ich bin **ihn** endlich los.	*I am at last rid of him.*
Er ist **meine Art und Weise** (nicht) gewohnt.	*He is (not) used to my ways.*
Ich bin **es** müde.	*I am tired of it.*
Es ist nicht **den hohen Preis** wert.	*It's not worth the high price.*
Ich habe/bin **die Arbeit** satt.	*I have had enough of work.*

(g) In certain phrases:

vielen Dank; guten Tag!	*many thanks; good day*

(h) After certain prepositions, see *84, 87.*

28 The Genitive

The genitive is used:

(a) To denote **possession**:

das Haus **meines Vaters**   *my father's house*

(b) To denote **indefinite time when**:

Eines Tages besuchte er mich.   *One day he visited me.*

Des Nachts konnte er nicht *He could not sleep at night.*
schlafen.

(c) To denote **manner**:

Er fährt nur **erster Klasse**.   *He only travels first class.*

Sei **guten Mutes**!   *Be of good courage.*

Wir gingen **unseres Weges**.   *We went our way.*

(d) With certain adjectives:

Ich bin mir **dessen** bewußt.   *I am aware of it.*

jeder Tat fähig   *capable of any action*

des Wartens müde   *tired of waiting*

des Erfolgs sicher   *sure of success*

des Bergsteigens ungewohnt   *unused to climbing*

dieser Tat schuldig   *guilty of this deed*

eines Besuchs wert (würdig)   *worth a visit*

Er war voll **des Lobes**.   *He was full of praise.*

(e) In certain expressions:

Es lohnt **der Mühe** (nicht).   *It is (not) worth the trouble.*

Ich bin **der Meinung** (*or* *I am of the opinion*
Ansicht)

(f) After certain prepositions, see *85*.

(g) After certain verbs, see *117, 118*.

29 The Dative

The dative is used:

(a) To denote the **indirect object**:

Er gab **mir** das Buch.   *He gave me the book.*

(b) To denote **interest** or **advantage**:

Du mußt es **mir** kaufen.   *You must buy it for me.*

(c) To denote **possession**:

Er rettete **mir** das Leben.   *He saved **my** life.*

Ich wusch **mir** die Hände.   *I washed **my** hands.*

(d) With certain adjectives:

seiner Mutter ähnlich	*like his mother*
mir (un)bekannt	*(un)known to me*
seinen Eltern dankbar	*grateful to his parents*
Das ist **ihm** eigen.	*That is peculiar to him.*
seinem Herrn gehorsam	*obedient to his master*
Das ist **mir** langweilig, lästig.	*That bores me.*
dem Tode nahe	*at the point of death*
dem Menschen nützlich/schäd- lich	*useful/harmful to man*
seinem Versprechen treu	*faithful to his promise*
Er sieht **seiner Mutter** sehr ähnlich.	*He looks very like his mother.*
Es ist **mir** ganz gleich.	*It is all the same to me.*

(e) In certain idioms:

Mir ist kalt/warm.	*I feel cold/warm.*
Mir ist schlecht/wohl.	*I feel bad/well.*

(f) After certain prepositions, see *86, 87*.

(g) After certain verbs, see *105, 115, 116*.

30 Apposition

(a) The noun in apposition is always in the same case as the noun to which it stands in apposition:

N. **Mein Freund, der Arzt,** kommt nicht.	*My friend the doctor is not coming.*
A. Kennst du **meinen Freund, den Arzt**?	*Do you know my friend, the doctor?*
G. Das ist das Haus **meines Freundes, des Arztes**.	*That is the house of my friend, the doctor.*
D. Ich sprach mit **meinem Freund, dem Arzt**.	*I spoke to my friend, the doctor.*

(b) In measurements the noun denoting the object measured is usually in apposition to (and therefore in the same case as) the noun denoting the measure (cf. *50*). 'Of' is then not translated. The construction with the genitive, when the second noun is qualified by an adjective, is now restricted to literary use:

ein Glas Wasser	*a glass of water*
ein Glas voll Wasser	*a glass full of water*
Er kam mit vier Dutzend Eiern.	*He came with four dozen eggs.*

ein Glas heiß**es** Wasser (*or* heiß**en** Wassers)	*a glass of hot water*
BUT ein Glas voll heiß**es**/heiß**em** Wasser (*or* heiß**en** Wassers)	*a glass full of hot water*
eine Anzahl jung**e** Leute (*or* jung**er** Leute)	*a number of young people*
mit einer Anzahl jung**en** Leuten (*or* jung**er** Leute)	*with a number of young people*
Er trank ein Glas süß**en** Wein (*or* süß**en** Weines).	*He drank a glass of sweet wine.*

NOTE die Stadt Berlin   *the town of Berlin*
       der Monat Mai   *the month of May*

Adjectives

31 The Predicative Adjective

The adjective used predicatively, i.e. coming after the verb (usually *sein, werden* or *bleiben*) or in apposition coming before or after a noun or pronoun, is indeclinable:

Das Papier ist **weiß**.   Der Mann, **alt** und **krank**, . . .

32 The Attributive Adjective

(a) The adjective used attributively, i.e. before the noun, may be declined either weak or strong:

Weak Declension				**Strong Declension**			
sing.			pl.	sing.			pl.
m.	f.	n.	m.f.n.	m.	f.	n.	m.f.n.
N. **-e**	**-e**	**-e**	**-en**	**-er**	**-e**	**-es**	**-e**
A. **-en**	**-e**	**-e**	**-en**	**-en**	**-e**	**-es**	**-e**
G. **-en**	**-en**	**-en**	**-en**	**-es**[1]	**-er**	**-es**[1]	**-er**
D. **-en**	**-en**	**-en**	**-en**	**-em**	**-er**	**-em**	**-en**

NOTE 1: The attributive adjective is declined **weak** if preceded by an article or other word declined strong. Otherwise the adjective is declined **strong**. (Thus: strong + **weak** + noun; otherwise, weak (or nothing) + **strong** + noun.)

NOTE 2: Two or more adjectives preceding the noun have each the same endings.

---

[1] The strong form *-es* of the **adjective** in the genitive singular masculine and neuter is now almost always replaced by the weak form *-en* because the noun usually shows the genitive case quite clearly.

(b) The adjective is declined **weak** after:

der	*the*	solcher	*such*
dieser	*this*	jeder (*sing.*)	*each, every*
jener	*that*	alle (*plur.*)	*all*
welcher	*which*	mancher (*sing.*)	*many a*

sing.

	m.		f.		n.	
N.	dieser	gute Junge	diese	gute Frau	dieses	gute Kind
A.	diesen	guten Jungen	diese	gute Frau	dieses	gute Kind
G.	dieses	guten Jungen	dieser	guten Frau	dieses	guten Kindes
D.	diesem	guten Jungen	dieser	guten Frau	diesem	guten Kind

pl.

m.f.n.

N.	diese	guten	Jungen,	Frauen,	Kinder
A.	diese	guten	Jungen,	Frauen,	Kinder
G.	dieser	guten	Jungen,	Frauen,	Kinder
D.	diesen	guten	Jungen,	Frauen,	Kindern

(c) The adjective is declined **strong** (except in the genitive singular masculine and neuter) if it stands alone before a noun:

	sing.						*pl.*	
	m.		f.		n.			
N.	guter	Wein	frische	Milch	frisches	Obst	reife	Äpfel
A.	guten	Wein	frische	Milch	frisches	Obst	reife	Äpfel
G.	guten	Weines	frischer	Milch	frischen	Obstes	reifer	Äpfel
D.	gutem	Wein	frischer	Milch	frischem	Obst	reifen	Äpfeln

(d) The adjective is declined partly **weak** and partly **strong** after:

ein	*a, one*	ihr	*her, its, their*
kein	*not a, no*	unser	*our*
mein	*my*	euer	*your* (pl. of *dein*)
dein	*your, thy*	Ihr	*your* (polite form)
sein	*his, its*		

	m.			f.		n.	
			sing.				
N.	kein	guter	Mann	keine	gute Frau	kein	gutes Kind
A.	keinen	guten	Mann	keine	gute Frau	kein	gutes Kind
G.	keines	guten	Mannes	keiner	guten Frau	keines	guten Kindes
D.	keinem	guten	Mann	keiner	guten Frau	keinem	guten Kind

pl.

m.f.n.

N.	keine	guten	Männer,	Frauen,	Kinder
A.	keine	guten	Männer,	Frauen,	Kinder
G.	keiner	guten	Männer,	Frauen,	Kinder
D.	keinen	guten	Männern,	Frauen,	Kindern

sing.

	m.		f.		n.	
N.	unser	alter Dom	unsere	alte Kuh	unser	altes Rad
A.	unseren	alten Dom	unsere	alte Kuh	unser	altes Rad
G.	unseres	alten Domes	unserer	alten Kuh	unseres	alten Rades
D.	unserem	alten Dom	unserer	alten Kuh	unserem	alten Rad

pl.

			m.	f.	n.
N.	unsere	alten	Dome,	Kühe,	Räder
A.	unsere	alten	Dome,	Kühe,	Räder
G.	unserer	alten	Dome,	Kühe,	Räder
D.	unseren	alten	Domen,	Kühen,	Rädern

NOTE: Below the line the adjective is declined weak.

(e) The adjective is declined strong after the cardinal numbers (no genitive except with 2 and 3) and after the following indefinite numerals (plural):

ein paar (indecl.)	*one or two*	manche	*a fair number of*
einige	*some, a few*	viele	*many*
mehrere	*several*	wenige	*few*

N.	viele	reiche	Leute
A.	viele	reiche	Leute
G.	vieler	reicher	Leute
D.	vielen	reichen	Leuten

(f) The demonstrative or possessive adjective following *alle* has the same endings as *alle*. The adjective following the demonstrative or possessive adjective is itself declined weak since both *alle* and the demonstrative or possessive adjective have strong declension:

N.	alle	diese	(jene)	reichen Leute
A.	alle	diese	(jene)	reichen Leute
G.	aller	dieser	(jener)	reichen Leute
D.	allen	diesen	(jenen)	reichen Leuten
N.	alle	meine	schönen	Bücher
A.	alle	meine	schönen	Bücher
G.	aller	meiner	schönen	Bücher
D.	allen	meinen	schönen	Büchern

33 Some very common Adjectives [1]

(a)

allein, *alone*
alt, *old*
ander-, *other, different*
angenehm, *pleasant*
arm, *poor*
ausländisch, *foreign*
bedeutend, *important*
bekannt, *well-known*
bequem, *comfortable*
bereit, *prepared*
beschäftigt, *busy*
braun, *brown*
durstig, *thirsty*
edel,[3] *noble*
eigen, *own*
einzig, *sole, unique*
elend, *wretched*
entfernt, *distant*
erfolgreich, *successful*
ernst, *serious*
erst-, *first*
fleißig, *diligent*
froh,[2] *glad, pleased*
ganz, *whole, entire*
geheim, *secret*

gelb, *yellow*
glücklich, *lucky, happy*
grau, *grey*
grün, *green*
halb, *half*
heiß, *hot*
hungrig, *hungry*
inner-, *inner*
interessant, *interesting*
jährlich, *annual*
jung, *young*
komisch, *funny*
langweilig, *boring*
laut, *loud*
leise, *soft, gentle*
letzt-, *last*
lieb, *dear, beloved, kind*
link-, *left*
mächtig, *powerful*
meist-, *most*
modern, *modern*
müde, *tired*
mutig, *brave*
nächst-, *next, nearest*
national, *national*
neugierig, *inquisitive*

nördlich, *northern*
nötig, *necessary*
östlich, *eastern*
praktisch, *practical*
recht, *right*
reich, *rich*
reizend, *charming*
ruhig, *quiet*
schlecht, *bad, wicked*
schlimm, *bad, sore*
schmutzig, *dirty*
spät, *late*
stolz,[2] *proud*
südlich, *southern*
täglich, *daily*
teuer,[3] *dear, expensive*
tot, *dead*
übel, *evil, ill*
übrig, *remaining*
voll,[2] *full*
vorig-, *previous*
vorsichtig, *cautious*
weiß, *white*
wert, *worthy, esteemed*
zahm,[2] *tame*
zornig, *angry*

[1] The hyphen after an adjective indicates that it can only be used in inflected form
[2] Does not modify in the comparative and superlative (see *38(b) note*)
[3] Drops penultimate 'e' when inflected

(33)

(b) Adjectives from which feminine abstract **nouns** are derived:

i. By adding -e and modifying the vowel if possible (see *19(c)iii(α)*)

blaß,[1] *pale*	groß, *big, great, tall*	sauer,[2] *sour*
blau, *blue*	gut, *good*	scharf, *sharp*
breit, *wide, broad*	hart, *hard*	schnell, *fast*
dicht, *thick, dense*	hell, *bright, light*	schwach, *weak*
dick, *thick, fat*	hoch,[3] *high*	schwarz, *black*
dünn, *thin*	hohl,[4] *hollow*	schwer, *heavy; difficult*
eben, *level*	kalt, *cold*	spitz, *pointed*
eng, *narrow, tight*	kühl, *cool*	stark, *strong*
fern, *distant*	kurz, *short*	still, *still*
fest, *firm*	lang, *long*	streng, *severe*
flach,[4] *flat, shallow*	leer, *empty*	süß, *sweet*
fremd, *strange, alien*	nah, *near*	tief, *deep, profound*
frisch, *fresh*	naß,[1] *wet*	treu, *loyal, faithful*
früh, *early*	reif, *ripe, mature*	warm, *warm*
glatt,[1] *smooth*	rot,[1] *red*	weit, *far, wide*

ii. By adding -heit (see *19(c)iii(β)*):

berühmt, *famous*	gewiß, *certain, sure*	schön, *beautiful, lovely*
besonder-, *special*	gleich, *like, equal*	selten, *rare*
bestimmt, *definite*	hübsch, *pretty*	sicher, *safe, certain,*
blind, *blind*	kahl,[4] *bald, bare*	*secure*
böse,[5] *bad, evil; angry*	klar,[4] *clear*	stumpf,[4] *blunt*
bunt,[4] *colourful*	klein, *small, little*	träge,[6] *indolent, idle*
dumm, *stupid*	klug, *clever, wise*	trocken, *dry*
dunkel,[7] *dark*	kompliziert, *compli-*	verschieden, *different,*
einfach, *simple*	*cated*	*diverse*
einzeln,[8] *single*	krank, *ill, sick*	vollkommen, *perfect*
falsch,[4] *false, wrong*	krumm, *crooked*	vornehm,
faul, *lazy; rotten*	leicht, *light; easy*	*distinguished*
fein, *fine, choice*	neu, *new*	wahr,[4] *true*
frei, *free*	offen, *open*	weich, *soft*
gemein, *common,*	rasch,[4] *quick*	weise,[6] *wise*
mean; vulgar	rein, *pure, clean*	wild, *wild*
gerade,[6] *straight*	rund,[4] *round*	zufrieden, *content,*
gesund,[9] *healthy, well*	schmal,[1] *narrow*	*satisfied*

[1] With or without modification in the comparative and superlative
[2] *Säure* (sourness, acid)   [3] *Höhe* (height)
[4] Does not modify in the comparative and superlative (see *38(b)*, note)
[5] *Bosheit* (malice, naughtiness)   [6] Drops final -e before adding suffix
[7] Drops penultimate 'e' when inflected   [8] *Einzelheit* (detail)
[9] Modifies in the comparative and superlative (see *38(b)*, note)

iii. By adding **-keit** (see *19(c)iii(γ)*:

ähnlich, *similar*	heiter, *serene, cheer-*	pünktlich, *punctual*
aufmerksam, *atten-*	*ful*	richtig, *right, correct*
tive	herrlich, *magnificent*	sauber, *clean*
billig, *cheap*	herzlich, *hearty,*	schläfrig, *sleepy*
bitter, *bitter*	*cordial*	schrecklich, *terrible*
dankbar, *grateful*	höflich, *polite*	schuldig, *guilty, due*
deutlich, *clear, distinct*	langsam, *slow*	schwierig, *difficult*
ehrlich, *honest*	lebendig, *alive, lively*	sichtbar, *visible*
einsam, *lonely*	lieblich, *charming*	sonderbar, *peculiar,*
ewig, *eternal*	lustig, *merry*	*strange*
fähig, *able, capable*	mächtig, *powerful*	traurig, *sad*
fertig, *ready, finished*	mäßig, *moderate*	vollständig, *complete*
freundlich, *friendly*	menschlich, *human*	wahrscheinlich,
fröhlich, *joyful, merry*	möglich, *possible*	*probable*
gefährlich, *dangerous*	natürlich, *natural*	wichtig, *important*
gemütlich, *snug*	niedrig, *low*	wirklich, *real*
gewöhnlich, *usual*	notwendig, *necessary*	wunderbar, *wonder-*
grausam, *cruel*	nützlich, *useful*	*ful, marvellous*
gründlich, *thorough*	öffentlich, *public*	würdig, *dignified,*
häßlich, *ugly*	ordentlich, *respectable,*	*worthy*
häufig, *frequent*	*tidy*	zuverlässig, *reliable*
heilig, *holy, sacred*	plötzlich, *sudden*	

(c) Negative adjectives:

unangenehm,	ungenau, *inaccurate*	unnötig, *unnecessary*
unpleasant	ungesund, *unhealthy*	unnütz(lich), *useless*
unbedeutend,	ungewiß, *uncertain*	unordentlich, *untidy*
unimportant	ungewöhnlich,	unpraktisch,
unbekannt, *unknown*	*unusual*	*unpractical*
unbequem, *uncom-*	unglücklich, *unhappy*	unpünktlich,
fortable	unhöflich, *impolite*	*unpunctual*
unbeschäftigt,	uninteressant,	unrecht, *wrong*
unoccupied	*uninteresting*	unreif, *unripe*
unbestimmt, *inde-*	unklug, *unwise*	unrein, *impure*
finite	unmäßig, *immoderate*	unruhig, *restless*
undankbar, *ungrateful*	unmenschlich,	unschuldig, *innocent*
unehrlich, *dishonest*	*inhuman*	unsicher, *unsafe*
unfähig, *incapable*	unmöglich,	unsichtbar, *invisible*
unfreundlich,	*impossible*	untreu, *unfaithful*
unfriendly	unnatürlich,	unvollkommen,
ungefährlich, *safe*	*unnatural*	*imperfect*

unvollständig,	unwichtig,	unzuverlässig,
incomplete	*unimportant*	*unreliable*
unvorsichtig,	unwirklich, *unreal*	
imprudent	unwürdig, *unworthy*	
unwahrscheinlich,	unzufrieden,	
improbable	*discontented*	

34 The Adjective-Noun

Adjective-nouns are declined like ordinary adjectives as in *32*. They are mostly written with a capital. (NOTE: *Der Junge* is **not** an adjective-noun.)

sing.

	m.		*f.*		*n.*
N.	der Alte	ein Alter	die Alte	eine Alte	das Neue
A.	den Alten	einen Alten	die Alte	eine Alte	das Neue
G.	des Alten	eines Alten	der Alten	einer Alten	des Neuen
D.	dem Alten	einem Alten	der Alten	einer Alten	dem Neuen

	m. f. pl.		*n. sing.*
N.	die Alten	Alte	Neues
A.	die Alten	Alte	Neues
G.	der Alten	Alter	Neuen
D.	den Alten	Alten	Neuem

The most common nouns of this type are:

der Alte	*old man*	der Gesandte	*ambassador*
der Angeklagte	*accused man*	der Kranke	*patient*
der Angestellte	*employee*	der Reiche	*rich man*
der Anwesende	*bystander, person present*	der Reisende	*traveller*
		der Schuldige	*guilty man*
der Arbeitslose	*unemployed man*	der Sterbliche	*mortal*
der Arme	*poor man*	der Verwandte	*relative*
der Beamte[1]	*official*	der Wahn-	*madman*
der Bekannte	*acquaintance*	sinnige	
der Blinde	*blind man*	die Elektrische	*tram*
der Deutsche	*German*	das Äußere	*exterior, appearance*
der Eingeborene	*native*		
der Erwachsene	*adult*	das Böse	*evil*
der Fremde	*stranger*	das Innere	*interior*
der Gefangene	*prisoner*	das Neue	*the new, news*
der Geistliche[2]	*clergyman*	das Schöne	*the beautiful*

[1] Feminine equivalent: *die Beamtin*   [2] No feminine equivalent

35 The Adjective-Noun after *etwas, viel, wenig, nichts, allerlei* and after *alles*

After *etwas, viel, wenig, nichts* and *allerlei* the adjective-noun is declined like a strong neuter adjective; after *alles*, like a weak neuter adjective. The adjective-noun is written, with few exceptions only, with a capital.

N.	nichts Neues (*nothing new*)	alles Gute (*all the best*)
A.	nichts Neues	alles Gute
G.	nichts Neuen	alles Guten
D.	nichts Neuem	allem Guten

Er sagte viel Liebes von dir.	*He said a lot of nice things about you.*
Anstatt etwas Neuen.	*Instead of something new.*
Er sah sich nach etwas Neuem um.	*He looked round for something new.*
Ich wünsche dir alles Gute.	*I wish you all the best.*

NOTE Er tat etwas and(e)res/alles mögliche. *He did something else/everything possible*

36 Adjectives derived from Place-names

Such adjectives are formed by the addition of *-er*[1] to the place-name, are invariable and are written with a capital.

Jenaer Glas	*Jena glass*
im Kölner Dom	*in Cologne Cathedral*
die Berliner Polizei	*the Berlin police*

37 Adjectives in Titles

Adjectives in titles are attributive, although they follow the noun; they are declined weak and are written with a capital.

N.	Karl	der	Große
A.	Karl	den	Großen
G.	Karls	des	Großen
D.	Karl	dem	Großen

38 Comparison of Adjectives

(a) Predicative:

warm	wärmer	am wärmsten
breit	breiter	am breitesten[2]

---

[1] If the place-name ends in *-e* only *-r* is added, e.g. *Haller* from *Halle*
[2] Adjectives ending in *-d, -s, -sch, -st, -t, -x, -z* add *-est* in the superlative

Der Fluß ist breit.	*The river is wide.*
Dieser Fluß ist breiter.	*This river is wider.*
Hier ist der Fluß am breitesten.	*Here the river is widest.*
Im Sommer sind die Tage am wärmsten.	*The days are warmest in summer.*

(b) Attributive:

der warme	der wärmere	der wärmste
der breite	der breitere	der breiteste

Das ist ein breiter Fluß.	*That is a wide river.*
Das ist ein breiterer Fluß.	*That is a wider river.*
Das ist der breiteste Fluß.	*That is the widest river.*
Dieser Fluß ist der breiteste.	*This river is the widest (one).*
Die wärmsten Tage des Jahres sind im Juli.	*The warmest days of the year are in July.*

NOTE: Adjectives of **one** syllable usually modify the vowel **a**, **o** or **u** (but not **au**) in the comparative and superlative. (Cf. list, *33*, in which exceptions are indicated.)

(c) Irregular Comparisons:

groß	größer	am größten	(der größte)	*big*
gut	besser	am besten	(der beste)	*good*
hoch	höher	am höchsten	(der höchste)	*high*
nah	näher	am nächsten	(der nächste)	*near*
viel	mehr[1]	am meisten	(das meiste)	*much, many*
wenig	{weniger[1] {minder	{am wenigsten {am mindesten	{(das wenigste) {(das mindeste)	*little* *few*

(d) Examples of Comparison of Adjectives:

i.

Er ist (nicht) **so** alt **wie** ich.	*He is (not) as old as I (am).*
Er ist **ebenso** alt **wie** ich.	*He is just as old as I.*
Er ist bei weitem **nicht so** alt **wie** ich.	*He is far from being as old as I.*
Da er **so** alt ist **wie** ich, ist er . . . (*Word order!*)	*As he is as old as I (am) he is . . .*
Wir sind gleich alt.	*We are both the same age.*

ii.

Er ist **älter als** ich.	*He is older than I (am).*
Er ist **weniger** reich **als** ich.	*He is less rich than I.*

[1] Indeclinable

Er ist zwei Jahre **älter als** ich.	*He is two years older than I.*
Er ist noch **ärmer als** ich.	*He is even poorer than I.*
Er ist viel/bei weitem **klüger als** ich.	*He is much/far cleverer than I.*
Er wird immer dicker.	*He is getting fatter and fatter.*
Er ist **mehr** fleißig **als** klug.	*He is industrious rather than clever.*
mehr oder minder gut	*more or less good*
Da er **älter** ist **als** ich, hat er . . . (*Word order!*)	*As he is older than I (am) he has . . .*
desto/um so besser	*all the better*

iii. Er ist der klügste von allen. — *He is the cleverest of all.*

Er ist mit[1] der klügste in der Klasse. — *He is among the cleverest in the form.*

Das schönste aller Kleider.	
Das schönste von (*or* unter) allen Kleidern.	*The prettiest of all the dresses.*

iv.

Die Zugspitze ist sehr hoch.	*The Zugspitze is very high.*
Er war höchst erstaunt.	*He was most surprised.*
Er ist außerordentlich klug.	*He is extraordinarily clever.*
Er ist ungemein klug.	*He is uncommonly clever.*
Er ist äußerst dumm.	*He is exceedingly stupid.*

NOTE:

ein älterer Herr	*a fairly old/elderly gentleman*
eine längere Reise	*a fairly long/lengthy journey*
die neuere Geschichte	*modern history*
die meiste Zeit	*most of the time*
die meisten Leute	*most people*
die meisten von uns	*most of us*

Adverbs

39 Formation of Adverbs

(a) The predicative adjective may generally be used as an adverb:

Sie singt schön.   *She sings beautifully.*

(b) Some adverbs are formed from adjectives and other parts of speech by the addition of certain endings, e.g., *-erweise, -weise, -lings, -wärts, -s, -e, -lang, -lich*:

[1] A dative (e.g. *anderen*) is understood in such phrases

glücklicherweise, *fortunately*	teilweise, *partly*
blindlings, *blindly*	vorwärts, *forwards*
abends, *of an evening*	teils, *partly*
lange, *for a long time*	wochenlang, *for weeks*
namens, *by name, called*	reichlich, *richly*

40 Comparison of Adverbs

(a) Adverbs have the same comparison as predicative adjectives (cf. *38(a)*). Note, however, the following irregular comparisons:

bald	{ eher { früher	{ am ehesten { am frühesten	*soon*
gern	lieber	am liebsten	*willingly*
gut (wohl)	besser	am besten	*well*
oft	{ häufiger { öfter	{ am häufigsten { am öftesten	*often*
viel (sehr)	mehr	am meisten	*much*
wenig	{ weniger { minder	{ am wenigsten { am mindesten	*little*

Sie sang besser, als sie es je getan hatte.	*She sang better than she had ever done.*

(b) Adverbs have in addition an absolute superlative.

aufs wärmste   aufs beste   aufs tiefste

Compare:

Er war **am tiefsten** beleidigt.	*He was the most deeply offended (of them all).*
Er war **aufs tiefste** beleidigt.	*He was most deeply offended (=mortally offended).*

(c) Notice the following forms of the superlative:

i.

erstens	*in the first place*
frühestens (*or* ehestens)	*at the earliest*
höchstens	*at the most*
letztens	*in the last place*
meistens (*or* meist)	*mostly*
spätestens	*at the latest*
strengstens (verboten)	*strictly (forbidden)*
wenigstens (*or* mindestens)	*at least*

ii.

höchst überrascht	*most surprised*
äußerst klug	*exceedingly clever*
möglichst schnell	*as fast as possible*

41 Adverbs of Time

ab und zu	*now and again*	längst	*long ago, long since*
anfangs ⎫		manchmal ⎫	
zuerst ⎬	*at first*	zuweilen ⎬	*sometimes*
zunächst ⎭		bisweilen ⎭	
bald (darauf)	*soon (afterwards)*	monatelang	*for months*
bis dahin	*till then, by then*	nachher ⎫	*after(wards) (123)*
bisher	*hitherto, till now*	danach ⎭	
damals	*then (123)*	nie ⎫	
dann	*then (123)*	niemals ⎬	*never*
darauf	*thereupon*	nimmer ⎭	
(so)eben ⎫	*just*	noch ⎫	*still (124)*
gerade ⎭		noch immer ⎭	
einst/einmal	*once; some day*	noch nicht	*not yet*
einstweilen ⎫	*for the time being*	nun	*now, well, then, why*
vorläufig ⎭		von nun an	*henceforth, from now on*
endlich ⎫			
schließlich ⎬	*finally, at last*	oft	*often*
zuletzt ⎭		schon	*already (124)*
erst	*only, not until (123)*	seitdem ⎫	*since then*
erst dann	*only then*	seither ⎭	
früher	*formerly*	sofort ⎫	
heutzutage	*nowadays*	sogleich ⎬	*immediately*
immer/stets	*always*	gleich ⎭	
inzwischen ⎫	*meanwhile*	stundenlang	*for hours*
unterdessen ⎭		tagelang	*for days*
jahrelang	*for years*	von jeher	*from time immemorial*
je	*ever*		
jetzt	*now*	vorher	*before (123)*
kaum	*scarcely, hardly*	vorhin	*a little while ago*
kürzlich ⎫	*recently*	wieder ⎫	*again, once again*
unlängst ⎭		noch einmal ⎭	
neulich	*the other day*	wochenlang	*for weeks*
lange	*for a long time*	zugleich	*at the same time*

42 Adverbs of Manner and Degree

anders als	*differently from*	durchaus ⎫	*by no means*
auswendig	*by heart*	nicht ⎬	
beinahe/fast	*almost*	keineswegs ⎭	
besonders	*especially*	ebenso wie	*just like*
dicht	*close*	eigentlich	*strictly speaking*

erst recht	*all the more*	nein	*no*
etwa	*approximately,*	nicht	*not*
ungefähr	*about*	nur	*only (123)*
ferner	*further*	plötzlich	*suddenly*
ganz	*quite, right*	schön	*certainly, all right*
überhaupt	*altogether, at all*	sehr	*very*
gar nicht		selbst/sogar	*even (123)*
überhaupt	*not at all*	sicher(-lich)	*certainly*
nicht		so	*so, in this way*
genug	*enough*	sonst	*otherwise*
gern(e)	*willingly (122(k))*	sowieso	*anyhow*
gleich	*equally*	umsonst	*in vain; gratis*
glücklicher-	*fortunately*	vergebens	*in vain*
weise		vergeblich	
hoffentlich	*I (etc.) hope so*	vielleicht	*perhaps*
ja	*yes (124)*	wirklich	*really*
kaum	*scarcely, hardly*	wohl	*well (124)*
lauter	*nothing but*	ziemlich	*rather, fairly*
leider	*unfortunately*	zu	*too*
natürlich		zufällig	*by chance*
selbstver-	*of course*		
ständlich			

Er spricht ebenso wie sie.	*He speaks just like her.*
Er denkt anders als ich.	*He thinks differently from me.*
Das macht's erst recht schlimm.	*That makes it all the worse.*
Hoffentlich kann er kommen.	*I hope he can come.*
Ich war zufällig da.	*I happened to be there.*

43 Adverbs of Place

(a) Definite:

i.	hier	Er ist hier.	*He is here.*
	hierhin	Legen Sie es hierhin!	*Put it here.*
	hierher	Kommen Sie hierher!	*Come here.*
	von hier	Er geht von hier weg.	*He goes away from here.*
	dort (da)	Er ist dort.	*He is there.*
	dorthin (dahin)	Er geht dorthin.	*He goes there.*
	dorther (von da)	Er kommt dorther.	*He comes from there.*

draußen	Er ist draußen.	*He is outside.*
nach draußen (hinaus)	Er geht nach draußen (hinaus)	*He goes outside.*
von draußen	Er kommt von draußen.	*He comes from outside.*

Likewise:

drinnen (*inside*)	nach drinnen (hinein)	von drinnen
oben (*up(stairs)*)	nach oben (hinauf)	von oben
unten (*down(stairs)*, *below*)	nach unten (hinunter)	von unten
vorn (*in front*)	nach vorn (vorwärts) (*to the front*)	von vorn
hinten (*behind*)	nach hinten (rückwärts)	von hinten
rechts (*on the right*)	nach rechts (*to the right*)	von rechts
links (*on the left*)	nach links (*to the left*)	von links
drüben (*over there*)	nach drüben (hinüber)	von drüben

ii. **hin** (*away from the speaker*) **her** (*towards the speaker*)

Ich gehe **hin**.	*I go there.*	Er kommt **her**.	*He comes here.*
Ich gehe **hinan**.	*I go (up) to.*	Er kommt **heran**.	*He comes (up) to.*
Ich gehe **hinaus**.	*I go out.*	Er kommt **heraus**.	*He comes out.*
Ich gehe **hinein**.	*I go in.*	Er kommt **herein**.	*He comes in.*
Ich gehe **hinauf**.	*I go up.*	Er kommt **herauf**.	*He comes up.*
Ich gehe **hinab/ hinunter**.	*I go down.*	Er kommt **herab/ herunter**.	*He comes down.*
Ich gehe **hinüber**.	*I go across, over.*	Er kommt **herüber**.	*He comes across, over.*
Ich gehe den Berg **hinauf**.	*I go up the mountain.*	Er kommt den Berg **herab/herunter**.	*He comes down the mountain.*

NOTE also the following examples:

Er ging **hin** und **her**.	*He walked to and fro.*
Er kommt **hinter** dem Baum **hervor**.	*He comes out from behind the tree.*
Er kommt **unter** dem Stuhl **hervor**.	*He comes out from under the chair.*
Er ging **in** das Haus **hinein**.	*He went into the house.*
Er sah **zum** Fenster **hinaus**.	*He looked out of the window.*
Ich ging **hinter** ihm **her**.	*I went along behind him.*
Ich ging **vor** ihm **her**.	*I went along in front of him.*
Er sah **vor** sich (A) **hin**.	*He looked straight in front of him.*
Herein!	*Come in!*

53

(43)

iii. Cf. *102(b)*

ab	*off, down*	Der Brief geht ab (*goes off*). Er steigt ab (*gets down*).
an	*on*	Er zieht die Schuhe an (*puts on*).
auf	*up, open*	Er steht auf (*gets up*). Er macht die Tür auf (*opens*).
aus	*out, off*	Er geht aus (*goes out*). Er zieht den Mantel aus (*takes off his coat*).
ein	*in*	Er steigt ein (*gets in*).
fort	*away, on*	Er geht fort (*goes away*). Er lebt fort (*lives on*).
heim	*home*	Er geht heim (*goes home*).
nieder	*down*	Er fällt nieder (*falls down*).
vor	*forward*	Er tritt vor (*steps forward*).
voran } voraus }	*on ahead*	Er geht voran/voraus (*goes on ahead*).
vorbei } vorüber }	*past*	Er geht vorbei (*goes past*). Er geht vorüber (*goes past*).
weg	*away*	Er geht weg (*goes away*).
zu	*to, shut*	Er nickt mir zu (*nods to me*). Er macht die Tür zu (*shuts*).
zurück	*back*	Er geht zurück (*goes back*).

NOTE: auf und ab
auf und nieder } *up and down*   bergauf *uphill*
bergab *downhill*

(b) Indefinite:

i.
überall	*everywhere*	Sie sind überall.
überallhin	*(to) everywhere*	Sie gehen überallhin.
überallher	*from everywhere*	Sie kommen überallher.
irgendwo	*somewhere*	Sie sind irgendwo.
irgendwohin	*(to) somewhere*	Sie gehen irgendwohin.
(von) irgend- woher	*from somewhere*	Sie kommen (von) irgend- woher.
nirgends } nirgendwo }	*nowhere*	Sie sind nirgends. Sie sind nirgendwo.
nirgendwohin	*(to) nowhere*	Sie gehen nirgendwohin.
(von) nirgend- woher	*from nowhere*	Sie kommen (von) nirgend- woher.
anderswo } woanders }	*elsewhere*	Sie sind anderswo. Sie sind woanders.

54

| anderswohin | (to) somewhere else | Sie gehen anderswohin. |
| (von) anders-
woher | from somewhere else | Sie kommen (von) anders-
woher. |

ii.

zusammen	together	Wir spielen zusammen.
beisammen	together (in one spot)	Wir sitzen beisammen.
unterwegs	on the way	Er ist unterwegs. *He is on his way.*
vorhanden	present, existent	Eisen ist hier vorhanden. *Iron exists here.*
herum	round, about (=around)	Das Rad läuft herum. *The wheel turns round.*
		Er lief um den Tisch herum. *He ran round the table.*
		Sie lagen überall herum. *They lay about everywhere.*
umher	about (=hither and thither)	Er irrte in der Stadt umher. *He wandered about the town.*
ringsum	all (a)round	Die Wälder ringsum. *The woods all around.*

NOTE: rings um   *all round* (prep.)   rings um das Schloß *all round the castle*

44 Interrogative Adverbs

wann	*when*	wo	*where*
wie lange	*how long*	wohin	*where (to)*
wie oft	*how often*	woher	*where from*
wie	*how, what . . . like*	worin	*in what*
warum }	*why*	worein	*into what*
weshalb }		etc.	

Wo bist du?	*Where are you?*
Wo gehst du hin? (Wohin gehst du?)	*Where are you going (to)?*
Wo kommt er her? (Woher kommt er?)	*Where does he come from?*

Worin hast du das?	*What do you have that in?*
Worein soll ich das tun?	*What shall I put that in?*

NOTE: Wie ist das schön!⎫
      Wie schön ist das!⎬ *How beautiful it is!*
      Wie schön das ist!⎭

Numerals, Dates, Etc.

45 Cardinals

0 null	40 vierzig
1 ein(s)	43 dreiundvierzig
2 zwei	50 fünfzig
3 drei	54 vierundfünfzig
4 vier	60 **sechzig**
5 fünf	65 fünfundsechzig
6 sechs	70 **siebzig**
7 sieben	76 sechsundsiebzig
8 acht	80 achtzig
9 neun	87 siebenundachtzig
10 zehn	90 neunzig
11 elf	98 achtundneunzig
12 zwölf	100 hundert/einhundert
13 dreizehn	101 hundertein(s)/hundertundein(s)
14 vierzehn	200 zweihundert
16 **sechzehn**	202 zweihundert(und)zwei
17 **siebzehn**	1 000 **tausend** (=**one** *or* **a** thousand)
20 zwanzig	1 001 tausend(und)ein(s)
21 einundzwanzig	1 100 tausendeinhundert
30 **dreißig**	1 000 000 eine Million
32 zweiunddreißig	

2 654 937 zwei Millionen sechshundertvierundfünfzigtausendneun-
hundertsiebenunddreißig.

46 Notes on the Cardinals

(a) In counting the forms **eins, hunderteins**, etc., are used.
(b) **Ein** preceding a noun is declined like the indefinite article (*12*).

(c) **Ein** is not inflected in certain expressions:

um **ein** Uhr	*at one o'clock*
vor ein oder zwei Tagen	*one or two days ago*
mit ein paar Freunden	*with one or two friends*
von hundertein Städten	*of 101 towns*

(d) **Noch** preceding a numeral means *more, another*:

noch ein/zwei Glas Bier	*another glass/two glasses of beer*

(e) **Zwei** and **drei** have a genitive form, viz. **zweier, dreier**:

die Freundschaft **zweier** groß**er** Völker	*the friendship of two great peoples*

This form may be, and often is, replaced by **von** and uninflected **zwei** and **drei**:

der Herr **von zwei** Dienern	*the master of two servants*

(f) Numbers from **zwei** to **zwölf** when used without the noun add **-en** or **-t** for the dative after *zu*:

Wir gingen zu vier**en**.	*We went in fours (groups of four).*
Wir gingen zu vier**t**.	*Four of us went (as a group).*

(g) Decades are indicated by the addition of **-er(n)** to the suffix -zig:

in den vierzig**er** (*indeclinable*) Jahren	*in the 'forties (i.e. 1940–49)*
Er steht in den Vierzig**ern**.	*He is in his forties.*

(h) When used as nouns **hundert** and **tausend** are written with capital letters and declined like Group IA neuter nouns:

zu Hunderten und Tausenden	*in hundreds and thousands*
einige Hunderte von Menschen	*some hundreds of people*
BUT einige hundert Menschen	*a few hundred people*

(i) Notice the use of **beide**:

Ein Mann hatte zwei Söhne; beide hatte er gleich lieb.	*A man had two sons: he was equally fond of both (= the two).*
meine beiden Brüder	*my two brothers*
die beiden Brüder	*the two brothers*
welcher von beiden?	*which of the two?*
keiner von beiden	*neither (of the two)*

wir beide	*both of us*
Wir gingen beide dorthin.	*We both went there.*
Ich mag beide nicht.	*I don't like either.*
Beides ist möglich.	*Either is possible.*

47 Ordinals

1st	der, die, das **erste**	19th	der neunzehn**te**
2nd	der, die, das zwei**te**	20th	der zwanzig**ste**
3rd	der, die, das **dritte**	21st	der einundzwanzig**ste**
4th	der, die, das vier**te**	100th	der hundert**ste**
7th	der, die, das **sieb**(en)**te**	101st	der hundert**erste**
8th	der, die, das **achte**	1000th	der tausend**ste**

48 Notes on the Ordinals

(a) Ordinals from *zweite* to *neunzehnte*, *hundertzweite* to *hundertneun-zehnte*, etc., are formed from the cardinals by the addition of **-t-** together with inflexion (*erste*, *dritte*, *achte* are exceptions). All other ordinals are formed from the cardinals by the addition of **-st-** together with inflexion.
(b) The ordinals are declined like ordinary adjectives (*32*).
(c) After names of kings, etc., they are written with capital letters:

Friedrich der Zweite; Elisabeth die Zweite

49 Fractions, etc.

(a) $\frac{1}{2}$ = halb/ein halb $\qquad\qquad$ $1\frac{1}{2}$ = anderthalb (*or* eineinhalb)
$\frac{1}{3}$ = ein Drittel $\qquad\qquad\qquad$ $2\frac{1}{2}$ = zweieinhalb
$\frac{1}{4}$ = ein Viertel $\qquad\qquad\qquad$ $3\frac{1}{2}$ = dreieinhalb
$\frac{1}{5}$ = ein Fünftel, etc. $\qquad\quad$ $4\frac{1}{4}$ = viereinviertel, etc.

NOTE: eine halbe Stunde	*half an hour*
eine Viertelstunde	*a quarter of an hour*
eine Viertelmeile	*a quarter of a mile*
alle halbe Stunde	*every half-hour*
anderthalb Stunden	*an hour and a half*
eine halbe Flasche	*half a bottle*
die halbe Flasche } die Hälfte der Flasche }	*half the bottle*
halb Berlin, halb Deutschland	*half Berlin, half Germany*

(b) einmal, zweimal, dreimal, etc. $\qquad$ *once, twice, three times, etc.*
(c) einfach, zweifach (zwiefach), drei- $\quad$ *onefold (simple), twofold, three-*
$\quad\;$ fach, etc. $\qquad\qquad\qquad\qquad\qquad$ *fold, etc.*
$\quad$ doppelt so viel $\qquad\qquad\qquad\qquad$ *double as much*

(d) einerlei, zweierlei, dreierlei	*of one, two, three kinds*
vielerlei Schiffe	*many kinds of ships*
allerlei Leute	*all sorts of people*
auf mancherlei Art	*in various ways*
Mir war das ganz einerlei.	*That was all the same to me.*
keinerlei Unterschied	*no distinction of any kind*
(e) einzig, einzeln, einsam	*single, separate(ly), solitary*
sein einziges Kind	*his only child*
Der einzelne ist machtlos.	*The individual is powerless.*
Sie werden einzeln verkauft.	*They are sold separately.*
ein einsamer Reiter	*a solitary rider*
(f) erstens, zweitens, drittens, etc.	*in the first, second, third place, etc.*

50 Measurements

Masculine and neuter nouns denoting measurements remain uninflected; feminine nouns, however, usually inflect.

zehn Pfund (n.)	*ten pounds (weight or sterling)*
ein Heer von 10 000 Mann	*an army of 10,000 men*
Der Tisch ist 4 Fuß lang.	*The table is 4 feet long.*
Das Zimmer ist 7 Meter im Quadrat (n.).	*The room is 7 yards square.*
Das Zimmer ist 20 Quadratmeter groß.	*The room is 20 square yards in size.*
drei Paar Handschuhe	*three pairs of gloves*
mit drei Paar Handschuhen	*with three pairs of gloves*
zwei Tassen Tee	*two cups of tea*
drei Meilen	*three miles*
BUT zwanzig Mark (f.)	*twenty marks*

51 Time of Day

| Wieviel Uhr ist es? | |
| Wie spät ist es? | *What is the time?* |

1^{00}	Es ist **ein** Uhr (es ist **eins**).
1^{05}	Es ist fünf Minuten nach eins, ein Uhr fünf.
1^{15}	Es ist Viertel **zwei**, (ein) Viertel nach eins.
1^{30}	Es ist halb **zwei**.
1^{40}	Es ist zwanzig Minuten vor zwei.
1^{45}	Es ist drei Viertel **zwei**, (ein) Viertel vor zwei.

Es ist 3 Uhr nachts/nachmittags, 6 Uhr morgens/abends, 11 Uhr
  vormittags/nachts, 12 Uhr mittags.
Es ist Mittag (*noon*)/Mitternacht (*midnight*).
Es ist halb **zwölf** (mittags/nachts).

Um wieviel Uhr stehen Sie auf?	*At what time do you get up?*
Ich stehe um 7 (Uhr) auf.	*I get up at 7 (o'clock).*
Der Zug fährt 14³⁰ ab.	*The train leaves at 2.30 p.m.*
Der Film beginnt Punkt 5 Uhr.	*The film begins punctually at 5.*
um/am Mittag; um Mitternacht	*at about noon; at about midnight*

NOTE 1 : Die Uhr geht vor.   *The clock is fast.*
          Die Uhr geht nach.   *The clock is slow.*
          Die Uhr geht richtig.   *The clock is right.*

NOTE 2 : ein Uhr   *one o'clock*
          eine Uhr   *a (or one) clock*
          eine Stunde   *an (or one) hour*

52 Dates, Days

der Januar, der Februar, der März, der April, der Mai, der Juni, der
Juli, der August, der September, der Oktober, der November, der
Dezember
der Sonntag, der Montag, der Dienstag, der Mittwoch, der Donnerstag, der Freitag, der Sonnabend (*or* der Samstag)

Der wievielte ist heute?	
Den wievielten haben wir heute?	*What is the date today?*
Heute ist der erste Januar.	
Heute haben wir den ersten Januar.	*It is January 1st today.*
am zweiten März	*on March 2nd*
am Dienstag, dem (*or* den) 8. Mai	*on Tuesday, May 8th*
(Im Jahre) 1939 brach der Krieg aus.	*War broke out in 1939.*
Berlin, den 2. März 1965	*Berlin, 2/3/65 (date at be-*
Berlin, 2.3.65	*ginning of letter)*
am Sonntagmorgen	*on Sunday morning*

53 Age

Wie alt bist du?	*What is your age?*
Ich bin vierzehn (Jahre alt).	*I am fourteen (years of age).*
Mit fünf Jahren ging ich zur Schule.	*I went to school when I was five.*
Wann wurde/ist er geboren?	*When was he born?*
Ich wurde/bin 1930 geboren.	*I was born in 1930.*

54 Useful Expressions of Time (cf. 41)

heute	*today*	acht Tage	*a week*
heute morgen	*this morning*	vierzehn Tage	*a fortnight*
heute nach- mittag	*this afternoon*	vor acht Tagen	*a week ago*
heute abend	*tonight (before bedtime)*	heute in 8 Tagen	*today week*
heute nacht	*last night (i.e., during the night)* *tonight (after bedtime)*	heute vor 14 Tagen	*a fortnight ago to- day*
		dieser Tage	*the other day*
morgen	*tomorrow*	morgens	*in the morning(s)*
morgen früh	*tomorrow morning*	vormittags	*in the forenoon*
morgen nach- mittag	*tomorrow afternoon*	nachmittags	*in the afternoon(s)*
		abends	*in the evening(s)*
morgen abend	*tomorrow evening*	bis nachts um eins	*till one in the morn- ing*
gestern	*yesterday*	tags zuvor	*the day before*
gestern morgen	*yesterday morning*	tags darauf	*the day after*
		voriges Jahr	*last year*
gestern nachmittag	*yesterday afternoon*	nächstes Jahr	*next year*
		am Donners- tag	*on Thursday*
gestern abend	*yesterday evening, last night (before bedtime)*	an demselben Tage	*(on) the same day*
übermorgen	*the day after to- morrow*	am nächsten Morgen	*(on) the next morning*
vorgestern	*the day before yes- terday*	am andern/ folgenden Tage	*the following day*
diese Nacht	*last night (after bedtime)*	am vorigen Abend	*the night (i.e. even- ing) before*
nächsten Mittwoch	*next Wednesday*	in der vorigen Nacht/ Woche	*the previous night/ week*
letzten/ vorigen Dienstag	*last Tuesday*	am Tage vorher	*the day before*
diesen Sommer	*this summer*	am Tage darauf	*the day after*
im Frühling	*in spring*		

Pronouns

55 Declension of Personal Pronouns, Possessive Adjectives and Pronouns

Pers. Pron.	Possessive Adj. (*Declension,* see *32(d)*)	Possessive Pronoun (*Declension:* (a) *Strong;* (b), (c) *Weak;* see *32(a)*)
N. ich (*I*)	mein, meine, mein	(a) meiner, meine, mein(e)s
A. mich	(*my*)	(b) der, die, das meine (*mine*)
G. meiner		(c) der, die, das meinige
D. mir		
N. du (*thou, you*)	dein, deine, dein	(a) deiner, deine, dein(e)s
A. dich	(*thy, your*)	(b) der, die, das deine (*thine*)
G. deiner		(c) der, die, das deinige
D. dir		
N. er (*he, it*)	sein, seine, sein	(a) seiner, seine, sein(e)s
A. ihn	(*his, its*)	(b) der, die, das seine (*his, its*)
G. seiner		(c) der, die, das seinige
D. ihm		
N. sie (*she, it*)	ihr, ihre, ihr	(a) ihrer, ihre, ihr(e)s
A. sie	(*her, its*)	(b) der, die, das ihre (*hers, its*)
G. ihrer		(c) der, die, das ihrige
D. ihr		
N. es (*it*)	sein, seine, sein	(a) seiner, seine, sein(e)s
A. es	(*its*)	(b) der, die, das seine (*its*)
G. seiner		(c) der, die, das seinige
D. ihm		
N. wir (*we*)	**unser**, uns(e)re, **unser**	(a) uns(e)rer, uns(e)re, uns(e)res
A. uns	(*our*)	(b) der, die, das uns(e)re (*ours*)
G. unser		(c) der, die, das uns(e)rige
D. uns		
N. ihr (*you*)	**euer**, eu(e)re, **euer**	(a) eurer, eu(e)re, eures
A. euch	(*your*)	(b) der, die, das eu(e)re (*yours*)
G. euer		(c) der, die, das **eurige**
D. euch		

N. sie (*they*)	ihr, ihre, ihr	(a) ihrer, ihre, ihr(e)s	
A. sie	(*their*)	(b) der, die, das ihre	(*theirs*)
G. ihrer		(c) der, die, das ihrige	
D. ihnen			

N. Sie (*you*)	Ihr, Ihre, Ihr	(a) Ihrer, Ihre, Ihr(e)s	
A. Sie	(*your*)	(b) der, die, das Ihre	(*yours*)
G. Ihrer		(c) der, die, das Ihrige	
D. Ihnen			

NOTE: The possessive pronouns of type (a) are now the usual spoken forms.

56 Notes on the Personal Pronouns

(a) The familiar forms of address, i.e. those used in addressing relatives, close friends, children and animals are *du* (sing.) and *ihr* (pl.). The polite form of address is *Sie* (sing. and pl.).

NOTE: In letters *du, ihr* (=you), *dein, euer*, etc., are always written with capitals, e.g. *Du, Ihr, Euer*, etc.

(b) **Er** (der Apfel) ist reif.	It (*the apple*) *is ripe.*
Sie (die Birne) ist reif.	It (*the pear*) *is ripe.*
Es (das Obst) ist reif.	It (*the fruit*) *is ripe.*

(c) Es waren **ihrer** drei.	*There were three of them.*
Wir waren **unser** sieben.	*We were seven of us.*

(d) When **things** are referred to, *seiner* and *ihrer*, i.e. the genitive of *er, es* and *sie*, are usually replaced by **dessen** (m. and n. sing.) and **deren** (f. sing. and m.f.n. pl.). For clarity *dessen* and *deren* are also sometimes preferred to the possessive adjectives *sein* and *ihr*.

Ich schäme mich **seiner**.	*I am ashamed* **of him** (or **of it**, e.g. child).
Er ist **ihrer** nicht würdig.	*He is not worthy* **of her.**
BUT Er schämt sich **dessen**.	*He is ashamed* **of it.**
ihr Land und **dessen** Volk	*their country and the people of it/its people*

(e) With most prepositions **da-** (**dar-** before a vowel) is usually used instead of the accusative and dative of the personal pronoun when referring to **things**. Compare:

Er interessiert sich **für ihn**.	*He is interested* **in him.**
Er interessiert sich **dafür**.	*He is interested* **in it/that/them.**

63

| Er erzählte **von ihnen**. | *He spoke **about them** (=persons).* |
| Er erzählte **davon**. | *He spoke **about it/that** (or **about them** (=things)).* |

NOTE 1: Such compounds are not possible with the prepositions *außer*, *außerhalb*, *entlang*, *gegenüber*, *ohne* and *seit*.

NOTE 2: In addition to their literal meanings some of these compounds have acquired other quite distinct meanings, e.g., **dabei** (*in doing so*), **dafür** (*in return*), **dagegen** (*on the other hand*), **darauf** (*thereupon*), **obendrein** (*into the bargain*), **darum** (*therefore*), **dazu** (*in addition*).

NOTE 3: deswegen *on account of it* (*them*)

(f) Note the following uses of **es**:

Es regnet; es schneite.	*It is raining; it was snowing.*
Es sind meine Freunde.	*They are my friends.*
Ich bin es; sind sie es?	*It is I; is it they?*
Dort gibt es Konzerte (*A*).	*There are concerts there.*
Es gibt **einen** Gott (*A*).	*There is (=exists) a God.*
Es ist **kein** Mensch da (*N*).	*There is nobody there* (i.e. present)
Es sind keine Menschen da.	*There are no people there.*
Es blühen die Blumen.	*The flowers are in bloom.*
Es wurde lange getanzt.	*Dancing went on for a long time.*

NOTE 1: In sentences like the last four *es* is **omitted** unless it is the first word in the clause. Compare:

Es ist kein Mensch da.⎫
BUT Kein Mensch ist da. ⎭ *There is nobody there.*

NOTE 2: Es war einmal ein König. *There was once (upon a time) a king.*

57 Notes on the Possessive Pronoun

(a) The possessive pronoun agrees in **gender** and **number** with the noun to which it refers.

(b) All three forms are still used though *der meine/der meinige*, etc. are now mainly restricted to the written language.

Dein Aufsatz ist besser als **meiner**/der mein(ig)e.	*Your essay is better than mine.*
Dies ist mein Buch, das ist **dein(e)s**.	*This is my book, that is yours.*
Dies sind meine Bücher, das sind **deine**.	*These are my books, those are yours.*

(c) The genitive rarely occurs, being mostly replaced by a construction with *von* + dative.

Das ist eins **von meinen.**   *That is one of mine.*

(d) Except when the subject is *es*, *das* or *dies* the possessive pronouns (but not *ihr* or *Ihr*) used predicatively are not inflected. These uninflected forms tend now to be replaced by the construction with *gehören* (belong):

Das ist meiner/meine/mein(e)s.   *That is mine.*
Das Buch/der Hut ist mein.   *The book/hat is mine.*
Die Uhr gehört ihr/Ihnen.   *The watch is hers/yours.*

(e) When written with capitals the possessive pronouns have special meanings:

die Seinen, die Seinigen   *his people* (or *family*)
das Seine/Seinige   *his property* (or *business, concern*)
die Seine   *his wife* (or *fiancée*)

NOTE: ein Freund von mir }
      einer meiner Freunde   *a friend of mine*

58 Reflexive Pronouns

sing.	*pl.*	*Polite Form (sing. and pl.)*
A. mich (*myself*)	uns (*ourselves*)	
D. mir	uns	
A. dich (*yourself*)	euch (*yourselves*)	sich (*yourself, yourselves*)
D. dir	euch	sich
A. sich (*him-, her-,*	sich (*themselves*)	
D. sich *it-self*)	sich	

Ich wasche mich.   *I wash myself.*
Ich wasche mir die Hände.   *I wash my hands.*
Ich sah unter mir das Meer.   *I saw the sea beneath me.*
Er sah unter **sich** das Meer.   *He saw the sea beneath him.*
Du schreibst nichts von dir.   *You write nothing about yourself.*

59 Reciprocal Pronouns

Wir lieben uns (*or* einander).   *We love one another.*
Sie schreiben sich (*or* einander).   *They write to one another.*
Sie denken aneinander.   *They think of one another.*
Sir sprechen miteinander.   *They speak to one another.*
Sie trennten sich voneinander.   *They separated from one another.*

60 Welcher, welche, welches

Strong declension (*32(a)*).

Welches Gedicht ist das beste?	*Which poem is the best?*
Von welcher Frau sprechen Sie?	*Which woman are you speaking of?*
Welch**es** ist der höchste Berg?	*Which is the highest mountain?*
Welch**es** sind die höchsten Berge?	*Which are the highest mountains?*

NOTE: Welch ein guter Mann!   *What a good man!*
Welch schlechtes Wetter!   *What bad weather!*

61 Was für einer (pron.); was für (ein) (adj.)

The pronoun is declined strong (*32(a)*), *welche* being substituted for
einer in the plural; the adjective is declined like the indefinite article (*12*),
ein being omitted in the plural.

Was für einer ist es?	*What sort of one is it?*
Was für **welche** haben Sie?	*What sort of ones have you?*
Was für ein Mann ist er?	*What sort of a man is he?*
Was für Männer sind das?	*What sort of men are those?*
Mit was für einem Bleistift schreibt er?	*With what sort of a pencil is he writing?*
Was für Holz ist das?	*What (sort of) wood is that?*

NOTE: Was für ein guter Mann er ist!   *What a good man he is!*
Was für schlechtes Wetter!   *What bad weather!*

62 Wer, was

	m.f.	*n.*
N.	wer	was
A.	wen	was (an was, woran)
G.	wessen	wessen
D.	wem	— (wovon, woraus, etc.)

Wer ist da? Was ist das?	*Who is there? What is that?*
Wer/was sind diese Leute?	*Who/what are these people?*
Wen liebt er? Was tut er?	*Whom does he love? What does he do?*
Wessen Hund ist das?	*Whose dog is that?*
Wessen hat man ihn angeklagt?	*What has he been accused of?*
Wem schreibst du?	*To whom are you writing?*
Woran/an was denkst du?	*What are you thinking of?*

63 Der, die, das (welcher, welche, welches)

	sing.		*pl.*
m.	*f.*	*n.*	*m.f.n.*
N. der (welcher)	die (welche)	das (welches)	die (welche)
A. den (welchen)	die (welche)	das (welches)	die (welche)
G. dessen	deren	dessen	deren
D. dem (welchem)	der (welcher)	dem (welchem)	denen (welchen)

(a) Note the following points:

i. The relative pronoun agrees with its antecedent in **gender** and **number**, but its case depends on the part it plays in its own clause.

ii. The finite verb has **final** position in a relative clause.

iii. The relative must **never** be omitted in German.

iv. *Der*, etc. (not *welcher*, etc.), **must** be used if the antecedent is a personal or indefinite pronoun.

v. *Der*, etc., is **generally** preferred to *welcher* except when otherwise an ugly repetition would result.

Die Frau, **die** vor mir stand, war alt.	*The woman who stood in front of me was old.*
Der Mann, **den** ich vor mir sah, war jung.	*The man I saw in front of me was young.*
Das Mädchen, **dessen** Vater krank war, mußte schwer arbeiten.	*The girl whose father was ill had to work hard.*
Die Leute, **denen** wir geholfen haben, sind dankbar.	*The people we helped are grateful.*
Die Kinder, mit **denen** wir spielten, waren sehr jung.	*The children we were playing with were very young.*
Die Jungen, mit **deren** Lehrer ich sprach, arbeiteten fleißig.	*The boys with whose master I spoke were working hard.*
Das Kind, **welches** (*not* das) das Brot aß, weinte.	*The child who ate the bread was weeping.*

(b) The forms compounded with **wo(r)-** and a preposition are used with indefinite antecedents, but never when the antecedent is a person or animal and rarely nowadays when it is a thing.

Das einzige, **wovon** er sprach, . . .   *The only thing he spoke of . . .*
Der Tisch, an **dem** (*rather than*   *The table he sat at . . .*
woran) er saß, . . .

NOTE 1: worauf, *whereupon*   wobei, *in doing which*   wodurch, *whereby*
NOTE 2: der Grund, warum   *the reason why*

(c) When the antecedent is a personal pronoun of the first or second person it is repeated immediately after the relative pronoun, and the verb agrees with it.

Du, der **du** das nicht **glaubst**, . . .   *You who do not think that . . .*
Wir, die **wir** das nicht **glau-**   *We who do not think that . . .*
ben, . . .
BUT Ich bin es, der (*or* die) angerufen   *It was I who rang up.*
hat.

64 Was

The relative pronoun is **was** when its antecedent is:

(a) A singular indefinite pronoun:

Das ist alles, **was** ich weiß.   *That is all I know.*
Vieles/nichts, **was** er sagt, . . .   *Much/nothing that he says . . .*
BUT Das ist etwas, **das** (*or* **was**) ich   *That is something I don't know.*
nicht weiß.

(b) An adjective used as a neuter noun:

Das Beste, **was** er tun kann, . . .   *The best thing he can do . . .*
Das einzige, **was** er tun kann, . . .   *The only thing he can do . . .*

(c) A whole clause:

Er arbeitet nicht, **was** ich nicht   *He does not work, a fact which I*
verstehe.   *don't understand.*

(d) Equivalent to **that which**:

Tue, **was** du kannst.   *Do what you can.*
Denke an das, **was** ich dir sagte.   *Think of what I told you.*

NOTE: Forms like *daran* should not be made the antecedent of *was*.

65 Wer

Declension: see *62*.

Wer sucht, findet.	*He who seeks shall find.*
Wen ich liebe, dem vertraue ich.	*Whom I love I trust.*
Wem nicht zu raten ist, dem ist auch nicht zu helfen.	*Who won't be told can't be helped.*

66 Wo, da

Die Stadt, **wo** ich wohne, . . .	*The town in which I live . . .*
Überall, **wo** man hingeht, . . .	*Wherever one goes . . .*
Jetzt aber, **wo** (*or* **da**) er fort war, . . .	*But now that he had gone . . .*

67 Dieser, jener

Strong declension, see *32(a)* and (*b*).

Dieses Buch kostet mehr als jenes.	*This book costs more than that one.*
Mit diesem Bleistift kann man besser schreiben als mit jenem.	*With this pencil one can write better than with that one.*
K. und H. waren Brüder; **dieser** blieb zu Hause, **jener** fuhr nach Amerika.	*K. and H. were brothers; the latter stayed at home, the former went to America.*

NOTE: *Jener* is used normally only with *dieser* expressed or understood. However, when an object can be pointed at, the demonstrative *der*, etc. (see **69**) is normally used, in the spoken language particularly, to render 'that', e.g. *der* (*Berg*) *da/dort*.

68 Solcher

Strong declension, see *32(a)*, except when preceded by *ein*, when it is declined as in *32(d)*. It is uninflected when followed by *ein*.

Ich habe solchen Hunger.	*I am so hungry.*
Ich habe solche Schmerzen.	*I have such pain(s).*
ein solcher Mensch⎫ solch ein Mensch ⎭	*such a man*
Solche, die das sagen . . .	*Those who say that . . .*

69 Der, die, das (Demonstrative Pronoun)

Declension: see *63*, but note that the genitive pl. is **derer** when followed by a **relative pronoun**. The demonstrative, unlike the definite article, is always stressed.

War es **der** Mann/Baum (da)? – Nein, nicht **der**.	*Was it **that** man? No, not **that** one.*
Die (dort) kenne ich nicht.	*I don't know **her/that one**.*
Ich bin mir dessen bewußt.	*I am aware of it.*
Der, der das sagt, lügt.	*He who says that lies.*
Viele **derer**, die . . .	*Many of those who . . .*
Unter denen, die . . .	*Amongst those who . . .*
Ihr Hut ist schöner als der ihrer Freundin.	*Her hat is prettier than her friend's.*
Er erzählte von seinem Freund und dessen Frau.	*He spoke of his friend and his (i.e. the friend's) wife.*
Er erzählte von seinem Freund und seiner Frau.	*He spoke of his friend and his (i.e. own) wife.*

NOTE: **Das (dies)** ist mein Buch. *That (this) is my book.*
Das (dies) sind meine Bücher. *Those (these) are my books.*

70 Derselbe, dieselbe, dasselbe

	sing.		*pl.*
	m.	*f.*	*n.*	*m.f.n.*
N.	derselbe	dieselbe	dasselbe	dieselben
A.	denselben	dieselbe	dasselbe	dieselben
G.	desselben	derselben	desselben	derselben
D.	demselben	derselben	demselben	denselben

Sie hat immer denselben Hut auf.	*She always has the same hat on.*
an demselben/am selben Tage	*(on) the same day*
Das ist dasselbe.	*That is the same thing.*

71 Derjenige, diejenige, dasjenige

	sing.		*pl.*
	m.	*f.*	*n.*	*m.f.n.*
N.	derjenige	diejenige	dasjenige	diejenigen
A.	denjenigen	diejenige	dasjenige	diejenigen
G.	desjenigen	derjenigen	desjenigen	derjenigen
D.	demjenigen	derjenigen	demjenigen	denjenigen

derjenige, der ...	*he who* ...
diejenige, die ...	*she who* ...
diejenigen Leute, die ...	*those people who* ...
mit allen denjenigen, deren ...	*with all those whose* ...

72 Selbst, selber

Indeclinable.

ich selbst, wir selbst (*or* selber)	*I myself, we ourselves*
Gott selbst (*or* selber)	*God Himself*
von selbst	*of its own accord*

73 Man

N.	man
A.	einen
G.	—
D.	einem

Man ißt.	*One eats, you eat, people eat.*
Man sagt, daß ...	*It is said/they say that* ...
Man klopft, klingelt.	*There is a knock, a ring.*
Sie sollten einen in Ruhe lassen.	*They ought to leave one alone.*
Das kann einem alle Tage begegnen.	*That can happen to one any day.*

74 Einer, eine, ein(e)s

Strong declension, see *32(a)*.

Eine(r) von euch hat es getan.	*One (f. or m.) of you has done it.*
eines der Bücher	*one (n.) of the books*
Das ist das Haus eines meiner Söhne/ einer meiner Töchter.	*That is the house of one of my sons/of one of my daughters.*
Ich zeigte es einem von euch.	*I showed it to one (m.) of you.*
eins von beiden	*one of the two (things)*
Es kommt auf eins heraus.	*It comes to the same thing.*
irgendeiner	*someone or other*

NOTE 1: *Einer*, etc., agrees in gender with the noun for which it stands.

NOTE 2: **One** is not translated when it occurs after an adjective:

Das ist das schönste.	*That is the finest one.*

75 Keiner, keine, kein(e)s

Strong declension, see *32(a)*.

Keiner will es ihm sagen.	*Nobody will tell him.*
keines der Bücher	*none of the books*
Er war keines Freund.	*He was nobody's friend.*

NOTE: *Keiner*, etc., agrees in gender with the noun for which it stands.

76 Jemand

Jemand ist gekommen.	*Somebody has come.*
Kennen Sie jemand(en), der . . .?	*Do you know anybody who . . .?*
Das muß jemand(e)s Hut sein.	*That must be somebody's hat.*
Er spricht mit jemand(em), der . . .	*He speaks to somebody who . . .*
Jemand anders hat es getan.	*Somebody else did it.*
irgend jemand	*somebody or other*
Sonst (noch) jemand?	*Anyone else* (i.e. in addition)*?*

77 Niemand

Niemand hat Sie gesehen.	*Nobody saw you.*
Ich habe niemand(en) gesehen.	*I saw nobody.*
Das ist niemand(e)s Sache.	*That is nobody's business.*
Das gehört niemand(em).	*That belongs to nobody.*
Niemand anders weiß davon.	*Nobody else knows about it.*

78 Jeder, jedermann

Jeder is declined like a strong adjective (*32(a)*); **jedermann** is declined like a strong masculine noun (*15*), though without -*e* in the dative. There is no plural.

Jeder junge Mann weiß das.	*Every young man knows that.*
Er sitzt jeden Tag zu Hause.	*He stays at home every day.*
Das kann jeden Tag geschehen.	*That can happen **any** day.*
jede dritte Woche	*every third week*
Jeder (*or* jedermann) weiß es.	*Everybody knows it.*
Das ist jedem bekannt.	*That is known to everybody.*
jedermanns Sache	*everybody's business*

79 Alles, alle (cf. *35*)

Strong declension (see *32(a)*), except before the genitive singular of masculine and neuter nouns ending in -*s* when it is now usually weak (i.e. *allen*). Before the definite article, the demonstrative and possessive adjective the contracted form *all* is now normally used with singular masculine nouns and often with plural and feminine singular nouns.

Alles ist vergebens.	*Everything is in vain.*
Alles war auf den Beinen.	*Everybody was astir.*
Alles umsteigen!	*All change!*
alles übrige	*all the rest; all that's left*
ohne allen Grund	*without **any** reason*
trotz allen Lärms	*in spite of all the noise*
alles in allem; vor allem	*all in all; above all*
all mein Geld	*all my money*
Wozu all der Lärm?	*Why all the noise?*
mit aller Kraft	*with all one's strength*
bei all(er) dieser Arbeit	*with all this work*
Alle waren eingeladen.	*All were invited.*
Alle/all(e) die Gäste kamen.	*All the guests came.*
Bitte warten Sie alle!	*Please wait all of you.*
alle drei Wochen	***every** third week, **every** three weeks*
all(e) seine Verwandten	*all his relations*
unter allen Umständen	*in all circumstances*

80 Etwas, was (cf. *35*)

Indeclinable.

Ich will dir (et)was sagen.	*I will tell you something.*
etwas Neues; etwas Komisches	*something new; something odd*
So etwas ist unmöglich.	*That sort of thing is impossible.*
Man kann so etwas nicht tun.	*One cannot do anything of the sort.*
etwas and(e)res	*something else/different*
etwas ganz and(e)res	*something quite different*
irgend etwas	*something or other*

81 Nichts (cf. *35*)

Indeclinable.

alles oder nichts	*all or nothing*
Ich weiß nichts davon.	*I know nothing about it.*
nichts and(e)res	*nothing else* (i.e. different)
Sonst nichts?	*Nothing else* (i.e. in addition)*?*
gar/überhaupt nichts	*nothing at all*

82 Welcher, welche, welches

Strong declension, see *32(a)*.

Welcher, used as an indefinite pronoun, means 'some' or 'any'. It agrees with the noun to which it refers in **gender** and **number**, but its case depends on the part it plays in its own clause.

Er hat keinen **Tee**; hast du welch**en**?	*He hasn't any tea; have you any?*
Er hat keine **Milch**; hast du welch**e**?	*He hasn't any milk; have you any?*
Er hat kein **Wasser**; gib ihm welch**es**!	*He hasn't any water; give him some.*
Er hat keine **Blumen**; hast du welch**e**?	*He hasn't any flowers; have you any?*

83 Indefinite Numeral Adjectives and Pronouns

Those in group (*a*) are indeclinable; those in group (*b*) are all plural and declined strong (see *32(a)*); and those in group (*c*) are declined weak, strong or not at all.

(a) **etwas** Zucker; **genug** Wasser	*some sugar; enough water*
mehr Tee; **weniger** Milch	*more tea; less milk*
ein wenig Brot; **ein bißchen** Brot; **ein paar** Leute	*a little bread; a bit of bread; one or two people*
(b) **viele** Leute; **mehrere** Leute	*many people; several people*
wenige Leute; **einige** Leute	*few (=only a few) people; a few (=some) people*
verschiedene Gründe; **manche** Leute	*various reasons; a fair number of people*

NOTE: manch liebes Kind ⎫
       manches liebe Kind ⎭   *many a dear child*

       mit manch liebem Kind ⎫
       mit manchem lieben Kind ⎭ *with many a dear child*

(c) das **ganze** Dorf	*the whole village*
den **ganzen** Monat	*the whole of the month*
eine **ganze** Menge	*quite a lot*
sein **ganzes** Geld	*all his money*
(in) **ganz** Deutschland	*(in) the whole of Germany*
Er ist mit **wenigem** zufrieden.	*He is satisfied with little.*
Ich nehme nur **wenig** Zucker.	*I only take a little sugar.*
mit **wenig** Mühe	*with little trouble*

Vielen Dank!	*Many thanks.*
Ich nahm (**zu-)viel** Milch.	*I took (too) much milk.*
Ich weiß **viel.**	*I know a lot.*
Viel Vergnügen!	*Enjoy yourself.*
BUT Mit **großem** Vergnügen!	*With much pleasure!*
Wieviel? Wieviel Leute?	*How much? How many people?*

(d) **Die einen** mögen es, **die an-   *Some like it, others don't.*
deren** nicht.

Prepositions

84 Prepositions governing the Accusative

ausgenommen, *except*
bis, *till, as far as, by, to*
durch, *through, by*
entlang, *along*
für, *for*

gegen, *against, towards, compared to*
ohne, *without*
um, *round, at, for*
wider, *against*

NOTE 1: Durchs = durch das; fürs = für das; ums = um das.
NOTE 2: *Entlang* and *ausgenommen* mostly follow the nouns they govern.

(a) BIS

Er bleibt bis Ostern.	*He is staying till Easter.*
Er fuhr bis Berlin.	*He went as far as Berlin.*
zwei bis drei Stunden	*two to three hours*
Er sprang bis an die Decke.	*He jumped up to the ceiling.*
Bis Mittwoch bin ich wieder da.	*By Wednesday I shall be back.*

(b) DURCH

| Er ging durchs Zimmer. | *He went through the room.* |
| Er wurde durch Gift getötet. | *He was killed by poison.* |

(c) ENTLANG

| Er ging die Straße entlang. | *He walked along the street.* |

(d) FÜR

Er tat es für mich.	*He did it for me.*
Er ist fürs Vaterland gestorben.	*He died for his country.*
Er kaufte für 50 Pfennig Äpfel.	*He bought 50 pfennigs worth of apples.*
jahr für Jahr	*year after year*

75

(e) GEGEN

Wir flogen gegen den Wind.	*We flew against the wind.*
Er tat es gegen meinen Wunsch.	*He did it against my wish.*
gegen Ende des Monats	*towards the end of the month*
gegen Osten; gegen Westen.	*towards the east; towards the west.*
gegen 4 Uhr	*about 4 o'clock*
Ich bin nichts gegen ihn.	*I am nothing compared to him.*
Er ist grausam/(un)gerecht gegen sie.	*He is cruel/(un)just to her.*
Er ist streng gegen sie.	*He is severe with them.*
Er ist (un)höflich gegen sie.	*He is (im)polite to them.*

(f) OHNE

Ich bin ganz ohne Mittel.	*I am entirely without any means.*

(g) UM

Wir saßen um den Tisch.	*We were sitting round the table.*
Er ging um die Stadt herum.	*He went right round the town.*
um 4 Uhr	*at four o'clock*
Ich tät' das um alles in der Welt nicht.	*I would not do that for anything in the world.*
um so besser; um so mehr	*all the better; all the more*
ein Jahr ums andere	*year after year*

(h) WIDER

Er tat es wider meinen Willen.	*He did it against my will.*

85 Prepositions governing the Genitive

(an)statt, *instead of*	mittels, *by means of*
außerhalb, *outside*	oberhalb, *above, higher up*
diesseits, *on this side of*	trotz,[1] *in spite of*
infolge, *as a result of*	um . . . willen, *for the sake of*
inmitten, *in the midst of*	unterhalb, *below, lower than*
innerhalb, *inside, within*	unweit, *not far from*
jenseits, *on the other side of, beyond*	während, *during*
	wegen, *because of*

[1] Also occasionally with the dative

(an)statt des Weins	*instead of the wine*
diesseits des Meeres	*on this side of the ocean*
inmitten dieser Leute	*in the midst of these people*
innerhalb der Stadt	*inside the town*
innerhalb eines Jahres	*within a year*
oberhalb der Brücke	*above the bridge* (i.e. *higher up the river*)
trotz des schönen Wetters	*in spite of the fine weather*
Um Gottes willen!	*For Heaven's sake!*
wegen des schlechten Wetters	*because of the bad weather*
berühmt wegen ihrer Schönheit	*famous for her beauty*

86 Prepositions governing the Dative

(a) aus, *out of*
    außer, *except (for), besides*
    bei, *at, near, with*
    entgegen, *towards, contrary to, against*
    gegenüber, *opposite*
    mit, *with*

nach, *to(wards), after, according to*
seit, *since*
von, *from, of, by (agent in passive)*
zu, *to*

NOTE 1: Beim = bei dem; vom = von dem; zum = zu dem; zur = zu der.
NOTE 2: *Entgegen* and *gegenüber* usually follow the nouns they govern, as does *nach* when it means 'according to'.

i. AUS

Er lief aus dem Hause.	*He ran out of the house.*
Er kommt aus Berlin.	*He hails from Berlin.*
aus Holz, Eisen (gemacht)	*(made) of wood, iron*
Aus welchem Grunde?	*For what reason?*
aus Mangel an Geld	*through lack of money*
Er tat es aus Liebe.	*He did it for love.*
Ich weiß es aus Erfahrung.	*I know it from experience.*
aus dem Englischen ins Deutsche übersetzt	*translated from English into German*

ii. AUSSER

Außer dir habe ich niemand.	*Apart from you I have nobody.*

iii. BEI

Er wohnt bei seinem Onkel.	*He lives at his uncle's/with his uncle.*
die Schlacht bei Hastings	*the Battle of Hastings*
bei meiner Ankunft	*on my arrival*
Er hat kein Geld bei sich.	*He has no money on/with him.*
bei schlechtem Wetter	*in bad weather*
bei jedem dritten Wort	*at every third word*
bei dieser Gelegenheit	*on this occasion*
Er hilft bei der Arbeit.	*He helps with the work.*
beim Aussteigen	*on getting out*

iv. ENTGEGEN

allen Regeln entgegen	*contrary to all rules*

v. GEGENÜBER

Er wohnt dem Bahnhof gegenüber/ gegenüber dem Bahnhof.	*He lives opposite the station.*

vi. MIT

Er kam mit seinem Vater.	*He came with his father.*
mit dem Auto; mit der Bahn	*by car; by rail*
mit der Elektrischen	*by tram*
mit dem Zug; mit dem Flugzeug	*by train; by aeroplane*
mit dem Schiff; mit der Post	*by boat; by post*
mit leiser/lauter Stimme	*in a soft/loud voice*
Er nickte mit dem Kopf.	*He nodded his head.*
mit zehn Jahren	*at the age of ten*
mit ihm bekannt/zufrieden	*acquainted/pleased with him*

vii. NACH

nach der Stadt; nach Paris	*to the town; to Paris*
nach Europa; nach England	*to Europe; to England*
nach Süden; nach Norden	*to the south; to the north*
Er geht nach Hause.	*He is going home.*
nach der Stunde	*after the lesson*
meiner Meinung nach	*in my opinion*
in der Richtung nach London	*in the direction of London*
der Reihe nach	*in turn*

viii. SEIT

seit dem Krieg.	*since the war.*
Schon seit 2 Jahren lerne ich Deutsch.	*I have been learning German for 2 years now* (cf. 94(c)).
Seit langem wartete ich darauf.	*I had been waiting for it for a long time* (cf. 95(c)).

ix. VON

Der Zug kommt von Berlin.	*The train comes from Berlin.*
der König von England	*the King of England*
Er aß von dem Brot.	*He ate some of the bread.*
ein Mann von 40 Jahren	*a man of 40*
ein Bild von Dürer	*a picture by Dürer*
von Anfang an	*from the beginning*
von nun an	*from now on*
südlich von; nördlich von	*to the south of; north of*
westlich von; östlich von	*to the west of; east of*
von mir geschlagen	*beaten by me*
müde von der Arbeit	*tired by the work*
Ich bin davon überzeugt.	*I am convinced of it.*
Es war keine Spur von ihm da.	*There was no sign of him there.*
Was sieht man von dort aus?	*What can one see from there?*

x. ZU

Er geht zum Bahnhof/zur Post.	*He goes to the station/to the post.*
Er geht zur Schule/zur Kirche.	*He goes to school/to church.*
Er geht zum Arzt.	*He goes to the doctor('s).*
Er geht zu Bett.	*He goes to bed.*
Er bleibt/ist zu Hause.	*He stays/is at home.*
Er kommt zu Hause an.	*He arrives (gets) home.*
zu Fuß; zu Pferde	*on foot; on horseback*
Er ißt bei uns zu Mittag (zu Abend).	*He has lunch (dinner) with us.*
zu Weihnachten; zu Ostern	*at Christmas; at Easter*
das Wirtshaus zum Weißen Löwen	*the White Lion Inn*
Eier zu 10 Pfennig das Stück	*eggs at a penny each*
Er hat Geld zur Reise nötig.	*He requires money for the journey.*
zu allem bereit	*ready for anything*
freundlich zu mir	*kind (friendly) to me*

(b) Less common prepositions governing the Dative.

binnen, *within (of time)*

dank, *thanks to*

gemäß, *according to*

längs, *along*

nächst, *next to*

nebst⎫

samt⎭ *together with*

zufolge, *according to*

zuwider, *repugnant, contrary to*

NOTE I: *Gemäß, zufolge* and *zuwider* follow the nouns they govern.

NOTE 2: *Längs, binnen, dank* and *zufolge* are also used with the genitive.

87 Prepositions governing the Accusative or Dative

(a) After the following prepositions the **accusative** is used to show movement **to** a place, the **dative** to show rest or movement **at** a place.

an, *on, at, to, by*

auf, *on (horizontal surface only)*

außer, *out of, beside*

hinter, *behind*

in, *in, into*

neben, *near, next to, beside*

über, *over*

unter, *under, among*

vor, *in front of, before*

zwischen, *between*

NOTE: ans = an das; am = an dem; aufs = auf das; ins = in das; im = in dem; übers = über das; überm = über dem; vors = vor das; vorm = vor dem

Er hängt es an **die** Wand.	*He hangs it on the wall.*
Das Bild hängt an **der** Wand.	*The picture hangs on the wall.*
Er setzt sich auf **den** Stuhl.	*He sits down on the chair.*
Er saß auf **dem** Stuhl.	*He was sitting on the chair.*
Ich geriet außer **mich** vor Wut.	*I got beside myself with rage.*
Ich war außer **mir** vor Wut.	*I was beside myself with rage.*
Er stellte sich hinter **mich**.	*He came and stood behind me.*
Er stand hinter **mir**.	*He was standing behind me.*
Er trat in **das** Zimmer.	*He came into the room.*
Er arbeitete in **dem** Zimmer.	*He was working in the room.*
Er ging **im** Zimmer auf und ab.	*He walked up and down in the room.*
Er setzte sich neben **mich**.	*He sat down beside me.*
Er saß neben **mir**.	*He was sitting beside me.*
Er hängt es über **das** Sofa.	*He hangs it over the sofa.*
Es hängt über **dem** Sofa.	*It hangs over the sofa.*

Er sank unter **den** Tisch.	*He sank down under the table.*
Er lag unter **dem** Tisch.	*He was lying under the table.*
Er legte es vor **mich** hin.	*He put it down in front of me.*
Es lag vor **mir**.	*It lay in front of me.*
Er setzte sich zwischen **sie**.	*He sat down between them.*
Er saß zwischen **ihnen**.	*He sat between them.*

(b) Idiomatic expressions involving these prepositions:

i. AN + ACCUSATIVE

Wir reisen ans Meer (an die See).	*We are going to the seaside.*
Er kommt jetzt an die Reihe.	*It is now his turn.*
Es ist ein Brief an Sie da.	*There is a letter for you here.*
Ich habe eine Bitte an Sie.	*I have a request to make to you.*
Er setzte sich ans Feuer.	*He sat down by the fire.*

ii. AN + DATIVE

Wir sind am Meer (an der See).	*We are at the seaside.*
Die Reihe ist an ihm. ⎫	*It is his turn.*
Er ist an der Reihe/dran. ⎭	
ein Lehrer an unserer Schule	*a master at our school*
Er saß am Feuer.	*He was sitting by the fire.*
am Tage, am Morgen	*in the daytime, in/on the morning*
am Nachmittag, am Abend	*in the afternoon, in/on the evening*
am Tage vor/nach seiner Ankunft	*the day before/after his arrival*
Er verdient 5 Mark am Tage.	*He earns 5 marks a day.*
Er kommt einmal am Tage.	*He comes once a day.*
Er ist noch am Leben.	*He is still alive.*
an Ihrer Stelle	*in your place/if I were you*
die Sterne am Himmel	*the stars in the sky*
Er ist reich an Erfahrung.	*He is rich in experience.*
Sie ist arm an Ideen.	*She hasn't many ideas.*
Er ist jung an Jahren.	*He is young in years.*
Er hat keinen Mangel an Zeit.	*He has no lack of time.*

iii. AUF + ACCUSATIVE

Er ging auf die Post/die Bank.	*He went to the post/bank.*
Er ging auf den Markt; auf die Straße.	*He went to the market; into the street.*
Eine Antwort auf die Frage/auf den Brief.	*An answer to the question/to the letter.*
Er macht sich auf den Weg nach ...	*He sets off for ...*
Er fuhr aufs Land.	*He went into the country.*
Er hat es auf 3 Jahre gemietet.	*He has rented it for 3 years.*
Alle kamen bis auf einen.	*All came except one.*
auf diese Weise	*in this way*
auf jeden Fall/auf alle Fälle	*in any case/anyhow*
auf den ersten Blick	*at first sight*
Sage es auf deutsch!	*Say it in German.*
Ich bin stolz auf ihn.	*I am proud of him.*
Ich bin böse auf ihn.	*I am angry with him.*

iv. AUF + DATIVE

Er war auf dem Markt.	*He was in/at the market.*
Er war auf der Straße.	*He was in the street.*
Er ist auf dem Bahnhof.	*He is at the station.*
Er wohnt auf dem Lande.	*He lives in the country.*
Auf dem Bild sehen wir ...	*In the picture we see ...*
Wann waren Sie auf der Schule?	*When were you at school?*

v. IN + ACCUSATIVE

Er fuhr in die Schweiz.	*He went to Switzerland.*
Er kam in die Nähe.	*He came near.*
Er ging ins Freie.	*He went into the open.*
Er reiste ins Ausland.	*He went abroad.*
Er ging ins Theater, ins Kino.	*He went to the theatre, cinema.*
Er ging ins Büro.	*He went to the office.*
Er brachte es wieder in Ordnung.	*He put it right again.*
Er arbeitet bis spät in die Nacht hinein.	*He works till late at night.*

vi. IN + DATIVE

Er wohnt ganz in der Nähe.	*He lives quite near (by).*
Wir sind jetzt im Freien.	*We are now in the open.*
Er lebt im Ausland.	*He lives abroad.*

Der Junge ist heute in der Schule.	*The boy is at school today.*
Er lernt nichts in der Schule.	*He does not learn anything at school.*
Es ist alles in Ordnung.	*Everything is all right.*
in der Frühe; in der Nacht	*early in the morning; at night*
in **dem**/diesem Augenblick	*(at) that/this moment*
im nächsten Augenblick	*the next moment*
50 km in der Stunde	*50 km an hour*
Er verdient 800 DM im Monat.	*He earns 800 marks a month.*
einmal in der Woche	*once a week*
Er kommt im Büro an.	*He arrives at the office.*
im Gegenteil	*on the contrary*
im allgemeinen	*in general/as a rule*
im Radio	*on the wireless/radio*

vii. ÜBER + ACCUSATIVE

Er fuhr über Ostende nach B.	*He went to B. via Ostend.*
Er ist über 90 Jahre alt.	*He is over 90 years old.*
Er blieb über Nacht bei uns.	*He spent the night with us.*
Tränen liefen ihr über die Wangen.	*Tears ran down her cheeks.*
Ich bin froh/traurig über die Nachricht.	*I am glad/sorry about the news.*
Ich bin erstaunt/zornig darüber.	*I am surprised/angry at it.*
eine Rechnung über 10 Pfund	*a bill for £10*

viii. UNTER + DATIVE

unter den Leuten	*among the people*
unter ander(e)m	*among other things*
unter dieser Bedingung	*on this condition*
unter seiner Regierung	*in his reign*
unter uns (gesagt)	*between ourselves*
unter diesen Umständen	*in these circumstances*

ix. VOR + DATIVE

vor vielen Jahren	*many years ago*
heute vor einem Jahre	*a year ago today*
vor langer Zeit	*a long time ago*
vor allem (vor allen Dingen)	*above all*
Er lachte/weinte vor Freude.	*He laughed/wept for joy.*
Er zitterte vor Angst.	*He trembled with fear.*
vor der Stadt	*just outside the town*

Verbs

88 Conjugation of the Auxiliary Verbs: *haben, sein* and *werden*

Infinitive

haben (*to have*)　　　sein (*to be*)　　　werden (*to become*)

Participles

PRESENT	habend	seiend	werdend
PAST	gehabt	gewesen	geworden

Imperative

2ND SING.	hab(e)!	sei!	werd(e)!
2ND PLUR.	habt!	seid!	werdet!
POLITE FORM	haben Sie!	seien Sie!	werden Sie!

Present

	Ind.	Subj.	Ind.	Subj.	Ind.	Subj.
ich	habe	—	bin	sei	werde	—
du	hast	—	bist	sei(e)st	**wirst**	—
er, sie, es	hat	habe[1]	ist	sei	**wird**	werde[1]
wir	haben	—	sind	seien	werden	—
ihr	habt	—	seid	—	werdet	—
sie (Sie)	haben	—	sind	seien	werden	—

Imperfect

	Ind.	Subj.	Ind.	Subj.	Ind.	Subj.
ich	hatte	hätte	war	wäre	wurde	würde
du	hattest	hättest	warst	wärst	wurdest	würdest
er, sie, es	hatte	hätte	war	wäre	wurde	würde
wir	hatten	hätten	waren	wären	wurden	würden
ihr	hattet	hättet	wart	wärt	wurdet	würdet
sie (Sie)	hatten	hätten	waren	wären	wurden	würden

Perfect

Ind.	Subj.
ich habe gehabt, bin gewesen, bin geworden, etc.	er habe[1] gehabt; ich sei gewesen, sei geworden, etc.

Pluperfect

ich hatte gehabt, war gewesen, war geworden, etc.	ich hätte gehabt, wäre gewesen, wäre geworden, etc.

[1] Only the third person singular is now used

84

Future

ich werde haben, werde sein, werde werden, etc.

er werde[1] haben, werde[1] sein, werde[1] werden, etc.

Future Perfect

ich werde gehabt haben, werde gewesen sein, werde geworden sein, etc.

er werde[1] gehabt haben, werde[1] gewesen sein, werde[1] geworden sein, etc.

Conditional

ich würde haben, würde sein, würde werden, etc.

Conditional Perfect (replaced often by Plpf. Subj.)

ich würde gehabt haben, würde gewesen sein, würde geworden sein, etc.

89 Notes on *haben, sein* and *werden*

(a) **Haben** is used to form the perfect tenses of **all transitive** and **reflexive** verbs and modal auxiliaries, and of those intransitive verbs which do **not** describe a change of place or state.

Ich habe es gekauft.	*I have bought it.*
Ich hatte mich gesetzt.	*I had sat down.*
Er hat es gemußt.	*He has had to.*
Er hat kommen müssen.	*He has had to come.*
Es hat geregnet.	*It has rained.*
Er hat mir gedient.	*He has served me.*

(b) **Sein** is used to form the perfect tenses of those **intransitive** verbs which **do** describe a change of place or state.

Er ist gegangen.	*He has gone.*
Er war eingeschlafen.	*He had fallen asleep.*

NOTE: Common exceptions to the rule are: **bleiben** (*stay*); **sein** (*be*); **geschehen** (*happen*); **gelingen** (*succeed*). These are all conjugated with **sein**.

(c) **Werden** is used with the **infinitive** of verbs to form the **future** tenses, and with the **past participle** of verbs to form the **passive voice**. (Cf. *110*.)

[1] Only the third singular is now used

85

Er wird tragen.	*He will carry* (future).
Er **würde** tragen.	*He would carry* (conditional).
Er wird getragen.	*He is being carried* (pres. passive).
Er **würde** getragen.	*He was carried* (impf. passive).

NOTE: The forms *ward* and *wardst* are still occasionally used, especially in poetry, instead of the more usual forms *wurde*, *wurdest*.

90 Conjugation of Regular Verbs

WEAK			STRONG

Infinitive

sag-**en** (*to say*)   trag-**en** (*to carry*)

Participles

	WEAK	STRONG
PRESENT	sag-**end**	trag-**end**
PAST	ge-sag-t	ge-trag-en

Imperative (cf. *107*)

	WEAK	STRONG
2ND SING.	sag(-e)!	trag(-e)!
2ND PLUR.	sag-t!	trag-t!
POLITE FORM	sag-en Sie!	trag-en Sie!

Present

	Ind.	Subj.	Ind.	Subj.
ich	sag-**e**	—	trag-**e**	—
du	sag-**st**	—	träg-**st**	—
er, sie, es	sag-**t**	sag-**e**[1]	träg-**t**	trag-**e**[1]
wir	sag-**en**	—	trag-**en**	—
ihr	sag-**t**	—	trag-**t**	—
sie (Sie)	sag-**en**	—	trag-**en**	—

Imperfect

	Ind.	Subj.	Ind.	Subj.
ich	sag-**te**	sag-**te**	trug	trüg-**e**
du	sag-**test**	sag-**test**	trug-**st**	trüg-**st**
er, sie, es	sag-**te**	sag-**te**	trug	trüg-**e**
wir	sag-**ten**	sag-**ten**	trug-**en**	trüg-**en**
ihr	sag-**tet**	sag-**tet**	trug-**t**	trüg-**t**
sie (Sie)	sag-**ten**	sag-**ten**	trug-**en**	trüg-**en**

[1] Only the third person singular is now used

Perfect

Ind.	Subj.	Ind.	Subj.
ich habe gesagt etc.	er habe[1] gesagt	ich habe getragen etc.	er habe[1] getragen

Pluperfect

Ind.	Subj.	Ind.	Subj.
ich hatte gesagt etc.	hätte gesagt	hatte getragen etc.	hätte getragen

Future

Ind.	Subj.	Ind.	Subj.
ich werde sagen etc.	er werde[1] sagen	ich werde tragen etc.	er werde[1] tragen

Future Perfect

Ind.	Subj.	Ind.	Subj.
ich werde gesagt haben, etc.	er werde[1] gesagt haben	ich werde getragen haben, etc.	er werde[1] getragen haben

Conditional

ich	würde sagen etc.	würde tragen etc.

Conditional Perfect (replaced often by Plpf. Subj.)

ich	würde gesagt haben, etc.	würde getragen haben, etc.

91 Notes on the Conjugation of Verbs [2]

(a) STRONG verbs (see 93 and 127) change their stem vowel, and the past participle ends in **-en**.

tragen: trägt trug getrag-**en**

(b) In **regular** STRONG verbs, if the infinitive has as its stem vowel **a, e, o** or **au**, these usually change in the 2nd and 3rd pers. sing. pres. ind. to **ä, i** or **ie, ö** and **äu** respectively.

tragen: trägt	geben: gibt	lesen: liest
stoßen: stößt	laufen: läuft	

[1] Only the third person singular is now used
[2] See 93(l) and 127 for the conjugation of irregular strong and weak verbs; and see 111 for the subjunctive form

(c) WEAK verbs (see *92*) do not change their stem vowel, and the past participle ends in **-t**:

  sagen: **sagt**   **sagte**   gesag-**t**

(d) Verbs ending in **-ern** and **-eln** (all weak) are conjugated in the pres. ind. as follows:

ich zitt-**(e)re**	wir zitt-**ern**		ich samm-**(e)le**	wir samm-**eln**
du zitt-**erst**	ihr zitt-**ert**		du samm-**elst**	ihr samm-**elt**
er zitt-**ert**	sie zitt-**ern**		er samm-**elt**	sie samm-**eln**

(e) Weak verbs whose stem ends in **-t** or **-d, -chn, -ckn, -dn, -fn, -gn** or **-tm** retain the **-e-** of the 1st pers. sing. pres. throughout the conjugation except in the 2nd pers. sing. impf. of strong verbs with stems ending in **-t** or **-d**:

wartest	badet	rechnete	trocknetest
ordnet	öffnetet	geregnet	atmet
BUT	fandst	botst	

(f) Verbs ending in the suffixes **-ieren** and **-eien** (all weak) and verbs compounded with inseparable prefixes (see *102(a)*) have no **ge-** in the past participle:

er hat studiert   sie hat prophezeit   wir haben versucht.

(g) Verbs whose stem ends in **-s, -ß, -z** and **-tz** now usually drop the **-es-** of the 2nd pers. sing. present indicative; those whose stem ends in **-sch** drop the **-e-** only:

du liest (*for* liesest);   du faßt   du sitzt   du wäsch**st**

(h) A few verbs – **brennen** (*burn*), **bringen** (*bring*), **denken** (*think*), **kennen** (*know*), **nennen** (*name*), **rennen** (*run*), **senden** (*send*), **wenden** (*turn*), and their compounds – are of mixed conjugation, i.e. though the stem vowel changes (to **-a-**) the past participle ends in **-t**:

brennen: brennt   brann-**te**   gebrann-**t**

92 Some very common Weak Verbs

(*a*)

antworten, *answer*	blühen, *bloom, flourish*	bringen, *bring*
arbeiten, *work*	borgen, *borrow*	(*91(h)*)
atmen, *breathe*	brauchen, *need, want*	denken, *think*
baden, *bathe*	brennen, *burn*	(*91(h)*)
blicken, *glance*	(*91(h)*)	dienen, *serve*

drucken, *print*
drücken, *press;*
  oppress
enden, *end; die*
fehlen, *be lacking*
fürchten, *fear*
glauben, *believe*
grüßen, *greet*
hassen, *hate*
heiraten, *marry*
  (123)
herrschen, *rule*
hindern, *prevent*
holen, *fetch, get*
  (123)
hören, *hear; listen*
interessieren,
  interest
irren, *err*
(*)jagen, *chase, hunt;*
  hurry
kämpfen, *fight*
kaufen, *buy*
kennen, *know*
  (91(h) and
  123)
kleben, *stick*
klopfen, *knock*
knien,[1] *kneel*
kochen, *cook, boil*
kosten, *cost; taste*
  (tr.)
küssen, *kiss*
lächeln, *smile*

lachen, *laugh*
leben, *live*
leeren, *empty*
legen, *lay, put*
  (123)
lernen, *learn*
loben, *praise*
lohnen, *reward*
machen, *make, do*
malen, *paint*
merken, *note, notice*
*nahen, *approach*
nähen, *sew*
passen, *fit, suit*
putzen, *clean; dress*
  up
rauchen, *smoke*
reichen, *reach out;*
  hand
reizen, *charm,*
  provoke
*rennen, *run (91(h))*
(*)rollen, *roll*
schaden, *injure,*
  harm
schauen, *look at,*
  see
schenken, *give,*
  present
schicken, *send*
schmecken, *taste*
  (intr.)
schmerzen, *ache*
schütteln, *shake*

schützen, *shelter,*
  protect
setzen, *set, put*
  (123)
sparen, *save,*
  economise
*spazieren, *stroll*
spielen, *play*
stecken, *set, put*
  (123)
stricken, *knit*
studieren, *study*
(*)stürzen, *fall;*
  dash; overthrow
tanzen, *dance*
töten, *kill*
trauen, *trust; marry*
  (123)
träumen, *dream*
trocknen, *dry*
trösten, *console*
urteilen, *judge*
wagen, *dare, venture*
wählen, *choose, vote*
wechseln,
  (ex)change
wecken, *wake up*
  (tr.)
wissen, *know*
  (123 and 127)
wünschen, *wish*
zählen, *count*
zeigen, *show, point*
zittern, *tremble*

(b) Verbs from which feminine **nouns** are derived by the omission of the last letter of the infinitive (see *19(b)v(α)*):

bürsten, *brush*
dauern, *last*
decken, *lay (table);*
  tile (roof)

ehren, *honour*
*eilen, *hurry*
ernten, *harvest, reap*
feiern, *celebrate*

(*)folgen, *follow; obey*
fragen, *ask, question*
füllen, *fill*
klagen, *complain*

[1] *er kniet, kniete, hat gekniet*

klingeln, *ring*	regeln, *regulate, settle*	stimmen, *vote, tune;*
lehren, *teach*	reihen, *set in rows*	*be correct*
lieben, *love, like*	*reisen, *travel*	strafen, *punish*
mieten, *hire, rent*	ruhen, *rest*	strecken, *stretch (tr.)*
pflanzen, *plant*	sagen, *say, tell*	stützen, *prop, support*
pflegen, *tend, nurse;*	sorgen, *take care of*	suchen, *seek, try,*
be accustomed to	spitzen, *point, sharpen*	*search for*
proben, *test, sample*	stellen, *place, put*	wachen, *be awake;*
reden, *speak, talk*	*(123)*	*watch over*

(c) Verbs from which feminine **nouns** are derived by the addition of -*ung* to the stem (see *19(b)v(β)*):

achten, *esteem; pay*	meinen, *say, mean,*	senden, *send (91(h))*
attention	*think*	stärken, *strengthen*
ahnen, *suspect*	mischen, *mix*	stellen, *place,put(123)*
ändern, *alter, change*	neigen, *incline*	stimmen, *vote, tune;*
bilden, *form, cultivate*	nennen, *name (91(h))*	*be correct*
(mind)	öffnen, *open*	stören, *disturb*
decken, *cover*	ordnen, *put in order*	teilen, *share, divide,*
dichten, *write (poetry)*	packen, *seize; pack*	*separate*
drehen, *turn*	prüfen, *examine*	trennen, *separate*
drohen, *threaten*	räumen, *vacate*	üben, *practise*
fassen, *seize; contain*	rechnen, *calculate,*	*wandern, *wander,*
fordern, *demand*	*count*	*hike*
fühlen, *feel*	regeln, *regulate, settle*	warnen, *warn*
füllen, *fill*	regieren, *govern*	wenden, *turn (91(h))*
handeln,[1] *act; bargain*	retten, *save, rescue*	wirken, *effect, work*
heizen, *heat*	richten, *judge; direct*	*(tr.)*
hoffen,[2] *hope*	rühren, *move, stir;*	wohnen, *dwell, live*
kleiden, *dress, clothe*	*touch*	zahlen, *pay*
lösen, *solve; buy*	sammeln,[1] *collect*	zeichnen, *draw, design*
(ticket)	*(things)*	zögern, *hesitate*

93 Some very common Strong Verbs

(a) **Group I** (ie – o – o, e.g. bi**e**gt, b**o**g, geb**o**gen):

(*)biegen, *bend, turn*	(*)fliegen, *fly*	*fließen, *flow*
bieten, *offer, bid*	(*)fliehen, *flee*	(*)frieren, *be cold, freeze*

[1] The '*e*' of the stem is omitted before -*ung* is added
[2] Adds -*nung* to the stem

riechen, *smell*	(*)schießen, *shoot*	wiegen, *weigh* (*intr.*)
gießen, *pour*	schließen, *shut, con-*	(*)ziehen,[1] *pull, draw;*
schieben, *shove, push*	clude	move, go

(b) Group II (*a*) (**ei – i – i,** e.g. beißt, biß, gebissen):

beißen, *bite*	(*)reißen, *tear*	(*)streichen, *stroke,*
gleichen, *resemble*	(*)reiten,[1] *ride* (*horse*)	smear; roam
greifen,[1] *seize, grab*	schneiden,[1] *cut*	streiten,[1] *argue*
leiden,[1] *suffer*	*schreiten,[1] *stride,*	*weichen, *yield, give*
pfeifen,[1] *whistle, pipe*	step out, proceed	way to

(c) Group II (*b*) (**ei – ie – ie,** e.g. bleibt, blieb, geblieben):

*bleiben, *remain*	scheinen, *seem;*	*steigen, *rise, climb;*
leihen, *lend*	shine	increase
reiben, *rub*	schreiben, *write*	(*)treiben, *drive, do;*
(*)scheiden, *part;*	schreien, *shout*	drift
separate	schweigen, *be silent*	weisen, *show, point*

(d) Group III (*a*) (**i – a – o,** e.g. bricht, brach, gebrochen):

beginnen, *begin*	nehmen,[1] *take*	*sterben, *die*
(*)brechen, *break*	(*)schwimmen, *swim*	treffen,[1] *strike; meet*
gelten, *be worth*	sprechen, *speak*	werben, *woo, recruit*
helfen, *help*	stechen, *sting, stab*	werfen, *throw*

(e) Group III (*b*) (**ie – a – o,** e.g. stiehlt, stahl, gestohlen):

| befehlen, *order* | empfehlen, *recommend* | stehlen, *steal* |

(f) Group IV (**i – a – u,** e.g. bindet, band, gebunden):

binden, *bind, tie*	finden, *find*	*springen, *jump*
(*)dringen, *penetrate;*	singen, *sing*	trinken, *drink*
(in + A) *urge s.b.*	*sinken, *sink*	zwingen, *compel*

(g) Group V (*a*) (**i – a – e,** e.g. gibt, gab, gegeben):

bitten,[1] *ask, request*	geben, *give*	(*)treten,[1] *step, walk;*
essen,[1] *eat*	messen, *measure*	tread
fressen, *eat* (*of animals*)		

(h) Group V (*b*) (**ie – a – e,** e.g. liest, las, gelesen):

| *geschehen, *happen* | liegen, *lie* | sehen, *see* |
| lesen, *read* | | |

[1] Somewhat irregular, see *127*

(i) **Group VI** (*a*) (**ä – i – a,** e.g. fängt, fing, gefangen):

fangen, *catch, capture*   hängen, *hang* (*intr.*)

(j) **Group VI** (*b*) (**ä – ie – a,** e.g. fällt, fiel, gefallen):

blasen, *blow*	lassen, *let, leave*	schlafen, *sleep*
fallen,[1] fall	*laufen, run*	
halten,[1] *hold, stop*	raten,[1] *advise*	

(k) **Group VII** (**ä – u – a,** e.g. fährt, fuhr, gefahren):

(*)fahren, *ride, drive,*	laden, *load, invite*	*wachsen, grow*
go	schlagen, *strike, beat*	waschen, *wash*
graben, *dig*	tragen, *carry, bear, wear*	

(l) **Group VIII** (Irregular, see *127*):

*gehen, *go, walk*	*kommen, *come*	sitzen, *sit*
hauen, *chop; strike*	rufen, *call, shout*	stehen, *stand*
heben, *lift, raise*	schaffen, *create*	tun, *do*
heißen, *be called, bid*		

94 The Present

(a) Ich schreibe jeden Tag einen   *I **write** a letter every day.*
Brief.

Ich schreibe jetzt einen Brief.
Ich bin jetzt dabei, einen Brief zu } *I **am writing** a letter now.*
schreiben.

Ich hoffe (sehr/doch), daß er kom-   *I **do hope** he will come.*
men wird.

(b) The present is sometimes used to impart vividness to narrative:

Er schaltete das Licht an. Da **sieht** er plötzlich einen Fremden vor sich stehen. Er **greift** in die Tasche und **will** seinen Revolver herausziehen; in diesem Augenblick aber **fühlt** er sich von hinten ergriffen.

He switched on the light. Then he suddenly saw a stranger standing in front of him. He put his hand in his pocket and was about to pull out his revolver, but at that moment he felt himself seized from behind.

[1] Somewhat irregular, see *127*

(c) The present with *seit* or *schon* expresses what has been going on and is still going on:

Er **wohnt** (schon) seit zwei Jahren hier.	*He **has been living** here for two years (now).*
Er **wartet** schon eine Stunde auf Sie.	*He **has been waiting** an hour for you.*
Seit wann **wartet** er auf ihn?	*How long **has** he **been waiting** for him?*

(d) The present is often used to express the future especially when the idea of futurity is already indicated by an adverb or by the sense:

Morgen reise ich nach Deutschland.	*I am going to Germany tomorrow.*
Wenn ich Zeit habe, hole ich dich ab.	*If I have time I shall call for you.*

(e) Es ist höchste Zeit, daß er **kommt**. *It is high time he **came**.*

95 The Imperfect

(a) Er schrieb jeden Tag einen Brief. Er pflegte jeden Tag einen Brief zu schreiben.	*He **wrote** (**used to write**) a letter every day.*
Er schrieb einen Brief, als . . . Er war dabei, einen Brief zu schreiben, als . . .	*He **was writing** a letter when . . .*
Ich hoffte so sehr, daß er kommen würde.	*I **did** so **hope** he would come.*
Er wollte eben aufstehen, als . . .	*He was just about to get up when . . .*
Er war eben im Begriff aufzustehen, als . . .	*He was just on the point of getting up when . . .*

(b) The imperfect is the tense of narrative:

Er setzte sich an den Tisch, nahm eine Feder in die Hand und schrieb ein paar Seiten.

He sat down at the table, took a pen in his hand and wrote a few pages.

(c) The imperfect with *seit* or *schon* expresses what had been going on and was still going on:

93

Er **wohnte** seit zwei Jahren dort.	*He* **had been living** *there for two years.*
Er **wartete** schon eine Stunde auf Sie.	*He* **had been waiting** *an hour for you.*
Seit wann **wartete** er auf mich?	*How long* **had** *he* **been waiting** *for me?*

(d) The imperfect is used for one action or fact in relation to another:

Er war im Bett, als ich ihn sah.	*He was in bed when I saw him.*
Während er sprach, hörte sie zu.	*While he spoke she listened.*

96 The Perfect

(a) The perfect is used for isolated acts in the past, often implying that such acts took place in the presence of the speaker or writer. (In S. Germany and Austria the perfect, especially in conversation, is used in narrative instead of the imperfect.)

Sie haben uns geschlagen.	*They beat us.*
Er hat es mir gesagt.	*He told me so.*
Ich habe es nur einmal getan.	*I have only done it once.*
Er hat sich das Bein gebrochen.	*He has broken his leg* (and it has not yet mended).
Sind Sie je in Berlin gewesen?	*Have you ever been to Berlin?*

(b) The perfect expresses what took place before something happening in the present or future:

Nachdem/wenn ich gegessen habe, lese ich die Zeitung (werde ich die Z. lesen).	*After/when I have eaten I read the paper* (*I shall read the paper*).

97 The Pluperfect

The pluperfect expresses what took place before a past event:

Nachdem/als ich gegessen hatte, las ich die Zeitung.	*After/when I had eaten I read the paper.*
Kaum hatte er sich hingesetzt, da hörte er es klopfen.	*Hardly had he sat down when he heard a knock.*

98 The Future

(a) The future is used of an action that is to take place at some time yet to come (cf., however, *94(d)*):

Ich weiß, daß er kommen wird.   *I know he will come.*

(b) The future is often used to indicate probability:

Er wird schon da sein.   *I expect he is there already.*

NOTE: When **will** expresses determination or desire the present of **wollen** is used:

Er will nicht kommen.	*He* **won't** (=*refuses to*) *come.*
Wollen Sie kommen?	*Will you come?*

99 The Conditional (Future in the Past)

(a) The future in the past is used of an action that was to take place at some future time:

Ich wußte, daß er kommen würde.   *I knew he would come.*

(b) The conditional is used in the main clause of a conditional sentence (cf. *113(b)*):

Ich würde es machen, wenn . . .   *I should do it if . . .*

NOTE: When **would** expresses determination, the imperfect of **wollen** is used:

Er wollte nicht kommen.   *He* **would** *not* (=*refused to*) *come.*

100 The Future Perfect

The future perfect is generally avoided except to indicate probability in the past:

Er wird es getan haben.   *I expect he did it.*

101 The Conditional Perfect

The conditional perfect is used in the main clause of a conditional sentence, though it is nowadays usually replaced by the pluperfect subjunctive (cf. *113(c)*):

Ich würde es gemacht haben,   *I should have done it if . . .*
wenn . . .

102 Compound Verbs

(a) INSEPARABLE[1] verbs are compounded with the prefixes **be-, emp-, ent-, er-, ge-, miß-, ver-** and **zer-**. These prefixes are **never** stressed.

Er besucht uns nicht. (*Present*)	*He doesn't visit us.*
Er besuchte uns nicht. (*Imperfect*)	*He didn't visit us.*
Er hat uns nicht **besucht**. (*Perfect*)	*He hasn't visited us.*
Er wünscht uns zu besuchen.	*He wishes to visit us.*
(*Infinitive with* zu)	
Obgleich er uns nicht besucht, ...	*Although he doesn't visit us ...*
(*Subordinate clause*)	

NOTE: There is **no** ge- in the past participle.

WEAK

bedecken, *cover*
bedeuten, *mean, signify*
begleiten, *accompany*
behandeln, *treat*
behaupten, *maintain, assert*
bemerken, *notice, remark*
beobachten, *observe, watch*
bereiten, *prepare*
bestellen, *order (123)*
bestimmen, *fix, determine, destine*
besuchen, *visit*
bewegen, *move (tr.)*
entdecken, *discover*
entschuldigen, *excuse, pardon*
entwickeln, *develop, evolve*
erblicken, *catch sight of*
erfüllen, *fulfil*
erkennen, *recognise (91(h))*
erklären, *declare; explain*
erobern, *conquer*
erreichen, *reach, attain, catch (train)*
erschrecken, *frighten*
(*)erstaunen, *(be) astonish(ed)*
*erwachen, *awake, wake up (intr.)*
erwähnen, *mention*
erwarten, *expect*

STRONG (see 127)

befehlen, *order (123), command*
beginnen, *begin*
begreifen, *grasp, understand*
behalten, *keep*
bekommen, *get, obtain, receive*
beschließen, *decide, resolve*
beschreiben, *describe*
besitzen, *possess*
besprechen, *discuss*
besteigen, *climb, mount, board*
betreten, *enter, set foot on*
empfangen, *receive, welcome*
enthalten, *contain*
entlassen, *dismiss*
entscheiden, *decide*
*entstehen, *come about, arise*
erfahren, *experience, learn*
erfinden, *invent*
ergreifen, *seize*
erhalten, *get, receive; preserve*
erheben, *raise*
*erscheinen, *appear*
*erschrecken, *be frightened*
ertragen, *stand, bear*
erwerben, *acquire*
erziehen, *bring up, educate*
gefallen (D), *please*

[1] Cf. *15(c)v(β)*

WEAK	STRONG (see *127*)
erwidern (D), *answer, reply*	genießen, *enjoy*
erzählen, *tell, relate*	*geschehen (D), *happen*
gebrauchen, *use*	gewinnen, *win, gain*
*gelangen, *come to, arrive, get to*	mißfallen (D), *displease*
verbessern, *correct*	verbergen, *conceal*
verbringen, *spend (time) (91(h))*	verbieten, *forbid*
verdienen, *deserve, earn*	verbinden, *connect, unite*
verfassen, *compose*	(*)verderben, *spoil*
verkaufen, *sell*	vergeben, *forgive*
verlangen, *ask, want, demand*	*vergehen, *pass, elapse*
verletzen, *hurt, injure*	vergessen, *forget*
vermieten, *let, hire out*	vergleichen, *compare*
verpassen, *miss, lose (train)*	verlassen, *leave, forsake, quit*
versammeln, *gather (people) (tr.)*	verlieren, *lose*
versuchen, *try, attempt; tempt*	vermeiden, *avoid*
verteidigen, *defend*	*verschwinden, *disappear*
verwandeln, *transform, change*	versprechen, *promise*
verweigern, *refuse*	verstehen, *understand*
zerstören, *destroy*	verzeihen, *pardon*
	(*)zerbrechen, *smash*

(b) SEPARABLE[1] verbs are compounded with the following prefixes (cf. *43(a)iii*): **ab-, an-, auf-, aus-, bei-, daher-, dahin-, dar-, ein-, empor-, entgegen-, entzwei-, fort-, her-** and **hin-** and their compounds (see *43(a)ii*), **inne-, los-, mit-, nach-, nieder-, statt-, teil-, vor-, voran-, voraus-, vorbei-, vorüber-, weg-, zu-, zurück-** and **zusammen-**. These prefixes, unlike the inseparable ones, all have an independent meaning and are **always** stressed.

Er macht die Tür **zu**. (*Present*)	He shuts the door.
Er machte die Tür **zu**. (*Imperfect*)	He shut the door.
Er hat die Tür **zu**gemacht. (*Perfect*)	He has shut the door.
Er versuchte, die Tür **zu**zumachen.	He tried to shut the door.
(*Infinitive with* zu).	
Als er die Tür **zu**machte, . . .	When he shut the door . . .
(*Subordinate clause*).	

NOTE 1: *Ge-* is retained in the past participle.
NOTE 2: *Zu* is inserted between the prefix and the verb.
NOTE 3: The prefix rejoins its verb in subordinate clauses in the present and imperfect.

[1] Cf. *19(c)v(β)*

WEAK	STRONG (see *127*)
abholen, *fetch, meet*	*abfahren, *set off, start*
ablehnen, *decline*	anfangen, *begin*
*abreisen, *leave* (*intr.*), *set off*	angreifen, *attack*
abschicken, *send off, dispatch*	*ankommen, *arrive*
anschalten, *switch on*	annehmen, *accept, suppose*
anstellen, *turn on* (e.g. *wireless*); *employ*	anrufen, *ring up*
	ansehen, *look at*
anzünden, *light, kindle*	anziehen, *dress* (*tr.*), *put on* (*clothes*); *attract*
auffassen, *comprehend, conceive*	aufgeben, *give up, assign; post*
aufhören, *cease, stop*	*aufgehen, *rise* (*sun*); *open* (*intr.*)
aufmachen, *open* (*tr.*)	aufheben, *pick up; keep; abolish*
aufpassen, *look out, pay attention*	aufschließen, *unlock*
aufsetzen, *put on* (*hat*)	*aufstehen, *get up, stand up*
ausdrücken, *express*	aufziehen, *wind up* (*watch*)
ausführen, *carry out, execute*	ausgeben, *spend* (*money*)
ausschalten, *switch off*	*ausgehen, *go out*
beiwohnen (D), *be present at*	aussehen, *look, appear, seem*
*dahereilen, *hurry along*	aussprechen, *pronounce; express, utter*
*dahinstürzen, *dash along, off*	
darstellen, *represent*	*aussteigen, *get out, get off*
einholen, *overtake, catch up*	ausziehen, *undress* (*tr.*), *take off* (*clothes*); *extract*
einstecken, *pocket; post*	beitragen, *contribute*
emporblicken, *look up*(*wards*)	einladen, *invite*
*entgegeneilen (D), *hurry towards*	*einschlafen, *fall asleep, go to sleep*
fortsetzen, *continue* (*tr.*)	*einsteigen, *get in, get on*
herstellen, *produce, restore*	*entzweibrechen, *break in two*
hinzufügen, *add*	(*)fortfahren, *drive away; continue*
mitteilen, *inform*	innehalten, *stop* (*intr.*) (*123*)
nachdenken, *consider, reflect*	*loswerden, *get rid of*
niederlegen, *lay down*	stattfinden, *take place*
*voraneilen (D), *hurry on ahead*	teilnehmen, *take part*
*vorauseilen (D), *hurry on ahead*	*vorkommen, *seem, occur*
*vorbeieilen, *hurry past*	vorlesen, *read aloud*
vorbereiten, *prepare* (*in advance*)	vorschlagen, *suggest, propose*
vorstellen, *introduce, personate*	*vorüberziehen, *pass*
weglegen, *lay aside*	vorziehen, *prefer*
zubringen, *spend* (*time*) (*91*(*h*))	*weglaufen, *run away*
zuhören (D), *listen*	zurückgeben, *give back, return*
zumachen, *shut*	zuschließen, *lock*
*zurückkehren, *return* (*intr.*)	
zusammensetzen, *put together*	

(c) Verbs[1] with the prefixes **durch-, hinter-, über-, um-, unter-, voll-, wider-** and **wieder-** may be either SEPARABLE or INSEPARABLE or, usually with different meanings, both.

Er setzte ihn über.	*He ferried him across.*
Er übersetzte das Buch.	*He translated the book.*

NOTE I: Verbs compounded with these prefixes are usually separable if they can be translated literally.

NOTE 2: When separable the prefix is stressed; when inseparable the stem of the verb is stressed.

SEPARABLE	INSEPARABLE
i. WEAK	
*durch-reisen, *travel through*	durchreisen, *travel all over*
hinter-legen, *put (s. th.) behind*	hinterlegen, *deposit*
(*)über-setzen, *ferry across; jump across*	übersetzen, *translate*
	überraschen, *surprise*
	überreden, *persuade*
	überzeugen, *convince*
um-spannen, *change horses*	umspannen, *encompass*
	umarmen, *embrace*
unter-breiten, *lay (spread) under*	unterbreiten, *submit (plan, etc.)*
	unterrichten, *instruct*
	untersuchen, *investigate, examine*
voll-füllen, *fill full*	vollenden, *complete*
wider-hallen, *echo*	widersprechen (D), *contradict*
wider-spiegeln, *reflect*	widerstehen (D), *resist*
	widerlegen, *refute*
wieder-holen, *bring back*	wiederholen, *repeat*
ii. STRONG (see *127*)	
*über-fahren, *pass over (intr.)*	überfahren, *run over (s.b.)*
	übertreiben, *exaggerate*
	überwinden, *overcome*
*um-gehen, *associate (with); circulate, go round (intr.)*	umgehen, *walk (get) round (tr.); evade*
	umgeben, *surround*
*um-steigen, *change (trains, etc.)*	
um-werfen, *knock over*	
(*)um-ziehen, *move (residence); change (clothes)*	

[1] Cf. *19(c)v(β)*

SEPARABLE	INSEPARABLE
unter-halten, *hold (s.th.) under* *unter-gehen, *set (of sun), sink*	unterhalten, *entertain; maintain,* *keep going (s. th.)* unterbrechen, *interrupt* unternehmen, *undertake* unterscheiden, *distinguish*

103 Reflexive Verbs

PRES.	ich	wasche	mich	wasche	mir	die Hände
	du	wäschst	dich	wäschst	dir	die Hände
	er, sie, es	wäscht	sich	wäscht	sich	die Hände
	wir	waschen	uns	waschen	uns	die Hände
	ihr	wascht	euch	wascht	euch	die Hände
	sie (Sie)	waschen	sich	waschen	sich	die Hände
	(I wash myself, etc.)			*(I wash my (lit. to myself the) hands, etc.)*		

IMPF.	ich wusch mich	wusch mir die Hände
PF.	ich **habe** mich gewaschen	ich **habe** mir die Hände gewaschen
FUT.	ich werde mich waschen	ich werde mir die Hände waschen
IMPER.	wasch(e)dich! wascht euch! waschen Sie sich!	wasch(e) dir die Hände! wascht euch die Hände! waschen Sie sich die Hände!

104 Some common Reflexive Verbs

WEAK	STRONG (see *127*)
sich amüsieren, *enjoy o.s.*	sich anziehen, *dress (intr.)*
sich ändern, *change, alter (intr.)*	sich aufhalten, *stay, sojourn*
sich anstrengen, *make an effort*	sich aussprechen, *express o.s.*
sich aufregen, *get excited*	sich ausziehen, *undress (intr.)*
sich ausruhen, *rest*	sich befinden, *be (situated), feel*
sich beeilen, *hurry up*	sich benehmen, *behave*
sich bewegen, *move (intr.)*	sich entschließen, *resolve, decide*
sich drehen, *turn (intr.)*	sich ergeben, *surrender, resign*
sich entfernen, *move away (intr.)*	*o.s. (to)*
sich ereignen, *occur, take place*	sich erheben, *get up, rise*

WEAK	STRONG (see *127*)
sich erholen, *recover (health)*	sich schlagen, *fight*
sich erkälten, *catch cold*	sich schließen, *shut, close (intr.)*
sich freuen, *be glad*	sich streiten, *quarrel*
sich fühlen, *feel (123)*	sich um-sehen, *look round*
sich nennen, *be called (91(h))*	sich um-ziehen, *change (clothes)*
sich niederlegen, *lie down*	sich unterhalten, *enjoy o.s.;*
sich öffnen, *open (intr.)*	*converse*
sich rühren, *stir (intr.)*	sich verlaufen, *lose one's way*
sich setzen, *sit down*	sich waschen, *wash (intr.)*
sich verspäten, *be late (123)*	
sich verstecken, *hide (intr.)*	
sich (D) vorstellen, *imagine*	
sich weigern, *refuse (123)*	

105 Impersonal Verbs

(a)

blitzen, *lighten*	frieren, *freeze*
dämmern, *dawn; grow dusk*	hageln, *hail*
donnern, *thunder*	regnen, *rain*
dunkeln, *grow dark*	schneien, *snow*

Es regnet/schneit heute.   *It is raining/snowing today.*

(b) Verbs used impersonally:

i. Es heißt, daß . . .   *It is said/reported that . . .*
   Es macht/schadet/tut nichts.   *It does not matter.*

ii. Mir fällt ein, daß . . .   *It occurs to me that . . .*
   Mir fehlt nichts.   *I am quite well.*
   Was fehlt dir?   *What's the matter with you?*
   Mir ist warm/kalt.   *I am, feel warm/cold.*
   Mir ist (nicht) wohl zumute.   *I feel in good/poor spirits.*
   Mir ist, als ob . . .   *I feel as if . . .*
   Or: Es fällt mir ein, daß, etc.

iii. Mir fehlt **es** an nichts (D).   *I lack nothing.*
   Mich freut **es**, daß . . .   *I am glad that . . .*
   Mir gefällt **es** (nicht) bei ihm.   *I (dis-)like staying with him.*
   Mir geht **es** gut/schlecht.   *I am well/unwell.*
   Wie geht's Ihnen?   *How are you?*
   Mir gelingt **es**, das zu tun.   *I succeed in doing it/manage to do it.*

   Dir geschieht **es** recht.   *It serves you right.*

Heute gibt **es** Fisch zum Mittag-essen.	*Today there is fish for lunch.*
Mir mißfällt **es** zu warten.	*I dislike waiting.*
Mir tut **es** leid.	*I am sorry.*
OR Es fehlt mir an nichts, etc.	

NOTE: Er tut mir leid/es tut mir leid *I am sorry for him.*
um ihn.

106 The Infinitive with and without *zu*.

(a) The simple infinitive stands after the modal auxiliaries (cf. *109*):

Er kann/muß/will kommen.	*He is able/has/wants to come.*

(b) The simple infinitive stands after *bleiben, fühlen, gehen, hören, lassen, machen* and *sehen* (cf. *122(c)*, note):

Er blieb dort stehen.	*He remained standing there.*
Ich fühlte mein Herz schlagen.	*I felt my heart beating.*
Ich gehe tanzen/schlafen.	*I'm going dancing/to bed.*
Ich hörte/sah ihn kommen.	*I heard/saw him coming.*
Ich ließ sie noch spielen.	*I let them go on playing.*
Er machte sie erröten.	*He made her blush.*

(c) When *lernen, lehren* and *helfen* follow their dependent infinitive **zu** is not used.

Sie hat kochen gelernt.	*She has learnt to cook.*
Er hat den Korb tragen **helfen**.	*He helped to carry the basket.*

(d) When *lernen, lehren* and *helfen* precede their dependent infinitive **zu** is usually required:

Er hat mir geholfen, den Korb zu tragen.	*He helped me to carry the basket.*

(e) Further uses of the simple infinitive:

i. Aufstehen! Bitte einsteigen!	*Get up everybody! All aboard please!*
ii. Warum arbeiten?	*Why work?*
Er weiß nicht, wohin gehen/was tun.	*He doesn't know where to go/what to do.*

(f) After all other verbs and verbal expressions the dependent infinitive must be immediately preceded by **zu**:

Er wünschte zu gehen.	*He wanted to go.*
Er bat mich zu kommen.	*He asked me to come.*

Es ist leicht, das zu sagen. *It is easy to say that.*
Er hat (nicht) die Absicht, morgen *He intends (does not intend) to*
zu kommen. *come tomorrow.*

NOTE: With separable verbs **zu** is inserted between the prefix and the verb:
Er bat mich, ihn ab**zu**holen. *He asked me to call for him.*

(g) To express purpose **um . . . zu** with the infinitive is required:

Er sagte es mir, um mich zu trösten. *He said it to console me.*

(h) Note the use of **zu** and infinitive after *ohne* and *(an)statt*:

Er kam ins Zimmer, ohne mich zu *He came into the room without*
sehen. *seeing me.*
(An)statt mir zu helfen, tut er *Instead of helping me he does*
nichts. *nothing.*

107 The Imperative

(a) The 2nd person singular of the imperative of all weak verbs, except
those ending in *-eln, -ern* and *-igen* (which always add *-e* to the stem),
and of most strong verbs is either the stem alone or with **-e** added:

sag(e)! mach(e)! lauf(e)! geh(e)! handle!

(b) Those strong verbs that change the **e** of the stem to **ie** or **i** in the
2nd and 3rd person singular present form the 2nd person singular of the
imperative by dropping the ending **-(s)t** from the 2nd person singular
present:

du gibst > gib! du nimmst > nimm! du liest > lies!

(c) The 2nd person plural of the imperative of **all** strong and weak verbs
corresponds to the 2nd person plural of the present indicative, but
there is **no** pronoun:

sagt! lauft! gebt! nehmt!

(d) The polite form (cf. *56(a)*) of the imperative is simply an inversion
of the corresponding person of the present subjunctive; there is no
hyphen:

sagen Sie! laufen Sie! seien Sie!

(e) The 1st person plural of the imperative is expressed in any one of
the following ways:

> Gehen wir! Wir wollen gehen!
> Laß (laßt, *or* lassen Sie) uns gehen! } *Let us go.*

(f) To qualify the force of the imperative **mal** (emphasising), **doch** (urging), **nur** (persuading or threatening) or **ja** (reminding) may be added:

Kommen Sie mal her!	*Just come here.*
Bitte kommen Sie doch!	*Please do come.*
Grabt nur!	*Just dig.*
Lachen Sie nur!	*Go on, laugh away.*
Komm ja nicht zu spät!	*See that you aren't late.*

(g) For the imperative of *haben, sein* and *werden*, see *88*.
For the imperative of reflexive verbs, see *103*.
For the passive imperative, see *110(a)*.
For the imperative of the 3rd person singular and plural, see *114(a)*i.
For position of *nicht* in the negative imperative, see *5(c)*.

NOTE: The imperative is usually followed by an exclamation mark.

108 The Interrogative

In questions **not** introduced by an interrogative adverb (*44*) or interrogative pronoun (or adjective) (*60–2*) the interrogative is shown by inversion of the verb and subject **and** by the question mark:

Siehst du ihn?	*Do you see him?*
(Siehst du ihn, so sage ihm . . .)	*(If you see him tell him . . .)*
Hast du ihn (nicht) gesehen?	*Have(n't) you seen him?*
Hat der Mann dich gesehen?	*Did the man see you?*
Wollen wir ins Theater?	*Shall we go to the theatre?*
Kommen Sie?	*Are you coming?*
(Kommen Sie!)	*(Come!)*

Note the form of the question with **ja, nicht wahr** and **doch**:

Du hast ihn gesehen, ja/nicht wahr?	*You've seen him,* **haven't you?**
Du kennst ihn, ja/nicht wahr?	*You know him,* **don't you?**
Du bist müde, ja/nicht wahr?	*You are tired,* **aren't you?**
Du wirst kommen, ja/nicht wahr?	*You will come,* **won't you?**
Er hat es doch nicht gemacht? Doch!	*He didn't do it,* **did he? Yes, he did.**

109 Auxiliary Verbs of Mood and *lassen*

(a) Conjugation:

PRES. IND.	dürfen	können	mögen	müssen	sollen	wollen
ich	darf	kann	mag	muß	soll	will
du	darfst	kannst	magst	mußt	sollst	willst
er, sie, es	darf	kann	mag	muß	soll	will
wir	dürfen	können	mögen	müssen	sollen	wollen
ihr	dürft	könnt	mögt	müßt	sollt	wollt
sie (Sie)	dürfen	können	mögen	müssen	sollen	wollen

PRES. SUBJ.[1]

ich/er	dürfe	könne	möge	müsse	solle	wolle

IMPF. IND.

ich	durfte	konnte	mochte	mußte	sollte	wollte

IMPF. SUBJ.

ich	dürfte	könnte	möchte	müßte	sollte	wollte

PF. IND.

ich habe	gedurft	gekonnt	gemocht	gemußt	gesollt	gewollt

PLPF. IND.

ich hatte	gedurft	gekonnt	gemocht	gemußt	gesollt	gewollt

PLPF. SUBJ.

ich hätte	gedurft	gekonnt	gemocht	gemußt	gesollt	gewollt

FUT.

ich werde dürfen	können	mögen	müssen	sollen	wollen

NOTE 1: The modal auxiliaries have two past participles: preceded by the infinitive of another verb, **dürfen** is used for **gedurft**, **können** for **gekonnt**, etc.:

Ich habe nicht kommen **können**.	*I have not been able to come.*
Ich hätte nicht schwimmen **sollen**.	*I should not have swum.*

NOTE 2: Neither *sollen* nor *wollen* ever modify.

(b) Examples of use:

i. **dürfen**

Er darf es tun.	*He may (is allowed to) do it.*
Er darf es nicht tun.	*He must not do it.*
Er durfte es tun.	*He was allowed to do it.*

[1] Only the 1st and 3rd pers. sing. subj. are now used

Er dürfte es tun.	*He would be allowed to do it.*
Er hat/hatte es tun dürfen.	*He has/had been allowed to do it.*
Er hat es gedurft.	*He has been allowed to.*
Er hätte es (nicht) tun dürfen.	*He would (not) have been allowed to do it.*
Er wird es tun dürfen.	*He will be allowed to do it.*
wenn ich bitten darf	*if you please*
Morgen dürfte schönes Wetter sein.	*Tomorrow it will probably be fine.*
So etwas hätte nie geschehen dürfen.	*A thing like that should never have happened.*

ii. können

Er kann es tun.	*He may, can do it.*
Er konnte es tun.	*He could (=was able to) do it.*
Er könnte es tun.	*He could (=would be able to) do it.*
Er hat/hatte es tun können.	*He has/had been able to do it.*
Er hat es gekonnt.	*He has been able to.*
Er hätte es (nicht) tun können, wenn . . .	*He could (not) have done it (= would (not) have been able to do it), if . . .*
Er wird es tun können.	*He will be able to do it.*
Das kann sein.	*That may be.*
Es könnte wahr sein.	*It might be true.*
Er kann (kein) Deutsch.	*He knows (does not know) German.*
Damals hat er Deutsch gekonnt.	*He knew German at that time.*
Er kann nichts dafür.	*He cannot help it.*
Er kann es getan haben.	*He may have done it.*
Er könnte es getan haben.	*He might possibly have done it.*

iii. mögen

Er mag es tun.	*He may possibly do it.*
Er mag es nicht tun.	*He does not like doing it.*
Er mochte es tun.	*He might well do it.*
Er mochte es nicht tun.	*He didn't like doing it.*
Er möchte es tun.	*He would like to do it.*

Er hat es nicht tun mögen.	*He didn't like doing it.*
Er hat es gemocht.	*He has liked it.*
Er hätte es (nicht) tun mögen.	*He would (not) have liked to do it.*
Er wird es tun mögen.	*He will like to do it.*
Das mag wohl sein.	*That may be so.*
Was er auch tun mag, ...	*No matter what he does...*
Ich mag nicht abreisen.	*I don't want to go away.*
Ich mag (gern) Äpfel.	*I like apples.*
Es mochte schon 11 Uhr sein.	*It may have been as late as 11.*
Ich möchte eine Tasse Tee.	*I should like a cup of tea.*
Er mag es getan haben.	*He may possibly have done it.*

iv. müssen

Er muß es tun.	*He must/has to do it, cannot help doing it.*
Er muß es nicht tun.	*He does not have to do it; he must not do it.*
Er mußte es tun.	*He had to do it.*
Er müßte es tun.	*He would have/ought to do it.*
Er hat/hatte es tun müssen.	*He has/had had to do it.*
Er hat es gemußt.	*He has had to.*
Er hätte es (nicht) tun müssen.	*He would (not) have had to do it; he ought (not) to have done it.*
Er wird/würde es tun müssen.	*He will/would have to do it.*
Ich muß fort.	*I must go.*
Er muß/mußte lachen.	*He can't/couldn't help laughing.*
Er muß es noch nicht wissen, sonst hätte er . . .	*He **cannot** know it yet or else he would have . . .*
Er muß (mußte) es getan haben.	*He must have done it.*

v. sollen

Er soll es tun.	*He is (said) to do it.*
Er sollte (ind.) es tun.	*He was (destined, said) to do it.*
Er sollte (subj.) es tun.	*He ought to do it.*
Er hat/hatte es tun sollen.	*He has/had been called upon to do it.*

Er hat es gesollt.	*It has been required of him.*
Er hätte es (nicht) tun sollen.	*He ought/should (not) have done it.*
Er wird es tun sollen.	*He will be called upon to do it.*
Was soll das?	*What is the meaning of that?*
Er soll reich sein.	*He is supposed to be rich.*
Du sollst nicht stehlen.	*Thou shalt not steal.*
Er wußte nicht, was er tun sollte.	*He did not know what to do.*
Sollte er vielleicht krank sein?	*Do you think he is ill?*
Sollte er kommen, . . .	*If he should come . . .*
Er soll/sollte es getan haben.	*He is/was said to have done it.*

vi. wollen

Er will es tun.	*He will do it, intends to do it.*
Er wollte es tun.	*He wanted, intended to do it.*
Er wollte es nicht tun.	*He would not/refused to do it.*
Er hat/hatte es tun wollen.	*He has/had been willing to do it.*
Er hat es gewollt.	*He has wanted it.*
Er hätte es (nicht) tun wollen.	*He would (not) have been willing/ have wanted to do it.*
Er wird es tun wollen.	*He will want to do it.*
Er würde es tun wollen.	*He would be willing to do it.*
Er will nichts davon hören.	*He won't hear of it.*
Was wollen Sie damit sagen?	*What do you mean by that?*
Wollen wir ins Theater?	*Shall we go to the theatre?*
Wir wollen ins Theater!	*Let us go to the theatre.*
Wir wollen eben ausgehen.	*We are just going out.*
Da er es eben tun wollte, . . .	*As he was just going to do it . . .*
Er will ein großer Gelehrter sein.	*He sets up/claims to be a great scholar.*
Er will es getan haben.	*He claims that he did it.*
Er wollte es getan haben.	*He maintained he did it.*
Das will ich nicht gesagt haben.	*I did not mean that.*

vii. lassen[1]

Er läßt mich warten.	*He makes me wait, keeps me waiting.*

[1] *Lassen*, though not an auxiliary verb of mood, tends to be used like one

Er läßt auf sich warten.	*He keeps people waiting for him.*
Er ließ den Arzt kommen.	*He sent for the doctor.*
Ich ließ es mir von ihm erzählen.	*I got him to tell me it.*
Er hat es zu Hause gelassen.	*He has left it at home.*
Er hat ihn kommen lassen.	*He has sent for him.*
Er hat es fallen lassen.	*He has dropped it.*
Ich habe mir eben die Haare schneiden lassen.	*I have just had my hair cut.*
Das läßt sich (A) leicht machen.	*That can easily be done.*
Er läßt Ihnen sagen, daß . . .	*He wants me to tell you that . . .*
Er läßt sie herzlich grüßen.	*He sends her his kindest regards.*

110 Passive Voice

(a) Conjugation (subjunctive forms given in brackets):

PRES.	Es wird (werde) getragen.	*It is (=is being) carried.*
IMPF.	Es wurde (würde) getragen.	*It was (=was being) carried.*
PF.	Es **ist** (sei) getragen **worden**.	*It has been carried.*
PLPF.	Es **war** (wäre) getragen **worden**.	*It had been carried.*
FUT.	Es wird (werde) getragen werden.	*It will be carried.*
COND.	Es würde getragen werden.	*It would be carried.*
FUT. PF.	Es wird (werde) getragen **worden sein**.	*It will have been carried.*
PF. COND.	Es würde getragen **worden sein**. (But cf. *101*.)	*It would have been carried.*
IMPER.	Sei gegrüßt!^{1}	*Greetings!*

With a **modal** verb:

Es muß gemacht werden.	*It must be done.*
Es mußte gemacht werden.	*It had to be done.*
Es müßte gemacht werden.	*It would have to be done.*
Es hat gemacht werden müssen.	*It has had to be done.*
Es muß gemacht **worden sein**.	*It must have been done.*
Es hätte gemacht werden müssen.	*It would have had to be done.*
Es wird gemacht werden müssen.	*It will have to be done.*

---

[1] The imperative is literary, and only possible with one or two verbs. The English negative imperative can often be rendered by a construction with *lassen*, e.g. *laß dich nicht betrügen/beirren* (don't be deceived/put off).

(b) Most **transitive** verbs (but **no** reflexives) can be used **passively**. The direct object of the active verb becomes the subject of the passive verb; the subject of the active verb becomes the agent:

Er tötete den Löwen.	*He killed the lion.*
Der Löwe wurde von ihm getötet.	*The lion was killed by him.*

(c) The **agent** is expressed by:

i. **von** + D, if animate or actively responsible for the action.

ii. **durch** + A, if inanimate, particularly when not **actively** responsible for the action.

BUT iii. it is omitted when *man* is the subject of the corresponding active.

Er wurde **von** seiner Mutter geweckt.	*He was woken up by his mother.*
Er wurde **durch** den Lärm geweckt.	*He was woken up by the noise.*
BUT Er muß geweckt werden.	*He must be woken up.*

(d) The **instrument** is expressed by **mit** + dative:

Der Brief wurde **mit** der Hand geschrieben.	*The letter was written by hand.*
Der Brief wurde von ihm **mit** diesem Bleistift geschrieben.	*The letter was written by him with his pencil.*

NOTE: The instrument remains the instrument in the active, whereas the agent becomes the subject in the active.

(e) The **infinitive** + **zu** preceded by **sein** has **passive** force:

Es war niemand zu sehen.	*There was nobody to be seen.*
Nichts war zu machen.	*There was nothing to be done.*

(f) With those neuter verbs (i.e. verbs that have no object, direct or indirect) that express some human activity, the **impersonal passive** is very common in German though impossible in English:

Es wurde jeden Abend gesungen.	*People sang every night.*
(Jeden Abend wurde gesungen.)	

NOTE: **Es**, the grammatical subject, is omitted in impersonal passive constructions unless it is the first word. (Cf. 56(e)).

(g) If the auxiliary **sein** is used instead of **werden** a state, not an action, is expressed. The past participle then has adjectival force:

Der Tisch **ist/war** gedeckt.	*The table is/was laid.* (= *state.*)
Der Tisch **wird/wurde** gedeckt.	*The table is/was being laid.* (=*action.*)
Das Lied **wird** überall gesungen.	*The song is* (**being**) *sung everywhere.*

(h) When a verb has two objects, one dative and the other accusative, the dative object **remains** in the dative case in the passive construction, while the accusative object becomes the subject of the passive construction:

Man gab mir einen Bleistift.	*They gave me a pencil.*
Mir wurde **ein** Bleistift gegeben.	I *was given a pencil.*

(i) Verbs governing the **dative** or followed by a **preposition** must be used **impersonally** in the passive:

Ihm ist nicht geholfen worden.	**He** *has not been helped.*
(Es ist **ihm** nicht geholfen worden.)	
An ihn ist nicht gedacht worden.	**He** *has not been thought of.*

NOTE: The passive may be (and often is) avoided altogether, especially in constructions like those shown in (*h*) and (*i*), by using *man* and the active voice.

(j) Cf. *lassen* (*109(b)*vii) for further ways of expressing the passive.

111 Formation of the Subjunctive

(a) Apart from *sein* (see *88*), the modal auxiliaries (see *109(a)*) and one or two other verbs, the present subjunctive is nowadays restricted to the third person singular (see *90*), the ending of all verbs except *sein* being -e added to the stem of the infinitive. Hence, the perfect subjunctive of verbs conjugated with *haben* (see *88*) and the future subjunctive of all verbs (see *90*) is likewise limited to the third person singular, the ending of the auxiliary being **-e**:

er **sag-e**	er **trag-e**	er **handel-e**
er **hab-e gesagt**	er **werd-e tragen**	
BUT ich **sei gekommen**	wir **sei-en geblieben**	ich **könn-e kommen**

(b) The imperfect subjunctive of weak verbs is, with few exceptions (see *111(e)* below), the same as the imperfect indicative:

er **mach-te** du **wart-etest** sie **sag-ten**

(c) The imperfect subjunctive of strong verbs is, with few exceptions (see *111(e)* below), formed by adding the endings **-e, -st, -e, -en, -t, -en** to the first person singular imperfect indicative. The vowel is modified if possible:

ich **trug: trüg-e** du **gabst: gäb-st** er **schlief: schlief-e**

(d) The pluperfect subjunctive of all verbs is formed by the imperfect subjunctive of *haben* or *sein* together with the past participle:

ich **hätte gesagt** ihr **hättet getragen** du **wärst gekommen**

(e) Irregular forms of the imperfect subjunctive:

befehlen	beföhle[1]	schwimmen	schwömme[1]
beginnen	begönne[1]	senden	sendete
brennen	brennte	spinnen	spönne[1]
bringen	brächte	stehen	stünde[1]
denken	dächte	sterben	stürbe
empfehlen	empföhle[1]	verderben	verdürbe
helfen	hülfe[1]	wenden	wendete
kennen	kennte	werben	würbe
nennen	nennte	werfen	würfe
rennen	rennte	wissen	wüßte
schelten	schölte[1]		

112 The Subjunctive in Indirect Speech

Direct Speech		*Indirect Speech*
Pres. Indic.	becomes	Pres. or Impf. Subj.
Imp. Indic. ⎫		
Pf. Indic. ⎬ (=Past)	become	Pf. or Plpf. Subj.
Plpf. Indic. ⎭		

[1] Has also the regular form

Direct Speech	*Indirect Speech*

Fut. Indic.
Conditional $\Big\}$ (=Future) become Fut. Subj. or Conditional

NOTE: Since, with few exceptions (see *III(a)*), only the third person singular present, perfect and future subjunctive is in current use, for all other persons the alternative tenses, i.e. the imperfect subjunctive, the pluperfect subjunctive and the conditional, must be used in indirect speech. Otherwise, modern usage tends to prefer the pluperfect subjunctive and the conditional, but, except in N. Germany, not the imperfect subjunctive. In any case all possible consistency in the use of tenses should be aimed at.

(a) STATEMENTS

Direct Speech	*Indirect Speech*
Mein Freund schrieb mir:	Mein Freund schrieb mir,
„Ich **bin** krank"	er **sei/wäre** krank. daß er krank **sei/wäre**.
„Ich **habe** Fieber gehabt."	er **habe/hätte** Fieber gehabt. daß er Fieber gehabt **habe/hätte**.
„Man **hat** den Arzt kommen lassen."	man **habe/hätte** den Arzt kommen lassen. daß man den Arzt **habe/hätte** kommen lassen.
„Sobald er mich untersucht **hatte, fühlte** ich mich schon besser."	sobald er ihn untersucht **habe/hätte, habe/hätte** er sich besser gefühlt. daß, sobald er ihn untersucht **habe/hätte**, er sich besser gefühlt **habe/hätte**.
„Ich **werde** bald an die See fahren."	er **werde/würde** bald an die See fahren. daß er bald an die See fahren **werde/würde**.
„Meine Eltern **kommen** mit."	seine Eltern **kämen** mit. daß seine Eltern **mitkämen**.
„Sie **machen** schon alles fertig."	sie **machten** schon alles fertig. daß sie schon alles fertig **machten**.

NOTE: In a passage of indirect speech *daß* is usually omitted.

(112)

(b) QUESTIONS

If in the direct question there is an interrogative adjective, adverb or
pronoun (e.g. *welcher*, *wann*, *wer*) this is retained in the indirect question.
If there is no such interrogative word, **ob** (*whether*) must introduce the
indirect question.

Direct Speech	*Indirect Speech*
Er fragte den Fremden:	Er fragte den Fremden,
„Wo **sind** Sie zu Hause?"	wo er zu Hause **sei/wäre**.
„Wann **fahren** Sie wieder nach Hause?"	wann er wieder nach Hause **fahre/führe**.
„Wie **kommen** Sie nach Hause?"	wie er nach Hause **komme/käme**.
„Was **machen** Sie zu Hause?"	was er zu Hause **mache/machte**.
„Wer **war** mit Ihnen?"	wer mit ihm gewesen **sei/wäre**.
„**Schreiben** Sie Bücher?"	**ob** er Bücher **schreibe/schriebe**.

(c) COMMANDS

The present (or imperfect) subjunctive of **sollen** or **mögen** is used to
render indirect commands:

Direct Speech	*Indirect Speech*
Er sagte zum Diener:	Er sagte dem Diener,
„Wecken Sie mich um 7 Uhr!"	er **solle/möge** ihn um 7 Uhr **wecken**. daß er ihn um 7 Uhr **wecken solle/möge**.

NOTE 1: *Sollen* is more imperative than *mögen*.

NOTE 2: The above construction can be avoided by using **bitten** (*to ask*) or
befehlen (*to command*) to render **tell**:

Er bat den Diener, ihn um 7 Uhr zu wecken.
Er befahl **dem** Diener, ihn um 7 Uhr zu wecken.

(d) SUBJUNCTIVE OR INDICATIVE?

i. In indirect speech the indicative is used if there is no doubt about
the truth of an assertion. Otherwise the subjunctive is used:

Man hat mir erzählt, daß er gestorben **ist**. (=fact.)
Man hat mir erzählt, daß er gestorben **sei**. (=unconfirmed report.)

ii. The indicative is therefore generally used after verbs in the main clause like **wissen, beweisen, erfahren,** etc., which imply certainty:

Wir wußten, daß er gekommen war.

iii. The subjunctive is generally used after verbs of thinking and saying like **sagen, glauben, denken, behaupten, erklären** and **fürchten** which imply some degree of doubt:

Er behauptete, daß sie ausgegangen **sei**.
Ich glaubte, daß sie ausgegangen **sei**.
Er sagte, er **hätte** keine Zeit.

iv. The indicative, however, is sometimes used even after verbs of saying and thinking when the verb in the main clause is in the **present tense** (especially in the 1st person):

Ich glaube (er glaubt), daß sie ausgegangen **ist**.

113 The Subjunctive in Conditional Sentences

(a) In the present and future the **indicative** is used in both clauses:

Ich **helfe** dir, ⎫
Ich **werde** dir ⎬ wenn ich **kann**.   *I shall help you if I can.*
helfen, ⎭

Du **mußt** fleißiger arbeiten, wenn   *You must work harder if you*
du das Examen bestehen **willst**.   *want to pass the exam.*

(b) In unreal conditional sentences referring to the future the **imperfect subjunctive** is still preferred in the **subordinate clause**, though the use of the conditional here is very common in the spoken language; in the **main clause** (except when this contains a modal auxiliary) the **conditional** is nowadays preferred to the imperfect subjunctive:

Ich **würde helfen**, wenn ich   *I should help if I could.*
könnte.

Ich **würde** es dir **sagen**, wenn ich es **wüßte**.	*I should tell you if I knew.*
Ich **würde** mich freuen, wenn er **käme** (*or* **kommen sollte**).	*I should be glad if he came* (or *were to come*).
Er **könnte** es tun, wenn er **versuchte**.	*He could do it if he tried.*
Du **müßtest** fleißiger arbeiten, wenn du das Examen bestehen **wolltest**.	*You would have to work harder if you wanted to pass the exam.*

(c) In unreal conditional sentences referring to the past the **pluperfect subjunctive** is normally used in both the **main** and **subordinate** clause:

Ich **hätte** dir **geholfen**, wenn ich es **gekonnt hätte**.	*I should have helped you if I had been able to.*
Du **hättest** fleißiger arbeiten **müssen**, wenn du das Examen **hättest** bestehen **wollen**.	*You would have had to work harder if you had wanted to pass the exam.*

(d) The *wenn*-clause may precede the main clause:

Wenn ich kann, (so/dann) helfe ich dir.
Wenn ich könnte, (so/dann) würde ich dir helfen.
Wenn ich gekonnt hätte, (so/dann) hätte ich dir geholfen.

(e) In the past tenses the word *wenn* may be omitted when the subordinate clause precedes the main clause. The finite verb must then be the **first** word and *so/dann* links up the two clauses:

Könnte ich, so/dann würde ich dir helfen.
Hätte ich gekonnt, so/dann hätte ich dir geholfen.

114 Other uses of the Subjunctive

(a) In main clauses:

i. To express the imperative of the 1st person plural and 3rd person singular and plural:

Friede sei mit euch!	*Peace be with you.*
Es lebe der König!	*Long live the King!*
Gehen wir!	*Let us go.*
Er sei, wer er wolle.	*No matter who he may be.*
Es koste, was es wolle.	*Whatever it may cost.*

ii. To express wishes either not fulfilled or incapable of fulfilment:

Käme er doch bald!	*If only he would come soon.*
Wäre er nur früher gekommen!	*If only he had come sooner.*
Ich wäre gern länger geblieben.	*I should have liked to stay longer.*

iii. To express uncertainty:

Das wäre wohl das Beste.	*That is probably the best thing.*
Wäre das möglich?	*Is that possible, do you think?*
Sollte er vielleicht krank sein?	*Do you think he is ill?*
Es dürfte ein Leichtes sein.	*It is probably an easy matter.*

(b) In subordinate clauses:

i. In noun clauses introduced by *wünschen* or *wollen*:

Ich wünschte, ich wäre schon dort!	*I wish I were there now.*
Ich wollte, er wäre früher gekommen!	*I wish he had come sooner.*
Wir wollten, daß sie früher kämen/kommen sollten.	*We wanted them to come earlier.*
BUT Er will, daß sie sofort **kommt**.	*He wants her to come immediately.*

ii. In relative clauses dependent on a negative antecedent:

Ich kenne niemand, der eine bessere Stimme **hätte**.	*I know nobody who **has** a better voice.*
Ich kannte niemand, der eine bessere Stimme **gehabt hätte**.	*I knew nobody who **had** a better voice.*

iii. In clauses dependent on *als ob* or *als wenn*:

Er sieht aus,	als ob er krank sei/wäre. als **sei/wäre** er krank.	*He looks as if he is ill.*
Er sah aus,	als wenn er krank sei/wäre. als **sei/wäre** er krank.	*He looked as if he were ill.*
Er tat (so),	als ob er nicht verstanden hätte. als **hätte** er nicht verstanden.	*He pretended he had not understood.*

NOTE: If the words *ob* or *wenn* are omitted the verb immediately follows *als*.

iv. In clauses dependent on *als daß*:

Es ist zu kalt, als daß wir draußen   *It is too cold for us to (be able* sitzen könnten.   *to) sit outside.*

NOTE: Unless it is necessary to insist on the personal element involved the simpler construction with *um . . . zu* can be used:

Es ist zu kalt, um draußen sitzen zu   *It is too cold to sit outside.* können.

Es ist zu schön, um wahr zu sein.   *It is too good to be true.*

v. After *damit, (an)statt daß* and *ohne daß* the subjunctive is occasionally used with the past tense, but nowadays no longer with the present:

Er erhob sich, damit wir ihn sehen   *He stood up so that we could see* konnten/könnten.   *him.*

BUT Wiederhole es, damit er es nicht   *Repeat it so that he does not* vergißt.   *forget it.*

115 Verbs governing the Dative

WEAK	STRONG (see *127*)
antworten, *answer (s.b.)*	*einfallen, occur to (105)*
begegnen, meet	*entfliehen, escape from*
beiwohnen, *be present at*	*entkommen, escape from*
danken, *thank*	*erliegen, succumb to*
dienen, *serve*	gefallen, *please, like (105, 123)*
drohen, *threaten*	*gelingen, succeed (105)*
fehlen, *be missing; be wrong with*	gelten, *be meant for*
(*)folgen, *follow; obey*	*geschehen, happen (105)*
gehorchen, *obey*	gleichen, *resemble*
gehören, *belong to (s.b.)*	helfen, *help*
genügen, *suffice*	leid tun, *be sorry (for) (105)*
glauben, *believe (s.b.)*	mißfallen, *displease, dislike*
mißtrauen, *mistrust*	*(105)*
sich nähern, *approach*	*mißlingen, fail (105)*
passen, *suit, fit*	*nachlaufen, run after*
schaden, *harm*	*vorkommen, seem to*
schmecken, *taste (intr.), enjoy*	*weichen, yield to*
(123)	weh tun, *hurt, ache*
vertrauen, *trust*	widersprechen, *contradict*
zuhören, *listen*	zusehen, *watch*

Ich bin ihm eben begegnet.	*I have just met him.*
Er kommt mir ganz alt vor.	*He seems quite old to me.*

116 Verbs governing the Accusative and Dative

WEAK	STRONG (see *127*)
anvertrauen, *entrust*	anbieten, *offer* (e.g. *job, money*)
berichten, *report*	aufgeben, *assign, set a task*
bringen, *bring, take* (*91(h)*)	befehlen, *order, command*
erklären, *explain; declare*	beschreiben, *describe*
erlauben, *allow, permit*	beweisen, *prove*
erzählen, *tell, relate*	bieten, *bid, offer* (e.g. *arm*)
klagen, *complain about*	empfehlen, *recommend*
melden, *announce*	geben, *give*
mitteilen, *inform of*	gebieten, *command*
reichen, *reach, hand, pass*	leihen, *lend*
sagen, *say, tell*	raten, *advise*
schenken, *give, present*	schreiben, *write*
schicken, *send*	stehlen, *steal*
senden, *send* (*91(h)*)	verbieten, *forbid*
verkaufen, *sell*	vergeben, *forgive*
verweigern, *refuse*	versprechen, *promise*
vorspielen, *play* (e.g. *music*) *to*	verzeihen, *pardon*
vorstellen, *introduce*	vorlesen, *read aloud*
wünschen, *wish*	weisen, *show*
zahlen, *pay*	zurückgeben, *give back, return*
zeigen, *show, point out*	zurufen, *call out to*

Ich brachte ihm ein Glas Wasser.	*I took him a glass of water.*
Das rate ich dir.	*I advise you (to do) that.*

117 Verbs governing the Genitive

WEAK	STRONG (see *127*)
bedürfen, *require* (cf. *109 (a)*)	sich annehmen, *take charge*
sich erinnern, *remember*	(*care*) *of*
sich schämen, *be ashamed of*	sich enthalten, *abstain from*

Er schämt sich seines Sohnes.	*He is ashamed of his son.*
Sie konnte sich der Tränen nicht enthalten.	*She could not keep back her tears.*

118 Verbs governing the Accusative and Genitive

WEAK	STRONG (see *127*)
anklagen, *accuse of*	entheben, *relieve of*

> Man klagte ihn der Tat an.   *He was accused of the deed.*
> Man enthob ihn dieses Amtes.   *He was relieved of this office.*

119 Verbs governing Two Accusatives

WEAK	STRONG (see *127*)
kosten, *cost*	heißen, *call*
lehren, *teach*	schelten, *call (abusively)*
nennen, *call (91(h))*	

> Er lehrt mich Deutsch.   *He teaches me German.*
> Er hieß ihn einen Dummkopf.   *He called him a blockhead.*

120 Verbs followed by a Prepositional Object

WEAK   STRONG

(a) AN + ACCUSATIVE

denken, *think of (91(h))*	binden, *tie to*
erinnern, *remind of*	*herankommen, *get to, approach*
sich erinnern, *remember*	schreiben, *write to*
gewöhnen, *accustom to*	
sich gewöhnen, *get used to*	
glauben, *believe in*	
sich wenden, *apply to*	

> Er erinnert sich an ihn.   *He remembers him.*
> Er band das Tier an den Baum.   *He tied the animal to the tree.*

(b) AN + DATIVE

erkennen, *recognise by (91(h))*	leiden, *suffer from*
sich freuen, *take pleasure in*	*sterben, *die of (illness)*
hindern, *prevent from*	teilnehmen, *take part in*
zweifeln, *doubt*	*vorbeigehen, *go past*

> Er hindert mich am Lesen.   *He prevents me from reading.*
> Er ging an mir vorbei.   *He went past me.*

WEAK	STRONG

(c) AUF + ACCUSATIVE

achten, *pay heed to*	sich belaufen, *amount to*
antworten, *answer* (e.g. *question*)	sich beziehen, *refer to*
aufmerksam machen, *call s.b.'s attention to*	dringen, *urge s.th.*
	*kommen, *come upon*
aufpassen, *keep an eye on*	schießen, *shoot at*
blicken, *look at*	sehen, *look at*
sich freuen, *look forward to*	sich verlassen, *rely on*
hoffen, *hope for*	weisen, *point at*
hören, *listen to*	*zugehen, *go up to*
rechnen, *count on*	*zukommen, *come up to/come towards*
warten, *wait for*	
zeigen, *point to/at*	

> Er antwortete auf die Frage.
> Er machte sie darauf aufmerksam.

> *He answered the question.*
> *He called her attention to it.*

(d) AUF + DATIVE

bestehen, *insist on*

> Er besteht auf einer Antwort.

> *He insists on an answer.*

(e) AUS + DATIVE

*folgen, *follow from*	bestehen, *consist of*
übersetzen, *translate from*	*werden, *become of*

> aus dem Englischen übersetzt
> Was wird aus ihm werden?

> *translated from English*
> *What will become of him?*

(f) BEI + DATIVE

sich entschuldigen, *apologize to*	helfen, *help with*
wohnen, *live with*	nehmen, *take by* (e.g. *hand*)

> Er wohnt bei seiner Mutter.
> Er half mir bei der Arbeit.

> *He lives with his mother.*
> *He helped me with my work.*

(g) FÜR + ACCUSATIVE

danken, *thank for*	sich entscheiden, *decide for*
sich interessieren, *be interested in*	gelten, *be considered to be*
sorgen, *take care of, look after*	halten, *consider to be*

> Er dankte mir für den Brief.
> Er gilt für reich.

> *He thanked me for the letter.*
> *He is considered to be rich.*

WEAK	STRONG

(h) IN + ACCUSATIVE

sich mischen, *interfere with*	*ausbrechen, *break/burst* (*into*)
übersetzen, *translate into*	dringen, *urge s.b.*
verwandeln, *turn into* (*tr.*)	*einbrechen, *break into, burgle*
sich verwandeln, *turn into* (*intr.*)	*einfallen, *invade*
	*einsteigen, *get on* (*bus, etc.*)
	*eintreten, *enter*
	sich ergeben, *resign o.s. to*
	*geraten, *get into* (e.g. *difficulties*)

Er wurde in ein Tier verwandelt.	*He was turned into an animal.*
Sie brach in Tränen aus.	*She burst (out) into tears.*

(i) IN + DATIVE

sich irren, *be mistaken in*	*ankommen, *arrive at, in*
	bestehen, *consist in*

Er irrt sich in dir.	*He is mistaken in you.*
Er kam in dem Dorf an.	*He arrived at the village.*

(j) MIT + DATIVE

sich beschäftigen, *occupy o.s. with*	sprechen, *speak, talk to*
handeln, *trade in*	verbinden, *connect to* (*with*)
nicken, *nod*	vergleichen, *compare with*
zubringen, *spend* (*doing s.th.*)	
(*91(h)*)	

Er bringt seine Zeit mit Lesen zu.	*He spends his time reading.*
Er nickte mit dem Kopf.	*He nodded his head.*

(k) NACH + DATIVE

*abreisen, *set off for*	aussehen, *look like*
fragen, *enquire about*	greifen, *clutch at, seize*
schicken, *send for*	riechen, *smell of*
schmecken, *taste of*	schreien, *clamour for*
streben, *strive after*	sehen, *look after*
suchen, *search for*	sich sehnen, *long for*
urteilen, *judge by*	sich umsehen, *look round for*

Er schickte nach dem Arzt.	*He sent for the doctor.*
Es sieht nach Regen aus.	*It looks like rain.*

WEAK	STRONG

(l) ÜBER + ACCUSATIVE

sich freuen, *be glad, pleased about*

herrschen, *rule over*

klagen, *complain of*

lachen, *laugh at*

nachdenken, *think over (91(h))*

reden, *talk about*

urteilen, *pass judgment on*

wachen, *watch over*

weinen, *weep about*

sich wundern, *be surprised at*

sich aussprechen, *express o.s. about*

erfahren, *learn about/of*

schimpfen, *grumble about*

schreiben, *write about*

sprechen, *speak about*

streiten, *argue*

sich streiten, *quarrel about*

sich unterhalten, *converse about*

Er lachte über mich.

Er sprach lange darüber.

He laughed at me.

He spoke a long time about it.

(m) UM + ACCUSATIVE

bringen, *defraud, deprive of*
  (91(h))

sich handeln, *be a question*
  (matter) of

sich kümmern, *worry about*

verkaufen, *sell for*

sich bemühen, *try to help*

sich bewerben, *apply, compete for*

bitten, *ask for*

*kommen, *lose*

ringen, *struggle*

Er brachte mich um das Geld.

Er bat mich um Feuer.

He did me out of the money.

He asked me for a light.

(n) VON + DATIVE

denken, *think (e.g. well) of*
  (91(h))

erzählen, *relate/tell about*

leben, *live on*

sagen, *say s.th, tell about*

überzeugen, *convince of*

wissen, *know about (123)*

abhängen, *depend on*

gelten, *be true of*

halten, *think (e.g. well) of*

sprechen, *speak of*

verstehen, *know about (123)*

*weichen, *budge from*

Was halten/denken Sie von ihm? *What do you think of him?*

(o) VOR + DATIVE

Angst haben }
sich fürchten } *be afraid of*

sich hüten, *beware of*

*fliehen, *flee from*

sich in acht nehmen, *beware of,*
  mind, watch out for

WEAK	STRONG
schützen, *protect from*	*sterben, *die of* (*emotion*)
verstecken, *hide from*	verbergen, *conceal from*
warnen, *warn against*	*weichen, *give way to*
weinen, *weep for*	

Sie weinte vor Freude.   *She wept for joy.*
Nimm dich in acht vor dem Hund! *Beware of the dog.*

(p) WEGEN + GENITIVE

loben, *praise for*	schelten, *scold* (*chide*) *for*
tadeln, *blame for*	

Man lobte ihn wegen seines Mutes. *He was praised for his courage.*

(q) ZU + DATIVE

bestimmen, *designate as, destine for*	beitragen, *contribute to*
	einladen, *invite to*
brauchen, *need for*	sich entschließen, *resolve to* (*do*) *s.th.*
dienen, *serve as*	
gehören, *be required for*, *belong to* (*s.th.*)	verhelfen, *help to* (*get s.th.*)
	*werden, *become* (*s.th. different*)
machen, *make*	zwingen, *force to* (*do*) *s.th.*
passen, *match, go with*	
taugen, *be fit for*	
wählen, *elect*	
sich wenden, *turn round to*	

Ich gehöre zu meiner Familie.   *I belong to my family.*
Dazu gehört Zeit.   *That takes time.*
Er lud mich zum Mittagessen ein. *He invited me to lunch.*

121 Clauses or Gerunds as Prepositional Object of Verbs

Such clauses or gerunds are normally preceded by *da(r)*- together with
the appropriate preposition (cf. *120*):

Er freut sich **darauf**, daß du ihn besuchst.	*He is looking forward to your visiting him.*
Er dankt mir **dafür**, daß ich ihn gerettet habe.	*He thanks me for having saved him.*

Er spricht **davon**, daß er eine Reise machen will.	*He talks of being about to go on a journey.*
Er wunderte sich **darüber**, daß ich nicht gekommen war.	*He was surprised at my not having come.*
Ich erinnere mich **(daran)**, ihn gesehen zu haben.	*I remember having seen him.*
Er fürchtete sich **davor**, gehört zu werden.	*He was afraid of being heard.*
Sie sprachen miteinander **darüber**, wie sie es machen könnten.	*They discussed with one another how they might do it.*

122 Translation of English Verbal Forms in -ing

These forms may be rendered by:

(a) The present participle when used adjectivally:

Ein dauernder Erfolg.	*A lasting success.*
Ein unterhaltendes Buch.	*An entertaining book.*

(b) The infinitive used as a noun:

Das Rauchen ist verboten.	*Smoking is prohibited.*
Ich bin des Wartens müde.	*I am tired of waiting.*
Beim Aussteigen wurde er überfahren.	*Whilst getting out he was run over.*
Im Stehen kann ich besser sehen.	*I can see better standing.*

(c) The simple infinitive after *sehen, hören, fühlen, finden, lassen,* and *bleiben,* e.g.:

Ich sah ihn sich entfernen.	*I saw him moving away.*
Ich hörte sie singen.	*I heard her singing.*
Ich fühlte mein Herz schlagen.	*I felt my heart beating.*
Ich fand ihn dort liegen.	*I found him lying there.*
Ich ließ es dort liegen.	*I left it lying there.*
Er blieb dort stehen.	*He remained standing there.*

NOTE: The infinitive of *sehen, hören, lassen* and *helfen* is normally used instead of the past participle in the perfect tenses when another infinitive immediately precedes (cf. *109(a)*, note, and *106(c)*).

Ich habe ihn kommen sehen.
Ich hatte sie singen hören.
Ich hatte es dort liegen lassen.

(d) The infinitive with *zu* when there is no change of subject:

Es ist angenehm, hier zu sitzen.	*It is pleasant sitting here.*
Er hat die Absicht, mich bald zu besuchen.	*He intends visiting me soon.*
Es gelang mir, ein billiges Hotel zu finden.	*I succeeded in finding a cheap hotel.*
Ich liebe **es**/hasse **es**/ziehe **es** vor, zu Hause zu bleiben.	*I like/hate/prefer staying at home.*
Ich bestehe darauf, Ihnen zu helfen.	*I insist on helping you.*
Er kam ins Zimmer, ohne mich zu sehen.	*He came into the room without seeing me.*
Anstatt mir zu helfen, tut er nichts.	*Instead of helping me he does nothing.*

(e) A dependent clause introduced by *indem* (by -ing), *daß*, *ohne daß* or *anstatt daß*:

Man macht Tee, indem man heißes Wasser auf die Blätter gießt.	*Tea is made by pouring hot water on the leaves.*
Ich bestehe darauf, daß du mir hilfst (bestand . . . helfen solltest).	*I insist (insisted) on your helping me.*
Er kam ins Zimmer, ohne daß ich ihn sah.	*He came into the room without my seeing him.*
Anstatt daß er mir hilft, muß ich ihm helfen.	*Instead of his helping me I have to help him.*

(f) A dependent clause introduced by *da, wenn, als, nachdem, bevor, ehe* or *indem* (while):

Da er müde war, ging er zu Bett.	*Being tired he went to bed.*
Nachdem/als er sich umgezogen hatte, ging er aus.	*Having changed he went out.*
Ehe/bevor er zu Bett ging, las er die Zeitung.	*Before going to bed he read the paper.*
Indem er das sagte, starb er.	*Saying this, he died.*

(g) A dependent clause introduced by *wie* after verbs of seeing and hearing:

Ich sah, wie er an dem Haus vorübereilte.	*I saw him hurrying past the house.*

Ich hörte, wie er die Treppe heraufkam.	*I heard him coming up the stairs.*

(h) A relative clause:

Der Mann, der den Wagen fuhr, schlief ein.	*The man driving the car fell asleep.*

(i) A main clause introduced by *und*:

Er schlief ganz fest und erwachte erst um 9 Uhr.	*He slept quite soundly, not waking up till 9 o'clock.*

(j) The past participle of a verb of motion after *kommen*:

Er kam auf mich zugelaufen.	*He came running up to me.*

(k) The finite verb together with *gern, lieber, am liebsten*:

Ich spiele gern Tennis.	*I like playing tennis.*
Ich spiele lieber Fußball.	*I prefer playing football.*
Ich spiele am liebsten Golf.	*I like playing golf best.*

123 Translation of certain English Words

ABOUT

Es war gegen Mitternacht.	*It was about* (=preposition) *midnight.*
um das Jahr 1900 herum	*(round) about the year 1900*
etwa (*or* ungefähr) acht Tage	*about* (=adverb) *a week*
etwa (*or* ungefähr) 6 Fuß hoch	*about 6 feet high*
Wovon spricht er?	*What is he talking about?*
ein Buch über Goethe	*a book about Goethe*
Er wollte eben ausgehen.	*He was just about to go out.*

AFTER

Nach zwei Stunden ging er fort.	*After* (=preposition) *two hours he went away.*
Nachdem er zwei Stunden gearbeitet hatte, ging er fort.	*After* (=conjunction) *he had worked for two hours he went away.*
ein Jahr darauf (*or* später)	*a year after* (=adverb)
Nachher ging er fort.	*Afterwards* (or *after that*) *he went away.*

(123)

ANY

Hast du (etwas) Brot?	*Have you any bread?*
Ich habe kein(e)s.	*I haven't any.*
Hast du welches?	*Have you any?*
Ich habe keine Blumen.	*I haven't any flowers.*
Hast du welche?	*Have you any?*
Ich kenne keinen von ihnen.	*I don't know any of them.*
jeden Augenblick	*(at) any moment*
Es kann jedem passieren.	*It can happen to anybody.*
Ich kann nicht länger bleiben.	*I cannot remain any longer.*
irgendwo; irgend jemand	*anywhere; anybody*

ASK

Er bat mich zu kommen.	*He asked me to come.*
Er bat mich um Feuer.	*He asked me for a light.*
Er bat mich zum Tee.	
Er lud mich zum Tee ein.	*He asked me to tea.*
Er hat mich das/etwas gefragt.	*He asked me that/something.*
Er fragte mich um Rat.	*He asked my advice.*
Er fragte mich nach dem Weg.	*He asked me the way.*
Er fragte mich nach ihrem Befinden.	*He asked me how she was.*
Er fragte mich, wo ich zu Hause sei.	*He asked me where I lived.*
Er stellte mir dieselbe Frage.	*He asked me the same question.*
Er verlangte zehn Pfund.	*He asked for £10.*
Das ist zu viel verlangt.	*That is asking too much.*

NOTE: *Bitten* = to request; *fragen* = to make an enquiry; *verlangen* = demand

BE

Er ist klein.	*He is small.*
Es war keine Spur von ihm da.	*There was no sign of him there.*
Es war eine große Menge dort.	*There was a big crowd there.*
Es gibt Leute, die das sagen.	*There are (=exist) people who say that.*
Es gab viel zu tun.	*There was a lot to do.*
Eine Brücke führt über den Fluß.	*There is a bridge over the river.*
Der Eingang befindet sich dort.	*The entrance is there.*
Frankfurt liegt am Main.	*Frankfurt is on the Main.*
Hier sollte ein Tisch stehen.	*There should be a table here.*
Die Sonne steht hoch.	*The sun is high up.*
Die Wohnung steht leer.	*The flat is empty.*

Das ganze Tal stand unter Wasser.	*The whole valley was under water.*
Wo steckt er denn?	*Where on earth is he?*
Die Bäume hängen voller Früchte.	*The trees are full of fruit.*
Geht deine Uhr richtig?	*Is your watch right?*
Nein, sie geht vor (nach).	*No, it is fast (slow).*
Wie geht's Ihnen?	*How are you?*
Mach' schnell!	*Be quick.*

BEFORE

Er ging vor zwei Uhr fort.	*He went away before (=preposition) two o'clock.*
Bevor (or ehe) es zwei Uhr geschlagen hatte, ging er fort.	*Before (=conjunction) two o'clock had struck he went away.*
einige Tage vorher (or zuvor)	*a few days before (=adverb)*
Ich habe das früher (or schon) gemacht.	*I have done that before (=adverb).*
Er ist noch nie zu spät gekommen.	*He has never been late before.*

CALL

Er heißt Robert.	*He is called (=his name is) Robert.*
Wir nennen ihn Bob.	*We call him Bob.*
Er nennt sich einen Dichter.	*He calls himself a poet.*
Er schalt mich einen Narren.	*He called me a fool.*
Er rief den Kellner.	*He called (=summoned) the waiter.*
Was hat er dir zugerufen?	*What did he call out to you?*
Er sprach bei mir vor.⎫ Er besuchte mich. ⎭	*He called on me (=visited me).*
Ich holte meinen Freund ab.	*I called for my friend.*

CATCH

Er fing den Ball.	*He caught the ball.*
Der Dieb wurde gefangengenommen.	*The thief was caught.*
Er erreichte den Zug.	*He caught the train.*
Er hat sich erkältet.	*He has caught a cold.*
Er hat ihn plötzlich erblickt.	*He suddenly caught sight of him.*

(123)

CHANGE

Er hat sich umgezogen.	*He has changed (his clothes).*
Er ist in Hannover umgestiegen.	*He changed (trains) at Hanover.*
Er hat sich sehr verändert.	*He has changed much.*
Die Zeiten haben sich geändert.	*Times have changed.*
Er hat sein englisches Geld gewechselt.	*He has changed his English money.*
Können Sie mir einen Zehnmarkschein wechseln?	*Can you change a ten-mark note for me?*
Es tut mir leid; ich habe kein Kleingeld bei mir.	*I am sorry; I haven't any change on me.*
Ich bekam nur zwei Mark heraus.	*I only got two marks change.*
Behalten Sie den Rest!	*Keep the change.*
Er liebt Veränderung.	*He is fond of a change.*
Zur Abwechslung ging ich ins Theater.	*For a change I went to the theatre.*

ENJOY

Hat dir das Konzert gefallen?	*Did you enjoy the concert?*
Hast du dich (gut) amüsiert? ⎫ Hast du dich gut unterhalten? ⎭	*Did you enjoy yourself?*
Er weiß das Leben zu genießen.	*He knows how to enjoy life.*
Er erfreut sich guter Gesundheit (G).	*He enjoys good health.*
Das Essen hat uns gut geschmeckt.	*We enjoyed the meal.*

EVEN

Er ist noch größer als ich.	*He is even taller than I.*
sogar (*or* selbst) meine Freunde	*even my friends*
Wenn er auch klein ist, ...	*Even if he is small, ...*
Auch wenn er das täte, ...	*Even if he did so, ...*
Er kann nicht einmal lesen.	*He cannot even read.*

NOTE: Never use *eben* to translate the adverb **even**.

FEEL

Er fühlte (empfand) Schmerz.	*He felt pain.*
Er fühlte sein Herz klopfen.	*He felt his heart beating.*
Er fühlte, er hatte unrecht gehandelt.	*He felt he had acted wrongly.*
Er fühlte sich krank/glücklich.	*He felt ill/happy.*

FINISH

Die Schule ist um 1 Uhr aus.	*School finishes at one o'clock.*
Er las den Brief zu Ende.	*He finished (reading) the letter.*
Er hat den Brief fertiggeschrieben.	*He finished (writing) the letter.*
Er spielte das Stück zu Ende.	*He finished (playing) the piece.*
Er ist (mit seiner Arbeit) fertig.	*He has finished (his work).*
Er ist mit seinem Buch fertig.	*He has finished his book.*
Er hat sein Frühstück beendet.	*He has finished his breakfast.*

GET

Ich habe keine (Blumen).	*I haven't got any (flowers).*
Er hat den Brief eben bekommen.	*He has just got (=received, had) the letter.*
Ich bin alt geworden.	*I have got (=become) old.*
Wann ist er nach Hause gekommen/ zu Hause angekommen?	*When did he get (=come) home?*
Er ist herübergekommen.	*He has got across.*
Wir erreichten die Insel.	*We got to (=reached) the island.*
Wir kamen in Hamburg (D) an.	*We got to Hamburg.*
Wir stiegen aus (dem Schiff).	*We got out (off the boat).*
Wir stiegen in die Straßenbahn.	*We got on the tram.*
Er stieg ab.	*He got down (dismounted).*
Er ist in Schwierigkeiten geraten.	*He has got into difficulties.*
Er stand auf.	*He got up.*
Ich muß gehen.	*I have got to go.*
Willst du es mir besorgen?	*Will you get (=procure) it for me?*
Willst du mir den Brief holen?	*Will you get (=fetch) me the letter?*
Es ist verlorengegangen.	*It has got lost.*

GO

Er geht zur Schule.	*He goes to school (on foot).*
Er fährt mit dem Auto zur Schule.	*He goes to school by car.*
Er macht einen Spaziergang.⎫ Er geht spazieren. ⎬	*He goes for a stroll/short walk.*
Er ist spazierengefahren.	*He has gone for a ride/drive.*
Er macht einen Ausflug.	*He goes on an excursion.*
Er macht eine Wanderung.	*He goes for a hike/long walk.*

Wann fährt der Zug (ab)? ⎫	
Wann geht der Zug? ⎭	*When does the train go?*
Meine Uhr geht (nicht).	*My watch is (not) going.*
Meine Uhr ist fort.	*My watch has gone.*

JUST

Er hat dir eben geschrieben.	*He has just written to you.*
Er wollte eben sprechen.	*He was just going to speak.*
Er erreichte den Zug gerade noch.	*He just caught the train.*
Ich hatte gerade noch Zeit dazu.	*I just had time for it.*
Das ist einfach unmöglich.	*That is just (=simply) impossible.*
genau zwei Meilen breit	*just two miles wide*
Ich hätte genau so gut laufen können.	*I might just as well have walked.*
Einen Augenblick nur!	*Just one moment!*
Komm mal her!	*Just come here!*
Das ist reiner Unsinn.	*That is just nonsense.*
ein gerechter Krieg	*a just war*

KEEP

Er hielt sein Wort/Versprechen.	*He kept his word/promise.*
Sie hielt das Haus in Ordnung.	*She kept the house in order.*
Sie hielt alles sauber.	*She kept everything clean.*
Er hält sich (D) Pferde.	*He keeps horses.*
Behalten Sie Platz!	*Keep your seat.*
Er hat mich warten lassen.	*He kept me waiting.*
Links/rechts fahren!	*Keep to the left/right.*

KNOW

Ich kenne ihn (von Ansehen).	*I know him (by sight).*
Ich kenne Berlin.	*I know Berlin.*
Ich weiß, daß er nichts weiß.	*I know that he knows nothing.*
Ich weiß, wie er heißt.	*I know what his name is.*
Ich weiß seinen Namen.	*I know his name.*
Ich kenne den Namen.	*I know the name.*
Von Musik verstehe ich nichts.	*I know nothing about music.*
Er versteht zu reden.	*He knows how to talk.*
Ich weiß nichts von der Sache.	*I know nothing about the matter.*
Ich kann Deutsch.	*I know German.*

NOTE: *Kennen* = to be acquainted with personally. (*Kennen* cannot be followed by a clause, or the equivalent of a clause.)

Wissen = to know through having learnt, to know facts.

LATE

Er **kommt** immer **zu** spät	*He is always late.*
Komme ich zu spät?	*Am I late?*
Er hat sich (5 Minuten) verspätet.	*He is (5 minutes) late.*
Es ist spät.	*It is late.*
Der Zug hat (5 Minuten) Verspätung.	*The train is (5 minutes) late.*

LEARN

Er hat das Gedicht (auswendig) gelernt.	*He has learnt the poem (by heart).*
Er hatte die Wahrheit erfahren.	*He had learnt (=found out) the truth.*

LEAVE

Ich ließ den Schirm zu Hause (stehen).	*I left my umbrella at home.*
Ich ließ das Buch auf dem Tisch (liegen).	*I left the book on the table.*
Er ließ sein Gepäck zurück.	*He left his luggage behind.*
Ich verließ das Haus um 8 Uhr.	*I left (=quitted) home at 8.*
Ich bin heute morgen abgereist.	*I left (=departed) this morning.*
Sein Zug fährt um neun Uhr ab.⎫ Sein Zug geht um 9 Uhr (ab). ⎭	*His train leaves at 9.*
Er hinterließ ihr ein großes Vermögen.	*He left (=bequeathed) her a great fortune.*
Überlassen Sie das mir!	*Leave that to me (=I'll see to it).*
Es hörte auf zu regnen.	*It left off raining.*
Er hat eine Woche Urlaub.	*He has a week's leave.*
mit Ihrer Erlaubnis	*by your leave (=permission)*
Er nahm Abschied von uns.	*He took leave of us.*

LIE

Er legte sich auf das Bett.	*He lay down on the bed.*
Er liegt auf dem Bett.	*He is lying on the bed.*
Er lügt.	*He lies, i.e. tells lies.*

LIKE

Wie finden Sie dieses Bild?	*How do you like this picture?*
Das Bild gefällt mir (gut/sehr).	*I like this picture (very much).*
Es gefällt mir in Hamburg.	*I like being in Hamburg.*
Er spielt gern.	*He likes playing.*

Ich mag gern frische Luft.	*I like fresh air.*
Ich mag Äpfel nicht.	*I do not like apples.*
Ich möchte dort bleiben.	*I should like to stay there.*
Macht, was ihr wollt.	*Do what you like.*
Ich mag ⎱ ihn gern. Ich habe ⎰	*I like him.*

LOOK

Er sieht gesund aus.	*He looks well.*
Er sieht nicht so alt aus, wie er ist.	*He does not look his age.*
Er sah ihn genau an.	*He looked at him closely.*
Er blickte (*or* sah) empor.	*He looked up.*
Er sah sich um.	*He looked round (=about him).*
Sie muß nach dem Kranken sehen.	*She must look after the patient.*
Er suchte es überall.	*He looked (=searched) for it everywhere.*
Er schlug das Wort im Wörterbuch nach.	*He looked up the word in the dictionary.*
Achtung!/Vorsicht!	*Look out!*

LOSE

Ich habe das Geld verloren.	*I have lost the money.*
Ich habe den Zug verpaßt.	*I have lost (=missed) the train.*
Ich habe die Gelegenheit verpaßt.	*I have lost the opportunity.*
Ich habe mich verlaufen.	*I have lost my way.*

MARRY

Er hat geheiratet.[1] Er hat sich verheiratet. ⎰	*He has got married.*
Er hat sie geheiratet.[1] Er hat sich mit ihr verheiratet. ⎰	*He has married her.*
Er hat seine Tochter verheiratet.	*He has married (i.e. given away in marriage) his daughter.*
Er ist verheiratet.	*He is married.*
Der Priester hat das junge Paar getraut.	*The priest married the young couple.*
Sie haben sich trauen lassen.	*They got married (in church).*

[1] The more usual verb

MASTER

die Stimme seines Herrn	*his master's voice*
Der Lehrer unterrichtet Deutsch.	*The master teaches German.*
Er ist ein Meister der Sprache.	*He is a master of language.*
Der Hausherr ist nicht da.	*The master of the house is away.*
Ich werde nie der deutschen Sprache (G) mächtig sein.	*I shall never master the German language.*

NOW

Ich wohne jetzt in Hamburg.	*I now live in Hamburg.*
Wir kamen nun in die Stadt.	*We now (=then) came to the town.*
Nun, an demselben/am selben Tag ...	*Now (=well), on that same day ...*
bald dies, bald das	*now this, now that*

NUMBER

die Nummer des Hauses	*the number of the house*
die Zahlen von 1 bis 100	*the numbers from 1 to 100*
Eine große Anzahl Leute/von Leuten war da.	*A great number of people were there.*

ONLY

Es ist erst 8 Uhr.	*It is only 8 o'clock.*
Er kam erst um 8 Uhr an.	*He only arrived at 8. (He did not arrive till/before 8.)*
Es kostet nur 8 Mark.	*It only costs 8 marks.*
Es war nur ein Traum.	*It was only a dream.*
Der einzige Mann, der das weiß, ...	*The only man who knows that ...*
Er allein weiß das.	*Only he knows that.*

NOTE: *Erst* always refers to **time**, *nur* to **manner**, **degree** or **quantity**.

ORDER

Er befahl mir zu kommen.	*He ordered me to come.*
Er bestellte eine Tasse Tee.	*He ordered a cup of tea.*
Er erteilt gern Befehle.	*He likes giving orders.*
Die Bestellung wurde mir ins Haus geliefert.	*The order (i.e. the goods ordered) was delivered to my house.*

Er tat es im Auftrage der Regierung.	*He did it by order (on behalf) of the government.*
Sie hielt alles in Ordnung.	*She kept everything in order.*
Er tat es, um mich zu ärgern.	*He did it in order to annoy me.*

PASS

Er ging an der Kirche vorbei.	*He passed the church.*
Er überholte mich.	*He passed (=overtook) me.*
Die Zeit vergeht schnell.	*Time passes quickly.*
Er hat die Prüfung bestanden.	*He has passed the examination.*
Reichen Sie mir das Salz!	*Pass me the salt.*
Wie verbringen Sie die Zeit?	*How do you pass the time?*
Er fällte ein Urteil über den Angeklagten.	*He passed sentence on the defendant.*

PUT

Stell die Lampe auf den Tisch!	*Put the lamp on the table.*
Leg das Buch auf den Tisch!	*Put the book on the table.*
Setz das Kind auf den Stuhl!	*Put the child on the chair.*
Steck das Geld in deine Tasche!	*Put the money in your pocket.*
Tue Wasser in die Flasche!	*Put some water in the bottle.*
Er griff in die Tasche.	*He put his hand in his pocket.*
Zieh den Mantel an!	*Put your coat on.*
Setz den Hut auf!	*Put your hat on.*
Er begibt sich in Gefahr.	*He puts himself in danger.*

NOTE: *Stellen* = put in an upright position; *legen* = put in a lying position; *setzen* = put in a sitting position; *stecken* = poke or stuff into; *tun* = put in a general and vague sense; *anziehen* = put on any article of clothing except hats.

REFUSE

Er wollte nicht kommen. ⎫ Er weigerte sich zu kommen. ⎭	*He refused to come.*
Er verweigerte mir die Stelle.	*He refused me the job.*

REMEMBER

Ich werde den Namen behalten.	*I shall remember the name.*
Weißt du noch, wie . . .?	*Do you remember how . . .?*
Wenn ich mich recht erinnere, . . .	*If I remember rightly . . .*
Ich kann mich nicht (mehr) daran erinnern.	*I cannot remember it.*
Vergessen Sie nicht zu kommen!	*Remember to come.*
Grüßen Sie Ihre Frau von mir!	*Remember me to your wife.*

REST

Er hat sich ausgeruht.	*He has had a rest.*
Der Rest des Tages verging sehr schnell.	*The rest of the day went quickly.*
Ich bedarf der Ruhe (G).	*I need rest.*
Er blieb, die übrigen gingen fort.	*He stayed, the rest went away.*
Das übrige kannst du behalten.	*You can keep the rest.*

SIGHT

bei diesem Anblick	*at this sight/the sight of this*
Es ist in/außer Sicht.	*It is in/out of sight.*
Er hat uns erblickt.	*He caught sight of us.*

SIT

Er setzte sich auf den Stuhl.	*He sat down on the chair.*
Er saß auf dem Stuhl.	*He was sitting on the chair.*

SO

Wer hat es Ihnen gesagt?	*Who told you so (=this)?*
Deshalb bin ich fortgelaufen.	*And so I ran away.*
Er ist so müde.	*He is so tired.*
Bist du müde? – Ich auch.	*Are you tired? – So am I.*

SPEND

Er gibt viel Geld aus.	*He spends a lot of money.*
Er verbrachte den Abend bei uns.	*He spent the evening with us.*
Er bringt seine Zeit mit Lesen zu.	*He spends his time reading.*
Er vertreibt sich die Zeit mit Lesen.	

NOTE: *Spenden* = to dispense, bestow.

START

Wir reisten früh ab.	*We started early.*
Wir brachen früh auf.	
Wann fährt der Zug ab?	*When does the train start?*
Wann geht der Zug (ab)?	
Wann fahren wir ab?	*When do we start (by car, etc.)?*

Der Zug setzte sich langsam in Bewegung.	*The train slowly started moving.*
Er setzte das Auto in Gang.	*He started (up) the car.*
Bei jedem Geräusch fährt er zusammen.	*He starts at every noise.*

STILL

Halte still!	*Keep still.*
Es ist noch Zeit.	*There is still time.*
Sie ist immer noch (*or* noch immer) nicht da.	*She is still not here.*
Immerhin könnte es wahr sein.	*Still, it might be true.*

STOP

Der Regen hat aufgehört.	*The rain has stopped (=ceased).*
Hör auf zu weinen!	*Stop crying.*
Der Zug hat gehalten.	*The train has stopped (=made a halt).*
Meine Uhr ist stehengeblieben.	*My watch has stopped (= ceased working).*
Wir müssen jetzt Schluß machen.	*We must stop (e.g. playing) now.*
Wir dürfen nicht auf halbem Wege stehenbleiben.	*We must not stop (=cease going) half-way.*
Wir dürfen uns nicht aufhalten.	*We must not stop (=stay).*
Er hielt plötzlich inne.	*He suddenly stopped (e.g. talking).*
Er hat den Wagen angehalten.	*He stopped the car.*
Was kann mich daran hindern, das zu tun?	*What's to stop (=prevent) me doing that?*
Er kann das Rauchen nicht (unter-) lassen.	*He cannot stop (=give up) smoking.*

TAKE

Bringen Sie ihm das Buch!	*Take the book to him.*
Er brachte mich nach Hause.	*He took me home.*
Trag das Paket auf die Post!	*Take the parcel to the post office.*
Nimm das Buch aus dem Schrank!	*Take the book out of the cupboard.*
Nimm mich mit ins Kino!	*Take me to the cinema.*
Führe mich den nächsten Weg!	*Take me the nearest way.*
Er holte es aus der Tasche.	*He took it out of his pocket.*

Er nahm den Zug, das Schiff.	*He took the train, the*
Er nahm die Medizin ein.	*He took the medicine.*
Er folgte meinem Rat.	*He took my advice.*
Hält er mich für einen Narren?	*Does he take me for a fo*
Es dauerte lange, bis wir dahin kamen.	*It took us a long time there.*
Man braucht nur wenig Zeit, um so einen Roman zu lesen.	*It does not take long to read a novel.*
Es gehört Zeit dazu.	*It takes time.*
Dieser Platz ist besetzt.	*This seat is taken.*
Wann machst du dein Examen?	*When do you take your exam nation?*
Er zog den Mantel aus.	*He took off his coat.*
Er nahm (*or* zog) den Hut ab.	*He took off his hat.*
Er legte Mantel und Hut ab.	*He took off his coat and hat.*

NOTE: *Bringen* = to carry **from** as well as **to** the speaker.

THAT

Das sagte er nicht.	*He did not say that.*
Er sagte, daß er kommen würde.	*He said that he would come.*
Das Hotel dort/dieses H. ist sehr teuer.	*That hotel is very dear.*
Der beste Rat, den ich geben kann, ...	*The best advice that I can give ...*
Das einzige, was nötig ist, ...	*The only thing that is necessary ...*

THEN

Damals wohnte ich in B.	*Then (=at that time* (past)) *I lived in B.*
gerade dann	*just then (=at that moment)*
Dann ist es zu heiß.	*It is too hot then (=at that time* (present)).
Dann wird es zu heiß sein.	*It will be too hot then (=at that time* (future)).
Dann zog ich nach F. um.	*Then (=subsequently) I moved to F.*
selbst dann	*even then (=in that case)*
So ist es ihm denn gelungen?	*So he succeeded then (=after all)?*
Wo ist er denn?	*Where is he then?*
Ich weiß noch nicht, ob ich da Zeit haben werde.	*I don't yet know whether I shall have time then.*
Sie kommen also?	*Then you'll come?*

139

THING

Wir haben andere Dinge zu tun.	*We have other things to do.*
Ihr dummen Dinger!	*You stupid little things!*
Sind meine Sachen schon da?	*Have my things come?*
Das ist die Hauptsache.	*That is the chief thing.*
Das ist das einzige, was er ...	*That is the only thing (that) he ...*
So etwas gibt's nicht mehr.	*That sort of thing no longer exists.*

THINK

Er hat nicht daran gedacht.	*He has not thought of it.*
Was halten/denken Sie von ihm?	*What do you think of him?*
Sie hält viel auf Kleider.	*She thinks a lot of clothes.*
Ich halte ihn für einen Narren.	*I think him a fool.*
Er ist ein netter Kerl. – Finden Sie?	*He is a nice chap. – Do you think so?*

TIME

Ich habe keine Zeit zum Lesen.	*I have no time for reading.*
von Zeit zu Zeit (*or* ab und zu)	*from time to time*
mit der Zeit	*in time (=in course of time)*
zur rechten Zeit (*or* rechtzeitig)	*in time (=punctually)*
zur selben (*or* zu gleicher) Zeit zugleich	*at the same time*
zur Zeit (*or* einstweilen)	*for the time being*
zur Zeit Friedrichs des Großen	*at the time of Frederick the Great*
auf einige Zeit	*for some time (=future)*
eine Zeitlang	*for some time (=past)*
lange	*for a long time*
in kurzer Zeit (*or* bald)	*in a short time*
um diese Zeit (*or* zu dieser Zeit)	*at this/that time*
vor langer Zeit	*a long time ago*
nach einer Weile	*after a time*
schon (*or* bereits)	*by this/that time*
einmal, zweimal, dreimal	*once, twice, three times*
einigemal (*or* einige Male)	*a few times*
zuweilen (*or* manchmal)	*sometimes*
diesmal (*or* dieses Mal)	*this time*
das erstemal (*or* das erste Mal)	*the first time*
das nächste (letzte) Mal	*the next (last) time*

zum erstenmal/ersten Mal.	*(for) the first time*
zum letztenmal/letzten Mal	*(for) the last time*
Als ich ihn zum letztenmal sah, ...	*The last time I saw him ...*
Jedesmal, wenn er kommt, ...	*Every time (that) he comes ...*
damals	*at that time (=then)*
Um wieviel Uhr kommt er?	*At what time is he coming?*
Wie spät ist es?	*What is the time?*

VERY

Das ist sehr schön.	*That is very fine.*
genau das Gegenteil	*the very opposite*
Schon der Gedanke/Der bloße Gedanke macht mich böse.	*The very thought makes me angry.*

WAKE

Er hat ihn geweckt.	*He woke him.*
Er ist spät erwacht/aufgewacht.	*He woke (intr.) late.*

WORK

Er ist bei der Arbeit.	*He is (hard) at work.*
Goethes gesammelte Werke	*Goethe's collected works*
Er arbeitet fleißig.	*He works hard.*
Er ist arbeitslos.	*He is out of work.*
Er tut Wunder.	*He works wonders.*
Er bahnte sich seinen Weg durch die Menge.	*He worked his way through the crowd.*
Er arbeitete sich zu einem General empor (*or* herauf).	*He worked his way up to the rank of general.*

WOULD

Er wollte ihm nicht gehorchen.	*He would not (=refused to) obey him.*
Er würde dann besser arbeiten.	*He would work better in that case.*

124 Translation of some Difficult German Words

(a) DA

Da ich ihn nicht kenne, ...	**As** (*since*) *I don't know him ...*
Da bin ich.	**Here** *I am.*

hier und da	*here and* **there**
Da wußte ich, was er meinte.	**And then** *I knew what he meant.*
zu der Zeit, da . . .	*at the time* **when**

(b) DENN

Er ißt nichts, denn er ist krank.	*He eats nothing,* **for** *he is ill.*
Wo ist er denn?	**Why,** *where is he? Where is he* **then?**
Warum denn?	*Why?*
Er ist bedeutender als Gelehrter denn als Künstler.	*He is more important as a scholar* **than** *as an artist.*

(c) DOCH

Er ist doch nicht krank.	**Surely** *he isn't ill?*
Du hast es nicht gemacht? Doch!	*You didn't do it?* **Yes,** *I did.*
Hilf mir doch!	**Do** *help me.*
Nicht doch!	**Certainly** *not;* **don't.**
Du hast es doch gemacht?	*You did it* **after all?**
Es ist mir doch zu groß.	*It is too big for me* **anyhow.**
Es ist doch wahr.	*It* **is** *true.*

(d) IRGEND

irgendein Buch ⎱ irgendwelches Buch⎰	*some book or other; any book*
Irgendeiner hat es gesagt. ⎱ Irgend jemand hat es gesagt.⎰	*Somebody or other said so.*
irgendwas ⎱ irgend etwas⎰	*something or other; anything*
irgendwo	*somewhere; anywhere*
irgendwie	*somehow or other*
irgendwann	*sometime or other*

(e) JA

Es ist ja nicht weit.	**Why,** *it's not far.*
Komm ja nicht zu spät!	**See** *that you aren't late.*
Er ist ja mein Sohn.	*He is my son,* **you see.**
Ich sagte es ja.	*I told you so. (I said so,* **you know**).
Er wird ja wissen.	*He'll* **certainly** *know.*

(f) NOCH

Ist er noch da?	*Is he **still** there?*
Er ist noch nicht gekommen.	*He has not **yet** come.*
Das ist noch besser.	*That is **even** better.*
Er verlangte noch ein Glas Bier.	*He asked for **another** glass of beer.*

(g) SCHON

Sind Sie schon da gewesen?	*Have you been there **already**?*
Schon der Gedanke macht mich böse.	*The **very** thought makes me angry.*
Er hat schon genug.	*He has enough **as it is**.*
Er wird schon kommen.	*He'll come **all right**.*
Das ist schon wahr, aber . . .	*That is **quite** true, but . . .*

(h) WIE

Er ist so alt wie ich.	*He is as old **as** I.*
Wie er sagte, (es) war niemand da.	***As** he said, nobody was there.*
Wie er ins Zimmer trat, . . .	***When** he came into the room . . .*
Wie ist Ihr Name?/Wie heißen Sie?	***What** is your name?*
Wie sieht er aus.	***What** does he look **like**?*
Ich denke wie du.	*I think **like** you.*
Er stand wie versteinert da.	*He stood there **as if** petrified.*
Wie geht es Ihnen?	***How** are you?*
Wie ist das schön!	***How** beautiful it is!*
Wie heißt das?	***What** is that called?*
Sie trug ein Kleid, wie es ihre Großmutter getragen hatte.	*She wore a dress **such as (like that)** her grandmother had worn.*
Ich sah/hörte, wie er ins Zimmer kam.	*I saw/heard him coming into the room.*

125 Punctuation

(a) The **comma** (*das Komma*) is used in German:

i. To separate a subordinate clause from a main clause:

> Wenn er müde ist, geht er zu Bett.
> Georg, der müde war, ging zu Bett.

ii. To separate subordinate clauses which are not connected by *und* or *oder*:

> Er sagte, daß er es tun würde, wenn er Zeit hätte.

iii. To separate main clauses connected by *und* or *oder* when there is a change or necessary repetition of the subject or before an intercalated subordinate clause:

> **Er** las ein Buch, und **ich** schrieb Briefe.
> Er setzte sich, und dann las **er** den Brief.
> Ich kam herein, und da es dunkel war, schaltete ich das Liche an.

iv. To separate the infinitive phrase with *zu* from the rest of the sentence if the phrase is in any way qualified:

> Es ist leicht, das zu sagen.
> Er sagte es mir, um mich zu trösten.
> Anstatt zu laufen, blieb er stehen.

BUT Er versuchte zu arbeiten.

(b) Inverted commas (*die Anführungszeichen*) are used as in English but are written and printed differently:

> „Ich kann nicht länger warten", sagte er.

(c) The colon (*der Doppelpunkt*) is used in German to introduce direct speech:

> Er sagte zu mir: „Ich kann nicht länger warten."

(d) The exclamation mark (*das Ausrufezeichen*) is required after an imperative and after exclamations, and is still quite common after the person addressed at the beginning of a letter:

> Komm! Guten Tag! Auf Wiedersehen! Lieber Erich! Sehr geehrter Herr! (*Dear Sir*).

(e) The full stop (*der Punkt*), semicolon (*das Semikolon*) and question mark (*das Fragezeichen*) are used as in English.

(f) The hyphen (*der Bindestrich*) is chiefly used when it is necessary, as at the end of a line, to divide a word. The following rules governing the division of words in German should be observed:

i. In uncompounded words the syllable after the hyphen should, if possible, begin with a consonant. Note however, that *ch*, *sch*, *ß*, *st*, *ph* and *th* are never separated:

lie-gen	nä-hen	Bru-der	Lö-cher
Fi-scher	Mei-ster	pro-phezei-en	grö-ßer

ii. Of several consonants (except those in (i) above) the last follows the hyphen. Note that *ck* becomes *k-k*:

sin-gen　　　Som-mer　　　kämp-fen　　　wek-ken

iii. In compound words the division comes at the end of each constituent element, except with suffixes beginning with a vowel (e.g. *-in*):

be-ob-achten　　er-obern　　　aus-ein-ander　　Haus-tür
Ge-burts-tags-ge-schenk　　　Lehre-rin　　　da-rauf

NOTE: The hyphen is also used in German in words group like: *die Vor- und Nachteile* (= *die Vorteile und Nachteile*).

(g) The character ß is used in printing instead of *ss*:

i. Medially (or with apostrophe after it), when preceded by a long vowel or by a diphthong:

Māße　　Füße　　Größe　　fleißig　　Gott grüß' dich!
BUT Māsse　　Flüsse　　essen　　　　Lass' ihn kommen!

ii. At the end of a word or syllable, whatever the length of the vowel preceding:

Māß　　däß　　läß　　mußte　　mißlingen

iii. At the end of a word when immediately followed by *-t*:

laßt　　mußt　　gemußt

iv. In writing it is not necessary to use the character ß. If, however, it is used the rules given above should be observed.

126 The Alphabet

(a) Roman Type (*Antiqua*)

a b c d e f g h i j k l m n o p q r s ß t u v w x y z
A B C D E F G H I J K L M N O P Q R S T U V W X Y Z

(b) Gothic Type[1] (*Fraktur*)

a b c d e f g h i j k l m n o p q r s ß t u v w x y z

A B C D E F G H I J K L M N O P Q R S T U V
W X Y Z

[1] Only occasionally used nowadays, e.g. in headlines in some newspapers. Cf. p. 320.

(c) German Script[1]

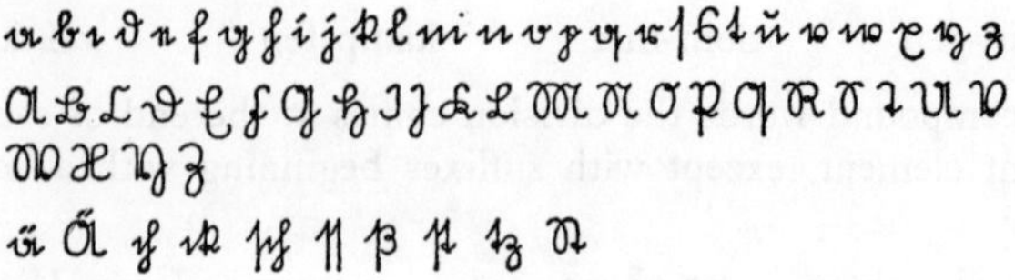

(d) Examples:

German Type	German Script	Roman Type
Aussicht	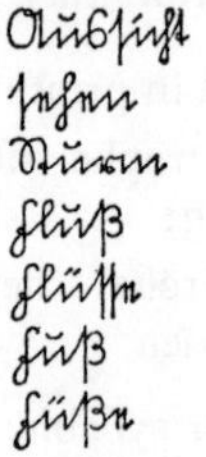 *(script)*	Aussicht
sehen	*(script)*	sehen
Sturm	*(script)*	Sturm
Fluß	*(script)*	Fluß
Flüsse	*(script)*	Flüsse
Fuß	*(script)*	Fuß
Füße	*(script)*	Füße

NOTE: The equivalent of italics in English is *Sperrdruck* (spaced type) in German, e.g.

D a s weiß ich nicht.   *That* I don't know.

127 List of Strong and Irregular Verbs

Infinitive	3rd Pers. Sing. Pres.	3rd Pers. Sing. Impf.	Past Part.	Meaning
backen	bäckt[2]	buk[2]	gebacken	*bake*
befehlen	befiehlt	befahl[3]	befohlen	*order, command*
beginnen	beginnt	begann	begonnen	*begin*
beißen	beißt	biß	gebissen	*bite*
*bersten	birst	barst	geborsten	*burst (intr.)*
betrügen	betrügt	betrog	betrogen	*deceive, cheat*
bewegen	bewegt	bewog	bewogen	*induce*
(*)biegen	biegt	bog	gebogen	*bend, turn*
bieten	bietet	bot	geboten	*offer, bid*
binden	bindet	band	gebunden	*tie*
bitten	bittet	bat	gebeten	*ask, request*
blasen	bläst	blies	geblasen	*blow, sound*
*bleiben	bleibt	blieb	geblieben	*remain, stay*

*(handwritten margin note: "to be →" pointing to *bersten)*

[1] No longer used except by very elderly people
[2] Also: *backt, backte.* (The form *buk* is now rare.)
[3] See *111(e)*

146

Verbrennen – burn to cinders
anbrennen – dinner burns.

Infinitive	3rd Pers. Sing. Pres.	3rd Pers. Sing. Impf.	Past Part.	Meaning
braten	brät	briet	gebraten	*roast*
(*)brechen	bricht	brach	gebrochen	*break*
ab brennen	brennt	brannte[1]	gebrannt	*burn*
bringen	bringt	brachte[1]	gebracht	*bring, take*
denken	denkt	dachte[1]	gedacht	*think*
(*)dringen	dringt	drang	gedrungen	*press (intr.); urge*
dürfen[2]	darf	durfte	gedurft	*be allowed to*
empfehlen	empfiehlt	empfahl[1]	empfohlen	*recommend*
*erlöschen[3]	erlischt	erlosch	erloschen	*be extinguished*
*erschrecken[4]	erschrickt	erschrak	erschrocken	*be frightened*
erwägen	erwägt	erwog	erwogen	*think over, weigh*
essen	ißt	aß	gegessen	*eat*
(*)fahren	fährt	fuhr	gefahren	*go (not on foot); drive*
*fallen	fällt	fiel	gefallen	*fall*
fangen	fängt	fing	gefangen	*catch*
fechten	ficht[5]	focht	gefochten	*fight, fence*
finden	findet	fand	gefunden	*find*
flechten	flicht[6]	flocht	geflochten	*wreathe*
(*)fliegen	fliegt	flog	geflogen	*fly*
(*)fliehen	flieht	floh	geflohen	*flee*
*fließen	fließt	floß	geflossen	*flow*
fressen	frißt	fraß	gefressen	*eat (of animals)*
(*)frieren	friert	fror	gefroren	*freeze, be cold*
gebären	gebiert	gebar	geboren	*give birth, bear*
geben	gibt	gab	gegeben	*give*
*gedeihen	gedeiht	gedieh	gediehen	*prosper, flourish*
*gehen	geht	ging	gegangen	*go, walk*
*gelingen[7]	gelingt	gelang	gelungen	*succeed*
gelten	gilt	galt	gegolten	*be valid, worth*
*genesen	genest	genas	genesen	*grow well, recover*
genießen	genießt	genoß	genossen	*enjoy*
*geschehen	geschieht	geschah	geschehen	*happen*
gewinnen	gewinnt	gewann	gewonnen	*win, gain*
gießen	gießt	goß	gegossen	*pour*
gleichen	gleicht	glich	geglichen	*resemble*
*gleiten	gleitet	glitt	geglitten	*glide, slide*
graben	gräbt	grub	gegraben	*dig*
greifen	greift	griff	gegriffen	*grasp, seize, grab*

[1] See *111(e)*
[2] See *109(a)*
[3] Weak = extinguish
[4] Weak = frighten
[5] 2nd Person Singular *du fichtst*
[6] 2nd Person Singular *du flichtst*
[7] See *105(b)*

Infinitive	3rd Pers. Sing. Pres.	3rd Pers. Sing. Impf.	Past Part.	Meaning
haben[1]	hat	hatte	gehabt	*have*
halten	hält	hielt	gehalten	*hold, stop (intr.)*
hängen[2]	hängt	hing	gehangen	*hang (intr.)*
hauen	haut	hieb[3]	gehauen	*hew, cut; strike*
heben	hebt	hob	gehoben	*raise, lift*
heißen	heißt	hieß	geheißen	*be called; bid*
helfen	hilft	half[4]	geholfen	*help*
kennen	kennt	kannte[4]	gekannt	*be acquainted with*
klingen	klingt	klang	geklungen	*sound*
*kommen	kommt	kam ·	gekommen	*come*
können[5]	kann	konnte	gekonnt	*can, be able to*
*kriechen	kriecht	kroch	gekrochen	*crawl*
laden	lädt	lud	geladen	*load; invite*
lassen	läßt	ließ	gelassen	*let, leave (behind)*
*laufen	läuft	lief	gelaufen	*run*
leiden	leidet	litt	gelitten	*suffer, bear*
leihen	leiht	lieh	geliehen	*lend*
lesen	liest	las	gelesen	*read*
liegen	liegt	lag ·	gelegen	*lie*
lügen	lügt	log ·	gelogen	*tell lies*
messen	mißt	maß	gemessen	*measure*
mögen[5]	mag	mochte	gemocht	*may; like*
müssen[5]	muß	mußte	gemußt	*must, have to*
nehmen	nimmt	nahm	genommen	*take*
nennen	nennt	nannte[4]	genannt	*name, call*
pfeifen	pfeift	pfiff	gepfiffen	*whistle; pipe*
preisen	preist	pries	gepriesen	*praise*
*quellen	quillt	quoll	gequollen	*spring, gush up*
raten	rät	riet	geraten	*advise; guess*
reiben	reibt	rieb	gerieben	*rub*
(*)reißen	reißt	riß	gerissen	*tear*
(*)reiten	reitet	ritt	geritten	*ride (on animal)*
*rennen	rennt	rannte[4]	gerannt	*run*
riechen	riecht	roch	gerochen	*smell*
ringen	ringt	rang	gerungen	*wrestle, struggle*
*rinnen	rinnt	rann	geronnen	*flow, trickle*
rufen	ruft	rief	gerufen	*call*
saufen	säuft	soff	gesoffen	*drink (of animals)*
saugen	saugt	sog	gesogen	*suck*
schaffen[6]	schafft	schuf	geschaffen	*create*
(*)scheiden	scheidet	schied	geschieden	*separate, part*

[1] See *88*
[2] Or, rarely, *hangen*. Weak = hang (tr.)
[3] Now usually *haute* = strike
[4] See *111(e)*
[5] See *109(a)*
[6] Weak = do, achieve

Infinitive	3rd Pers. Sing. Pres.	3rd Pers. Sing. Impf.	Past Part.	Meaning
scheinen	scheint	schien	geschienen	seem; shine
schelten	schilt	schalt[1]	gescholten	scold, blame
schieben	schiebt	schob	geschoben	shove, push
(*)schießen	schießt	schoß	geschossen	shoot
schinden	schindet	schund	geschunden	flay, rub off skin
schlafen	schläft	schlief	geschlafen	sleep
schlagen	schlägt	schlug	geschlagen	beat, strike
*schleichen	schleicht	schlich	geschlichen	creep
schließen	schließt	schloß	geschlossen	shut, conclude
schlingen	schlingt	schlang	geschlungen	coil; devour
schmeißen	schmeißt	schmiß	geschmissen	fling, chuck
(*)schmelzen	schmilzt[2]	schmolz	geschmolzen	melt
schneiden	schneidet	schnitt	geschnitten	cut
schreiben	schreibt	schrieb	geschrieben	write
schreien	schreit	schrie	geschrie(e)n	shout, shriek
*schreiten	schreitet	schritt	geschritten	stride, proceed
schweigen	schweigt	schwieg	geschwiegen	be(come) silent
*schwellen[3]	schwillt	schwoll	geschwollen	swell (intr.)
(*)schwimmen	schwimmt	schwamm[1]	geschwommen[4]	swim
schwingen	schwingt	schwang	geschwungen	swing
schwören	schwört	schwor[5]	geschworen	swear (on oath)
sehen	sieht	sah	gesehen	see
*sein[6]	ist	war	gewesen	be
senden	sendet	sandte[1, 7]	gesandt[7]	send
singen	singt	sang	gesungen	sing
*sinken	sinkt	sank	gesunken	sink (intr.)
sinnen	sinnt	sann	gesonnen	think, meditate
sitzen	sitzt	saß	gesessen	be sitting, sit
sollen[8]	soll	sollte	gesollt	be obliged to
speien	speit	spie	gespie(e)n	spit, spew out
spinnen	spinnt	spann[1]	gesponnen	spin, spin round
sprechen	spricht	sprach	gesprochen	speak
*sprießen	sprießt	sproß	gesprossen	sprout
*springen	springt	sprang	gesprungen	jump, spring
stechen	sticht	stach	gestochen	prick, sting; trump
stehen	steht	stand	gestanden	stand
stehlen	stiehlt	stahl	gestohlen	steal

[1] See *111(e)*   [2] Also *schmelzt* when transitive
[3] Weak = swell (tr.)
[4] Er **hat** über eine Stunde geschwommen (=directionless activity)
    Er **ist** über den Fluß geschwommen (=movement towards a place)
[5] Also: *schwur*   [6] See *88*   [7] Also: *sendete, gesendet*   [8] See *109(a)*

Infinitive	3rd Pers. Sing. Pres.	3rd Pers. Sing. Impf.	Past Part.	Meaning
*steigen	steigt	stieg	gestiegen	*mount, rise, increase*
*sterben	stirbt	starb[1]	gestorben	*die*
(*)stoßen	stößt	stieß	gestoßen	*push; stumble on*
(*)streichen	streicht	strich	gestrichen	*stroke; wander*
streiten	streitet	stritt	gestritten	*argue*
tragen	trägt	trug	getragen	*carry, bear; wear*
treffen	trifft	traf	getroffen	*meet; hit, strike*
(*)treiben	treibt	trieb	getrieben	*drive, do; drift*
(*)treten	tritt	trat	getreten	*step, go; kick*
trinken	trinkt	trank	getrunken	*drink*
tun	tut	tat	getan	*do*
verbergen	verbirgt	verbarg	verborgen	*hide, conceal*
(*)verderben	verdirbt	verdarb[1]	verdorben	*spoil, ruin*
verdrießen	verdrießt	verdroß	verdrossen	*vex*
vergessen	vergißt	vergaß	vergessen	*forget*
verlieren	verliert	verlor	verloren	*lose*
vermeiden	vermeidet	vermied	vermieden	*avoid*
*verschwin-den	verschwin-det	verschwand	verschwun-den	*disappear*
verzeihen	verzeiht	verzieh	verziehen	*pardon*
*wachsen	wächst	wuchs	gewachsen	*grow (intr.)*
waschen	wäscht	wusch	gewaschen	*wash (tr.)*
weben[2]	webt	wob	gewoben	*weave*
*weichen[3]	weicht	wich	gewichen	*give way to, yield*
weisen	weist	wies	gewiesen	*point, show*
wenden	wendet	wandte[1,4]	gewandt[4]	*turn (tr.)*
werben	wirbt	warb[1]	geworben	*woo, enlist, recruit*
*werden[5]	wird	wurde	geworden	*become*
werfen	wirft	warf[1]	geworfen	*throw*
wiegen[6]	wiegt	wog	gewogen	*weigh (intr.)*
winden	windet	wand	gewunden	*wind, twist*
wissen	weiß[7]	wußte	gewußt	*know (as a fact)*
wollen[8]	will	wollte	gewollt	*want to*
(*)ziehen	zieht	zog	gezogen	*draw, pull; grow (tr.); go, move*
zwingen	zwingt	zwang	gezwungen	*compel, force*

[1] See *111(e)*
[2] Usually weak except in non-literal sense
[3] Weak=soften
[4] Also: *wendete, gewendet* (= change direction of)
[5] See *88*
[6] Weak=rock
[7] Present tense irregular: *weiß weißt, weiß, wissen, wißt, wissen*
[8] See *109(a)*

Sentences and Phrases on Grammatical Points

(The numbers in brackets at the head of each exercise refer to the paragraphs of the Grammar Section.

Words enclosed in round brackets either (1) give in inverted commas the German equivalent for the preceding English word or (2) give an alternative form of wording for literal translation into German. Figures and letters enclosed in round brackets refer to the various paragraphs of the Grammar. Words enclosed in square brackets are to be omitted for purposes of translation into German.)

1 Word Order (*1–4*)

REWRITE IN GERMAN WORD ORDER:

1. He smokes a pipe. 2. Every day he smokes a pipe. 3. When is he at home? 4. Has he smoked his pipe? 5. Smoke your pipe. 6. He reads a book and smokes a pipe. 7. He reads a book or he writes letters. 8. He reads a book and smokes a pipe but I sit and write. 9. He smoked his pipe and then went to bed. 10. He sat by the (*87 (b)ii*) fire, for it was cold. 11. When it is cold he sits by the fire. 12. He sits by the fire when it is cold. 13. After he had read the book he went to bed. 14. Since it was late he went to bed. 15. He went to bed as it was late. 16. I write letters or read a book when I come home. 17. When she returned the money had gone (*123*). 18. Although he is young he is lazy. 19. Before he went he said goodbye. 20. I do not know (*123*) if it is true.

2 Word Order (*5*)

A. REWRITE IN GERMAN WORD ORDER:

1. He comes home at six o'clock. 2. He always comes home at six o'clock. 3. He comes home at six o'clock every day. 4. He goes to school every day. 5. He goes to school at eight o'clock every day. 6.

We go to school by train. 7. We go to school every day by train. 8.
We play outside in the garden. 9. He gave his son a car. 10. He gave
the car to his son. 11. He gave him a car. 12. He gave it to his son.
13. He gave him it. 14. He gave it to him. 15. He brought me the
letter. 16. He brought the letter to his wife. 17. He brought her it (55
and 56(b)). 18. He did not bring it to her. 19. That is not true. 20. I
have not read the book. 21. No, that is not true. 22. He has not
washed himself today. 23. He never washes himself. 24. He goes out
every morning. 25. Oh! I am so tired.

B. TRANSLATE EXERCISE 2.

C. TRANSLATE EXERCISE 1, SENTENCES 1–5.

3 Conjunctions (6–8)

A. TRANSLATING ONLY THE CONJUNCTIONS, REWRITE IN
GERMAN WORD ORDER:

1. I know (123) that this is true. 2. It is true for I read it in (87(a)) the
newspaper. 3. Before I go to bed I always read the newspaper. 4. But
it is not true. 5. When I was there last week she had no maid. 6.
When she is here I go out every evening. 7. When he spoke people
(73) always used to laugh. 8. If you (73) smoke too much you get (123)
ill. 9. Although he is rich he is not happy. 10. As you say, I haven't
worked. 11. As you haven't worked you don't deserve a prize (you
deserve no prize). 12. You have played but you haven't worked. 13.
He waited till I came. 14. As he said that he got (123) up. 15. While I
was waiting a car went (123: 'go') past. 16. After he had read the newspaper he gave it to me. 17. Since my brother came in the (87(b)ii)
afternoon we could not work. 18. Since my brother came I haven't
worked. 19. You must stay here as long as you can. 20. Unless you
can swim you must remain here. 21. He is so small that one does not
notice him. 22. Because he is so small one does not notice him. 23.
The master speaks slowly so that we can understand him. 24. The
train arrived late so that I had to hurry. 25. As soon as I know (it), I'll
tell you (it). 26. I don't know when the train goes (123). 27. I don't
know if he is at home now. 28. I don't know where he works now.
29. I don't know how old he is. 30. I don't know who was there. 31.
It's two years since I've seen him. 32. Scarcely had he gone when his

friend arrived. 33. There are moments when it is difficult to be silent.
34. However much he tries he makes no progress. 35. I don't know how
long he is staying here.

B. TRANSLATE EXERCISE 1, SENTENCES 6–20.

C. TRANSLATE EXERCISE 3.

4 Conjunctions (9–10)

A. TRANSLATING ONLY THE CONJUNCTIONS, REWRITE IN
GERMAN WORD ORDER:

1. He does not smoke, nor does he drink. 2. Both he and I were there.
3. So it makes no difference. 4. Besides, he is very rich. 5. Neither he
nor I knew (123) that. 6. It seems impossible, yet it is true. 7. The
longer he works the stupider he gets (123). 8. Now he looked (123) to
the right (43(a)i), now to the left (43(a)i). 9. You must go to bed or
else you will be (94(d)) tired tomorrow. 10. Either it is too cold or it is
too hot. 11. He is neither clever nor diligent. 12. And it is very far
too. 13. It was raining but nevertheless he came. 14. Then I knew that
it was true. 15. It was raining and so I stayed at home.

B. TRANSLATE EXERCISE 4.

5 The Articles (11–13)

TRANSLATE INTO GERMAN:

1. Life is very dull here. 2. Young George; little Mary; modern
England. 3. 2 marks a kilo; 4 marks a bottle; 2.50 marks a yard; 6 marks
each. 4. The Thames flows into the North Sea. 5. The Main (m.) is a
tributary of the Rhine. 6. The Zugspitze is a mountain in Germany.
7. He lives in (87(a)) Castle Street. 8. Berne is the capital of (86(a)ix)
Switzerland. 9. Do you know (123) Alsace? 10. We visited France in
autumn and Switzerland in winter. 11. In the morning we work. 12.
We did not work on Wednesday. 13. After breakfast I read the newspaper. 14. In June the days are very long. 15. He shook his head. 16.
He raised his hand. 17. I took (123) off my coat. 18. What have you
in your hand? 19. I saved his life. 20. He stood there with his hands
in his pockets. 21. I put (123) my hand in my pocket, for I wanted to

give the man [some] money. 22. Although I read the newspaper after breakfast I did not see that. 23. He took off his jacket because it was hot. 24. After he had washed his hands he wrote the letter. 25. Since it is not an interesting book I shall not read it.

6 The Articles (*14*)

TRANSLATE INTO GERMAN:

1. He is a teacher. 2. He wants to become a teacher. 3. He is a famous doctor. 4. He is an Englishman. 5. She is an Englishwoman. 6. He remained a porter all (*83(c)*) his life. 7. She is a teacher. ·8. Have you any milk? 9. I haven't any butter. 10. He has some bread. 11. I have some paper but no ink. 12. Do you feel inclined to go there (*43(a)i*)? 13. Whenever she saw a mouse she was afraid. 14. Although he spoke in a loud voice we did not understand him. 15. Even if I am thirsty I shall not drink. 16. In the morning I am always in a great hurry, for I have to (*109(b)iv*) catch (*123*) a train. 17. I cannot stay now as I have some visitors. 18. It is a pity that you cannot come. 19. Although he has a temperature he has a good appetite. 20. He wanted to have more because he was hungry.

7 Nouns (*18*)

TRANSLATE INTO GERMAN:

1. A man has two arms, a bird has two wings. 2. I like (*123*) apples, but I don't like cheese. 3. We have one tree in the garden; some gardens have several trees. 4. I don't drink tea with sugar. 5. The schoolboys found the pencils on (*87(a)*) the schoolmaster's table. 6. That is no consolation. 7. The tops of the mountains were covered with snow. 8. His head is big and his body is short. 9. He has no courage. 10. The landlord had many guests. 11. The messenger brought three letters in the morning. 12. Don't make so much noise. 13. The servant carried five or six suitcases. 14. The doctor's son paid (=made) me a visit. 15. I have two cousins but no brothers. 16. In the (*87(b)ii*) sky one could see the moon and the stars. 17. In London [there] is a lot of (much) traffic. 18. We saw many soldiers and sailors in (*87(a)*) the ports. 19. The branches of the trees were bare. 20. New York has many inhabitants. 21. He is the pride of his father. 22. The

baker, the butcher and the tailor are friends. 23. My husband has no enemies. 24. In the ('im') north it is very cold in winter. 25. The emperor has two sons and three grandsons. 26. You deserve your success. 27. That is no proof. 28. I need little sleep. 29. In (*87(b)iv*) the market [there] were many farmers. 30. This ring has no value. 31. At the ('am') edge of the wood the hunter saw a bear. 32. The count has had great losses. 33. I made many purchases. 34. There are ('es gibt') few kings nowadays. 35. I must buy some shoes and hats. 36. I don't know (*123*) my neighbours yet. 37. What is the name of the President of (G) the United ('Vereinigten') States? 38. All the seats are taken (*123*). 39. The chairs are not very comfortable. 40. *War and Peace* is the title of a novel by (*86(a)ix*) Tolstoy ('Tolstoi'). 41. On the lake we saw two boats. 42. Have you still pain (pl.)? 43. In summer one sees many foreigners in the shops in London. 44. The customer is always right. 45. What is the purpose of this comparison? 46. Since the cathedral is so beautiful one (*73*) always sees many visitors there. 47. If that is the case I shall not make the attempt. 48. I don't know if I have [any] tobacco. 49. When he saw the slave he was afraid. 50. You can go as soon as you have corrected the mistakes.

8 Nouns (*19*)

TRANSLATE INTO GERMAN:

A. (*19(a)i* and *ii* and *19(c)i*.)

1. This cat has caught (*123*) three mice already. 2. I don't like (*123*) pears. 3. The walls of the town are very thick. 4. Such opportunities are rare. 5. The door is white but the walls are yellow. 6. Have you any brothers and sisters? 7. He has two watches. 8. He does not smoke cigarettes. 9. That is your duty. 10. The king does not always wear a crown. 11. We have three meals every day (*27(c)*). 12. The earth was covered with snow. 13. Have you any stamps? 14. This jacket has three pockets. 15. In winter the nights are long. 16. His wife has no help in the kitchen. 17. Haven't you any nuts? 18. He bought a lot [of] flowers. 19. The frontier was quite near. 20. There was ('es war') not a soul in (*87(b)iv*) the street. 21. How many pages have you read? 22. I did not understand (the) half (of) the answer. 23. Her aunt spent a night in (the) town. 24. He knows (*123*) many languages. 25. The world is very small. 26. Clouds covered the sky so that we could not

see the sun. 27. After he had waited [for] two hours he left (*123*) the island. 28. Although the danger was very great they had no fear. 29. As they had no choice they remained on (*87(a)*) the bridge. 30. Before I go to (*87(b)iii*) the bank I shall buy a newspaper.

B. Derivatives: (*19(c)ii–v*):

1. All wanted to see the heroine. 2. The queen and the princesses visited the workwomen. 3. Our cook has many weaknesses. 4. Her beauty was unusual. 5. That is the truth. 6. He has great abilities. 7. Punctuality is a virtue. 8. He deserved his punishment. 9. The sentry was standing at (*87(a)*) the corner of the street. 10. What is the meaning of his sudden politeness? 11. He spoke without interruption. 12. She has a cold. 13. They have no hope of making (to make) his acquaintance. 14. Where is your flat? 15. The waitress brought him his bill. 16. Do you smoke a pipe? 17. This spot is very uncomfortable. 18. He is a man of (*86(a)ix*) honour. 19. That is a question of (the) time. 20. He made ('hielt') a speech for the government. 21. Rest after (the) work is very pleasant. 22. The rules of (the) society are not simple. 23. What will be the consequences of his action? 24. He accepted the invitation. 25. To be continued (continuation follows). 26. As soon as he heard the bell he opened the door. 27. Although the journey was [a] long [one] he made (use 'treffen') no preparations. 28. As he was in a great hurry he did not stop (*123*). 29. While he was showing me his collection I was examining my surroundings. 30. (The) experience has shown that few women have those qualities.

9 Nouns (*20*)

TRANSLATE INTO GERMAN:

1. The child sang a song. 2. We saw some cows and horses in (*87(b)iv*) the fields. 3. The houses of these villages are small. 4. The roofs of the houses in (*87(a)*) the village are red. 5. In winter many trees have no leaves. 6. The furniture in the room was (=were) very old. 7. Animals have four legs. 8. Birds build their nests in spring. 9. How much does the fruit cost? Two marks a pound. 10. I rarely go to (*87(b)v*) the theatre. 11. (The) man has two eyes, two ears, a nose, a mouth and a chin. 12. What was the result of your visit? 13. We saw many boys and girls. 14. What was his appearance like (*44*)? 15. I like

his novels but not his poems. 16. Silence is golden (gold). 17. She had three pictures on (*87(a)*) the walls of her room. 18. We found a lot [of] wood in the corner. 19. He finds the learning of the words very difficult. 20. Many faces were unknown to me (*29(d)*). 21. He is full [of] confidence. 22. I got (*123*) many presents. 23. Smoking is prohibited. 24. I have no paper but I have a knife. 25. I have left (*123*) my exercise books at home. 26. He did not keep (*123*) his promise. 27. Miss X brought him two parcels. 28. To my astonishment he did not reply. 29. I should like (*123*) a room with two beds. 30. Travelling costs money. 31. The lady bought a dozen eggs. 32. The valleys in (*87(a)*) this district are very beautiful. 33. Business is business. 34. I have said that many times (*123*). 35. From the bridge (add 'aus') we saw many ships and boats. 36. A litre costs 5 marks. 37. The weather was very fine yesterday. 38. We lay (*123*) in (*87(b)vi*) the grass round the fire. 39. He bought two shirts. 40. My nephew lived there [for] twenty years. 41. My sister bought two pair[s] [of] stockings. 42. Which fairy tales used your mother to tell you? 43. In spite of his age he still looks (*123*) young. 44. I heard him on the (*87(b)iv*) radio. 45. (The) living in England is very dear. 46. When the windows and doors are shut you (*73*) cannot hear anything. 47. Everybody knows (*123*) that a river has two banks. 48. The books were cheap, for they cost only three marks each. 49. Although he has all this poet's works in his library he has not read any of them. 50. As soon as his wife saw the dress she wanted to buy it.

10 Nouns (*21–23*)

TRANSLATE INTO GERMAN:

1. Where are you spending (*123*) the holidays? 2. My father goes (*123*) to the office every day by (*86(a)vi*) (the) car. 3. My parents are dead. 4. The cafés and restaurants are always full. 5. Many people wear good clothes. 6. He gave me some good advice. 7. Two policemen were standing at (*87(a)*) the corner of the market place. 8. Paris is the capital of (*86(a)ix*) France. 9. I must go to the dentist's tomorrow. 10. The four seasons are: spring, summer, autumn, winter (*13(f)*). 11. They are flying by (the) aeroplane to (*86(a)vii*) North America. 12. In (*87(a)*) this city the town hall is very small and ugly. 13. Our house has one sitting-room, one dining-room, three bedrooms, a bathroom

and a kitchen. 14. Have you a railway time-table? 15. He was sitting at his desk and writing letters. 16. Have you a headache? – No, but I have a sore throat. 17. We have three meals a *(87(b)ii)* day: breakfast, dinner and supper. 18. Have you seen my friend's stamp collection? 19. What *(124(h))* is your Christian name and surname? 20. That is not a fast train, that is a slow train. 21. My grandparents gave me a dictionary as a ('zum') birthday present. 22. I have no change. 23. My wife has lost her handbag. 24. I am looking *(123)* for a letter-box. 25. Every year we have a Christmas tree and sing Christmas carols. 26. I always forget my clothes brush and my toothbrush. 27. In this century we have already had two World Wars. 28. Tomorrow is full moon. 29. Actors and actresses are strange people. 30. When does the doctor have his consulting hours? 31. In the summer holidays the children usually go to *(87(b)i)* the sea[-side]. 32. He had to pay a fine. 33. Can I have a teaspoon? 34. We saw many aeroplanes at *(87(b)vi)* the airport. 35. I never wear gloves. 36. That *(123)* suggestion has its advantages and disadvantages *(125(f)iii*, note). 37. I have no intention *(106(f))* of becoming (to become) a member. 38. That made no impression on *(87(b)iii)* me. 39. He has made little progress (pl.). 40. What is the opposite of *(86(a)ix)* 'white'? 41. He had a very interesting career. 42. The surface of the lake was like a mirror. 43. He has no conception of *(86(a)ix)* the difficulty of his task. 44. In *(87(b)viii)* these circumstances (the) resistance is pointless (has no purpose). 45. The defeat of the enemy is certain. 46. As the maid is ill the house is not very clean. 47. Although it was raining hard (strongly) he had neither an umbrella nor a raincoat. 48. As soon as the porter came with the luggage he gave him a tip. 49. I know *(123)* that the postman will bring a postcard tomorrow. 50. While he was having (making) his stroll he smoked a cigarette.

11 Nouns *(24-25)*

TRANSLATE INTO GERMAN:

1. Frederick's soldiers. 2. Mary's aunt. 3. Fred's friends. 4. Mozart's works. 5. Brahms's songs. 6. The works of Conrad Ferdinand Meyer. 7. The death of Emperor Franz of Austria. 8. Aunt Martha's cars. 9. Uncle Robert's shop. 10. Mr. Smith's ('Schmidt') radio. 11. Professor Miller's ('Müller') flat. 12. The poems of Joseph von Eichen-

dorff. 13. The buildings of Paris. 14. The banks of the Neckar (m.). 15. The beginning of May. 16. The middle of October. 17. The end of March. 18. The victories of Henry the Lion. 19. Max's cousin. 20. Julia's library. 21. Not all Russians speak Russian. 22. People (73) speak German in Austria and parts of Switzerland. 23. He can neither write nor speak English. 24. Norway and Sweden have not many inhabitants. 25. In France [there] are still many peasants. 26. Spain is very poor but very proud. 27. The U.S.A., Russia, England, France and China were the Great Powers which fought against Germany in (87(a)) the Second World War. 28. People speak French and English in Canada. 29. His wife is a Frenchwoman but he is a German. 30. My father is an Australian and my mother is an Englishwoman.

12 The Cases (26–30)

TRANSLATE INTO GERMAN:

1. He is my friend. 2. He became a famous poet. 3. He remained their friend. 4. Next Tuesday my mother is coming. 5. One morning I woke (123) up quite suddenly. 6. Her husband is unknown to me. 7. He is very like his mother. 8. This town is worth a visit. 9. Some birds are useful to man. 10. She kept (123) the house in order for them. 11. It is not worth the trouble. 12. We met Mr Braun, my cousin's friend. 13. He is very grateful to the doctor. 14. That is the house of my friend the judge. 15. A crowd of people were standing in (87(b)iv) the square. 16. One day he will be well and strong again. 17. Smoking is harmful to the health. 18. He has remained faithful to his promise. 19. My uncle always travels first class. 20. This year we did not go to (86(a)vii) France. 21. When the doctor came the painter was at the point of death. 22. If you work hard you are sure of success. 23. As he was always ill he had become tired of life. 24. I am of the opinion that you are wrong. 25. After he had drunk a glass full of fresh cold water he felt (123) better.

13 Adjectives (31–32(d); 33)

TRANSLATE INTO GERMAN:

1. This red hat; my green hat; a brown hat. 2. These good friends; our clever friends; dear friends. 3. The little bottle; an empty bottle; his own bottle. 4. These wide streets; its charming streets; magnificent

streets. 5. This clean handkerchief; her pretty handkerchief; a bright-coloured handkerchief. 6. Which dirty knives? – your heavy knives; sharp knives; all blunt knives. 7. This deep lake; our round basket; not a smooth stick. 8. Little man; a famous man; this honest man. 9. These long letters; your frequent letters; sad letters; all polite letters. 10. Every short speech; her successful speech; not a bad speech. 11. Have you any foreign stamps? Yes, I have German, French, Italian and Spanish stamps. 12. January is the first month of the year and December is the last. 13. The old peasant's son had built a little white cottage. 14. Every big town has important buildings. 15. He gave his little sister a beautiful watch. 16. That is our little garden. 17. Have you a big garden? 18. These yellow flowers come from (*86(a)i*) our little garden. 19. We shall have fine weather. 20. In (*87(a)*) the middle of the little village stood a fine old church. 21. The high walls of the little town are very thick. 22. My old father helps our poor neighbours. 23. I have a big brother and a little sister. 24. This young poet writes very bad poems. 25. The old houses of the little village have red roofs. 26. Our old dog died last week. 27. In our little garden we have a very tall tree with very thin branches. 28. He has two ripe apples. 29. The old town has very narrow streets. 30. Which German town have you visited? 31. As these new books are very cheap I shall buy them. 32. We have both a black cat as well as two little dogs, for we like (*123*) animals. 33. Although he is not very well he has a good appetite. 34. He speaks in a loud voice so that we can understand him. 35. While I was out for a walk (*123*: 'go') I met our old doctor's little son.

14 Adjectives (*32(e)–37*)

TRANSLATE INTO GERMAN:

1. All our good friends were there. 2. The works of all these great writers are in his library. 3. Many clever boys are very lazy. 4. The opinions of several great men were well known. 5. All these wide streets are quite new. 6. He spoke to (with) the accused man. 7. He has many rich relatives. 8. He goes to school every day by tram. 9. I do not like (*123*) his appearance. 10. Have you no acquaintances in Cologne? 11. The patient still had a temperature. 12. He gave the traveller a ticket. 13. He examined the traveller's ticket. 14. Trams are

no longer modern. 15. In our little village strangers are rarely to be seen (*110(e)*). 16. Many rich men live in London. 17. That is the quarter of the poor. 18. We saw several fine cars. 19. The houses of many rich people are very simple. 20. There are ('es gibt') very few trams. 21. Many Germans live in London. 22. The streets of many old towns are very narrow. 23. In several old towns one sees many interesting old buildings. 24. You (*73*) do not see many strangers here. 25. In Germany [there] are everywhere officials. 26. He had to (*109(b)iv*) dismiss a hundred employees. 27. In England there are many unemployed. 28. She has never spoken evil of (*86(a)ix*) anybody. 29. I have a lot of news to tell you. 30. That is nothing unusual. 31. Cologne Cathedral is very high. 32. The London policemen are very friendly. 33. All these short sentences are very easy to translate. 34. Voltaire was a friend of Frederick the Great. 35. People (*73*) relate many stories about (*120(n)*) Frederick the Great. 36. Although Cologne Cathedral is very beautiful I prefer several other German cathedrals. 37. As he was a stranger nobody helped him. 38. If the patient feels (*123*) better tomorrow she may (*109(b)i*) get up. 39. Although England was rich [there] were many unemployed there. 40. I don't know whether my acquaintance will do everything possible.

15 Comparison of Adjectives (*33, 38*)

TRANSLATE INTO GERMAN:

1. This fine oak tree is very tall. 2. But the fir tree is much taller than the oak. 3. He is just as clever as you. 4. Are you older than he? 5. He is not so young as I. 6. The Thames is very wide. 7. The Thames is widest at (*87(b)ii*) this spot. 8. The Rhine is even wider than the Thames. 9. The knife is getting (*123*) blunter and blunter. 10. That is truer than you think. 11. That is a very tall building. 12. She has become weaker. 13. He is stronger than his friend. 14. He became even angrier. 15. She spoke in an even softer voice. 16. That is the best book. 17. He is most proud. 18. He is the proudest man in (*86(a)ix*) the world. 19. The river is deepest at this spot. 20. He has less money than you. 21. You have more money than he. 22. Most people say that. 23. In summer the days are longest. 24. The longest days of the year are in summer. 25. Young and elderly gentlemen were sitting in the cafés. 26. Although he is younger than she he knows (*123*) more

than she [does]. 27. When you are older you will understand better. 28. You can understand this better than your brother because you are older than he [is]. 29. Since he is exceedingly rich he gives a lot of money to the poor. 30. I always buy at (87(b)vi) that shop, for things are cheapest there.

16 Adverbs (39–41)

TRANSLATE INTO GERMAN:

1. He was then sixteen years old. 2. He welcomed me most warmly. 3. He goes to the (87(b)v) theatre very often. 4. He goes to the cinema even more often. 5. It is partly black, partly green. 6. At first he would (123) not come home. 7. Then he came. 8. Before [that time] he lived in Berlin. 9. Afterwards he moved to (86(a)vii) Hamburg. 10. Since then he has been living (94(c)) there. 11. At last he got (123) up. 12. He never writes. 13. He is always reading. 14. Now I know. 15. Well, what do you think? 16. He came immediately. 17. Now (123) this, now that. 18. They have just arrived. 19. I met him the other day. 20. He sometimes visits me. 21. Till now I have had no news from (86(a)ix) him. 22. Till then you must wait. 23. He will be there by then. 24. There was (56(f)) once a king called Peter. 25. You will know it some day. 26. I have been waiting (94(c)) a long time for (120(c)) my father. 27. He usually sleeps after lunch. 28. From now on I shall work. 29. At the same time he saw a faint (weak) light. 30. He is not coming till tomorrow. 31. He has not yet arrived. 32. Suddenly he got up. 33. I am sometimes right. 34. I rarely smoke before (123) lunch. 35. Meanwhile many people had arrived. 36. Although he is usually right he is sometimes wrong. 37. When he comes he always brings a present with [him]. 38. He did not come till it was too late. 39. Hardly had he gone to bed when he fell asleep. 40. 'Have you ever been in Germany?' he asked (123) the young man.

17 Adverbs (39, 42–44)

TRANSLATE INTO GERMAN:

1. He laughs just like you. 2. Germans think differently from Englishmen. 3. The town was about 3 kilometres away. 4. He is still fairly young. 5. In vain did he try. 6. I prefer dancing. 7. He is by no means stupid. 8. Unfortunately he cannot come. 9. Fortunately he could

come. 10. Perhaps it is true. 11. Probably he is ill. 12. There were (*56(f)*) almost fifty people there. 13. Even my friend has heard nothing. 14. Put (*123*) the money there. 15. He went upstairs. 16. He has gone outside. 17. He was standing at the back. 18. It is cold outside. 19. It is warm inside. 20. We went down the mountain. 21. He came down. 22. We went up the mountain. 23. He went to the left. 24. He came from over there. 25. The sun came out from behind the clouds. 26. The cat came out from under the table. 27. He had been (gone) everywhere. 28. It was nowhere to be found (*110(e)*). 29. I put the money somewhere else. 30. It must be somewhere. 31. On the way he met a peasant. 32. Where are you going to? 33. Where do you live? 34. Where do you come from? 35. He is going there now. 36. As he ran round the table he fell over. 37. I know that you find them everywhere. 38. When he came in he sat down. 39. While we were working together we heard a lot of (much) noise. 40. After he had wandered about in the town he went back to his hotel. 41. He walked (went) up and down. 42. He went past. 43. We are going home. 44. He stepped forward. 45. They got in. 46. He shut the door. 47. They opened the door. 48. He put on his coat. 49. He took off his shoes. 50. He drove off.

18 Numerals, Dates, etc. (*45-54*)

TRANSLATE INTO GERMAN:

1. He bought three apples and ate one. 2. There were (*56(f)*) thirty boys in (*87(a)*) the classroom. 3. The seventeenth page; the twentieth line. 4. I have brought back the two books. 5. Both their sons are at home now. 6. Neither of the two knew it. 7. What is your age? 8. I am fifty years of age. 9. He was born on the 21st January 1937 (*in full*). 10. He went to bed at half past ten. 11. What is the date today? It is the 16th May. 12. At what time did you see that man? 13. What is the time now? 14. The father of Frederick II was Frederick William I (*in full*). 15. Queen Victoria often wrote letters to her grandson William II (*in full*). 16. George V died in 1936 (*in full*). 17. There were all sorts of flowers on (*87(a)*) the table. 18. He drank another glass of milk. 19. He walked (went) [for] an hour and a half. 20. This bottle holds (contains) six-tenths [of a] litre. 21. She is his only child. 22. The guests came separately. 23. That is all the same to me. 24. That is very simple. 25. The policeman came past every half hour.

26. He has eaten half a loaf. 27. I have already eaten half the sausage. 28. Thousands of people were in (*87(b)iv*) the square. 29. Several hundred people were there. 30. One or two hours ago (*87(b)ix*). 31. He drank three cups of tea. 32. He came back with two pairs of shoes. 33. I bought two pounds of apples. 34. He spoke to (*120(j)*) a number (*123*) of young people. 35. 'I am twenty-seven,' he said, 'I was born in 1913.' 36. Yesterday morning; last night; tonight (before bedtime). 37. In the first place I don't feel inclined (*14(d)*), and in the second place I have no time (*123*). 38. A fortnight ago today; a week tomorrow. 39. *Write in German a list of the days of the week and a list of the months of the year.* 40. *Write down the German for the following times:* 7.30; 9.15; 11.20; 7.45; 1.0 a.m.; 2.0 p.m.; 12.30; 5.55; 4.5. 41. Although I was at home at a quarter past eight I heard nothing at all. 42. As he has lost his fortune he has to (*109(b)iv*) work now. 43. After she had sat there for half an hour she went to bed. 44. I know of course that you (*73*) can buy each article (piece) separately. 45. I was glad that I went there, for I met one of my friends there.

19 Personal and Reflexive Pronouns, etc. (*55-59*)

TRANSLATE INTO GERMAN:

1. He gave his son the money. 2. He lent his daughter a pencil. 3. She gave her little son an apple but he did not eat it. 4. He gave her a new car but she did not like (*123*) it. 5. Where is your watch? – I have lost it. 6. A friend of mine saw them yesterday. 7. I am ashamed of you. 8. Here is the pen. – Give it to me. 9. The stranger gave them the money. 10. He is not worthy of her. 11. She is not worthy of him. 12. He is ashamed of us. 13. The mother said to her child: 'You are a bad boy; I must punish you.' 14. The mother said to her children: 'You are bad children; I must punish you.' 15. I wrote a long letter to you. 16. That is our house but we do not live in it. 17. He put (*123*) the money on it. 18. I cannot write with it. 19. The dog went with (*86(a)vi*) him. 20. He took his dog with him. 21. In front of (*87(a)*) him stood his father. 22. In front of it stood the teacher. 23. They thanked (*115*) them for it. 24. It is I; it is we; it is they; is it you? 25. That is my book; that is yours. 26. This is my pencil; that is his. 27. I can write better with your pen than with mine. 28. I have lost my pencil; can I borrow yours? 29. There were no people in the hall.

30. There is no good music nowadays. 31. His grandmother is very old. 32. Her grandfather rarely said a word. 33. They saw nothing beneath them. 34. Do you hear steps behind (*87(a)*) you? 35. We write to one another every week. 36. Although he is a friend of ours we do not see him very often. 37. If the clock has stopped (*123*) wind it up. 38. Since he gave ('ließ') us no choice we had to (*109(b)iv*) accept his invitation. 39. I know (*123*) that I am not worthy of you. 40. After they had finished (*123*) their work they went to the (*87(b)v*) cinema.

20 Interrogative and Relative Pronouns, etc. (*60–66*)

TRANSLATE INTO GERMAN:

1. Which is the longest river in Germany? 2. Which German towns have you visited? 3. Who said that to you? 4. Whom did you meet in (*87(a)*) the town? 5. Whose book is that? 6. To whom did you give your old bicycle? 7. What have you read today? 8. What are you thinking of? 9. What am (*109(b)v*) I to thank (*115*) you for? 10. The man who brought me the letter is our neighbour. 11. The man we just saw is a great friend of mine. 12. The man whose son visited us last night is very poor. 13. I don't know (*123*) the woman you greeted. 14. The man you gave the money to is not very poor. 15. The little girl whose book you have taken is very unhappy. 16. The woman who brings us the eggs every day has a little farm quite near. 17. The shirt he was wearing had a big hole. 18. That is the woman whose son works in the shop. 19. The child he gave the prize to had worked hard (diligently). 20. That is the woman I gave the money to. 21. The child who was crying so loud had lost (*123*) its way. 22. Boys who go to school are called (*123*) schoolboys. 23. The people whose sympathy he won were very simple. 24. Those (*69, note*) are writers whose works are famous. 25. The postman with whose wife I spoke this morning is very ill. 26. The men with whom I was speaking were old acquaintances of his. 27. The table on which the books lay stood in the corner. 28. The table at which he was sitting (*123*) was covered with papers. 29. That was all he knew. 30. That is the best (thing) I can do. 31. Now that you have more time you can play with us. 32. He who works hard makes good progress. 33. Wherever I go I see this man. 34. Although the man I gave the money to is very poor he has a job. 35. Since the shirt he was wearing had many holes we gave him a new [one].

21 Demonstrative Adjectives and Pronouns (67-72)

TRANSLATE INTO GERMAN:

1. This hat is prettier than that. 2. This pen writes better than that.
3. This book is just as interesting as that. 4. I have such a headache.
5. This play is even more boring than that one. 6. I can write better
with this pencil than with that one. 7. Was it *that* woman? – No, not
that one. 8. *He* does not know anything. 9. That is true. 10. You are
not aware of that. 11. He who works hard will have success. 12. Those
who think that are wrong. 13. Those he said that to believed him. 14.
Of (*86(a)ix*) those who spoke he spoke best. 15. Amongst those who
came were three old acquaintances. 16. The number (*123*) of those
who have read this book is very large. 17. We have enough of ('von')
those already. 18. My suit is better than my brother's. 19. The only
car in the village is the doctor's. 20. That is my money. 21. Those are
your keys. 22. This is his watch. 23. These are my stockings, those are
hers. 24. That is all the same thing. 25. That is the same woman we
met yesterday. 26. All those who do not want to come can stay at
home. 27. They themselves said that. 28. I know that I saw her the
same day. 29. Although this dress is dearer than that one I like (*123*)
this one better. 30. Since my car is better than my sister's she always
borrows mine.

22 Indefinite Adjectives and Pronouns (73-83)

TRANSLATE INTO GERMAN:

1. There is a ring [at the door]. 2. You cannot know (*123*) everything.
3. This morning I met one of my friends. 4. It must be one of us. 5.
I haven't read any of his poems. 6. Some are very beautiful. 7. Somebody or other said that to me. 8. Did you see anybody last night? 9.
That is somebody else. 10. Nobody has read his novels. 11. He has
not told (said it to) anybody. 12. We go to school every day. 13. We
go away every year. 14. Everything you say is untrue. 15. Everybody
says the same thing. 16. He gave me something else. 17. He did not
say anything. 18. I haven't any bread. – Have you any? 19. Put (*123*)
a little sugar in the water. 20. He drinks a lot of tea. 21. He takes much
more sugar than I [do]. 22. There is only a little milk in the bottle.
23. The whole town was astir. 24. Many beautiful presents lay on

(*87(a)*)) the table. 25. I had invited a few of my friends. 26. Some presents were for me. 27. My sister has several German friends. 28. I have only a few friends. 29. One or two elderly guests left (*123*) our house early. 30. Some say this, others say that. 31. Although one of the books was very interesting the other was most boring. 32. As I have only seen a few plays, it is difficult to say. 33. When there is a knock we open the door. 34. Everybody knows that that is wrong. 35. 'Have you enough salt?' she asked.

23 Prepositions (*84–86*)

TRANSLATE INTO GERMAN:

1. Through the little wood. 2. At his old aunt's. 3. With your red pencil. 4. Without a single chair. 5. To France. 6. Opposite the new station. 7. Because of the severe cold. 8. Round the small town. 9. About half past seven. 10. On the other side of the frontier. 11. Against my will. 12. Out of the little glass. 13. Instead of a big present. 14. At a quarter to nine. 15. Since his arrival. 16. During the last holidays. 17. Along the narrow street. 18. Till next Wednesday. 19. From her old mother. 20. In spite of the bad weather. 21. Above the new bridge. 22. Except for him. 23. To her great surprise. 24. For my father. 25. During the summer. 26. On this side of the wide river. 27. From the house to the station. 28. In spite of the heavy (strong) rain. 29. Below the old bridge. 30. At Woolworth's. 31. After you. 32. Since the last war. 33. The President of France. 34. Not far from the station. 35. Through my help. 36. During the afternoon. 37. Without my intention. 38. Contrary to his parents' advice. 39. For the sake of your little son. 40. With his sister.

24 Prepositions (*87(a)*)

TRANSLATE INTO GERMAN:

1. He stood in front of the door. 2. He put (*123*) the pen on the table. 3. Berlin is (*123*) on the Spree (f.). 4. He built his house between the lake and the wood. 5. He was sitting (*123*) in the room. 6. He went and stood in front of the door. 7. He put the handkerchief in his pocket. 8. He sat down under a tree. 9. The dog lay under the table. 10. There is ('es ist') a great difference between him and her. 11. I found the letter among my papers. 12. The pen is lying on the table. 13. He

threw his hat on the floor. 14. He sat down at the table. 15. He jumped over the wall. 16. He sat down amongst the spectators. 17. A little bird perched (sat) on a branch of the big tree. 18. It flew on to the roof of our house. 19. He was sitting at the table. 20. He was sitting on the table. 21. The teacher held the book in his hand. 22. He came and stood behind me. 23. He threw the coat over his arm. 24. His house stood behind the old tower. 25. They were all sitting at the open window. 26. There were no beautiful pictures on the walls. 27. The waiter put the glass of wine on the table in front of the guest. 28. The servant put the old man's chair in front of the window. 29. He is always building castles in the air. 30. The picture hangs above the sofa between the door and the window.

25 Prepositions used idiomatically (84–87)

TRANSLATE INTO GERMAN:

1. We live in the country. 2. The next morning he got up early. 3. I saw him in Dresden a month ago. 4. Year after year we go to the seaside in the holidays. 5. Is it my turn? 6. Have you any money on you? 7. We went on (123: 'go') an excursion into the country. 8. How much does he earn a day? 9. I like (123) being in the open. 10. Tears ran down his cheeks. 11. My children go to school every morning at nine o'clock. 12. I must set off for home. 13. Amongst other things he noticed her pretty face and little hands. 14. I'll see you to the station. 15. Above all one must (109(b)i) not lose courage. 16. When he got (123) home he found the door open. 17. For what reason did he say that? 18. We went by tram to the station. 19. In my opinion he is wrong. 20. Who is that picture by? 21. He is very proud of his son. 22. At that moment he came into the room. 23. As a rule he comes home at half past four. 24. He has many friends abroad. 25. The First World War broke out in the reign of William the Second. 26. Many people were in the streets. 27. On the contrary he is still alive. 28. All the guests left early except one. 29. You will not make any progress in this way. 30. He was ready for anything. 31. He has been learning French for two years. 32. We want to go to Switzerland for three weeks. 33. Some people always speak in a loud voice. 34. I always stay at home in bad weather. 35. He nodded his head. 36. Although he only earns fifty marks a week he has already saved a lot of money. 37.

If you go to Germany via Ostend you will find it much cheaper. 38.
Before he set off for home he bought a newspaper at the station. 39.
When he came into the room he sat down at the table and wrote the
letter immediately. 40. As soon as she saw him she wept for joy.

26 Conjugation of Verbs (88–93)

TRANSLATE INTO GERMAN:

A. (88)

1. You have been (3 forms). 2. You have had (3 forms). 3. You have
become (3 forms). 4. We shall become. 5. I should have. 6. You were
(3 forms). 7. I had been. 8. She had become. 9. He became. 10. You
have (3 forms). 11. I should have become. 12. We should have had.
13. You are (3 forms). 14. Give (a) the pres. subj. of 'sein'; (b) the 3rd
pers. sing. pres. subj. of 'haben', 'werden'. 15. Give the impf. subj. of
'haben', 'sein', 'werden'.

B. Weak Verbs

1. I worked. 2. You fetch (3 forms). 3. It cost. 4. They paint. 5. They
fear. 6. They feared. 7. I hope. 8. We hoped. 9. I shall smoke. 10.
They have studied. 11. I change. 12. He changes. 13. He has killed.
14. They drew. 15. He opens. 16. He laughed. 17. He smiled. 18. I
have bought. 19. I should buy. 20. He has altered. 21. He has hesi-
tated. 22. He breathes. 23. We had knocked. 24. You have travelled
(3 forms). 25. I shall need. 26. He will disturb. 27. We should love.
28. I have followed. 29. He rented. 30. You have honoured (3 forms).
31. It lasts. 32. We waited. 33. He knows. 34. He knew. 35. I shake.
36. He would have brought. 37. You have practised (3 forms). 38. He
had ruled. 39. She boiled. 40. Share (3 forms).

C. Strong Verbs

1. I have found. 2. They have fallen. 3. We took. 4. He lets. 5. He
reads. 6. I requested. 7. He tore. 8. He broke. 9. He has died. 10.
He speaks. 11. We compelled. 12. He had seen. 13. You run (3 forms).
14. They held. 15. I lay. 16. You have swum (3 forms). 17. I should
eat. 18. We have remained. 19. He advises. 20. He has suffered. 21.
They shut. 22. We have struck. 23. They have come. 24. You help
(3 forms). 25. He dug. 26. It seemed. 27. He was sitting. 28. They
wore. 29. You have slept (3 forms). 30. He has grown. 31. He has

gone. 32. He wrote. 33. They have cut. 34. He was silent. 35. He met. 36. I threw. 37. We tied. 38. He catches. 39. He steps. 40. She washes.

27 Tenses of Verbs (94–101)

TRANSLATE INTO GERMAN:

1. He goes to bed every night at ten. 2. I am now writing the last few ('paar') pages. 3. Tomorrow we are going into the country. 4. If the weather is fine tomorrow we shall go (123) on an excursion into the mountains. 5. We are just going to the theatre. 6. How long have you been learning German? 7. I have been learning German for three years. 8. He came into the dining-room, saw an empty (free) table in the corner and sat down at it. 9. He went to the office every morning at half past nine. 10. I was in the United States when they elected the new President. 11. I went to the theatre last night. 12. I have never been in France. 13. Where were you when I called (123) you? 14. While he was working in the library his wife was cooking in the kitchen. 15. Who told you so (123)? 16. He was just having his lunch when someone knocked. 17. He was just on the point of speaking when he suddenly saw a policeman. 18. He had been sitting there for several hours. 19. After I have finished (123) reading the book I shall go to bed. 20. After we had solved the problem we were satisfied. 21. After he had sent the letter he knew that he had forgotten something important. 22. They had scarcely sat down at the table when they heard the bell ring. 23. I expect she is ill. 24. I expect he has done nothing. 25. As soon as we have finished our work we shall visit you.

28 Compound Verbs (102)

TRANSLATE INTO GERMAN:

A. Inseparable.

(a) Weak:

1. He has missed the opportunity. 2. I suddenly caught sight of his face at the window. 3. He tried to work. 4. He could not explain the word. 5. I will see (accompany) you to the station. 6. I shall not catch the train. 7. I did not expect that. 8. When did you wake up this morning? 9. How much do you want (demand) for it? 10. What does this sentence mean? 11. Have you fixed the day already? 12. He has

treated me very badly. 13. Who discovered this mistake? 14. His wife prepared a magnificent meal. 15. Where did you spend the holidays last year? 16. The big house at the corner is to be let (*110(e)*). 17. My uncle earns 250 marks a month. 18. 'That is quite true,' he answered. 19. Nothing excuses what he has done. 20. He maintained that he had (*112(d)(iii)*) no time to visit us.

(b) Strong:

1. We decided to spend our holidays in South Germany and Austria. 2. He ordered (*116*) me to come at once. 3. School begins at 9 o'clock. 4. What does this glass contain? 5. She has brought up her son very badly. 6. A face suddenly appeared at (D) the window. 7. He did not get an answer to his letter. 8. This book does not please me at all. 9. I have forgotten his name. 10. I could not understand a single word. 11. I leave the house at half past eight every morning. 12. Where did you lose the money? 13. How did you find that out (learn)? 14. The Russians won a great victory over (A) the Germans. 15. A railway connects the two towns. 16. We compared the two poems with one another. 17. The sun disappeared behind (D) the clouds. 18. He promised to come but he had (*109(b)(iv)*) to stay at home. 19. He raised his hand, as though he wanted to say something. 20. Although he possesses a large stamp collection he still buys quite a lot of stamps.

B. Separable.

(a) Weak:

1. The rain has not stopped yet. 2. He tried to shut the door. 3. You have expressed that badly. 4. We hoped to continue our journey the next day. 5. He had opened all the windows and turned on the wireless. 6. The soldiers have executed the emperor's orders. 7. The children hurried past. 8. He promised to meet me at the station. 9. At school you must pay attention (*add:* 'gut'). 10. What does this picture represent? 11. My cousin hurried towards me (D). 12. He has not yet sent off the parcel. 13. She put on her best hat. 14. When does your maid return? 15. The whole family is leaving on Monday, the 24th July. 16. He will not listen to me. 17. My grandfather had to (*109(b)iv*) decline the invitation. 18. 'Come early,' he added. 19. After the boy had put the watch together again he handed it to his sister. 20. They informed me that the country produces all sorts of goods.

(b) Strong:

1. He has just got up. 2. When does the train start? 3. My friends have invited me to spend a fortnight with them. 4. His father looked very ill yesterday. 5. At what time does the train arrive? 6. He has not yet returned me my pen. 7. My friend would (*123*) not accept the invitation. 8. As usual I have spent all my money. 9. He looked at the boy closely (exactly). 10. Germany attacked Russia in June 1941. 11. He wanted to begin a new life. 12. In summer the sun rises very early in England. 13. I tried in vain to fall asleep. 14. He took off his shoes. 15. He expressed his thanks. 16. The case seldom occurs. 17. That sort of thing has never taken place. 18. I could not get rid of the thought. 19. As he had given up all hope he left the town. 20. After he had put on his coat he opened the door and went out.

C. Separable or Inseparable.

(a) Weak:

1. They submitted the plan to us. 2. The train travels through without stopping (*122(d)*). 3. That surprised me very [much]. 4. Please repeat your question. 5. I am firmly convinced of it. 6. She spread a blanket under [him]. 7. You must have put it behind. 8. He tried to translate this page. 9. He fetched the dog back. 10. We have travelled all over the whole of (*83(c)*) Germany.

(b) Strong:

1. He always tries to evade the law. 2. A thick wall surrounds the town. 3. The wheels are going round very fast. 4. He entertained the whole company. 5. When does the sun set now? 6. He associates with actors and actresses. 7. We are moving tomorrow. 8. Hold your hand under. 9. Where did you change trains? 10. He interrupted me suddenly.

29 Reflexive and Impersonal Verbs (*103–105*)

TRANSLATE INTO GERMAN:

1. Did you enjoy yourself at the theatre last night? – No, not at all (*3 forms*). 2. You haven't washed your hands (*3 forms*). 3. He sat down on a chair and rested. 4. I cannot imagine that (*5(a)ii*). 5. In which street is the hotel situated? 6. We conversed a long time. 7.

Suddenly the door opened and a stranger came in. 8. He has behaved very badly. 9. How did you like being in Hamburg? (*3 forms*). 10. I am very sorry, I cannot go there tonight, I don't feel very well. 11. How are you? (*3 forms*). – I am (we are) very well, thank you. 12. I did not manage to see him. 13. He has hidden behind (D) the tree. 14. The ship moved away slowly. 15. Has he recovered [his health]? – No, he is still seriously ('schwer') ill. 16. The little girl has lost her way in the wood. 17. He lay down on the ground and immediately fell asleep. 18. I haven't undressed yet. 19. He stayed a month in the country. 20. Times have changed. 21. If you go out without a coat you will catch cold. 22. After he had dressed he went downstairs. 23. If it rains I shall not go out. 24. When he came into the room he looked round but did not notice the captain. 25. 'It serves you right,' she said (*3 forms*). 26. I hope that it will freeze. 27. As it was cold he got up and sat down by the fire. 28. I am glad that you can come. 29. Before she goes to the theatre she must change. 30. 'Do not move,' he cried.

30 The Infinitive (*106*)

TRANSLATE INTO GERMAN:

1. It is very hard to write German correctly. 2. She knows (*123*) [how] to dress. 3. He intends to visit us. 4. I saw him walking along the street. 5. He wants to learn. 6. They wished to leave (*123*) the house. 7. He invited me to spend a fortnight with him. 8. I have often asked (*123*) him at least to make the attempt. 9. I hope to find them well. 10. I was not able to speak. 11. He wished to help me. 12. I heard him get up early this morning. 13. He does not dare to ask (*123*) her. 14. Is it possible to get (*123*) wine here? 15. He makes the children believe what he wants. 16. Where did you learn to speak German so well? 17. You need not answer immediately. 18. The maid helped me to lay the table. 19. He came last night to ask (*123*) me something. 20. The doctor advised me to stay another week in bed. 21. We hope to see your father tomorrow. 22. I went to Germany to learn German. 23. It is quite impossible to hear the speaker. 24. My cousin promised to come the next day. 25. Mother forgot to wake (*123*) me this morning. 26. Although I had asked him to meet me at the station he did not come. 27. He ordered (*123*) the soldiers to stop (*123*), which they did at once. 28. As he remained at home instead of coming with us I

could not introduce him to my friend. 29. When I saw them coming my heart began to beat. 30. If you will help me to carry these parcels I shall be very grateful to you.

31 The Imperative and Interrogative (*107, 108; 44; 60–62*)

TRANSLATE INTO GERMAN:

(*Where possible give the three forms of the imperative.*)

1. Bring me a cup of tea. 2. Think of (*120(a)*) it before (*123*) it is too late. 3. Give me a bicycle for ('zu') my birthday. 4. Go into the town and buy a pound of apples. 5. Eat, drink and be merry. 6. Try this. 7. Don't run away. 8. Lend me a knife. 9. Read the first page aloud. 10. Take these books; you will find them very interesting. 11. Sleep well. 12. Shut your eyes and open your mouth. 13. Send an answer to their letter immediately. 14. See what uncle has sent you. 15. Come here. 16. Come in. 17. Don't forget to write to me at least once a week. 18. Wash your neck properly (thoroughly). 19. Throw the stone into the water. 20. Tie up the parcel securely (firmly). 21. Let us ring him up now. 22. Let us hide behind the tree. 23. Do stop crying. 24. Just imagine how I felt (*123*). 25. Be prepared. 26. You do know him, don't you? 27. Do you know him? 28. Don't you know him? 29. You went there, didn't you? 30. You are happy, aren't you? 31. When are you coming? 32. Where do you live? 33. Does your brother live in Cologne? 34. How old are you? 35. Are you older than your brother? 36. Whose bicycle is that? 37. What are you writing with? 38. Which novel did you choose? 39. What sort of wood is that? 40. Which is the best drawing?

32 Auxiliary Verbs of Mood (*109*)

TRANSLATE INTO GERMAN:

A. 1. May I open the window? – You may. 2. He cannot shut the door. 3. We do not like interrupting him. 4. I should like to help you. 5. They are to see (go to) the doctor tonight. 6. I won't say anything now. 7. You must not laugh. 8. You ought not to laugh. 9. I should like to know where he is. 10. I could not come yesterday. 11. I could come tomorrow perhaps. 12. He will never be able to swim. 13. Why hasn't he been allowed to come? 14. We haven't been able to. 15. You ought to have written earlier. 16. I could have lent you the money. 17. We shall not be allowed to go to the theatre. 18. Couldn't you see him this evening? 19. You will not be able to see him. 20. He has never had to work. 21. He would have liked to remain at home. 22. In any case you would have to go to the bank. 23. He was unable to go to school yesterday. 24. He would not give an answer. 25. He should not have given her the money. 26. We should not make so much noise. 27. We could never have done anything of the sort (*80*). 28. One has to be careful (cautious). 29. I should like to have two pounds of potatoes. 30. He had to leave (*123*) (the) school. 31. Will you shut the door please? 32. Can he understand you? 33. I shall send for the doctor. 34. Thou shalt not kill. 35. I did not like going there. 36. I have just had my hair cut. 37. He made the dog jump over the stick. 38. I could not say. 39. You ought to work harder. 40. She makes her pupils learn too much by heart.

B. 1. That may well be. 2. I could not help laughing. 3. Shall we go to the theatre tonight? 4. Do you like fruit? 5. What is the meaning of that? 6. I must go away. 7. The sun was just about to set. 8. He is supposed to be clever. 9. You must have done it. 10. We cannot help it. 11. I may have done it. 12. He only knows a little German. 13. Let's go to the theatre tomorrow. 14. Do you think she is ill? 15. She may have been as old as thirty-five. 16. He is supposed to have stolen the money. 17. He sends her his kindest regards. 18. He claims that he saw him last night. 19. We did not know what to do. 20. That cannot be described. 21. I won't hear of it. 22. He must have left the house at that moment. 23. He did not know what to say, for he was so surprised. 24. I may have done it but I don't think so (*123*). 25. He was just on the point of going to bed when there was a knock [at the door].

33 Passive Voice (*110(a)–(g)*)

TRANSLATE INTO GERMAN:

1. In this shop vegetables and fruit are sold. 2. The house was built last year. 3. The glass has been filled. 4. The money will soon be found. 5. The letter had been received yesterday. 6. The money was found soon afterwards (*41*). 7. A lot of wine is drunk every year in

France. 8. The fish has been caught. 9. The waiter was called (*123*). 10. The bill has been paid. 11. The foreigner had been killed. 12. I was beaten by him. 13. The picture has already been sold. 14. This problem has at last been solved. 15. The poem will soon be learnt by heart by the children. 16. Money is being collected in the streets by the unemployed. 17. The letter was written with a fountain-pen. 18. The letter has been written by your mother. 19. By whom was this play written? 20. The inhabitants of the town were awakened by the noise. 21. The ball was thrown by the boy through the window. 22. The letter to my tailor must be written today. 23. The bread ought to be cut tonight. 24. A beginning ought to have been made by now. 25. That must not be forgotten. 26. That might easily have been forgotten. 27. The child would like to be carried. 28. This exercise has to be done. 29. The shops are now being shut. 30. This shop is not yet shut. 31. There was singing and dancing all night long. 32. There was nothing to be seen. 33. The new house at the corner of the street is to be sold. 34. The dress cannot be altered now. 35. Supper is being prepared by the maid. 36. There was a knock [at the door]. 37. The doors will have to be opened. 38. The exercise is finished (*123*). 39. While the letters are being read I'll wait here. 40. The letter I had written this morning could not be sent off because nobody had any stamps.

34 Passive Voice (*110(h)–(j); 115–116*)

TRANSLATE INTO GERMAN:

1. I was given a lovely pencil for ('zu') my birthday. 2. I have not been told that. 3. The young student has been greatly helped by your good advice. 4. He was advised to go abroad. 5. We were warmly recommended this hotel. 6. He had been forbidden to drink beer. 7. I was offered a large sum of money. 8. We shall be shown the cathedral tomorrow. 9. I have been lent a most interesting play. 10. I wasn't allowed to enter the building. 11. They had been ordered to leave the town immediately. 12. He is not trusted any longer. 13. We have been followed. 14. He will never be pardoned. 15. He can never be forgiven. 16. He ought to be given the opportunity. 17. That cannot be proved. 18. That is easily said. 19. Although I had been told he would come I did not recognise him when I saw him. 20. Since I was offered the job I accepted it.

35 Indirect Speech (*111–112*)

TRANSLATE INTO GERMAN:

(*With* 'daß' *and without* 'daß' *where possible.*)

1. He told her that he had been ill. 2. He asked the soldier when he had got (*123*) home. 3. He said he was tired. 4. My friend wrote to me [to say] that he would arrive the next morning. 5. I know that that is not true. 6. He thought it was not true. 7. The official asked the traveller where he had lost his luggage. 8. An acquaintance of mine told me that he rarely went to the cinema. 9. The waiter asked the man if he wanted tea or coffee. 10. She told the maid to bring her a cup of tea at eight o'clock. 11. The judge asked the accused when his father had died. 12. The teacher told the boy to go to the blackboard and write his name on it. 13. He ordered his servant to wake him early the next morning. 14. The paper reported that many people had died as a result of the accident. 15. The doctor said that he would visit the patient the following evening. 16. A stranger asked me how far it was to the nearest station. 17. I told him I did not know. 18. The doctor asked the patient if he felt better. 19. He wanted to know if he had a good appetite. 20. My friend asked me to come to the theatre with him. 21. The old man said that although he had lived all his life in the same village he had been very happy. 22. He knows that my parents have gone away. 23. He learnt (*123*) that same day that his mother had died. 24. He saw that there was nothing to be done. 25. He was afraid I had not received his letter. 26. He hoped that he had acted rightly. 27. I think he has told the truth. 28. I maintained that he was a bad man. 29. He thinks my father is ill. 30. We are of the opinion that he has gone away.

36 Conditional Sentences (*111, 113*)

TRANSLATE INTO GERMAN:

1. If you work hard you will pass (*123*) the examination. 2. If you worked harder you would pass the examination. 3. If you had worked harder you would have passed the examination. 4. If the weather is fine tomorrow we can go (*123*) on an excursion into the mountains. 5. If the weather were fine tomorrow we could go for an excursion into the mountains. 6. If the weather had been fine yesterday we could have

gone on an excursion into the mountains. 7. If he is diligent he will succeed. 8. If he were more diligent he would succeed. 9. If he had been more diligent he would have succeeded. 10. If I have, time I shall visit the cathedral. 11. If I had time I should visit the cathedral. 12. If I had had time I should have visited the cathedral. 13. If we make progress we are praised. 14. If we made progress we should be praised. 15. If we had made progress we should have been praised. 16. If he had taken (*123*) my advice he would have gone to France long ago. 17. If he drank less he would be healthier. 18. We should be sorry if we had to do that. 19. If they had invited me I should have come. 20. If the letter had been sent off earlier I could have come in time (*123*). 21. If I had been allowed to do that I should have been happy. 22. If you had looked (*123*) at him closely (exactly) you would have seen that he looked very ill. 23. I will give you ten marks if you can give me the answer to this question. 24. If you practise a little every day you will soon learn the language. 25. If we had not discovered the mistake it would have been very serious. 26. You will have very little success if you miss every opportunity. 27. If I had more money I should spend a year in Italy. 28. If you had been able to come yesterday you would have enjoyed yourself thoroughly. 29. If you had wanted to swim you could have done so (*123*). 30. You would be tired, too, if you had had to push the car (*3(a)*).

37 Other Uses of the Subjunctive (*111, 114*)

TRANSLATE INTO GERMAN:

1. Long live the Queen! 2. Peace be with you! 3. If only I had time! 4. We should have liked to come later. 5. If only he had written earlier! 6. That would have been the best thing. 7. Had he only come earlier! 8. I wish it were true. 9. I wish I had never seen him. 10. He wished he had told me sooner. 11. I wish I had worked better. 12. The foreigner spoke German as if he had been a German. 13. He behaved as if he were alone in the room. 14. It looks as if it is going (*109(b)vi*) to rain. 15. She looks as if she is tired. 16. It was as if he had not understood what I had said. 17. He pretended to be asleep. 18. He pretended to be grateful. 19. I feel (*105(b)*) as if something terrible had happened to him. 20. Make yourself (do as if you were) at home. 21. He was too young to be told that. 22. We are too far away to be recognised here.

23. He is too stupid to understand this. 24. This discovery is too important to be ever forgotten. 25. The river was too deep for him to get across.

38 Government of Verbs (115–119)

TRANSLATE INTO GERMAN:

A. (Cf. 5(a)).

1. He gave him the book. 2. He gave it to him. 3. He gave the book to his brother. 4. He sent you the hat. 5. He sent it to you. 6. He sent the suit to your father. 7. He lent her the pen. 8. He lent it to her. 9. He lent the pen to her sister. 10. He brought me the eggs. 11. He brought them to me. 12. He brought the eggs to my mother. 13. He offered them some money. 14. He offered it to them. 15. He offered the money to their cousins. 16. He wrote the letter to me. 17. He showed his poems to me. 18. He passed me the salt. 19. I can recommend you a cheap hotel. 20. His parents promised him a bicycle.

B. 1. He met me in the street two days ago. 2. I told you so (*123*). 3. They accused the young man of the deed. 4. I did not answer him. 5. It was impossible to approach the bridge. 6. That cost me a lot of (much) trouble. 7. The old man ordered me to follow him. 8. The enemy at last succeeded in destroying the bridge. 9. The grandmother told the little child a fairy story every night. 10. To whom does this red pencil belong? – It belongs to me. 11. The guest paid the waiter the bill. 12. He is ashamed of his old car. 13. I cannot promise you anything. 14. I liked (*123*) the play very [much]. 15. A great crowd watched the game. 16. Do what I advise you. 17. He had served his master faithfully. 18. I'll teach you the difference. 19. We were very [much] helped by him. 20. He lent me a large sum of money. 21. She called her husband a fool. 22. You do not need to listen to him. 23. The waiter brought her a cup of coffee and a piece of cake. 24. As we approached the harbour the sea got (*123*) much calmer. 25. I do not want to forbid you [to do] that, but it would be better if you did not do it. 26. [If I were] in your place I should not trust him. 27. I had already informed them of the news. 28. He never forgave me [for] it. 29. She resembles her mother. 30. Pass me the bread, please. 31. The merchant showed the customer his goods. 32. He gave them (a) good advice. 33. Allow me to thank you. 34. We can strongly (very) recommend this wine to you. 35. We sent the poor man a big parcel. 36. He wrote his parents a long letter every week. 37. I was offered a very good job. 38. Give me all you have. 39. He stole my wallet from me. 40. He wished me a good day. 41. He refused me the job. 42. You must never contradict your parents. 43. He succeeded in escaping from the enemy. 44. The little dog ran after its master. 45. Give me back the money I lent you. 46. May I introduce him to you? 47. What did he call out to me? 48. He made me a present of a fountain pen. 49. Her face seems familiar to me. 50. Believe me, it is very easy. 51. We were present at the fête. 52. That would never have occurred to me. 53. He offered me his arm. 54. They threatened him with imprisonment if he would not speak. 55. He entrusted me with a lot of money. 56. We enjoyed (*123*) the lunch very much. 57. That can happen to anybody (*123*: 'any'). 58. Please read us a story. 59. Your new dress suits you well ('gut'). 60. He sold me four chairs and a table.

39 Verbs followed by a Prepositional Object (*120(a)–(j)*)

TRANSLATE INTO GERMAN:

1. He trades in sugar, tea and coffee. 2. What are you thinking of? – I am thinking of the money I lost. 3. We recognised him by his voice. 4. You can rely on my young brother. 5. Most people do not believe in dreams. 6. I insist on an answer. 7. Small boys are usually very much interested in stamps. 8. He is considered to be very rich. 9. We have never doubted your good will. 10. The bill amounted to a large sum of money. 11. You soon get used to the cold. 12. He suffers from a terrible disease. 13. We are hoping for a letter from you. 14. He looks after his employees. 15. We had to wait a long time for the train. 16. He has just this moment (*87(b)vi*) gone past us. 17. Will you please answer my question immediately? 18. We all think him a most stupid man. 19. The huntsmen arrived soon after in the village. 20. He died of a terrible disease. 21. As soon as I saw him I went up to him. 22. I applied to my friend. 23. The bill amounted to £10. 24. I cannot compare myself with him. 25. I no longer remember my grandparents. 26. The noise prevents me from reading. 27. He was mistaken in this point. 28. From which language was this story translated – and by

whom? 29. War turns many men into heroes. 30. He apologised to the master. 31. Many people wanted to get into the train. 32. He spends every night reading. 33. The water has turned to ice. 34. What will become of him? 35. A stranger entered the room. 36. He took me by the hand. 37. His family consisted of his wife and an only son. 38. I thank you very [much] for your great help. 39. We are looking forward to the holidays. 40. That reminds me of my uncle. 41. He has helped me very [much] with the work. 42. What does this refer to? 43. I had to wait an hour and a half for him. 44. Keep an eye on the children. 45. He called my attention to the stranger. 46. He tied the boat to the tree. 47. The Germans invaded Russia. 48. She burst out into tears. 49. It follows from this that he is dead. 50. He nodded his head.

40 Verbs followed by a Prepositional Object $(120(k)-(q), 121)$

TRANSLATE INTO GERMAN:

1. People judge by (the) success. 2. He always smells of tobacco. 3. They were pleased at the news. 4. Some people live on milk and eggs alone. 5. You need not be afraid of the dog. 6. Ebert was elected President of Germany in 1919. 7. He hid from his enemies. 8. I am very surprised at his opinion. 9. It is a question of life and death. 10. I warned you against that dealer long ago. 11. What were you speaking about? – I was speaking about the translation of Goethe's works. 12. We enquired about his wishes. 13. We laughed heartily at his mistake. 14. Our soldiers fled from the enemy. 15. We had to send for the doctor immediately. 16. That depends on you. 17. That depends on what he says. 18. They made him king. 19. He thought a long time over the problem. 20. The poor woman asked me for some money. 21. She was praised for her work. 22. We conversed about everything. 23. I know (123) nothing about music. 24. Beware of the dog. 25. He turned to me and said: 'How old are you?' 26. His slowness lost him his advantage. 27. He contributed much to the success we had. 28. He refused to budge from the spot. 29. The King of England ruled over many peoples. 30. Why should he blame me for my severity? 31. He said he knew nothing about it. 32. He sold the house for £9000. 33. They had to give way to the enemy. 34. I succeeded in convincing him of his error. 35. I must look after the children. 36. It looks like rain. 37. What do such people

live on? 38. Let this (5(a)ii) serve as a warning to you. 39. He ought not to have laughed at them. 40. I need time and money for that. 41. He does not think of visiting us. 42. He is looking forward to our visiting him. 43. He spoke of how he had made his great discovery. 44. I recognised him by the way he walked. 45. He complained of my not having replied to his letter. 46. He insists on your coming. 47. He is glad I can come. 48. I rely on your sending me the money by next Tuesday. 49. I don't doubt that you will pass (123) the examination. 50. I am surprised you did not come.

41 Translation of English Verbal Forms in -ing (122)

TRANSLATE INTO GERMAN:

1. Having read the newspaper I went to bed. 2. Having read the newspaper I go to bed. 3. Having no more friends in Berlin he went back to the village where he was born. 4. The man crossing the road did not notice the car and was run over. 5. Saying that, he left me. 6. She has a fine voice; I hear her singing every day. 7. Getting out of the train she fell and broke her (13(h)) leg. 8. Having worked all day he felt tired. 9. A boy riding a bicycle can go ('sein') faster than a man riding a horse. 10. I intended going (123) on at least one excursion before returning to England. 11. Without undressing I lay down on the bed and fell asleep. 12. He must have knocked [at the door] without our hearing it. 13. I always read whilst getting (123) up. 14. Eating and drinking keeps body ('Leib') and soul together. 15. I am very fond of dancing. 16. He succeeded in reaching the top of the mountain although the snow was very deep. 17. As he was very ill he stayed in bed all day, not getting up till the evening. 18. Having had very little to eat he still felt hungry. 19. They came running up to me. 20. Instead of saying nothing he shouted in a loud voice that the enemy was near. 21. Instead of my writing this letter why don't you do ('tun') it? 22. The cooking of vegetables is a great art. 23. It was dark, but I could feel the strange object lying on the table. 24. I saw him sitting at the window of his study. 25. I hate having to go out in the evening. 26. By shouting like that ('so') you merely frighten the child. 27. I had seen them coming and had hidden behind (D) a tree. 28. He went past me without seeing me. 29. He remained standing there for half an hour. 30. I prefer doing nothing.

Section Three

English Prose Passages for Translation into German

A. Annotated Passages

1 Our family

We are a small family consisting[1] only of father, mother, Fred and me. We have a small flat in Berlin. We have been living[2] in Berlin[3] for several years now[2]. But I was not born[4] in Berlin. I was born in Hamburg. We had to move to[5] Berlin because my father was offered[6] a better job there. Although our flat is quite small it is very comfortable. We live quite near one[7] of the stations of the Underground Railway and so[8] it does not take[8] us long to get[8] to[9] the centre of the town. Of course we never spend[8] July[10] in Berlin. It is much too hot at that time[8] of the year. We usually spend the whole of[11] July at the seaside[12].

[1] *122(h)* and *120(e)*. [2] Tense? *94(c)*. [3] Word order? *5(b)i*. [4] *53*. [5] *86(a)vii*. [6] Care! *110(h)* and *116*. [7] *74*. [8] *123*. [9] *87(b)v*. [10] *13(f)*. [11] *83(c)*. [12] *87(b)ii*.

2 A fine afternoon

As[1] it was very fine yesterday afternoon[2] we decided to hire a boat and go[3] down[4] the river. About[3] two miles below[5] the bridge there is[6] a pretty little island on which there is[6] a restaurant. When[1] we got[3] to the island we got[3] out of the boat and went to the restaurant. There was[7] a great crowd of people[8] eating[9] and drinking[9] there; but we succeeded[10] in finding an empty[11] table under a shady tree. When[1] the waiter came mother ordered[3] a glass of[8] milk for Fred and tea and cakes for us. It was very pleasant sitting[12] there in the open[13].

[1] *8*. [2] *5(b)iv*. [3] *123*. [4] *43(a)ii* and *102(b)*, note 2. [5] *85*. [6] Avoid *sein*; see *123*, 'be'. [7] *56(f)*. [8] *30(b)*. [9] *122(h)*. [10] *105(b)*. [11] Say 'free'. [12] *122(d)*. [13] *87(b)vi*.

Als - action in the past

183

3 We go to the theatre

Aunt Martha stayed for[1] a few days[1] with[2] us last month[3]. The night before she went away[4] she took[5] us to the theatre. I had never been to the theatre before[5] and so[5] I was very excited. Aunt Martha had booked[6] seats in the upper circle. We arrived of course much too early, for aunt hates being[7] late[5]. Still[5], there was[8] plenty to see before[5] the play began. At last the lights went out and the curtain went up[9]. I stood up in order to see better but somebody sitting[10] behind me told me in a loud voice[11] to sit down[12]. As a matter of fact[13] I could see just as well sitting down[14]. I enjoyed[5] the play very much, though some of the speeches were rather long.

[1] *27(b)* and *5(b)i* and *ii.* [2] *86(a)iii.* [3] *27(c).* [4] Say 'On the evening before her departure', *87(b)ii* and *123*: 'before'. [5] *123.* [6] Say 'ordered', *123.* [7] *122(d).* [8] *123*: 'be'. [9] *43(a)iii.* [10] *122(h).* [11] *14(d).* [12] *112(c).* [13] Say 'indeed', *13(j).* [14] *122(b).*

4 Our classroom

In my class there[1] are thirty boys. The classroom is quite big. There are many beautiful[2] pictures on the walls. In[3] summer it is very warm in our classroom, but in winter it is very cold in spite of the fact that we have central heating. We have desks but the master[4] sits[4] at[5] a table. Not all our[6] masters, however, sit at the table. Some stand in front of[5] the class, some walk up and down between[5] the desks, one[7] of them even[4] nearly always sits[4] down on[5] a boy's desk. Some masters like[4] fresh air. Then[4] all the windows, sometimes the door too, have to be opened[8] even[4] if it is snowing outside. Others on the other hand[9] do not like fresh air at all[10]. Then[4] all the windows have to be shut.

[1] *56(f)* and note 1. [2] *32(e).* [3] *13(f).* [4] *123.* [5] Case? *87(a).* [6] *32(f).* [7] *74.* [8] *110(a).* [9] *56(e)*, note 2; word order as in English. [10] *42.*

5 An invitation

Yesterday morning[1] I got[2] a letter from my uncle. He invited me to spend[2] a fortnight[1] with[3] him. I was of course very pleased, for he has a farm in[4] the country and I hate spending[5] my holiday in town[6]. My[7] parents were very pleased too. They say I make too much noise and will be glad to get rid[8] of me. They know[2] too that I shall enjoy[2] myself very much at my uncle's[3]. My uncle has a son who is a little older than I am[9]. His name is George, and he and I are good friends. George is not my only[10] cousin, for uncle has two other[11] children: Robert, who is twelve years old, and Mary, who is two years younger. I am very much looking forward[12] to the holidays.

[1] 54. [2] 123. [3] 86(a)iii. [4] 87(b)iv. [5] 122(d). [6] 13(j). [7] Say 'the'. [8] 102(b) and note 2. [9] Word order? 38(d)ii. [10] 49(e). [11] 46(d). [12] 120(c).

6 The stranger

Last night[1] I answered[2] my uncle's invitation. After[3] I had written the letter I put[3] it in an envelope on which[4] I had already written my uncle's name and address. Then I asked[3] my father for a stamp, which I stuck on[5] the envelope, and took[3] the letter to the nearest letterbox. As[6] I was going home[7] a stranger came[2] up to me and asked[3] me the way to[8] the station. He looked[3] very excited and seemed to be in a great hurry[9], for as soon as I had told him the way he dashed off[10] as fast as he could. This morning[1] we read in the paper that Mr Smith's house had been burgled[11] last night about[3] six o'clock. I wonder[12] whether it was[13] the same man!

[1] 54. [2] 120(c). [3] 123. [4] 63(b). [5] Case? 87(a). [6] 8. [7] 86(a)vii. [8] 86(a)x. [9] 14(d). [10] 102(b). [11] Say 'at Mr Smith's had been burgled', 110(a) and (f) and 112(a). [12] Say 'I should like to know,' 123: 'know'. [13] Indicative.

7 An illness

Last week[1] I fell[2] ill[3] quite suddenly. I woke[4] up one morning[5] with a sore throat. When I spoke to[6] mother about it[6] she told me to stay[7] in bed[8] and then[9] sent[10] for the doctor. He came an hour later and examined me thoroughly. He said that it was[11] nothing serious[12] but added that I should have[11] to stay in bed for a day or two. He sent me[13] some[14] medicine which I had to take[4] three times[4] a day[15] after[4] meals. It tasted very bitter and I did not like[4] it at all. After[4] three days I was allowed[16] to get[4] up again. It was very dull having to stay in bed all day[17]. Of course the weather was marvellous while I was ill and of course as soon as I had recovered[18] it began to rain.

[1] 27(c). [2] Say 'became'. [3] Place after 'quite suddenly'. [4] 123. [5] 28(b). [6] 120(j), 120(l) and 56(e). [7] 112(c). [8] 13(j). [9] 2. [10] 120(k). [11] 112(a). [12] Say 'dangerous', 35. [13] Case? 29(a) and 5(a). [14] 14(c). [15] 87(b)ii. [16] 109(b)i. [17] 27(b) and 5(b)i. [18] 104.

8 The departure

At last the holidays had come. Mother had packed my things[1] in my bag the night before[2] so that[3] all was ready. I was to[4] take[1] the 10.40 train[5]; I should have to[6] change[1] at Altdorf, but since[3] I had made the journey before[1] mother was not at all afraid. She knew too that uncle would be waiting for[7] me at Neuhausen with the car.

At a quarter past ten I left[1] the house with mother. She bought my ticket for me[8] and we went through the barrier on to the platform. At 10.38 the train arrived. Just[1] at that moment[9] I remembered[10] that I had left[1] uncle's present lying[11] on the table in the sitting-room. 'I'll[12] send it to you[13] by post[14],' said mother, 'and you can give it to him tomorrow. Do hurry up[15] or else[16] you will lose[1] the train.' I got[1] into the train and just[1] had time to say goodbye to mother before[1] the train started[1].

[1] 123. [2] 54. [3] 8. [4] 109(b)v. [5] Say 'the train at 10.40'. [6] 109(b)iv. [7] 120(c). [8] 29(b). [9] 87(b)vi. [10] 121. [11] 122(c). [12] 94(d). [13] 5(a)ii and 56(a). [14] 86(a)vi. [15] 104 and 107(f). [16] 9.

9 In the country

My uncle's farm is right[1] in the country. It[2] is a quarter of an hour by car[3] from the station[4]. There are other farms near by[5], some bigger, some smaller than my uncle's[6]. Uncle has a lot of black and white[7] cows and a few fat pigs; and of course chickens run about[8] everywhere. Behind the house there is a little wood. If we want to swim we have to go through the little wood till we come to a little lake. In summer the water is usually quite warm. We often have a bathe twice a day in[9] fine weather. My cousin George can swim like a fish but his younger brother Robert cannot swim yet. In the morning George, Robert and I help uncle in[10] the fields while[11] Mary helps in the kitchen. In the afternoon we are allowed to do what we like[12]. We sometimes go[12] for long walks through the woods and meadows. When it is very hot we just[12] lie[12] about[13] in the sun.

[1] *42.* [2] *56(b).* [3] *86(a)vi.* [4] Add 'distant'. [5] *87(b)vi.* [6] *69.* [7] Say 'many black-white', *32(e).* [8] *43(b)ii.* [9] *86(a)iii.* [10] *87(b)iv.* [11] *8.* [12] *123.* [13] Omit.

10 A friend is expected

John woke[1] late the next morning[2], for his mother had forgotten to wake[1] him. He jumped out of bed[3], ran to the bathroom, washed[4] quickly and hurried back to his bedroom. In three minutes he had dressed[4] and was running downstairs[5]. Why was he in such a great hurry[6]? He had promised to meet[7] his friend at[7] the station at a quarter to nine[8]. It was a quarter past eight already and it was a quarter of an hour to the[9] station, so that[10] he had no time to lose. Breakfast[11] was waiting for[12] him on the table. He greeted his mother, sat[1] down at the table and ate quickly. At half past eight he left[1] the house and reached the station just[1] before[1] his friend's train arrived.

[1] *123.* [2] *54.* [3] *13(j).* [4] *104.* [5] *43(a)ii* and *27(d).* [6] *14(d).* [7] Say 'fetch from', *102(b).* [8] *5(b)i* and *51.* [9] Say *bis zum.* [10] *8.* [11] *13(f).* [12] *120(c).*

11 Plans for the future

John's friend, whose names was Charles, lived in Hanover and John had invited him to spend three weeks with him in the country. John had come to the station to meet[1] him. Whilst[2] John was waiting for the train he made all sorts of[3] plans. He and his friend would[4] go[5] for long walks through the fields and meadows and woods near his home. They would[4] go[5] on at least[6] one excursion into the mountains which were not very far away, and every day[7] when[2] it was[8] fine they would[4] bathe in the river which was quite near. While[2] John was making all these plans the train arrived. Many people got[5] out of the train which then[5] went[9] off again. But there was[10] no sign of Charles there. He must[11] have lost[5] the train.

[1] *102(b).* [2] *8.* [3] *49(d).* [4] *99.* [5] *123.* [6] *40(c).* [7] *27(c).* [8] Indicative. [9] *123*: 'go'. [10] *123*: 'be'. [11] *109(b)iv.*

12 Berlin

A. Do you know[1] Berlin?

B. No, I have never been there[2]. I always intended to go there[2] when I was in Germany two years ago[3] but for[4] some[5] reason or other[5] I was never able to.

 A. How would[6] it be if you came[6] to Berlin this Easter[7]? Berlin is very pleasant at[8] Easter. The theatres are still open and sometimes there are[9] very fine concerts.

B. I should like[1] to go there[2] but I only get[1] three days' holiday at[7] Easter. But I could[10] go there[2] next summer.

A. I should not advise[11] you to come to Berlin in summer. Berlin is terribly hot then[1]. Everybody who can goes either[12] to the country[13] or[12] to the seaside[14]. Besides[15], we shall not be in Berlin then[1]. We are going to[14] the North Sea. Father has bought a little house on one[16] of the islands.

[1] *123*. [2] *43(a)i*. [3] *87(b)ix*. [4] *86(a)i*. [5] *124(d)*. [6] *113(b)*. [7] *22*, footnote 2. [8] *86(b)x*. [9] *56(f)*. [10] *109(b)ii*. [11] *116*. [12] *10*. [13] *87(b)iii*. [14] *87(b)i*. [15] *9*. [16] *74*.

13 The treasure

A peasant who was at the point of death[1] called[2] his sons to his bed and said[3], 'My children, after[2] me you[4] will[5] get[2] the field which my father possessed. Look[2] well and you will find a treasure there.' After[2] the old man's death his sons dug everywhere in the field but they found no sign of[6] the treasure. They found neither[7] gold nor[7] silver; but as[8] they had dug over the ground so thoroughly they had a very good harvest. Only then[9] did they understand what their father had meant[10]. Henceforth[9] they dug out[11] more and more[12] of[6] this treasure.

[1] *29(d)*. [2] *123*. [3] *125(b)* and *(c)*. [4] *56(a)*. [5] *94(d)*. [6] *86(a)ix*. [7] *10*. [8] *8*. [9] *41*. [10] Say 'had wanted to say', *3(a)*. [11] *43(a)ii*. [12] *38(d)ii*.

14 Stupid thieves

An old man lived in a little house. He was so poor that he did not even[1] have a bed but[2] had to[3] sleep on straw. In the room there were only[1] two chairs and an old table. One evening[4] he was very tired and went to bed early. He soon fell asleep. At midnight[5] two thieves broke[6] into the house in order to steal something. It was very dark and they did not have a light. One of them knocked over[7] a chair. The noise woke[1] the poor man. He saw the thieves and said[8], 'You are very stupid. You hope to find something here at nighttime[4] and I can't find anything here in the daytime[9].'

[1] *123.* [2] *8.* [3] *109(b)iv.* [4] *28(b).* [5] *51.* [6] *120(h).* [7] *102(c)ii.* [8] *125(b)* and (c). [9] *87(b)ii.*

15 A strange prescription

One day[1] a man from a distant farm stopped[2] his cart in front of a chemist's shop. Only with great difficulty did he manage to lift out of the cart a big heavy door which he then took[2] into the shop. The chemist opened his[3] eyes wide and said, 'Why[4], what are you doing here, my friend, with your door? The carpenter lives opposite the inn.' The man said that the doctor had[5] visited his wife who was[5] ill and had[6] wanted to prescribe her some medicine. 'As[7] there[8] was no pen, ink or paper in the house,' he continued[9], 'but[7] only a piece of[10] chalk, the doctor wrote the prescription on the door. Will you be so good as[11] to make me[12] up[11] the medicine?'

[1] *28(b).* [2] *123.* [3] *13(g).* [4] *124(b).* [5] *112(a).* [6] *3(a).* [7] *8.* [8] *56(f)*, note 1. [9] *2* [10] *30(b).* [11] Omit. [12] *29(b).*

16 Boring visitors

One day a famous actor paid[1] a visit to Prince[2] Bismarck. During their conversation he asked Bismarck how he managed to get rid of boring visitors so quickly. Bismarck replied, 'That is simpler than you think. My wife knows[3] all the people whose visits bore me[4]. Whenever[5] she learns[3] that one of these people is with[6] me she comes into the room after a certain time and calls[3] me out[7] under some[8] pretext or another[8].'

Hardly had Bismarck said this when[5] the door opened[9] and Bismarck's wife looked[3] in[7] saying[10], 'Dear Otto! It is high time that you[11] took[12] your medicine; you should have done[13] so[3] an hour ago[14].'

¹ Say 'made' and see *5(a)i*. ² Leave undeclined. ³ *123*. ⁴ *29(d)*. ⁵ *8*.
⁶ *86(a)iii*. ⁷ *43(a)ii*. ⁸ *124(d)*. ⁹ *104*. ¹⁰ *122(i)*. ¹¹ *56(a)*. ¹² *94(e)* and *123*.
¹³ *109(b)v*. ¹⁴ *87(b)ix*.

17 Good advice

A young man once came to Richard Strauss, the famous composer¹, to
play² to him a piece of music he had just³ written. Strauss listened
attentively. When the young man had finished³ the piece he asked
Strauss what he thought³ of it⁴. Without hesitating⁵ a moment Strauss
replied, 'My dear friend, I advise you not to write music any more in
future but to do something quite different⁶.'

Feeling⁷ beside⁸ himself with anger, the young man packed his
things³ together and left³ the room without saying⁵ another⁹ word.
Then Strauss ran¹⁰ after him and added¹¹, 'If I may give you another⁹
piece⁷ of⁷ advice, don't pay any heed¹² to what¹³ I have just³ said. I was
once told¹⁴ exactly the same thing¹⁵.'

¹ *30(a)*. ² *116*. ³ *123*. ⁴ *56(e)*. ⁵ *122(d)*. ⁶ *80*. ⁷ Omit. ⁸ *87(a)*. ⁹ *46(d)*.
¹⁰ *115*. ¹¹ *102(b)*. ¹² *120(c)*. ¹³ *64(d)*. ¹⁴ *110(i)*. ¹⁵ *70*.

18 A dull life

The waiter was looking out¹ of the dining-room window. He could see
from there² the little railway station. He knew that the train had³
arrived, for it was midday already. Life⁴ was very dull in this old inn
and he did⁵ so⁶ hope⁵ that one day some⁷ interesting stranger would
come. Every day he looked out of the window at this time⁸ in the hope
of seeing⁹ some⁷ new face, but rarely was¹⁰ this hope fulfilled. But who
was that approaching¹¹ the inn? That was somebody¹² he did not
know⁸. It was a young man with a heavy rucksack on his¹³ back and a
stout stick in his¹³ hand. He did not look⁸ as if¹⁴ he had much money.
Even⁸ if he were to come¹⁵ into the inn he would probably only⁸ want a
glass of beer and some¹⁶ bread and cheese. Still⁸, it might be interesting
talking⁹ to¹⁷ him. Anyhow¹⁸, he was better than nobody.

¹ *43(a)ii*. ² Add 'out'. ³ *112(d)ii*. ⁴ *13(b)*. ⁵ *95(a)*. ⁶ Add 'very'. ⁷ *124(d)*.
⁸ *123*. ⁹ *122(d)*. ¹⁰ *110(g)*. ¹¹ *115* and *122(h)*. ¹² *76* and *63(a)iii*. ¹³ *13(g)*.
¹⁴ *114(b)iii*. ¹⁵ *113(b)*. ¹⁶ *14(c)*. ¹⁷ *120(j)*. ¹⁸ *87(b)iii*.

19 Unpleasant consequences

Last night I had a lot of homework, more than usual even[1]. Soon after I had got home Robert arrived; Robert is a great friend of mine[2]. He has left[1] school, so[1] he does not need to do any homework. Robert wanted to know if I would go to[3] the cinema with him. I told him I had[4] a lot of work[1] to do still[1]. 'You[5] could[6] do it tomorrow before going[7] to school[8],' said Robert. 'It's supposed[9] to be a very good film.' 'All right[10],' I said, 'I'll[11] come. Just[1] one moment[12].' I quickly put[1] on my[13] raincoat and told mother where[14] we were going and then we left the house. I liked[1] the film very much but I got[1] home rather late.

This morning I was so tired that it was just[1] impossible to get[1] up any[15] earlier than usual. The consequence[16] was that I had no time to finish[1] my homework before school began and – well,[17] you can imagine[18] the rest[1].

[1] *123*. [2] *57(d)*, note. [3] *87(b)v*. [4] *112(a)*, note. [5] *56(a)*. [6] *109(b)ii*. [7] *122(f)*. [8] *13(j)*. [9] *109(b)v*. [10] *42*. [11] *94(d)*. [12] *27(b)*. [13] *13(g)*. [14] *44*. [15] Omit. [16] Add 'of it' and see *56(e)*. [17] *41*. [18] *104*.

20 The Radio

Some friends of ours[1] came to us to dinner[2] a few days ago. We wanted them to hear[3] our new radio, but when I turned[4] it on it made a most[5] unpleasant noise. I was very unhappy, for I am very proud of[6] my radio. I said I would send[7] for the dealer the next day to put the radio right[8] again. 'Why spend[9] money when we can put the radio right[8] ourselves[10]?' said my friend. Now[9], I don't know[11] anything about radios, but my friend, who sets up[12] to be an engineer, seemed to know what to do[13]. He took[9] out[14] one part after the other and put[4] them together again and after about[9] two hours he said he thought the radio was[15] all right[16] again. So[9] we turned on the radio again, but this time[9] there was nothing to be heard[17] at all.

When the dealer came the next morning he said that somebody who did not know anything about radios must[18] have been playing with it[19]. He put the radio right[8] in a quarter of an hour[20] and a week later I got[9] a bill for[21] two pounds[22].

[1] *57(d)*, note. [2] *13(f)*. [3] *114(b)i*. [4] *102(b)*. [5] *38(d)iv*. [6] *87(b)iii*. [7] *109(b)vii* or *120(k)*. [8] *87(b)v*. [9] *123*. [10] *72*. [11] *120(n)*. [12] *109(b)vi*. [13] *109(b)v*.

[14] *43(a)ii*. [15] *112(d)iii*. [16] *87(b)vi*. [17] *110(e)*. [18] *109(b)iv* and *112(a)*. [19] *56(e)*. [20] *49(a)*, note. [21] *87(b)vii*. [22] *50*.

21 A quick decision

A young man who wanted to go to Berlin came into a railway compartment and found all the seats taken[1] except one[2] on which an elderly[3] gentleman had put[1] his suitcase. The young man asked[1] the gentleman if he might[4] put[1] the case in[5] the rack. But the gentleman said that it[6] belonged to a friend of his who would come in a few minutes.

The young man was just going[7] to leave the compartment when the train started[1] moving. 'Your friend has lost[1] his train, but he must[8] not[9] lose[1] his luggage as well[9],' he said. Thereupon[10] he took the case, threw it[6] out[11] of the window on to the platform and calmly sat[1] down.

[1] *123*. [2] *86(a)ii*. [3] *38(d)iv*, note. [4] *109(b)i* and *112(b)*. [5] *87(b)v*. [6] *56(b)*. [7] *109(b)vi*. [8] *109(b)i*. [9] Say *nicht auch noch* and place before 'his luggage'. [10] *56(e)*, note 2. [11] *43(a)ii*, note.

22 Journey's end

It was still raining when the train stopped[1]. Peter opened the window and looked[1] out[2] to see where he was. He could not see the name of the station and, not being able[3] to understand what the other passengers were saying, he did not at first know what he ought to do. He had never been abroad[4] before and he was beginning to find out that you cannot really learn to speak foreign languages in[5] school. Soon he found that every one except himself had left[1] the compartment and he was alone. He guessed he must[6] have come to the end of his journey, got[1] out, gave his ticket to the official at the barrier and then went into[7] the street. The street in which he found himself was long and narrow with tall grey buildings on either[8] side. He felt[1] rather hungry and although he had very little German money in his pocket he went into the café opposite the station and ordered[1] two boiled eggs and a cup of coffee – fortunately the waiter understood English. He ate and drank very slowly and wondered[9] what he should say if he could[10] not pay the bill.

¹ *123*. ² *43(a)ii*. ³ *122(f)*. ⁴ *87(b)vi*. ⁵ *87(b)iv*. ⁶ *112(d)iii*. ⁷ *87(b)iii*.
⁸ *46(i)*. ⁹ Say 'asked himself'. ¹⁰ *113(b)*.

23 Burglars

As usual their parents had sent them to bed at nine o'clock; but the
moon was shining so brightly that the boys did not want to sleep yet.
They were both sitting at the open window. Down below them[1] they
could see the garden distinctly. Suddenly Edward said, 'Look! Do you
see that shadow moving[2] there?' Peter saw it too. 'It's a burglar,' he
said. 'I hope[3] so,' answered Edward. 'Let's[4] watch.'

They saw the shadow move[2] again and then they caught[5] sight of a
man. A moment later he had disappeared behind a tree[6]. 'That's
certainly a burglar,' said Edward. 'We must go downstairs[7] and tell[8]
father.' Without losing[9] a moment they went downstairs and opened the
door of the sitting-room. 'Father, there's a burglar outside[7] in the
garden,' said Peter. 'Nonsense! Go[10] back to bed at once. Why[11], it's
half past nine already.' 'But father, it's true[12], we saw him from our
window,' said Edward. 'Don't[12] be so silly,' their father replied. 'Can't
you recognise Charles when you see him? I told him to bring in the
chair[13] I had left in the garden.'

¹ *58*. ² *104* and *122(c)*. ³ *42*. ⁴ *107(e)*. ⁵ *102(a)*. ⁶ Dative. ⁷ *43(a)i*. ⁸ Add
'it'. ⁹ *122(d)*. ¹⁰ *56(a)* and *107(c)*. ¹¹ *124(e)*. ¹² *124(c)*. ¹³ *63(a)iii*.

24 A clever judge

A farmer bought a horse at[1] the market one day for two hundred
marks. He gave the dealer two hundred-mark notes, took the horse and
left the town. Scarcely had he gone a quarter of a mile[2] when[3] he was
overtaken[4] by a policeman who ordered[5] him to ride back to[6] the town
and appear before the judge. Here to his surprise he found the dealer.
The judge said to him, 'This man accuses you of having[7] stolen the
horse.' The farmer answered that he had paid two hundred-mark notes
for the horse. 'That is not true,' said the dealer, 'he is lying[5].' 'Take
out[8] your wallets and show me your money,' said the judge. Both men
put[5] their wallets on the table. In the farmer's wallet there[9] were only

fifty marks; in the dealer's two hundred-mark notes. The judge examined the notes closely[10], shook his[11] head and said, 'False! why[12], you can go[13] to[14] prison for that[15].' 'If anyone is to[16] go to prison,' said the dealer, 'then[17] it is the farmer. I got[5,12] the two hundred-mark notes from him.' 'What for[18]?' asked the judge. 'Why[19], for the horse – but since[3] they are false . . .' 'They are not false,' interrupted the judge; 'I merely wanted to know whether you had[20] received your money.'

[1] *87(b)iv*. [2] *49(a)*, note. [3] *8*. [4] *102(b)*. [5] *123*. [6] *87(b)v*. [7] *122(d)*. [8] *43(a)ii*. [9] *56(f)*, note 1. [10] Say 'exactly'. [11] *13(g)*. [12] *124(e)*. [13] Say 'come'. [14] Say 'into the' and see *87(a)*, note. [15] *56(e)*. [16] *109(b)v*. [17] *113(d)*. [18] *62* and *124(b)*. [19] *41*. [20] Indicative.

25 Mrs Brown

As[1] I was going home yesterday I met my neighbour[2], Mrs Brown. I hate[3] meeting her in the street, for she talks too much. It was already late and I did not want to keep[4] my husband waiting. But unfortunately Mrs Brown was not in a hurry[5] herself. She had just had news from her son who lives abroad[6]. Every[7] six months he writes her a letter and then Mrs Brown talks for hours[8]. I tried to explain to her that it was[9] already late, that my husband was[9] probably home already and getting[9] angrier and angrier. It was all in vain. Fortunately, however, I saw Mrs Smith coming[10] towards us. Her husband does not come home to lunch[11] and so[12] she has plenty of time. As soon as Mrs Smith had greeted us I said 'Goodbye[13], I must really go now,' and left[12] them both. I managed[14] to get[12] home just[12] before[12] my husband, who fortunately was ten minutes late[12]. When I went out again at half past two in the afternoon[15] to buy something I saw in the distance Mrs Brown and Mrs Smith still talking[16] with one another.

[1] *8*. [2] *19(c)ii*. [3] *122(d)*. [4] *109(b)vii*. [5] *14(d)*. [6] *87(b)vi*. [7] *79*. [8] *41*. [9] *112(d)*. [10] *122(c)* and *120(c)*. [11] *13(f)*. [12] *123*. [13] *125(d)*. [14] *105(b)*. [15] *5(b)ii* and *54*. [16] *122(c)* or *(g)*.

26 The precious stone

Shortly before his death my father tried to sell the precious stone in order to get money for the estate. He found a dealer in Amsterdam who was prepared to make the transaction[1]. The dealer came to Cologne in order to see the precious stone. My father asked[2] more for the stone than the dealer was willing to give for it, so the latter[3] went away without the stone. My father showed[4] him out, first putting[2,5] the stone in the drawer of his desk, which he could not lock since he did not have the key with[6] him[7]. My father was outside for not more than five minutes[8]. When he came back to[9] his room, he opened the drawer. To his astonishment the precious stone had gone[2]. He could not believe[10] his eyes. He opened the other drawers of his desk, looked[2] in the paper-basket, on the desk, on the floor, under the chairs. He looked[2] everywhere, but the precious stone was nowhere to be found[11]. What was[12] he to do? He did not believe that the police could[13] help him, but he saw no other possibility and so he applied[14] to them.

[1] Say 'business'. [2] *123*. [3] *67*. [4] Say 'accompanied'. [5] *122(f)*. [6] *86(a)iii*.
[7] *58*. [8] *5(b)i*. [9] *87(b)v*. [10] Say 'He did not trust' (*trauen* (D)). [11] *110(e)*.
[12] *109(b)v*. [13] *112(d)*. [14] *120(a)*.

27 Our house in the country

We have been living[1] in the country for three years now[2]. It is much pleasanter living[3] here in the open[4] than in[5] town although it is perhaps not so convenient. We do not go to[6] the theatre as often as before because we get[7] home so late. Father has[8] to go[7] to[6] town every morning[2]. He has to get up half an hour earlier now in order to catch[7] the train. If he loses[7] his train he has to wait a quarter of an hour[9] for[10] the next one[11]; and then of course he arrives late[7] at[4] the office. He does not like[12] arriving late. It sets[13] a bad example, he says. So he prefers[12] to run all[14] the way to[15] the station. Mother goes to town once a[4] week[2] to buy fish. Sometimes I am allowed[16] to go with her[17]. We both[18] went there[19] last week[2]. We left[7] our umbrellas at home because the weather looked[7] so fine and half an hour[9] after[7] we had left[7] the house it began of course to rain. It rained all day long[14] and we were quite wet when we got[7] home.

[1] *94(c)*. [2] *5(b)i*. [3] *122(d)*. [4] *87(b)vi*. [5] *13(j)*. [6] *87(b)v*. [7] *123*. [8] *109(b)iv*.
[9] *49(a)*, note. [10] *120(c)*. [11] *74*, note 2. [12] *122(k)*. [13] Say 'gives'. [14] *83(c)* and
27(b). [15] *86(a)x*. [16] *109(b)i*. [17] Omit 'her'. [18] *46(i)*. [19] *43(a)i*.

28 A letter from [1] England

London, 26th May, 1967[2]

Dear John[3],

I was very glad to have some news from you[4] at last. I was surprised to learn[5] that you had left school and were no longer in Berlin. How do you like[5] being in Hamburg? You probably know[5] that I have been there once too. Three years ago[6] I spent[5] two months there with a very charming family.

I am still at[7] school, but I hope to leave school at the end of this year. If I pass[5] my exam I shall try to get a job in a bank. Was it difficult for you to find your job? Is it an interesting one[8]? How long holidays do you get in[9] summer? I should be very glad if you could come over[10] to England, for I shall not be able to visit you in Germany this year. It really is not very far from Hamburg to England and you could come away with us to[11] the country. We are hoping to spend[5] the summer holidays somewhere[12] in Hampshire. We have some friends there who have a big farm. It would be magnificent if you could come too.

You did not say much about[13] yourself in your letter. Write to me again soon and tell me all that's[14] happened[15] to you since[16] you last[17] wrote. And do[18] try to come this summer.

Mother sends her kindest regards[19].

Yours sincerely[20],

FRED

[1] *86(a)i.* [2] *52.* [3] *125(d).* [4] *56(a)* and note. [5] *123.* [6] *87(b)ix.* [7] *87(b)iv.* [8] *74,* note 2. [9] *13(f).* [10] *43(a)ii.* [11] *87(b)iii.* [12] *43(b)i.* [13] *120(n).* [14] *64(a).* [15] *115.* [16] *8.* [17] *123*: 'time'. [18] *107(f).* [19] *109(b)vii.* [20] Say 'with best greeting'.

29 In the mountains

Although we had gone to bed fairly late the night before[1] we got up very early the following morning[1]. It was still dark as[2] we washed in the ice-cold water that flowed past[3] the little mountain hut. Eric prepared the breakfast which consisted of[4] rolls[5] and butter and hot coffee. A quarter of an hour after breakfast we were ready. Eric, George and I were going to climb[6] the Fernerkogel (*m.*). We intended to reach the top by[7] ten o'clock. We followed[8] the little stream for half an hour till we came to the end of the glacier from[9] which[9] it sprang and then[10] we skirted[11] the glacier. After climbing[12] for three hours we rested for half an hour and ate a second breakfast. The second half[13] of our climb was[14] over snow. On our way[15] we saw a most beautiful[16] lake. How clear and still the water was[17]! We got to the top finally at half past nine. What a[18] marvellous view we had! Not a cloud in[19] the sky. No sign of mist.

[1] 54. [2] 8. [3] 43(a)iii and cf. 120(b). [4] 120(e). [5] 15(c)iv, note. [6] 27(d). [7] 84(a). [8] 115. [9] Say 'where'. [10] 2 and 125(a)iii. [11] Say 'went along', 84(c). [12] 122(f). [13] 49(a), note. [14] Say 'went'. [15] 43(b)ii. [16] One word will translate the English. [17] 44, note. [18] 61, note. [19] 87(b)ii.

30 A letter from Berlin

BERLIN,
3rd June, 1967[1]

Dear Margaret[2],

Many[3] thanks for your kind letter and the invitation for the summer holidays. My parents have given me permission[4] to come. I am particularly glad, for mother is to[5] go to[6] the spa[7] again this year and I should have had[8] to accompany her. That would have been very dull. Please write and tell me when I am to come. Our holidays begin on the 4th July.

Our class is getting[9] smaller and smaller[10]. Grete Müller's parents are moving away[11] from here. Just[12] guess where to[13]! To[14] South America! I should not like[15] to go so far away[11] and leave all my[16] friends behind here.

The day before yesterday[17] Grete celebrated her birthday. The whole class was invited and Grete's brother had also invited a few friends. First of all we had tea in the garden and then we played games with one another[18]. Before we went home we had[19] some ice. It was wonderful; it's a pity[20] you weren't there.

I have still an essay to write. So I must stop[9] for today. Once again, thank you very much for the invitation. I am looking forward[21] to staying[22] with you.

Yours sincerely,
ERIKA

[1] 52. [2] 125(d). [3] 83(c). [4] Add 'the'. [5] 109(b)v. [6] 87(b)v. [7] Bad(n.). [8] 109(b)iv. [9] 123. [10] 38(d)ii. [11] 43(a)iii. [12] 107(f). [13] 44. [14] 86(a)vii. [15] 109(b)iii. [16] 32(f). [17] 54. [18] 59. [19] Say 'got' and see 123. [20] 14(d). [21] 120(c). [22] 121 and 122(d).

31 Snow White and the Dwarfs (i)

When it had got quite dark the masters of the little house[1] came home; they were the seven dwarfs who dug for[2] gold in the mountains. They lit their seven little[1] candles[3] and then they saw that somebody had been in[4], for it was no longer as they had left it. The first one[5] said, 'Who has been sitting in my little chair[1]?' The second said, 'Who has been eating from my little plate[1]?' The third said, 'Who has been eating some[6] of my little loaf[1]?' The fourth said, 'Who has been eating some[6] of my soup?' The fifth said, 'Who has been using my little fork[1]?' The sixth said, 'Who has been cutting with my little knife[1]?' The seventh said, 'Who has been drinking out of my little glass[1]?' Then the first one looked[7] round and saw that somebody had been sleeping in his little bed! The others came running[8] and cried, 'Somebody has been lying in my little[1] bed too.' But the seventh, when he looked[9] at his little bed, caught[9] sight of Snow White, who lay in it and slept. Then he called[9] the others who came running[8] up to him to look[9] at the child. But they did not wake[9] her up, for she looked[9] so beautiful, and so the seventh dwarf had to sleep with his companions, one hour with each.

[1] Use diminutive form, *17(d)* and *15(c)iv*, note. [2] Say 'after'. [3] Say 'lights'. [4] Add 'it'. [5] *74*, note 2. [6] *14(c)*. [7] *104*. [8] *122(j)*. [9] *123*.

32 Snow White and the Dwarfs (ii)

When it was morning Snow White woke[1] up and when she saw the seven dwarfs she was frightened. But they were friendly and asked[1], 'What is your name[2]?' 'My name is Snow White,' she answered politely. 'How did you get[1] into our house?' the dwarfs continued. Then she told them that her stepmother had[3] ordered[1] the huntsman to kill her, but the huntsman had[3] spared[4] her life and so she had[3] walked[5] all day till she had[3] finally found their little house. The dwarfs said, 'If you will[6] look after[7] the house for us[8], cook, make the beds, wash, sew and knit, and if you will keep[1] everything clean and tidy you can stay with us and you shall[9] lack[10] nothing.' 'Yes,' said Snow White, 'most willingly!' And she stayed with them. She kept[1] the house in order for them[8], in the morning they went into the mountains and looked[1] for gold, in the evening they came back and their food had to be ready. The whole day long the girl was alone; so the good dwarfs warned her, saying[11], 'Beware[12] of your stepmother, she will soon know that you are here; see[13] that you don't let anybody in[14].'

[1] 123. [2] 123: 'call'. [3] 112(a). [4] Say 'presented to her', 116. [5] Say 'run'. [6] 98(b), note. [7] Say 'lead'. [8] 29(b). [9] 109(b)v. [10] 105(b). [11] 122(i). [12] 120(o). [13] 107(f). [14] 43(a)ii.

33 Sleeping Beauty

But at[1] the moment when[2] she felt[3] the prick she fell down on the bed which stood there and lay in a deep sleep. And this sleep spread over[4] the whole castle, the King and the Queen who had just come home and entered the hall began to fall asleep and all their people with them. The horses in the stables, the dogs in the yard, the birds on the roof, the flies on the wall also slept, and even[3] the fire became still and fell asleep. But all around[5] the castle a thorn hedge began to grow which every year got[3] higher, until nothing could be seen of the castle any more. But people began to talk about Sleeping Beauty, as the King's daughter was called, and so from time to time princes came and tried to force their way[6] through the thorn hedge into the castle, but for a hundred[7] years none[8] succeeded[9] in doing so[3]. At last the day had come when[10] Sleeping Beauty was destined[11] to wake up again. And when the Prince approached[12] the thorn hedge it turned[13] immediately into lovely big flowers through which[14] he got[3] without difficulty.

[1] 87(b)vi. [2] 8. [3] 123. [4] 87(a). [5] 43(b)ii, note. [6] Say 'penetrate', 93(f). [7] 45 and 27(b). [8] 75. [9] 105(b). [10] Say 'on (87(b)ii) which', or see 66. [11] 109(b)v. [12] 115. [13] 120(h). [14] 63(b).

34 Hansel and Gretel (i)

When they had come to the middle of the forest their father told[1] the children to gather wood. 'I will make you a fire,' he said, 'so that[2] you won't[3] be cold[4].' Hansel and Gretel gathered together some wood. Their father kindled[5] it and when the flame burnt up high his wife said, 'Now, you children, lie[6] down by the fire and rest while we go into the forest and chop[7] wood. When we have finished[6] we shall come back and fetch[5] you.'

Hansel and Gretel sat[6] round the fire and when it was noon each ate his little piece[8] of bread. And because they could hear the blows of an axe they thought their father was[9] near[10]. But it was not the axe but a bough which he had tied[11] to a tree and which the wind blew[12] to and fro[13]. And when they had sat thus for a long time[6] their eyes closed from[14] weariness and they fell fast[15] asleep. When they woke[6] up at last it was quite dark. Gretel began to weep, saying[16], 'How[17] shall[18] we get[6] out of the wood?' But Hansel tried to console her by saying[19], 'Wait a little till the moon has risen, then we will find the way all right[20].'

[1] *112(c)*. [2] *8*. [3] *94(d)*. [4] Say 'freeze'. [5] *102(b)*. [6] *123*. [7] *93(l)*. [8] *15(c)iv*, and note. [9] *112(d)*. [10] *87(b)vi*. [11] *120(a)*. [12] Say 'knocked'. [13] *43(a)ii*, note. [14] *87(b)ix*. [15] Say 'firmly'. [16] *122(i)*. [17] *124(b)*. [18] *109(b)v*. [19] *122(e)*. [20] *124(g)*.

35 Hansel and Gretel (ii)

When it was noon they saw a beautiful snow-white bird sitting[1] upon a bough which sang so sweetly that they stopped[2] and listened[3] to it. When it had finished[2] it flew along in front[4] of them and they followed[3] it until they came to[5] a little house upon the roof of which[6] it perched[7], and when they got[8] close up to it[9] they saw that the little house was made of[10] bread and cakes and that the windows were made of sugar. 'Let's eat[11],' said Hansel. 'I will eat a piece of[12] the roof and you Gretel can eat some[13] of the window.' Hansel reached up[4] and broke off[14] a piece of[12] the roof to try what[15] it tasted like[15] and Gretel went and stood at[16] the window and ate some[9] of it. Then suddenly the door opened[17] and a very old woman came out[4]. Hansel and Gretel were so frightened that they dropped[18] what they held in their[19] hands. But the old woman merely said, 'Ah, you[20] dear children, who has brought you here[21]? Come in[4] and stay with me, no harm will befall[22] you here.' And she took[23] them both[24] by the hand and led them into her little house.

[1] *122(h)*. [2] *123*. [3] *115*. [4] *43(a)ii*. [5] *86(a)x*. [6] *63(a)*. [7] Say 'sat down', *123*. [8] *120(a)*. [9] Omit. [10] *86(a)i*. [11] *107(e)*. [12] *86(a)ix*. [13] *14(c)*. [14] *43(a)iii*. [15] *124(h)*. [16] *87(a)*. [17] Intransitive, see *104*. [18] *109(b)vii*. [19] *13(g)*. [20] *56(a)*. [21] *43(a)i*. [22] Say 'happen'. [23] *120(f)*. [24] *46(i)*.

36 Aladdin and the Lamp

The next moment[1] – he did not know at all[2] how it had happened – he was lying on the sofa at home with[3] his mother who, weeping for[4] happiness and joy, was embracing[5] and kissing him; as he had never come back with the 'uncle' she had thought[6] him dead. Under her care Aladdin recovered[7] again soon and was able to tell all that had happened to him. 'The wretched impostor!' cried his mother. 'And I really thought[6] he was a brother of your dear father! But wait, we will sell the old lamp which he thought[6] so much of and perhaps get a little money for it, if I clean it nicely; for I have no money to buy anything for[8] supper.' She took the lamp in[9] her hand, but scarcely had she begun to rub it when a terrible genie[10] stood before her and called[11] out to her in a voice of thunder[12], 'What do you want[13] of the slave[14] of the lamp, oh mistress[15]? Speak, and I will obey[16].' The poor woman could not utter[17] a word, so Aladdin quickly took the lamp and said to the genie, 'Get[6] us, above all[4], something to eat, for we are very hungry[18].'

[1] 87(b)vi. [2] 42. [3] One word conveys this meaning, 86(a)iii. [4] 87(b)ix. [5] 102(c)i. [6] 123. [7] 104. [8] Say 'to' 13(f). [9] 87(a). [10] Say 'spirit'. [11] 116. [12] Say 'in a thundering voice', 105(a) and 14(d). [13] See 'ask', 123. [14] 18(d). [15] 19(c)ii. [16] 94(d). [17] 102(b). [18] 14(d).

37 Ali Baba and the Forty Thieves[1] (i)

One day[2] when Ali Baba was working as usual in the wood he saw a great cloud of[3] dust in the distance and a number[4] of[3] horsemen coming[5] up to him[6]. Being[7] a very cautious man he drove his asses deeper into the wood and climbed up[8] a tree from which[9] he could see without being[10] seen. Scarcely had he got[11] up[11] when the horsemen stopped[4] close in front of him and got[4] down[12] from their horses. They were robbers, as[13] Ali Baba could easily tell[14] by their wild appearance[15]. Whilst[13] most[16] of them now began to count their booty their captain went up to the mountain and said in a loud voice, 'Open, Sesame,' whereupon[17] the mountain immediately opened and, after the captain and all his men together with their booty had disappeared inside, quickly shut again as if[18] of its own accord[19] behind them. Ali Baba hardly dared move on his tree for[20] fear the robbers might[21] come out again and find him. Finally the mountain opened again, all the robbers came out, but this time with empty hands; and after their captain had cried, 'Shut, Sesame,' the mountain closed. Then the robbers jumped on their horses and rode away.

[1] Say 'robbers'. [2] *28(b)*. [3] *30(b)*. [4] *123*. [5] *122(c)* and *120(c)*. [6] *58*. [7] *122(f)*. [8] Say 'on to', *87(a)*. [9] Add 'out'. [10] *122(d)*. [11] Say 'was' for 'had got', *43(a)i*. [12] Omit. [13] *8*. [14] Say 'recognise', *120(b)*. [15] *20(c)i(β)*. [16] *38(d)iv*, note. [17] *63(b)*, note. [18] *124(h)*. [19] *72*. [20] *86(a)i*. [21] *112(d)iii*.

38 Ali Baba and the Forty Thieves (ii)

When the robbers had disappeared Ali Baba came down from the tree, went and stood in front of the mountain and cried like[1] the captain, 'Open, Sesame,' and behold[2], the rock obeyed[3] him and let him in. To his surprise he did not find a dark cave, as[4] he had expected, but fine, lofty[5], light rooms full of[6] gold and silver and precious stones. Ali Baba lost no time and carried out as much of[7] the gold, which was in bags, as his asses could carry. He then whistled to his asses, put[8] the bags on them and covered the bags with wood so that[4] they could not be seen. When he had done this, he went up to the mountain again and cried, 'Shut, Sesame,' and the rock closed. He then drove his asses to town and as[4] it was already dark he got[8] home without anyone seeing[9] the bags of gold hidden under the wood. Then he shut all the doors and windows of his house, sent the children to bed and showed[10] his wife what he had brought[10] her. 'Now[8] just[11] go[12] and[12] buy yourself[13] something nice[14] with[15] it,' he said.

[1] *124(h)*. [2] Say 'see', singular imperative. [3] *115*. [4] *8*. [5] Say 'high'. [6] *30*. [7] *86(a)ix*. [8] *123*. [9] *122(e)* and say *man*. [10] *116*. [11] *107(f)*. [12] Omit. [13] *29(b)*. [14] *35*. [15] Say 'for'.

39 The Emperor's New Clothes (i)

Many years ago there[1] lived an emperor who thought[2] so much of new clothes that he spent[2] all[3] his money in order to be well dressed. He did not worry[4] about his soldiers, he did not worry[4] about his theatre and he only loved driving[5] about[6] in order to show his new clothes. In the great city in which he lived there[1] arrived one day two impostors, who pretended[7] to be weavers and said that they knew[2] how to weave the most beautiful stuff imaginable[8]. The colours and the pattern, they[6] said[6], were[9] not only unusually beautiful, but the clothes which were[9] sewn from this stuff possessed[9] the wonderful quality that they were[9] invisible to[10] every person who was[9] not fit[11] for his office[12] or who was[9] very, very stupid. 'Why[13], those are just[2] the clothes I want[14],' thought the Emperor, 'if I had them on I could find out which men in my realm are not fit for the office they have, I could distinguish the clever people from the stupid! Yes, the stuff must be woven for me immediately!' And he gave the two impostors a lot of money so that they might begin their work.

[1] 56(f), note 1. [2] 123. [3] 79. [4] 120(m). [5] 122(d) and 123: 'go'. [6] Omit. [7] 114(b)iii. [8] Say 'that one could imagine', 104. [9] Mood? [10] Say 'for'. [11] 120(q). [12] 20(b)ii. [13] 124(e). [14] Say 'need'.

40 The Emperor's New Clothes (ii)

They set[1] up[2] two looms and pretended[3] to work, but they had nothing at all on the loom. They demanded more money which they put[4] into their own pockets and worked at the empty looms till late at night[5].

'I *should*[6] like to know how far they have got[7] with the stuff!' thought the Emperor. But he felt[8] quite queer[9] when he thought[10] that he[11] who was[12] stupid or unfit[12] for his office wouldn't[12] be able to see it. To be sure[13] he believed that he had[12] nothing to fear for himself but he wanted nevertheless[13] to send somebody else first to see how matters[14] stood[12]. All the people in the whole town knew what special quality the stuff possessed and all wanted to see how bad or how stupid their neighbour was[12].

'I will[15] send my honest old minister to the weavers!' thought the Emperor.' He can tell best[16] what[17] the stuff is like[17], for he is clever and nobody is better fitted for his office than he.'

The good old minister went into the room where the two impostors sat and worked at the empty looms. 'Gracious me[18]!' thought the old minister and opened his eyes wide, 'why[19], I cannot see anything.' But he did not say so[4].

[1] Say 'put', 123. [2] 43(a)iii. [3] 114(b)iii. [4] 123. [5] 87(b)v. [6] 124(c). [7] Say 'are'. [8] 105(b). [9] Say 'peculiar'. [10] 120(a) and 121. [11] 71. [12] 112(d). [13] 9. [14] Say 'it' and add 'with it'. [15] 98(b), note. [16] 40(a). [17] 124(h). [18] Say 'thou dear God'. [19] 124(e).

41 Gulliver in Lilliput

Early next day I came out of my house and looked about me. The country was like a garden. The fields were about forty feet square[1]. The tallest trees seemed to be about seven feet[1] high. On the other side of me the town looked like a picture in a child's book[2]. In front of my church there was a very high house on the other side of the road, about twenty feet[1] from me[3]. As[4] I stood there the King came with many ladies and gentlemen. They went up[5] on to the top[6] of the house to look at me. After a time[7] the King came down. He got up on his horse and began to ride nearer to me. But the horse was afraid of such a sight[7], as if a mountain had moved before him. The King (who was a very good horseman) was not thrown off, but, when servants came and held the horse for him, he got[7] down.

SWIFT, *Gulliver's Travels*
(Simplified by Michael West)

[1] *50.* [2] *23(b)iii.* [3] Add 'distant'. [4] Say 'while'. [5] Say 'climbed'. [6] Say 'roof'. [7] *123.*

42 Victory

The King and all his great men had come down to meet me. When they first saw all the Blefusco[1] ships coming, they were greatly afraid. For they could not see me, because the sea was deep there, and only my head was above water. As I came nearer I stood up out of the water and held up the string so that they might see it, and I called out: 'Long live[2] the most powerful King of Lilliput!'

The King was so pleased[3] at this, that he asked[4] me to go[5] again and bring all the rest[4] of the ships from Blefusco. He wanted to conquer their whole country and to make[6] the people of it[7] his servants. I said that I would not help him to treat a free people in[8] this way. At[9] this he became angry. And from this time[10] certain of the King's friends[11] began to talk together how they might kill me or send me away.

SWIFT, *Gulliver's Travels*
(Simplified by Michael West)

[1] *blefuskosch.* [2] *114(a)i.* [3] *120(l).* [4] *123.* [5] Add 'there', *43(a)ii.* [6] *120(q).* [7] *56(d).* [8] *87(b)iii.* [9] *87(b)vii.* [10] *41.* [11] Say 'certain friends of the King'.

43 Gulliver's hat

One day when the King was sitting with me, there came a man with a note to the King. The note was from some people who had been riding near the place where I was first found.

'We were riding today near the place where the Man-Mountain was found and we saw there a very large black thing on the ground. It is as high as a man, and as large around[1] as a hut. Close about it there was a thing that was like a road. It may be some great sea-beast, but it is not alive, for it does not move. If it is a hut or house, there is no man or beast living in it, for we have climbed on to the top and can hear no sound inside it. Also we can see no door. We think that the Man-Mountain may know what it is. For this reason we have sent a note to the King telling him about it. Please send five horses to us and we will bring the thing to the city.'

SWIFT, *Gulliver's Travels*
(Simplified by Michael West)

[1] Say *im Umfang*.

44 Crusoe builds a house

Still seeking[1] a place for my hut, I found a little plain on the side of a hill. There was a hole in the side of the hill at the back[2] of this little plain, but this hole was small and did not go far into[3] the rock. I brought the sail of my boat here, and made of it a tent, which I set[4] up[5] on the plain. Then I drew a half-circle about the tent. In this half-circle I fixed[4] two lines[6] of strong sticks into the ground[7]. The sticks were about five and a half[8] feet[9] high and were pointed at the top. Then I began to cut away[10] the rock so as to make the hole in the hill larger; and I put the earth and stones within the fence, so that it raised the ground inside about a foot and a half[8]. Thus I had two rooms, my tent in which I would live, and the hole as a storeroom.

DANIEL DEFOE, *Robinson Crusoe*
(Simplified by Michael West)

[1] Say 'on the search after'. [2] Say 'end'. [3] *43(a)ii*, note. [4] Say 'struck'. [5] *43(a)iii*. [6] Say 'rows'. [7] Add 'in', *43(a)iii*. [8] *49(a)*. [9] *50*. [10] Say 'hew out'.

45 Crusoe gets a servant

When the man came to my tent, I gave him bread, some dried fruits, and a cup of water, for he was greatly tired by[1] his running. After that I made[2] him lie down and sleep.

After he had slept about half an hour he waked again and came out of the house to me. Then I began to speak to[3] him and to teach him to speak to[3] me. First, I told him that his name should be Friday, for that was the day on which I saved his life. I taught him to say 'Master'[4], and then let him know that this was to be my name. I taught him to say 'Yes' and 'No', and to know[5] the meaning of them[6]. Then I gave him some clothes, and a coat[7] made of the skin of a large animal and a cap made of rabbit skin. He was very well pleased to see himself in such clothes at first, for he was not used[8] to wearing[9] clothes. The coat rubbed his neck and the inside[10] of his arms, but I made it larger[11] and after that he became used[12] to the clothes very quickly.

DANIEL DEFOE, *Robinson Crusoe*
(Simplified by Michael West)

[1] *86(a)ix.* [2] *109(b)vii.* [3] *120(j).* [4] *123.* [5] Say 'understand'. [6] *56(d).* [7] Add 'which was'. [8] *120(a)* and *121.* [9] *122(d).* [10] Say *die Unterseite.* [11] Say 'wider'. [12] *120(a).*

46 Unexpected help

I went to my house and made all ready for a battle as before. Then I decided to show myself to the three prisoners, and learn something of their condition[1].

I came as near to them as I could without being seen, then I called out to them, 'Who are you, gentlemen[2]?'

They jumped up in surprise[3], but they were ten times more surprised when they saw me, for indeed I must have looked very strange. They made[4] no answer. 'Gentlemen[2],' said I again, 'do not be surprised at[5] me; perhaps you may[6] have a friend near you[6] when[7] you did not expect it[6].' 'The friend must[8] be[9] sent from heaven then,' said one of them very gravely, 'for our condition is beyond the help of man[10].' 'I am an Englishman,' said I, 'and I wish to help you. I have one servant only. We have guns and powder. Tell me freely[11]. Can we serve you? What has happened to you?'

DANIEL DEFOE, *Robinson Crusoe*
(Simplified by Michael West)

[1] Say 'situation'. [2] Add 'my'. [3] Say 'surprised'. [4] Say 'gave'. [5] *87(b)vii.*
[6] Omit. [7] Say 'whom'. [8] Subjunctive, *109(b)iv.* [9] *110(g).* [10] Say 'beyond human help'. [11] Say 'openly'.

47 A fine young fellow

It was a beautiful summer morning. The sun shone on[1] the trees of the forest which lies round the castle of Plessis-les-Tours in France. A youth was seen[2] coming from the north-east towards a little river, on the bank of which were standing two men.

As the youth came nearer, it could be seen that he was dressed[3] in[4] the national dress of Scotland. His age was twenty. When he came to the bank of the stream, he stopped and shouted, asking whether the water was too deep for him[5] to cross.

Not receiving an answer, the young man jumped into the water. But it was deeper than he had expected, and he was forced to swim.

'Ha!' cried the older man, 'he is a fine young fellow, he swims well. Run and give him your help when he reaches the bank. He looks as if he might belong[6] to our company of Scottish soldiers.'

WALTER SCOTT, *Quentin Durward*
(Simplified by Michael West)

[1] *87(b)iii.* [2] *110(i)*, note. [3] *92(c).* [4] *87(b)v.* [5] *114(iv).* [6] *120(q).*

48 Just in time

He looked round at[1] the faces of the crowd, and saw one face among them which seemed to stand out from the others – a good Scottish face – and, as he looked[2] again, he saw that the man was dressed as one of the King's guard.

'Help!' he cried. 'I am your countryman. Will no man help me? Balafré is my uncle. Call him quickly!'

The man raised his[3] hand and gave[4] a loud shout. . . . Could it be that Balafré was near? Would he come in time[5]?

One of the soldiers climbed up the tree and was fixing[6] the rope firmly[6] to[7] a strong branch.

Quentin heard far off an answering shout. The soldiers pushed him towards the tree. The Scotsman had disappeared. Perhaps he had run down the hillside to meet his companions.

They were fixing[8] the rope round his neck. Then a shout sounded nearer. Quentin felt the rope become tight. It was a matter[9] of moments. Would help come in time[5]? He closed his eyes, thinking[10] all hope lost . . .

Then he heard the sound of horsemen. He opened his eyes and saw Balafré standing in front of him and heard his voice.

WALTER SCOTT, *Quentin Durward*
(Simplified by Michael West)

[1] Say 'among', *87(b)viii.* [2] Add 'thither', *43(a)ii.* [3] *13(g).* [4] Say 'uttered'. [5] *123.* [6] Say 'making fast (firm)', *95(a).* [7] *87(b)ii.* [8] Say 'laying'. [9] *120(m).* [10] Say 'in the opinion that'.

49 Dangerous times

The Duke put his hand on his sword. All rose from their seats. The Duke's servants shut the doors of the great hall. Several of the French lords ran to the King's side and stood by him ready to defend him. King Louis sat calmly on[1]. He said not one word. The Duke of Burgundy still stood with his hand on his sword, and his men waited for the sign to begin a fight which must have ended in[2] the killing of the King of France and all his followers.

Then Crèvecœur rushed forward[3]. 'My master,' he cried, 'think[4] what you are doing! This is your hall. Are you not loyal to your King? Would you kill him in your own castle? For the honour of[5] your house, do not do this thing.'

'He is right,' said Louis calmly. 'Gentlemen,' he added, turning[6] to his own followers, 'my friend the Duke is angry at the news of the death of the Bishop of Liège. Put back[7] your swords. If he wishes to kill me, it will do no good for you[8] to fight against these greater numbers[9].'

WALTER SCOTT, *Quentin Durward*
(Simplified by Michael West)

[1] Say 'remained sitting', *122(c)*. [2] Say 'with'. [3] *43(a)iii*. [4] Use 2nd pers. plur., *107(c)* and *64(d)*. [5] Say 'for the sake of', *85*. [6] *120(q)* and *122(f)*. [7] Say 'in', *43(a)iii*. [8] Say 'it will not help you anything'. [9] Say 'superior force', *23(e)*.

50 The King speaks

When the Duke began he spoke calmly, but, as he reached the end[1] his voice became wild and angry. It seemed as if there was a trace of fear in the King's face, but in a moment this passed and the King spoke to the gathering far more calmly than the Duke had done[2].

'Noble lords of France and Burgundy,' he said, 'it is a strange thing[3] that a king should be called upon to defend himself in this way. There is no reason why I should not speak plainly[4], although the Duke has not done so. It was quite clear to all of you[5] that he was speaking of me. I ask you whether I should have come here and put[6] myself in the power of the Duke, if I thought that the Duke was my enemy. I am as grieved as he is at the terrible events which have happened[7] in Liège. But I fail to[8] understand in what way[9] I am to be blamed[10] for them[11].'

WALTER SCOTT, *Quentin Durward*
(Simplified by Michael West)

[1] *14(d)*. [2] Add 'it'. [3] *35*. [4] Say 'freely. [5] Use 2nd pers. pl. and cf. *79*. [6] *123*. [7] Say 'taken place', *102(b)*. [8] Say 'I cannot at all'. [9] Say 'how'. [10] *120(p)* and *110(e)*. [11] *56(e)*, note 3.

B. Unannotated Passages

51 On the Baltic

Last summer we spent our holidays on the Baltic. As usual our grandparents, who have a house on the shore there, invited us for three weeks in July. We had a wonderful time. The first few days the weather was very bad and on the second day of our stay it rained without stopping. That was very dull, at least in my opinion, for I had to read a book which I did not like at all. But soon the weather got finer and the last two weeks we had sunshine every day. As the sea was so warm we bathed twice and often three times a day. Although Fred is only five years old he has now learned to swim. He likes swimming so much that we cannot get him out of the water. Sometimes we went on an excursion into the country, but on most days we stayed on the beach all day; when we had swum enough we would play tennis on the beach or just lie in the sun.

52 My birthday present

Guess what father gave me for my birthday. He gave me a puppy. It was a nice surprise. He is a funny little thing. He is entirely white except for his nose, which is black. He looks very funny. We call him Bob. He is very friendly though he makes a good deal of noise. When we play with him he pretends to bite, but he does not do so really. He is especially fond of father's shoes. In fact, the other day he bit a hole in one of them. Fortunately it was not a big hole, but nevertheless father was very angry at first. Later he said it did not matter much for the shoes were very old and he would have had to buy a new pair very soon anyhow. Still, Bob was beaten because of it. I must say it seems to have had no effect. He still bites everything and he is especially fond of things made of leather.

53 Times have changed

Hitherto we have spent our holidays every year in the same village but we are afraid that that soon will no longer be possible. Three years ago the little village was almost unknown, being five miles away from the nearest station. Only a few strangers ever came to it, none stayed there. In fact, there was nowhere where one could stay. If father had not bought a small cottage we should not have been able to go there either, for at that time there was no inn and the inhabitants of the village had no rooms to let. Two years ago, however, people began to build a new road which was to connect two main roads, and this new road goes right through our little village. Last year somebody began to build a large hotel, which will probably be finished before the summer. And then I suppose crowds of visitors will come, cars will speed through the village and there will be no more peace and quietness in the village. Father will probably sell his cottage.

54 An excursion

It was the last day of the holidays. Since the weather was so fine we decided to go on an excursion into the Bruchwald, which is about twenty miles away from our town. We left at half past eight and went to the main station where we booked tickets to Langerode. We had not long to wait for the train. We managed to find an empty compartment and sat down in the corner seats. We arrived at Langerode at a quarter past nine. From there we had an hour's walk to the forest. It was still fairly cool and it was very pleasant walking along the narrow road. We soon saw the forest in the distance looking rather dark and unfriendly. When we got to the edge of the forest it was already beginning to get quite warm and we were glad to be able to sit and rest in the shade of the trees. The trees there are very lovely. There are a few oaks there as well as firs. I am very fond of oaks. They give such lovely shade.

55 To Germany by boat

We sometimes spend our holidays abroad. Last summer, for example, we went to Germany. We had long wanted to go by one of the Hapag liners, and so we went to Berlin via Southampton–Hamburg. There were many people waiting for the train when we arrived at Waterloo. Still, we succeeded in getting a fairly empty compartment. After about an hour and a half we reached Southampton. There we found the tender waiting for us, but it took us more than half an hour to get on the boat. At last we said goodbye to England and after about twenty minutes we saw the *New York (f.)*, the liner that was to take us to Hamburg. The liner looked so big in comparison with the very small boat on which we were. We came very near to the *New York* and soon it was possible to board her. Almost immediately we were told the number of our cabin and the number of our table in the dining-room.

As the weather was fine we had a calm crossing and reached the German port of Cuxhaven at six o'clock on the following morning.

56 Elizabeth is late

On Wednesday morning Frederick rang his sister up, asking her to meet him at the station on Thursday at 8.30 p.m. He said that his train was due to arrive at 8.18 at the Lehrter Bahnhof, but that he thought it would be late. The train arrived punctually but it was not till a quarter to nine that Elizabeth appeared. 'As usual,' thought Frederick, and sat down at a table in the waiting-room to read his newspaper. He was tired and hungry and in a bad mood. At twenty to nine Frederick decided to wait no longer. He put his paper into his rucksack and looked out of the waiting-room window. 'Everybody in Berlin seems to be here except Elizabeth,' he was thinking. 'If only I'd told her to come half an hour earlier we'd have begun eating by now.' He got up, left the waiting-room and was walking slowly out on to the platform when he recognised Elizabeth, who came running towards him. 'You look terribly hot and dirty,' she shouted to him, still running. 'Why didn't you have a wash while you were waiting for me? You're even too dirty to kiss!'

57 Our friends in the country

This morning I woke up at six o'clock. I jumped out of bed immediately and went to the window to see what the weather was like. The sky was covered with clouds and although the sun must have risen it was still rather dark. We were going by car to visit some friends of ours who have a little house in the country about fifty miles away from London.

At eight we were just going to set off, but father had some difficulty at first in starting the car. Still, he managed to put it right again and we were soon travelling along in the direction of Newbury.

When we got to our friends' house there wasn't a cloud in the sky, so after all we were able to spend a lovely day in the country. We went for a long walk through the woods and had our lunch in the open. After lunch we had a swim in a lake and then walked back to our friends' house where we had tea in the garden under a shady tree. We spent the evening indoors talking about old times. But meanwhile it had got dark and it was time to return to town.

58 The accident

'Where is John?' asked father. 'He is playing in the street with his friends,' mother answered. 'But I told him not to play in the street,' said father. 'It is much too dangerous nowadays. When I was a boy it was quite safe, but now it is different. There is much too much traffic. Why doesn't the boy obey me? It is not far to the meadows where he and his friends can play without running the danger of being run over.' Just at that moment a loud cry was heard. Both parents rushed out of the house. A car had stopped in front of the gate and the car driver had got out and was kneeling beside a small boy who lay on the ground. 'It's John!' shrieked mother. She rushed up to the child. 'Are you hurt, my darling?' she cried. 'I don't think he's hurt,' said the man, 'I was going fairly slowly and was just able to stop in time.' John managed to get up and walk into the house. He looked very pale but was otherwise unhurt. Still, he had to go to bed early that night. 'That's the last time you play in the street, do you understand?' said his father.

59 A conversation

A. At what time do you get up?

B. In summer I get up usually at half past seven but in winter I don't get up till a quarter to eight. It is so dark in the morning that I don't like getting up.

A. And when do you have to be at school?

B. School begins at nine o'clock.

A. Is the school far away from here? How do you get there: by tram, by rail or on foot?

B. No, it is not very far away. When the weather is fine I go to school on my bicycle, but when it rains I usually go by bus. It is quicker by bicycle than by bus. If I don't go by bicycle I have to walk five minutes to catch the bus. Sometimes I have to wait a long time for the bus.

A. Where do you have lunch: at school, or at home?

B. I nearly always come home to lunch. School finishes at twelve o'clock and doesn't begin again till two o'clock. So I have plenty of time to go home.

A. And at what time do you get home in the afternoon?

B. School finishes at a quarter past four so I am usually home soon after half past four.

60 If I were rich

If I were rich I should not live in this house nor in this town. The house is too small and most inconvenient, the town is dirty and dull. I should live, I think, in London which, although it is dirty, is not dull, but I should not stay there all the time. The winter, for instance, I should spend, at least now and then, in the South of France, in the spring I should go to Paris or to Italy, and part of the summer I should spend in South Germany, Austria and Switzerland, for I am very fond of the mountains. As you see, I should not spend much time in London, but it is pleasant to have a house of one's own somewhere, and London has advantages of its own too. I don't think I should buy a car, nor even an aeroplane. I think too many people will have them, and it will certainly be no pleasure driving a car in England. If I had to get anywhere quickly I could always hire a car; but in the country I prefer walking. You see so much more of the country when you walk and you have time to stop and look at the trees, the flowers and the birds.

Section Four

Free Composition

Hints on Writing Free Composition

Your compositions should run to about 150 words. You should aim at simplicity and accuracy. If you attempt anything complicated you will almost certainly be inaccurate. Do not therefore write out or think out your composition first in English and then translate it into German, for that will only make your task far harder, since your English composition, though it may seem simple to you, will certainly be far more difficult than the German you can be expected to write at this stage.

Simplicity will make for accuracy, but it does not necessarily follow that your German will in fact be accurate merely because it is simple. It is also essential to have at your command a vocabulary which, though quite small, is yet thoroughly known. You may know that the German for 'dog' is '*Hund*', but that knowledge alone is of very little use to you when writing German – you must in addition know the gender and declension of '*Hund*'; or you might know that 'to see' is '*sehen*', but in writing German you must also know exactly how '*sehen*' conjugates; or you may know that 'to wait' is '*warten*' though you may not be able to use your knowledge to any real purpose because you don't know its proper construction and cannot say 'he is waiting for you' in German.

You must, therefore, for German free composition, have much the same sort of intimate knowledge of German as is required for translating into German. But there is one great difference: in free composition you have a chance to show what you know, since you can decide what you are going to write. Do not therefore use words or expressions which you are not quite certain of, but replace them by others that you really know.

When given a subject it is perhaps a good plan to write down first a number of the simplest, barest statements which will form, as it were, the skeleton of your composition. When this has been done you can begin to elaborate. Adjectives can be added to nouns, adverbs can be inserted into clauses and some of the simple statements can be welded into compound or complex sentences. This process can best be shown by an example.

Subject:

Ein Mann wachte mitten in der Nacht erschrocken auf. Er hatte einen furchtbaren Traum gehabt. Was hatte er geträumt?

	Conjunctions	*Relative Pronouns*	*Adjectives*	*Adverbs and Adverbial Phrases*
1. Es war dunkel.				jetzt
2. Der Mann ging durch einen Wald.		**der**	jung(e) dicht(en)	
3. Er war müde.				
4. Er war allein.	**da**			
5. Er hatte Angst.				
6. Er sah ein Licht.	aber		groß(e) hell(es)	plötzlich rechts
7. Er ging dorthin.	und			schnell bald
8. Er kam an ein Haus.			niedrig(es)	
9. Er klopfte.	**nachdem**			
10. Eine Frau öffnete die Tür.			klein(e) alt(e)	
11. Sie fragte ihn.				
12. „Was wollen Sie?"				
13. Er fragte sie.				
14. „Kann ich ein Zimmer für die Nacht haben?"				
15. Sie sagte.				
16. „Ja, kommen Sie herein!"				nur
17. Sie führte ihn in ein Schlafzimmer.	und		kahl(es)	
18. Sie wünschte ihm gute Nacht.			kalt(es)	
19. Er ging zu Bett.				sofort
20. Er wollte früh aufstehen.	**weil**			

	Conjunctions	Relative Pronouns	Adjectives	Adverbs and Adverbial Phrases
21. Die Tür öffnete sich.				nach einer halben Stunde
22. Eine Frau trat ein.	und		weiß-gekleidet(e)	
23. Sie hielt einen Revolver.		**den**	klein(en)	sehr in der Hand
24. Sie schoß ihn ab.				
25. Der Mann wachte auf.			jung(e)	erschrocken
26. Er war in seinem Zimmer.			eigen(en)	
27. Das Licht brannte.	und			noch
28. Sein Buch lag auf dem Fußboden.			schwer(es)	

The first column gives the barest outline of the dream in the form of short simple statements. If your composition were left in this state it would certainly be simple and, as far as it goes, it would be accurate. But it would sound very jerky and incoherent and bare. To make it run more easily the conjunctions and relatives suggested in the second and third columns could be used to link up clauses with one another, the brackets indicating which clauses could be so linked up. Great care must be taken with word order, which will be affected by the subordinating conjunctions and relative pronouns (printed in bold type), but not by the co-ordinating conjunctions. Sometimes too the tense of the verb will have to be altered. The fourth column suggests possible adjectives which would serve to make the narrative less bare. See that these adjectives have the right endings. In the fifth column there are given a number of adverbs and adverbial phrases which could be usefully employed to give further details as to the time, manner and place of the various actions. Remember that an adverb or adverbial phrase coming at the head of a main clause must be followed by the finite verb.

Applying all these modifications to our first draft we shall get something like this:

Jetzt war es ganz dunkel. Der junge Mann, der sehr müde **war**, ging durch einen dichten Wald. Da er allein **war**, hatte er große Angst. Plötzlich aber sah er rechts ein helles Licht. Er ging schnell dorthin, und bald kam er an ein niedriges Haus. Nachdem er geklopft **hatte**, öffnete eine kleine alte Frau die Tür. „Was wollen Sie?" fragte sie ihn. „Kann ich ein Zimmer für die Nacht haben?" fragte er sie. „Ja", sagte die Frau, „kommen Sie nur herein!" Sie führte ihn in ein kahles, kaltes Schlafzimmer und wünschte ihm gute Nacht. Er ging sofort zu Bett, weil er früh aufstehen **wollte**. Nach ungefähr einer halben Stunde öffnete sich die Tür, und eine weißgekleidete Frau trat ganz leise ein. In der Hand hielt sie einen kleinen Revolver, den sie **abschoß**. Der junge Mann wachte erschrocken auf. Er war in seinem eigenen Zimmer. Das Licht brannte noch, und sein schweres Buch lag auf dem Fußboden.

Now this is simple, straightforward and correct German, and you are not expected at your stage to be able to write anything more ambitious. It is obvious that you could have written something much more exciting in English – but you simply do not yet command the vocabulary, phrases and syntax that would enable you to do something comparable in German. Be content therefore, at first, with a plain simple narrative of the kind shown in the example above.

1

Erzählen Sie, was Sie heute morgen gemacht haben, bevor Sie zur Schule gekommen sind!

Use the perfect tense

*auf-stehen, *to get up*
das Badezimmer, *bathroom*
sich waschen, *to wash*
sich (D) die Zähne putzen, *to brush one's teeth*
sich an-ziehen, *to dress*
die Treppe *hinunter-gehen, *to go downstairs*
das Eßzimmer, *dining-room*

die Eltern, *parents*
begrüßen, *to say good morning to*
frühstücken, *to have breakfast*
der Speck, *bacon*
das Ei (-er), *egg*
auf Wiedersehen sagen, *to say goodbye*
zu Fuß, *on foot*
mit dem Fahrrad, *on a bicycle*

das Haus verlassen, *to leave home*	plaudern, *to chat*
*begegnen (D), *to meet*	der Freund ⎫ *friend* die Freundin ⎭

2

Die Mutter Ihres Freundes (Ihrer Freundin) hat Sie zum Tee eingeladen. Sie haben die Einladung vergessen. Schreiben Sie einen Entschuldingungsbrief!

Plan

Am Tage nach der Einladung werde ich krank – der Arzt kommt – ich muß drei Tage im Bett bleiben – am Mittwoch darf ich wieder ausgehen – ich freue mich auf die schönen Kuchen – ich ziehe mich um – ich will eben das Haus verlassen – ich sehe eine Zeitung auf dem Tisch liegen – ich bemerke das Datum – der 21. Februar war gestern – ich bitte um Entschuldigung – ich hoffe auf eine neue Einladung.

Sehr geehrte, gnädige Frau! *Dear Mrs P.*	der Fehler, *mistake*
untersuchen, *to examine*	verwechseln, *to confuse*
Fieber messen, *to take one's temperature*	wie schade, *what a pity!*
	verzeihen (D), *to forgive*
die Mandelentzündung, *tonsillitis*	Mutter läßt Sie schön grüßen, *mother sends her kind regards*
ernst, *serious*	mit vielen Grüßen, *with kind regards*
sich erholen, *to recover*	
zu meinem Entsetzen, *to my horror*	Ihr sehr ergebener, *yours sincerely*

3

Die Mutter erzählt Ihnen beim Mittagessen, warum Sie so lange auf die Mahlzeit haben warten müssen.

Use the imperfect tense
Plan

Ich verlasse das Haus – fahre mit dem Omnibus zur Stadt – kaufe ein – habe viele Pakete – überall viele Leute – habe den Omnibus gerade noch erreicht – plaudere mit einer Freundin – steige aus – komme zu Hause an – will das Fleisch braten – ist nicht mehr da – muß es verloren haben – steige in Omnibus ein – kaufe Fleisch – komme zurück – schon sehr spät.

219

die Haltestelle, *bus-stop*
halten, *to stop*
*ein-steigen, *to get on* (bus)
*aus-steigen, *to get off* (bus)
der Einkauf(÷e), *purchase*
das Geschäft(-e), *shop*
das Paket(-e), *parcel*
ein-wickeln, *to wrap up*
der Fleischer, *butcher*

der Grünwarenhändler, *green-grocer*
der Bäcker, *baker*
der Konditor, *pastry-cook*
das Lebensmittelgeschäft, *grocer's*
kaufen bei (D), *to buy at*
die Menge, *crowd*
großen Hunger haben, *to be very hungry*

4

Vorige Woche haben Sie sich im Gebirge verlaufen und haben die Nacht im Freien verbracht. Schreiben Sie einen Brief an Ihren Freund (Ihre Freundin) und erzählen Sie ihm (ihr), wie es war!

Use the du *form of address*

Plan

Mein Freund und ich machen einen Ausflug – am Nachmittag fängt es an zu schneien – die Nacht bricht ein – wir sind noch nicht am Ziel – können nicht mehr nach der Karte sehen – wollen nicht erfrieren – beschließen, die ganze Nacht auf und ab zu gehen – Erfrischungen im Rucksack – Morgendämmerung – wir wissen jetzt, wo wir sind – Wirtshaus eine Viertelstunde entfernt – wir essen und trinken – gehen zu Bett.

Lieber Fritz! *Dear Fred*
Liebe Paula! *Dear Paula*
die Wolke, *cloud*
dunkel, *dark*
der Schnee, *snow*
die Thermosflasche, *thermos flask*
der Kaffee, *coffee*
die Schokolade, *chocolate*
dämmern, *to dawn*

das Streichholz(÷er), *match*
naß, *wet*
der Sumpf(÷e), *quagmire*
in der Nähe, *near by*
die Erfrischung, *refreshment*
das Getränk(-e), *drink*
das Frühstück, *breakfast*
Dein treuer Freund ⎫ *yours*
Deine treue Freundin ⎭ *sincerely*

5

Sie sind Zeuge eines Unfalls. Sie beschreiben den Eltern, was Sie gesehen haben.

Plan

Vater und Mutter warten zu Hause – ich erzähle ihnen – auf dem Wege nach Hause – Schulkamerad fährt mit dem Fahrrad vorüber – Auto will ihn gerade überholen – Junge biegt plötzlich nach links ein – Auto stößt mit dem Fahrrad zusammen – Junge schwerverletzt – Menge – Schutzmann – Krankenhaus.

sich verspäten, *to be late*	der Zusammenstoß, *collision*
aufgeregt, *excited*	sich bilden, *to form (intr.)*
*geschehen, *to happen*	das Notizbuch, *notebook*
die Hauptstraße, *main road*	der Name(-ns, -n), *name*
der Verkehr, *traffic*	die Adresse, *address*
rechts *fahren, *to drive on the right*	fragen nach (D), *to ask for*
	das Krankenauto, *ambulance*
der Radfahrer, *cyclist*	bestellen, *to summon*
der Autofahrer, *motorist*	die Bahre, *stretcher*
(*)zerbrechen, *to break, smash*	ab-transportieren, *to drive off*

6

Während einer Schneeballschlacht zerbrechen Sie ein Fenster mit einem Schneeball. Erzählen Sie, wie es geschehen ist und was die Folgen davon sind!

Plan

Die Schule ist aus – es hat geschneit – Sie gehen mit anderen Schülern nach Hause – einer wirft einen Schneeball – andere folgen seinem Beispiel – richtige Schneeballschlacht – Sie zielen nach einem Jungen – Schneeball zerbricht Fensterscheibe – alle rennen davon – man ruft Ihnen nach – Sie kommen zu Hause an – Sie sagen nichts – man klingelt – Frau beschwert sich über Sie – Mutter bietet Schadenersatz (*damages*) an – Strafe.

das Ziel, *aim*	erkennen, *to recognise*
verfehlen, *to miss*	befragen, *to question*
erschrocken, *frightened*	ein-gestehen, *to confess*
zu Mittag essen, *to have lunch*	das Taschengeld, *pocket money*
die Nachbarin, *neighbour*	Schlittschuh *laufen, *to go skating*
wütend, *very angry*	verbieten (D), *to forbid*
böse auf (A), *angry with*	

7

Sie erzählen Ihrem Lehrer, warum Sie Ihre Schularbeit nicht gemacht haben.

Plan

Wir sitzen am Feuer – ich mache meine Übersetzung – das Abendessen ist fertig – ich lasse meine Arbeit am Fußboden liegen – wir gehen ins Eßzimmer hinunter – wir gehen ins Wohnzimmer hinauf – das Zimmer ist voll Rauch – glühende Kohle ist aus dem Kamin auf das Heft gefallen – der Teppich hat ein Loch – habe keine Zeit mehr, meine Arbeit wieder anzufangen – muß zu Bett gehen – zeige dem Lehrer das Heft.

übersetzen, *to translate*
aus dem Englischen ins Deutsche,
  from English into German
schwierig, *difficult*
das Wörterbuch, *dictionary*
nach-schlagen, *to look up* (*words*)
ins Reine schreiben, *to copy out*
dauern, *to last*

zu Ende schreiben, *to finish*
hungrig, *hungry*
guten Appetit haben, *to have a*
  good appetite
riechen nach (D), *to smell of*
tränen, *to water* (*of eyes*)
auf-heben, *to pick up*

8

Sie sind von der Flut abgeschnitten. Sie erzählen einem Schulfreund davon.

Plan

Die Familie macht einen Spaziergang am Strand – das Meer ist kaum sichtbar – Kinder sammeln Muscheln – Eltern plaudern – beschließen, zurückzugehen – unmöglich – versuchen, weiter zu gehen – Weg durch die Springflut abgeschnitten – müssen auf die Felsen hinaufklettern – Mutter sehr böse – müssen da bleiben – Flut steigt immer höher – endlich erreicht Wasser seinen Höchststand – haben Tee und Kuchen mitgebracht – können später zurückgehen.

der niedrigste Stand der Ebbe, *low*
  tide
der höchste Stand der Flut, *high*
  tide

die Flut kommt, *the tide comes in*
die Ebbe tritt ein, *the tide goes out*
der Felsen (-) *rock*
der Sand, *sand*

die Gefahr, *danger*
trocken, *dry*
steil, *steep*
sich an-halten an (A *or* D), *to*
  cling to

*hinunter-klettern, *to scramble*
  down
helfen (D), *to help*

9

Ihr Vater beschließt, seinen Kamin selbst zu reinigen. Beschreiben Sie, mit welchem Erfolg er es macht!

Plan

Mutter hängt Tücher vor den Kamin – Vater geht auf das Dach – reinigt den Schornstein – kommt wieder herunter – kein Ruß liegt in seinem Kamin – es klingelt – Nachbar kommt – Vater erzählt ihm von seinem sauberen Kamin – Nachbar bittet ihn, mit in sein Schlafzimmer zu kommen – Ruß im ganzen Zimmer.

der Schornsteinfeger, *chimney-*
  sweep
die Leiter, *ladder*
gleich aus-sehen, *to look alike*
die Bürste, *brush*
die Stange, *pole*
biegsam, *flexible*

sich wundern, *to be surprised*
schmutzig, *dirty*
bedecken, *to cover*
die Möbel (*pl.*), *furniture*
das Bett, *bed*
die Steppdecke, *eiderdown*
der Teppich, *carpet*

10

Sie sind Augenzeuge eines Überfalls. Machen Sie Ihre Aussage (*statement*) vor der Polizei!

Plan

Ich mache meine Schularbeiten – der Briefkasten steht meinem Fenster gegenüber – der Briefträger kommt – er pfeift – öffnet Briefkasten – hört auf zu pfeifen – ich blicke auf – Briefträger liegt am Boden – Mann ergreift Briefe – läuft davon – hinkt (*limps*) ein wenig – ich rufe Mutter herbei – sie ruft Polizei an – Schutzmann kommt – ich erzähle ihm den Vorfall.

der Schreibtisch, *desk*
der Nachmittag, *afternoon*

heiß, *hot*
schläfrig, *sleepy*

die Ecke, *corner*
erkennen an (D), *to recognise by*
das Pfeifen, *whistling*
ab-brechen, *to stop, interrupt*
das Lied, *song*
ein Meter 80, *5 ft. 11 in.*

breitschultrig, *broad-shouldered*
gutgekleidet, *well-dressed*
das linke Bein, *left leg*
das Gesicht, *face*
der Rücken, *back*

11

Sie fahren mit Ihrer Familie auf dem Schiff. Ein kleiner Junge fällt ins Wasser. Beschreiben Sie den Vorfall!

Plan

Junge klettert auf die Reling – fällt ins Wasser – Vater springt ins Wasser – Matrose wirft Rettungsring – Schiff fährt langsamer – hält – Boot wird heruntergelassen – Matrosen retten Vater und Jungen – Boot wieder heraufgeholt – Schiff fährt weiter – dankbare Mutter.

12

Sie sind im Zeltlager. Früh am Sonntagmorgen entdeckt man Knochen vor dem Lebensmittelzelt. Erzählen Sie, was geschehen ist und was gemacht wurde!

Plan

Zwanzig Jungen – großen Appetit! – am Sonnabend ist Fleisch für Sonntag und Montag (Bankfeiertag) geliefert worden – Zelt zuge-schnürt – Hunde – acht Meilen von der Stadt entfernt – Quartier-meister – Fahrrad – alle Läden zu – sucht Fleischer überall – bekommt Fleisch – Mittagessen verspätet.

13

Zwei befreundete Familien machen einen Ausflug mit Picknick (*n.*) im Wald. Beschreiben Sie den Hergang!

Plan

Jungen und Mädchen fahren mit dem Rad – die alten Herrschaften gehen zu Fuß – Beschreibung des Weges – kommen im Walde an – Feuer schon gemacht – zum Kochen bringen – Tuch ausbreiten – Tassen und Teller auspacken – belegte Brote – Kuchen – Tee trinken – nach Hause gehen.

14

Ihr Schulfreund schwänzt die Schule (*plays truant*). Sie erzählen Ihrer Mutter davon.

Plan

Willi – Schularbeiten nicht gemacht – beschließt, Schule zu schwänzen – Mutter nicht zu Hause – holt Angelrute – fängt Fische – Grundbesitzer erwischt ihn – führt ihn zum Schuldirektor – erzählt Vorfall – befragen – Strafe – Grundbesitzer droht mit Klage (*legal action*), wenn er ihn noch einmal findet.

15

Ihr Bruder erzählt Ihrem Vater, wie Sie beim Felsenklettern steckengeblieben sind und nicht weiterkommen konnten.

Plan

In den Felsen herumklettern – Fritz will Klippe bis nach oben hinaufklettern – ein Stück Felsen löst sich – Fritz kann weder nach oben noch nach unten – Küstenwache holen – Seil – zerschundene Knie – zerrissene Hosen – sonst heil.

16

Sie bringen Ihre Tante zum Zuge. Beschreiben Sie, was passiert!

Plan

Beschreibung der Tante – Taxi – Gepäckträger – Gepäck – Fahrkarte – Bahnsteigkarte – Sperre – Gepäckträger verschwunden – Tante aufgeregt – Zug fährt ein – Gepäckträger kommt – Trinkgeld – Handtasche fällt – Inhalt verstreut – Zugführer (*guard*) ungeduldig – aufheben – einsteigen – Zug fährt ab.

17

Beschreiben Sie Ihre erste Nacht im Zeltlager!

Plan

Zeltlager am Abhang eines Berges – kleines Zelt aufschlagen (*pitch*) – zu Bett gehen – Wind – Regen – nicht schlafen können – Zelt bricht zusammen – höchst unangenehm – Zelt wieder aufschlagen – Wasser fließt vom Berg ins Zelt – nicht wagen einzuschlafen – müde – Scheune (*barn*) vorziehen.

18

In der Nacht hören Ihre Eltern ein sonderbares Geräusch unten. Vater erzählt den Kindern beim Frühstück davon.

Plan

Kinder schlafen fest – Mutter wacht auf – aufwecken – zuhören – jemand im Hause? – aufstehen – Schlafrock anziehen – Treppe – Taschenlampe – warten – Geräusch kommt aus der Küche – Tür vorsichtig öffnen – Kopf der Katze steckt in Konservenbüchse (*tin*).

19

Sie machen einen Spaziergang mit Ihrem Vater im Wald. Sie haben einen unangenehmen Zwischenfall (*scene*) mit dem Förster. Erzählen Sie der Mutter davon!

Plan

Cäsar rennt überall umher – Unterholz – verschwindet – bellt – Vogel schreit – Cäsar kommt herangelaufen – hat einen Fasan (*pheasant*) in der Schnauze – Vater nimmt Fasan – tot – Förster kommt – böse – Erklärung des Vaters – Förster konfisziert Fasan – Warnung – Hund an der Leine führen.

20

Ihr Haus wird überschwemmt. Beschreiben Sie die Szene!

Plan

Einstöckig – am Ufer des Flusses – Frühling – sonderbares Geräusch – aus dem Bett springen – Wasser bis an die Knöchel (*ankles*) – Eltern aufwecken – Leiter – Boden (*attic*) – Betten, Lebensmittel, Kerzen, Streichhölzer, Spirituskocher (*primus*) – Wasser steigt – lange warten müssen – Rettungsboot – abholen.

21

Setzen Sie „Eingeschlossen im Theater" fort (Nr. 10, S. 240)!

Plan

Weiße Gestalt kommt näher – Heinrich erkennt Schauspielerin – Maske des Jungen zurückgestreift – Schauspielerin erkennt kleinen

Jungen – spät – Junge schläft am Fußende ihres Bettes – am folgenden
Morgen nach Hause gebracht – Heinrichs Mutter ängstlich – Theater-
besuch verboten – Schauspieler verlassen Stadt – Heinrich traurig.

22

Setzen Sie „Ertappt" fort (Nr. 14 S. 243)!

Plan

Diener für Baum verantwortlich (*responsible*) – böse – fragt Mozart aus –
Mozart will gehen – Diener unzufrieden – muß die Sache melden –
Mozart will Trinkgeld geben – kein Geld bei sich – Brief an Gräfin –
Gräfin kennt Mozarts Musik – bittet ihn, am Fest teilzunehmen.

23

Setzen Sie „Zu spät" fort (Nr. 18, S. 246)!

Plan

Ich muß hinunter – Reiter haben sich verirrt – wollen Weg nach B.
wissen – ich weiß nicht – ziehen Pistolen – ich wähle irgendeinen Weg –
lange Wanderung – Morgendämmerung – Reiter halten – drohen –
erkennen – Gärtner vom Schloß – wollen mich als Diener für Reise nach
Italien – mein Ziel Italien – einwilligen.

24

Setzen Sie „Schiff in Not" fort (Nr. 19, S. 247)!

Plan

Effi geht zum Hafen – kommt zur rechten Zeit – erster Schuß – Rakete
mit Fangseil (*lasso*) – kleine Leine – dickes Seil – Korb – Korb kommt
mit Matrosen zurück – viele Male, bis alle gerettet sind – bald darauf
sinkt Schiff.

25

Setzen Sie „Das Wiedersehen" fort (Nr. 20, S. 248)!

Plan

Kutscher mit Wagen – große Koffer aufgegeben – zu schwer – Kutscher
muß sie morgen holen – Handgepäck – Axel bezahlt Gepäckträger –

Bruder und Schwester steigen ein – Reisedecke – abfahren – bekannte Wege – kommen zu Hause an – Mutter auf der Treppe – Begrüßung – Tee.

26

Setzen Sie „Verletzter Stolz" fort (Nr. 22, S. 250)!

Plan

Anton kommt zurück – sagt nichts – Angestellte gehen nach Hause – Anton spricht mit Jordan – Jordan will Antons Herausforderung (*challenge*) Fink überbringen – Jordan hat Unterredung mit Fink – Fink entschuldigt sich bei Anton – will sich vor allen entschuldigen – Anfang einer Freundschaft.

27

Setzen Sie „Schwacher Vorsatz" fort (Nr. 24, S. 252)!

Plan

Junge wacht um 7 auf – keine Schularbeit – an der Reihe – wird er Ostern sitzenbleiben? – zur Schule ohne Frühstück – kommt zu spät an – Morgenandacht (*morning prayers*) – allein im Klassenzimmer – andere Schüler – Lehrer kommt – Stunde beginnt – wird Johann Buddenbrook gefragt werden?

28

Setzen Sie „Die Wand hat Ohren" fort (Nr. 25, S. 253)!

Plan

Wirt geht aufs Schloß – berichtet Donna Elena – Entführung (*abduction*) – Donna Elena schwört Rache – nimmt Dolch – ruft Männer zusammen – alle gehen zum Gasthaus – Schlafzimmer – Donna Elena will Don Enrique töten – ruhiges Gesicht des Schlafenden – verliebt sich – verheiraten sich.

29

Setzen Sie „Die freundliche Alte" fort (Nr. 33, S. 261)!

Plan

Lampe – Leiter – Kämmerchen – Alte bringt Essen – Bett – kann nicht schlafen – laute Stimmen – steht auf – durchschreitet anstoßendes (*adjoining*) Zimmer – legt Auge an Türspalte – sieht Männer – hört Unterredung – man plant, seinen Freund zu töten – beschließt, ihn davor zu warnen.

30

Setzen Sie „Das Kreuzverhör" fort (Nr. 50, S. 279)!

Plan

Mütze im Korridor – Haus verlassen – Hoffnung – heute Sonntag – Läden zu – nach Haagers Wohnung – verzweifelt – langer Weg – ankommen – nicht mehr aushalten – Junge will nicht hineingehen – nicht bei Haager gekauft – wieder nach Hause – eingestehen – im Schlafzimmer des Vaters gefunden – den ganzen Nachmittag in dunkler Dachkammer eingesperrt.

31

Continue "A Fine afternoon" (No. 2, p. 183).

Plan

Mother pays bill – somebody has taken their boat – mother at a loss – Fred suggests telephoning – another boat sent – same boat as the one they had hired – explanation – boat had drifted back.

32

Continue 'An invitation' (No. 5, p. 184).

Plan

Preparations for the holiday – mother sees me off – change at S. – uncle's car is waiting at D. station – arrival at farm – excursion planned for following day – disappointment – rains all day.

33

Continue 'The stranger' (No. 6, p. 185).

Plan

I tell father about stranger – father rings up police – policeman comes – I tell him all I know – man arrested in neighbouring town – am asked to say whether it is the same man.

34

John receives letter from Charles explaining why he was not able to come (No. 11, p. 187).

Plan

Charles's father has returned to England after long stay abroad – cannot yet come home – invites wife and son to come to London for few days – Charles hopes to visit John a week later.

35

Describe the summer holiday A. spends on one of the North Sea islands (No. 12, p. 188).

Plan

Fine weather on the whole – swimming – sunbathing – fishing – boating – exploring – difficulty in understanding the islanders – one violent storm – rough sea – return sunburnt and well – Berlin very dull in comparison.

36

Continue 'A dull life' (No. 18, p. 190).

Plan

Young man orders lunch – wine – chats with waiter – famous film star (*Filmstar*) – would like to stay for a week – his friend arrives tomorrow – wants to walk a lot – waiter much happier.

37

Continue 'The precious stone' (No. 26, p. 194).

Plan

Police arrive – ask questions – search house – find nothing – interrogate everybody in house – go away – father desperate – goes back to study – opens drawer – finds precious stone! – how did it get back?

38

Continue 'In the mountains' (No. 29, p. 196).

Plan

We stay on top till midday – lunch – rope together (*sich miteinander anseilen*) – way down more difficult – snow soft – Eric suddenly disappears – crevasse (*die Spalte*) – George holds firm – we pull Eric out – get back safely to mountain hut – tired and hungry.

39

Continue 'Snow White and the Dwarfs' (No. 32, p. 198).

Plan

Queen goes to mirror – learns that Snow White is still alive – disguises herself (*verkleidet sich*) as a peasant woman – knocks at door – Snow White refuses to open – Queen offers half of apple through window – Snow White eats – dies – Queen goes away – dwarfs return.

40

Continue 'The Emperor's New Clothes' (No. 40, p. 203).

Plan

Minister tells Emperor about beautiful cloth – Emperor goes to see it – looms empty – dares not say so – cloth finished – clothes made – Emperor puts them on – procession – crowd admires clothes – child says, 'He's got nothing on!'

41

Beschreiben Sie einen Film, den Sie kürzlich gesehen haben!

42

Sie verbringen die Nacht in einem alten Haus, in dem angeblich ein Gespenst umgeht. Erzählen Sie einem Freund davon!

43

Sie schreiben im Auftrag Ihres Vaters an ein Hotel, um Zimmer für die Familie für die Sommerferien zu bestellen und sich nach Einzelheiten zu erkundigen.

44

Sie gewinnen das Große Los in einer Lotterie. Welchen Einfluß hat das auf Ihr Leben?

45

Ein Affe ist aus dem Zoo entsprungen. Beschreiben Sie seine Abenteuer!

46

Beschreiben Sie einen Tag, den Sie bei dichtem Nebel in einer Groß-
stadt verbringen!

47

Heute war Ihr Geburtstag. Sie schreiben Ihrer Großmutter einen
Dankesbrief für ihr Geschenk.

48

Sie gehen zum ersten Mal ins Theater. Beschreiben Sie Ihre Eindrücke!

49

Beschreiben Sie Ihre Heimatstadt oder Ihr Heimatdorf!

50

An einem Ferientag regnete es den ganzen Tag so stark, daß Sie nicht
ausgehen konnten. Beschreiben Sie, wie Sie sich amüsiert haben!

Section Five

German Prose Extracts

(A) Passages for Translation or Comprehension

i *Easy*

1 Eine schlaflose Nacht

Wir ziehen uns bei Lichte an, um mit Tagesanbruch wieder hin-
unterzugehen. Diese Nacht habe ich ziemlich unruhig zugebracht.
Ich lag kaum im Bett, so kam mir vor, als wenn ich über und über
mit einer Nesselsucht[1] befallen wäre; doch merkte ich bald, daß es
5 ein großes Heer hüpfender Insekten war, die den neuen Ankömmling blutdürstig überfielen. Diese Tiere befinden sich manchmal in
den hölzernen Häusern in großer Menge. Die Nacht wurde mir
sehr lang, und ich war zufrieden, als man uns am Morgen Licht
brachte.

nach JOHANN WOLFGANG VON GOETHE (1749–1832),
Briefe aus der Schweiz

1 Was taten sie nach dem Aufstehen?
2 Warum hatte man ein Licht nötig?
3 Warum stand man so früh auf?
4 Hat Goethe gut geschlafen?
5 Was fand Goethe in seinem Bett?
6 Was machten die Insekten?
7 In was für einem Hause brachte Goethe die Nacht zu?
8 Was ist ein Ankömmling?
9 Warum wurde Goethe die Nacht sehr lang?
10 Woher wissen Sie, daß das Haus nicht im Tal lag?

2 Das Waisenkind

„Warte, Johannes", sagte Friedrich stolz, „ich will dir mein halbes
Butterbrot geben, es ist mir doch zu groß." – „Laß doch", sagte

[1] die Nesselsucht: *nettle-rash*

Margret, „er geht ja nach Hause." – „Ja, aber er bekommt nichts
mehr; Onkel Simon ißt um sieben Uhr." Margret wandte sich zu
5 dem Knaben: „Hebt¹ man dir nichts auf?¹ Sprich, wer sorgt für
dich?" – „Niemand", stotterte das Kind. – „Niemand?" wiederholte sie; „da nimm, nimm!" fügte sie heftig hinzu; „du heißt
Niemand, und niemand sorgt für dich! Das sei Gott geklagt! Und
nun mach dich fort! Friedrich, geh nicht mit ihm, hörst du, geht
10 nicht zusammen durchs Dorf." – „Ich will ja nur Holz holen aus
dem Schuppen", antwortete Friedrich.

ANNETTE VON DROSTE-HÜLSHOFF (1797–1848), *Die Judenbuche*

1 Warum wollte Friedrich dem Jungen sein halbes Butterbrot geben?
2 Warum fand Margret, daß das nicht nötig war?
3 Warum würde Johannes nichts mehr zu Hause bekommen?
4 Bei wem wohnte er?
5 Was für ein Junge war Johannes?
6 Wie hieß Johannes?
7 Was tat Margret, als sie erfuhr, daß niemand für Johannes sorgte?
8 Was sollte Friedrich nicht tun?
9 Was ist ein Schuppen?
10 Wo befindet sich gewöhnlich der Schuppen?

3 Besuch bei den Bergarbeitern

Die meisten Bergarbeiter² wohnen in Klausthal und in dem damit
verbundenen Bergstädtchen Zellerfeld. Ich besuchte mehrere
dieser guten Leute, sah ihre kleinen Zimmer, hörte einige ihrer
Lieder, die sie mit der Zither, ihrem Lieblingsinstrumente, gar
5 hübsch begleiten, ließ mir alte Bergmärchen von ihnen erzählen,
und auch die Gebete hersagen, die sie alle zusammen zu halten
pflegen, ehe sie in den dunkeln Schacht³ hinuntersteigen, und
manches gute Gebet habe ich mit gebetet. Ein alter Bergarbeiter

¹ aufheben: *keep*   ² der Bergarbeiter: *miner*
³ der Schacht: *shaft*

meinte sogar, ich sollte bei ihnen bleiben und Bergmann[1] werden; und als ich dennoch Abschied nahm, gab er mir einen Brief an 10 seinen Bruder mit, der in der Nähe von Goslar wohnt, und viele Küsse für seine liebe Nichte.

nach HEINRICH HEINE (1797–1856), *Die Harzreise*

1 Was ist ein Bergarbeiter?
2 Mit welchem Instrument begleiten die Bergarbeiter ihre Lieder?
3 Was erzählten die Bergarbeiter Heine?
4 Wann sagen sie ihre Gebete her?
5 Woher wissen Sie, daß die Bergarbeiter Heine gern mochten?
6 Wollte Heine Bergmann werden?
7 Wie kommt man ins Bergwerk?
8 Wohin wollte Heine gehen?
9 Um was bat man Heine beim Abschied?
10 Was ist eine Nichte?

4 Unangenehme Reise

Es war Mitternacht, als ich in die Barke stieg; die Menge des Gepäcks und der Passagiere machten den Platz unbequem. Die Nacht, bald stürmisch, bald still, war jedesmal der Fahrt zuwider; gänzlicher Mangel an Schutz gegen die unerträglichen Strahlen der 5 Sonne ließ den folgenden Tag unangenehm vorübergehen. Bei Anbruch der Nacht zogen Gewitter herauf, ein mächtiger Regen drohte uns zu durchweichen[2], der Sturm wuchs, und der Schiffer beschloß, das Gewitter auf offner See mit ausgeworfenem Anker abzuwarten, weil die Felsen der nächsten Küste die Landung un- 10 sicher machten. Glücklich zog ohne Regen das Gewitter vorüber, doch konnte man erst um Mitternacht weitersegeln. Am Abend des zweiten Tages stiegen endlich die Türme Venedigs aus den Wellen des Meeres.

nach KARL FRIEDRICH SCHINKEL (1781–1841), *Briefe*

[1] der Bergmann: *miner*   [2] durchweichen: sehr naß machen

235

1 Wann stieg Schinkel in die Barke?
2 Warum war es ihm unbequem in der Barke?
3 Warum kam man in der Nacht nicht schnell vorwärts?
4 Wie war das Wetter am folgenden Tage?
5 Warum bestand die Gefahr, daß man naß werden könnte?
6 Warum wollte der Schiffer nicht landen?
7 Sind die Passagiere naß geworden?
8 Wie lange mußte man warten, bis man weitersegeln konnte?
9 Wie lange dauerte die Fahrt?
10 Wohin wollten die Passagiere fahren?

5 Die Nacht im Schulhause

Endlich war es Zeit zum Gehen. Man führte ihn über die Straße:
das Pfarrhaus war zu eng, man gab ihm ein Zimmer im Schulhause.
Er ging hinauf. Es war kalt oben, eine weite Stube, leer, ein hohes
Bett im Hintergrund. Er stellte das Licht auf den Tisch und ging
5 auf und ab. Er dachte wieder an den Tag, wie er hergekommen, wo
er war. Das Zimmer im Pfarrhause mit seinen Lichtern und lieben
Gesichtern, es war ihm wie ein Schatten, ein Traum, und es wurde
ihm leer, wieder wie auf dem Berg; aber er konnte es mit nichts
mehr ausfüllen, das Licht war erloschen, die Finsternis verschlang
10 alles. Eine unnennbare Angst erfaßte ihn. Er sprang auf, er lief
durchs Zimmer, die Treppe hinunter, vors Haus; aber umsonst,
alles finster, nichts – er war sich selbst ein Traum.

nach GEORG BÜCHNER (1813–37), *Lenz*

1 Wo mußte Lenz übernachten?
2 Warum konnte er nicht im Pfarrhause schlafen?
3 Was ist ein Pfarrhaus?
4 Wo stand das Schulhaus?
5 Womit war die Stube beleuchtet?
6 Was war in der Stube zu sehen?
7 Warum ging Lenz auf und ab?
8 Warum hatte ihm das Zimmer im Pfarrhause gefallen?
9 Warum lief er plötzlich die Treppe hinunter?
10 Was hoffte er unten vor dem Hause zu finden?

6 Der unzufriedene Gast

Das Leben in einem solchen Boarding house will mir gar nicht
gefallen... Um 9 Uhr läutet's zum Frühstück. Dieselbe Versammlung,
dasselbe englische Gestammel, dieselbe Langeweile. Dazu die Wahl
zwischen Tee, der mir nicht bekommt, und Kaffee, den man hier
5 nicht zu bereiten versteht. Brot mit Butter, die mich krank macht.
Kaltes Fleisch, das ich nicht verdaue.[1] Ich greife jedoch zu, bis auf
das Fleisch, das mir zuerst noch zu englisch war, was, wie ich wohl
sah, die Hausfrau etwas beleidigte. Ein paar Engländer, die auch da
wohnten und die, wie alle ihrer Nation, im Anfange einer Bekannt-
10 schaft höchst unangenehm sind, vermehrten mein Mißbehagen.[2]
Ich wünschte mich auf tausend Meilen fort, wußte aber noch nicht,
wohin. Nach dem Frühstück ging ich in mein Zimmer zurück, in
das der kalte Wind in Strömen einzog durch ein Fenster, das nicht
schloß, wie ich erst später bemerkte.

nach FRANZ GRILLPARZER (1791–1872), *Tagebuch auf der Reise
nach Frankreich und England*

1 Um wieviel Uhr nahm man das Frühstück?
2 Warum trank Grillparzer nicht gern Tee?
3 Warum war der Kaffee schlecht?
4 Wie war das Fleisch?
5 Warum war die Hausfrau beleidigt?
6 Hatte Grillparzer eine interessante Unterhaltung mit den anderen
Gästen?
7 Warum sind die Engländer im Anfange einer Bekanntschaft höchst
unangenehm?
8 Warum wünschte sich Grillparzer auf tausend Meilen fort?
9 Wohin ging er, nachdem er gefrühstückt hatte?
10 Warum kam der kalte Wind ins Zimmer?

7 Gute Vorsätze

Tief in der Nacht saß Eduard in seinem einsamen Zimmer, mit
vielfachen Gedanken beschäftigt. Um ihn lagen unbezahlte Rech-
nungen, und er häufte die Summen daneben auf, um sie am folgenden Morgen zu bezahlen. Es war ihm gelungen, unter guten Bedin-

[1] verdauen: *digest*   [2] das Mißbehagen: *displeasure, uneasiness*

5 gungen ein Kapital auf sein Haus aufzunehmen,[1] und obgleich er
sich arm erschien, so war er doch schon in dem Gefühl zufrieden,
welches ihm sein fester Vorsatz[2] gab, künftig auf andere Weise zu
leben. Er sah sich in Gedanken schon tätig, er machte Pläne, wie er
von einem kleinen Amte zu einem wichtigeren emporsteigen und
10 sich in diesem zu einem noch besseren vorbereiten wolle. „Die
Gewohnheit", sagte er, „wird ja zu unserer Natur, im Guten wie im
Schlimmen, und wie mir Nichtstun bisher notwendig gewesen ist,
um mich wohl zu befinden, so wird es in Zukunft die Arbeit nicht
weniger sein."

nach JOHANN LUDWIG TIECK (1773–1853), *Die Gemälde*

1 War Eduard allein?
2 Woher wissen Sie, daß Eduard Schulden gemacht hatte?
3 Wie hatte er Geld bekommen?
4 Was wollte er mit dem Geld machen?
5 Warum fühlte er sich zufrieden?
6 Wie hoffte er, es zu vermeiden, neue Schulden zu machen?
7 War er arbeitslos?
8 Wie wollte er im Leben weiterkommen?
9 Woran hatte er sich gewöhnt?
10 Woran hoffte er sich in Zukunft zu gewöhnen?

8 Die Heimkehr

Im Hafen von Hamburg lag das Schiff, *The Witch of the Waves*,
welches eben von London angekommen war, und die Passagiere
warteten ungeduldig auf die Boote, welche sie ans Land setzen
sollten. Es gab auf dem ganzen Schiff nur ein en Menschen, der
5 ruhig inmitten der Hast und des Getümmels[3] blieb. Etwas abseits
dem Haufen der Reisegefährten stand er unbeweglich und blickte
nach der nahen Stadt und der langverlassenen Vaterlandserde
hinüber. Sein Gesicht war von fremder Sonne gebräunt, sein Haar
gebleicht vom Alter, das Auge müde. Er lehnte etwas gebückt an
10 einem Stock und war der Letzte, der langsam hinabstieg in den
Kahn, welcher ihn ans Land tragen sollte. Erst als er den Fuß auf

[1] Kapital aufnehmen: sich Geld borgen   [2] der Vorsatz: die Absicht
[3] das Getümmel: *turmoil, bustle*

238

den deutschen Boden setzte, kam ein seltsames Leben in seine
Züge, ein leises Zittern überlief seinen Körper; er atmete aus tiefer
Brust auf, lüftete dann ein wenig, wie grüßend, den Hut.

WILHELM RAABE (1831–1910), *Die alte Universität*

1 Wo hatten die Passagiere das Schiff bestiegen?
2 Warum warteten sie ungeduldig auf die Boote?
3 Wie zeigte sich ihre Ungeduld?
4 Wo war der Passagier geboren, der ohne Ungeduld wartete?
5 Woher wissen Sie, daß er Deutschland lange nicht gesehen hatte?
6 Wo hatte er wahrscheinlich gelebt?
7 Welche Farbe hatten seine Haare?
8 Warum lehnte er an einem Stock?
9 Blieb er immer noch ruhig, als er ans Land kam?
10 Warum lüftete er den Hut?

9 Der Langschläfer

„Du Langschläfer", sagte der Vater, „wie lange sitze ich schon hier
und feile. Ich habe deinetwegen nichts hämmern dürfen; die
Mutter wollte den lieben Sohn schlafen lassen. Aufs Frühstück habe
ich auch warten müssen. Klüglich hast du den Stand des Lehrers
5 erwählt, für den wir wachen und arbeiten. Indes ein fleißiger
Gelehrter, wie ich mir habe sagen lassen, muß auch Nächte zu
Hilfe nehmen, um die großen Werke der Vorfahren[1] zu studieren."
„Lieber Vater", antwortete Heinrich, „werdet nicht böse über
meinen langen Schlaf, den Ihr sonst nicht an mir gewohnt seid. Ich
10 schlief erst spät ein und habe viele unruhige Träume gehabt, bis
zuletzt ein schöner Traum mir erschien, den ich lange nicht vergessen werde und den ich für mehr als einen bloßen Traum halte."
„Lieber Heinrich", sprach die Mutter, „du hast dich gewiß auf den
Rücken gelegt oder beim Abendgebet fremde Gedanken gehabt. Du
15 siehst auch noch ganz sonderbar aus. Iß und trink, daß du munter
wirst."

nach NOVALIS (FRIEDRICH VON HARDENBERG) (1772–1801),
Heinrich von Ofterdingen

[1] der Vorfahr: *ancestor*

1 Was war der Stand des Vaters?
2 Warum hatte er nichts hämmern dürfen?
3 Woher wissen Sie, daß der Vater hungrig war?
4 Was wollte Heinrich werden?
5 Was muß ein fleißiger Gelehrter tun?
6 Stand Heinrich oft spät auf?
7 Warum war Heinrich an diesem Morgen spät aufgestanden?
8 Warum würde er den Traum nicht vergessen?
9 Warum dachte die Mutter, daß er Träume gehabt hatte?
10 Sah er aus, als hätte er gut geschlafen?

10 Eingeschlossen im Theater

Als ich wieder erwachte, war das Theater leer und still, die Lampen
ausgelöscht, und der Vollmond goß sein Licht zwischen den
Kulissen[1] über die seltsame Unordnung herein. Ich wußte nicht, wo
ich mich befand; doch als ich meine Lage erkannte, ward[2] ich voll
5 Furcht und suchte einen Ausgang, fand aber die Türen verschlossen,
durch welche ich hereingekommen war. Nun begann ich von
neuem, alle Seltsamkeiten dieser Räume zu untersuchen. Ich legte
das Mäntelchen und den Degen[3] des Mephistopheles, welche auf
einem Stuhle lagen, über mein Meerkatzenkleid[4] um. So spazierte
10 ich in dem hellen Mondschein auf und nieder, zog den Degen und
fing an zu gestikulieren. Da rührte es sich im Dunkel, atemlos sah
ich hin, und jetzt stand eine weiße Gestalt in der Ecke. Einen leisen
Schritt tat ich näher; da rief es mit gebieterischer Stimme: „Halt!
kleines Ding! was bist du?" und streckte drohend den Arm gegen
15 mich aus. Leise antwortete ich: „Ich heiße Heinrich Lee und bin
eine von den Meerkatzen; man hat mich hier eingeschlossen!"

nach GOTTFRIED KELLER (1819–90), *Der grüne Heinrich*

1 Wo waren die Zuschauer?
2 Was konnte Heinrich sehen?
3 Warum hatte Heinrich Angst?

[1] die Kulisse: *scenery flat*   [2] ich ward: ich wurde
[3] der Degen: *sword*   [4] die Meerkatze: *(long-tailed) monkey*

4 Warum konnte er nicht hinaus?
5 Wie war er angezogen?
6 Was tat Heinrich mit dem Degen?
7 Was sah er plötzlich im Dunkel?
8 Warum trat er näher?
9 Was befahl ihm die weiße Gestalt zu tun?
10 Warum war Heinrich immer noch im Theater?

Zum Fortsetzen (Umriß, S. 226)

ii *More Difficult*

11 Das Erdbeben

Am 1. November 1755 ereignete sich das Erdbeben von Lissabon
und verbreitete über die ganze Welt einen ungeheuren Schrecken.
Eine große prächtige Stadt wird ungewarnt von dem furchtbarsten
Unglück betroffen. Die Erde bebt und schwankt, das Meer braust
5 auf, die Schiffe schlagen zusammen, die Häuser stürzen ein, Kirchen
und Türme darüber her, der königliche Palast zum Teil wird vom
Meere verschlungen, die geborstene Erde scheint Flammen zu
speien, denn überall meldet sich Rauch und Brand in den Ruinen.
Sechzigtausend Menschen, einen Augenblick zuvor noch ruhig und
10 behaglich, gehen miteinander zugrunde, und der Glücklichste
darunter ist der zu nennen, dem keine Empfindung über das Unglück mehr gestattet ist.

JOHANN WOLFGANG VON GOETHE (1749–1832),
Dichtung und Wahrheit

1 Wo ist Lissabon?
2 In welchem Jahrhundert ereignete sich das Erdbeben von Lissabon?
3 Wußte man in Lissabon, daß ein Erdbeben bevorstand?
4 Woher wissen Sie, daß Lissabon eine Hafenstadt ist?
5 Was für Gebäude wurden zerstört?
6 Wodurch wurden sie zerstört?
7 Was verbreitete sich schnell in den Ruinen?
8 Wieviel Einwohner kamen bei dem Unglück um?

9 Wie lebten die Einwohner von Lissabon kurz vor dem Erdbeben?
10 Übersetzen Sie: Der Glücklichste darunter ist der zu nennen, dem keine Empfindung über das Unglück mehr gestattet ist.

12 Die Erkenntnis

Auf einer Bank am See saß Klein friedlich und sah dem vorübertreibenden Volk zu. Er entfaltete im hellen Laternenlicht eine italienische Zeitung und versuchte zu lesen. Er verstand nicht alles, aber jeder Satz, den er zu übersetzen vermochte, machte ihm Spaß.
5 Erst allmählich begann er, über die Grammatik weg, auf den Sinn zu achten, und fand mit einem gewissen Erstaunen, daß der Artikel eine heftige, erbitterte Schmähung seines Volkes und Vaterlandes war. Wie seltsam, dachte er, das alles gibt es noch! Die Italiener schrieben über sein Volk, genau so wie die heimischen Zeitungen es
10 immer über Italien getan hatten, genau so richtend, genau so empört, genau so unfehlbar vom eigenen Recht und fremden Unrecht überzeugt!

HERMANN HESSE (1877–1962), *Klein und Wagner*

1 In welchem Land befand sich Klein?
2 Womit beschäftigte er sich?
3 Warum entfaltete er die Zeitung?
4 Wo muß die Laterne gestanden haben?
5 Woher wissen Sie, daß Klein kein Italiener war?
6 Was machte ihm Spaß?
7 Warum war er erstaunt?
8 In welcher Sprache waren die heimischen Zeitungen gedruckt?
9 Was hielt man in Deutschland von Italien?
10 Wovon ist jedes Volk überzeugt?

13 Das verlassene Haus

Ich lernte den Wald gut kennen, denn ich wohnte ja mittendrin. Die Bauern hatten eine Straße durch den Wald geleitet. Ich ging und ging. Und gerade als ich umkehren wollte, fand ich zwischen den Eichen ein verfallenes Haus. Rundum mochte ehemals ein

5 schmaler Streifen urbar gemachten Landes gewesen sein. Jetzt war er gänzlich versumpft[1]. Ich ging in das tote Haus hinein. Rechts und links über den Viehständen hing das Dach in Fetzen herunter. Dahinter die Küche hatte nur noch drei Wände. Aus der vierten war die Backsteinfüllung herausgefallen. Aber die Schlafkammer
10 gefiel mir gut. In einem der beiden in die Wand eingebauten Betten richtete ich mir aus Schilf und Stroh ein leidliches Lager her.

MANFRED HAUSMANN (1898–), Die Frühlingsfeier

1 Wo wohnte der Schriftsteller?
2 Was hatten die Bauern gebaut?
3 In welchem Zustand war das Haus mitten im Walde?
4 Woran erkennen Sie, daß ein Bauer früher im Haus gewohnt haben muß?
5 Womit war das Haus früher umgeben?
6 Warum wird das Haus „tot" genannt?
7 Was tut man in einer Küche?
8 Woraus war das Haus gebaut?
9 Wieviel Leute müssen im Haus gewohnt haben?
10 Was tat der Schriftsteller, um sein Bett bequem zu machen?

14 Ertappt!

Da hört er Tritte in der Nähe, er erschrickt, und das Bewußtsein, wo er ist, was er getan, stellt sich urplötzlich bei ihm ein. Schon im Begriff, die Pomeranze[2] zu verbergen, hält er doch gleich damit inne, sei es aus Stolz, sei's, weil es zu spät dazu war. Ein großer
5 breitschulteriger Mann in Livree, der Gärtner des Hauses, stand vor ihm. Derselbe hatte wohl die letzte verdächtige Bewegung noch gesehen und schwieg betroffen einige Sekunden. Mozart, gleichfalls sprachlos, auf seinem Sitz wie angenagelt, schaute ihm halb lachend, unter sichtbarem Erröten, doch gewissermaßen keck und
10 groß mit seinen blauen Augen ins Gesicht; dann setzte er – für einen Dritten wäre es höchst komisch anzusehen gewesen – die scheinbar unverletzte Pomeranze . . . in die Mitte des Tisches.

EDUARD MÖRIKE (1804–75),
Mozart auf der Reise nach Prag

[1] versumpft: *boggy*   [2] die Pomeranze: *orange*

1 Warum erschrak Mozart?
2 Was hatte Mozart mit der Pomeranze tun wollen?
3 Warum wollte er die Pomeranze zuerst verbergen?
4 Aus welchen Gründen verbarg er die Pomeranze nicht?
5 Wer stellte sich vor ihn?
6 Warum hatte der Gärtner Mozart in Verdacht?
7 Was sagte er?
8 Woher wissen Sie, daß Mozart sich verlegen fühlte?
9 Wohin setzte er die Pomeranze?
10 Woraus schließen Sie, daß die Pomeranze nicht mehr heil war?

Zum Fortsetzen (Umriß, S. 227)

15 Abend auf dem Dorfe

Klein aß Gemüsesuppe und Brot, der Wirt kam heim, an den
grauen Steindächern des Dorfes verglühte die späte Sonne. Er
fragte nach einem Zimmer, es wurde ihm eines angeboten, eine
Kammer mit dicken, nackten Steinwänden. Er nahm es. Noch nie
5 hatte er in einer solchen Kammer geschlafen, sie kam ihm vor wie
das Gelaß[1] aus einem Räuberdrama. Nun ging er durch das abendliche Dorf, fand einen kleinen Kramladen noch offen, bekam
Schokolade zu kaufen und verteilte sie an Kinder, die in Mengen
durch die Gasse schwärmten. Sie liefen ihm nach, Eltern grüßten
10 ihn, jedermann wünschte ihm gute Nacht, und er gab es zurück,
nickte allen den alten und jungen Menschen zu, die auf den Schwel-
len und Vortreppen der Häuser saßen.

HERMANN HESSE (1877–1962), *Klein und Wagner*

1 Wo aß Klein?
2 Woraus bestand seine Mahlzeit?
3 Wo wollte er die Nacht zubringen?
4 Warum gefiel ihm die angebotene Kammer nicht?
5 Was kann man in einem Kramladen kaufen?
6 Was ist eine Gasse?

[1] das Gelaß: Zimmer

7 Was beweist, daß Klein Kinder liebte?
8 Warum liefen die Kinder ihm nach?
9 Welche Jahreszeit war es?
10 Was machten die Dorfbewohner am Abend?

16 Emanuel verläßt sein Heim

An einem Sonntagmorgen, im Monat Mai, erhob sich Emanuel
Quint von seiner Lagerstätte auf dem Boden des kleinen Hüttchens,
das der Vater mit sehr geringem Recht sein Eigen nannte. Er wusch
sich mit klarem Gebirgswasser, draußen am Steintrog, indem er
5 die hohlen Hände unter den kristallenen Strahl hielt, der aus einer
hölzernen, vermorschten[1] und bemoosten Rinne[2] floß. Er hatte die
Nacht kaum ein wenig geschlafen und schritt nun, ohne die Seinen
zu wecken oder etwas zu sich zu nehmen, in der Richtung gegen
Reichenbach. Ein altes Weib, das auf einem Feldweg ihm entgegen-
10 kam, blieb stehen, als sie von fern seiner ansichtig wurde. Denn
Emanuel ging mit seinem langen, wiegenden[3] Schritt und in einer
sonderbar würdigen Haltung, die mit seinen unbekleideten Füßen,
seinem unbedeckten Kopf, sowie mit der Armseligkeit seiner
Bekleidung überhaupt in Widerspruch stand.

GERHART HAUPTMANN (1862–1946),
Der Narr in Christo, Emanuel Quint

1 Wo schlief Emanuel Quint?
2 Waren seine Eltern reich?
3 Woher kam das Wasser, mit dem er sich wusch?
4 Warum war er früh aufgestanden?
5 Woher wissen Sie, daß er keinen großen Hunger hatte?
6 Was machten die Seinen?
7 Wohin wollte Emanuel gehen?
8 Drücken Sie anders aus: als sie seiner ansichtig wurde.
9 Was hatte Emanuel an den Füßen? Und auf dem Kopf?
10 Wie war er angezogen?

[1] vermorscht: *rotten*   [2] die Rinne: *conduit*
[3] wiegend: *springy, swinging*

17 Anfang einer Freundschaft

Er wagte ihn kaum von nahe anzusehen, so sehr bewunderte er ihn. Sein Vater hatte einen Palast und viele Autos. Er wurde in einem Auto zur Schule gebracht und nahm bei der Rückfahrt stets einen Kameraden mit, den er nach Hause fuhr. Einmal lud er Axel ein,
5 aber Axel lehnte erschreckt ab, denn erstens war das Haus, in dem sie wohnten, schlecht und hatte einen häßlichen Eingang, vor dem immer schwatzende Weiber standen. Und dann fühlte er sich gedemütigt und wurde trotzig. „Wenn du mit mir zusammen sein willst, warum gehst du nicht mit mir?" hatte er geantwortet. Da war
10 der vornehme Junge stumm abgefahren. Am nächsten Tage kam er ohne Automobil. Als die Schule zu Ende war, fragte er Axel, ob sie ein Stück miteinander gehen wollten; nur so ganz nebenbei, als sei es ihm gerade eingefallen. Axel erbebte. Ja, sagte er gleichgültig, er habe wohl noch etwas Zeit und könne ihn begleiten. Dann gingen
15 sie und sprachen nichts.

FRANK THIESS (1890–   ), *Die Verdammten*

1 Warum wagte Axel nicht, den vornehmen Jungen von nahe anzusehen?

2 Woher wissen Sie, daß der vornehme Junge reich war?

3 Was ist ein Palast?

4 Wie kam der vornehme Junge zur Schule?

5 Wen fuhr er jeden Tag nach Hause?

6 Warum weigerte sich Axel, mit ihm zu fahren?

7 Was für einen Eingang hatte Axels Haus?

8 Wollte der vornehme Junge Axel demütigen?

9 Warum kam er am folgenden Tage ohne Automobil?

10 Warum erbebte Axel?

18 Zu spät

Wie ich noch immer so dasitze, höre ich auf einmal aus der Ferne Hufschlag im Walde. Ich hielt den Atem an und lauschte, da kam es immer näher und näher, und ich konnte schon die Pferde schnauben hören. Bald darauf kamen auch wirklich zwei Reiter unter den
5 Bäumen hervor, hielten aber am Rande des Waldes an und sprachen heimlich sehr eifrig miteinander ... Ich streckte mich nun an dem Lindenbaume, unter dem ich gesessen hatte, ganz unmerklich so

lang aus, als ich nur konnte, bis ich den ersten Ast erreicht hatte und
mich geschwinde hinaufschwang. Aber ich baumelte noch mit
10 halbem Leibe über dem Aste und wollte soeben auch meine Beine
nachholen, als der eine von den Reitern rasch hinter mir über den
Platz dahertrabte. Ich drückte nun die Augen fest zu in dem dunklen
Laube und rührte und regte mich nicht. „Wer ist da?" rief es auf
einmal dicht hinter mir. „Niemand!" schrie ich aus Leibeskräften
15 vor Schreck. „Ei, ei", sagte der Räuber wieder, „wem gehören denn
aber die zwei Beine, die da herunterhängen?"

JOSEPH VON EICHENDORFF (1778–1857),
Aus dem Leben eines Taugenichts

1 Was tat der Taugenichts, um besser hören zu können?
2 Warum schnaubten die Pferde?
3 Drücken Sie anders aus: sie sprachen heimlich miteinander.
4 Wo stand der Lindenbaum?
5 Warum streckte sich der Taugenichts lang aus?
6 Was beweist, daß der Taugenichts Angst vor den Reitern hatte?
7 Stiegen die Reiter von den Pferden ab?
8 Warum drückte der Taugenichts die Augen fest zu?
9 Woher wissen Sie, daß es Sommer war?
10 Woher wußte der Reiter, daß jemand im Baum war?

Zum Fortsetzen (Umriß, S. 227)

19 Schiff in Not

Seit Silvesternacht ging ein scharfer Nordost, der sich in den nächsten Tagen fast bis zum Sturm steigerte, und am 3. Januar nachmittags hieß es, daß ein Schiff draußen mit der Einfahrt nicht
zustande gekommen und hundert Schritt vor der Mole gescheitert
5 sei; es sei ein englisches, von Sunderland her, und soweit sich
erkennen lasse, sieben Mann an Bord; die Lotsen[1] könnten beim
Ausfahren, trotz aller Anstrengung, nicht um die Mole herum, und
vom Strande aus ein Boot abzulassen, daran sei nun vollends nicht
zu denken, die Brandung[2] sei viel zu stark. Das klang traurig genug.
10 Aber Johanna, die die Nachricht brachte, hatte doch auch Trost bei
der Hand: Konsul Eschrich, mit dem Rettungsapparat und der Raketenbatterie, sei schon unterwegs, und es würde gewiß glücken; die

[1] der Lotse: *pilot*   [2] die Brandung: *breakers*

Entfernung sei nicht so weit wie anno 75, wo's doch auch gegangen, und sie hätten damals den Pudel mit gerettet, und es wäre ordentlich
15 rührend gewesen, wie sich das Tier gefreut und die Kapitänsfrau und das liebe, kleine Kind immer wieder mit seiner roten Zunge geleckt habe.

THEODOR FONTANE (1819–98), *Effi Briest*

1 Wann ist Silvester?
2 Warum ist das Schiff gescheitert?
3 Wieviel Leute waren an Bord?
4 Was ist ein Lotse?
5 Wozu dient eine Mole?
6 Warum konnten die Lotsen nicht um die Mole herum?
7 Was wäre geschehen, wenn ein Boot vom Strand abgelassen worden wäre?
8 Warum war die Lage nicht hoffnungslos?
9 Woraus besteht ein Rettungsapparat?
10 Was tut man mit einer Rakete?
11 Wie weit von der Mole war das Schiff im Jahre 1875 gescheitert?
12 Wie hatte der Hund seine Freude gezeigt?

Zum Fortsetzen (Umriß, S. 227)

20 Das Wiedersehen

Der Zug hält.

Es steigen nicht allzu viele aus. Auf sie zu kommt ein Herr in schwarzen Koteletten[1]. Er sieht sie fragend an. Sie bleibt stehen. Er – geht weiter. Sie sieht ihm nach. Er fällt irgendeinem Frauenzimmer[2]
5 in die ausgebreiteten Arme. Gott sei Dank. Indessen: wo ist Axel? Sie läuft zur Sperre. Da drängen sich Menschen. Nein, hier ist er gewiß nicht. Wie dumm, daß wir kein Erkennungszeichen abgemacht haben! Gewiß werden sie aneinander vorüberlaufen.

Plötzlich bleibt ihr zwei Sekunden lang das Herz stehen. Sie
10 sieht einen ganz fremden Herrn mit breitem Reisemantel und Mütze drei Schritte vor sich. Er gibt einem Gepäckträger den Handkoffer und zeigt ihm einen Zettel. Der Gepäckträger sagt etwas und deutet nach rechts. Dabei dreht er sich um und sieht auf Ursula.

[1] die Koteletten (*pl.*): *mutton-chop whiskers* [2] das Frauenzimmer: *female*

Und Ursula sieht auf ihn. Ein, zwei, drei Sekunden starren sich
15 beide an. Dann sagt der fremde Herr mit etwas englischem Akzent:
„Ich habe dich zuerst erkannt."
„Axel . . ."
Er gibt ihr die Hand. Hinter seiner Hornbrille sehen zwei dunkle
Augen sie erstaunt und ganz merkwürdig an. Muings[1] Augen.
20 „Du hast Muings Augen, Axel."

FRANK THIESS (1890–), *Die Verdammten*

1 Wieviel Menschen stiegen aus?
2 Warum freute sich Ursula, daß der Herr nicht Axel war?
3 Was tut man an der Sperre?
4 Wieviel Leute waren an der Sperre?
5 Warum konnte Ursula Axel nicht erkennen?
6 Was hatte der fremde Herr auf dem Kopf?
7 Warum gab er dem Gepäckträger einen Zettel?
8 Warum drehte er sich um?
9 Wo hatte Axel wahrscheinlich gelebt?
10 Was für Augen hatte Muing?

Zum Fortsetzen (Umriß, S. 227)

21 Der Anfang des Buches

Um das Jahr 1450 lebte zu Mainz Meister Johann Gensfleisch,
genannt Gutenberg, ein Mann aus einem vornehmen Bürgergeschlecht der Stadt. Sein Vater hatte aber in einem Aufstand der
unteren Bürger all sein Vermögen verloren. Daher war Johann
5 Gutenberg ein armer Mann und mußte allerlei Handwerk treiben,
sich und seine Hausfrau zu ernähren. Er war ein geschickter und
kluger Mann und hatte in den Werkstätten zu Mainz und Straßburg
mancherlei Künste gelernt. Er verstand es, glänzende Spiegel aus
Kristall und Glas zu schleifen und edle Steine zu schneiden. Sein
10 Hauptgewerbe aber war es, allerlei Bildwerk in Holz einzugraben,
das Bild mit Schwärze zu überziehen und auf Papier oder Leinwand

[1] Muing: Ursulas Name für die Mutter

abzudrucken. Von einem solchen Bildstock¹ konnte man viele Bilder abziehen und also um billigeres Geld verkaufen, als die mit der Hand gemalten und gezeichneten Bilder. Band man viele der-
15 gleichen mit einem Band zusammen, so wurde es ein Buch. Und dies waren die ersten gedruckten Bücher, die es gab. Es waren aber nur Bilderbücher mit wenigen verzierten Worten und Sprüchen. – Alle anderen Bücher wurden noch wie von altersher mit Tinte und Feder auf Pergament und das neumodische Papier geschrieben.

WILL VESPER (1882–1962), *Die Flügel der Gedanken*

1 In welchem Jahrhundert lebte Gutenberg?
2 Warum war sein Vater arm gewesen?
3 Wie ernährte sich Gutenberg?
4 Was konnte er machen?
5 Wozu dient ein Spiegel?
6 Hatte Gutenberg immer in Mainz gelebt?
7 Warum waren seine Bilder billiger?
8 Wie konnte man aus den Bildern ein Buch machen?
9 Wer hat die ersten gedruckten Bücher gemacht?
10 Welchen Nachteil hatten die ersten gedruckten Bücher?

22 Verletzter Stolz

Als Anton an das Pult des Prokuristen² trat, um den Brief in Empfang zu nehmen, sah Fink von seinem Platz auf und sagte zu Jordan: „Schicken Sie ihn doch gleich einmal zum Büchsenmacher, der Taugenichts soll ihm mein Gewehr mitgeben." Da sagte Anton zu
5 Jordan: „Geben Sie mir den Auftrag nicht, ich werde ihn nicht ausrichten." – „So?" fragte Fink und sah verwundert auf, „und warum nicht?" – „Ich bin nicht Ihr Diener", antwortete Anton. „Hätten Sie mich gebeten, den Gang für Sie zu tun, so würde ich ihn vielleicht gemacht haben, aber einem Auftrage von Ihnen folge
10 ich nicht." – „Einfältiger Junge", brummte Fink und schrieb weiter.

Das ganze Kontor hatte die schmähenden Worte gehört, alle Federn hielten still, und alle Herren sahen auf Anton. Dieser war in der größten Aufregung, er rief mit etwas bebender Stimme, aber

¹ der Bildstock: *engraved block from which prints were made*
² der Prokurist: *head clerk*

15 mit blitzenden Augen: „Sie haben mich beleidigt. Sie werden mir
heute abend darüber eine Erklärung geben." – „Ich prügele nie-
manden gern", sagte Fink friedfertig. – „Es ist genug", rief Anton
totenbleich, „Sie sollen mir Rede stehen", ergriff seinen Hut und
stürzte mit dem Brief des Herrn Jordan hinaus.

GUSTAV FREYTAG (1816–95), *Soll und Haben*

1 Warum trat Anton an das Pult des Prokuristen?
2 Wie hieß der Prokurist?
3 Was macht ein Prokurist?
4 Was ist ein Büchsenmacher?
5 Warum wollte Anton das Gewehr nicht abholen?
6 Was für ein Mann war Fink?
7 Warum hielten alle Federn still?
8 Warum sprach Anton mit bebender Stimme?
9 Was verlangte Anton von Fink?
10 Warum wurde Anton totenbleich?
11 Übersetzen Sie: Sie sollen mir Rede stehen.

Zum Fortsetzen (Umriß, S. 228)

23 Zukunftspläne

Er glitt in seine frühere Lage zurück. „Dies frühzeitige Aufstehen",
dachte er, „macht einen ganz blödsinnig. Der Mensch muß seinen
Schlaf haben. Andere Reisende leben wie Haremsfrauen. Wenn ich
zum Beispiel im Laufe des Vormittags ins Gasthaus zurückgehe, um
5 die erlangten Aufträge zu überschreiben, sitzen diese Herren erst
beim Frühstück. Das sollte ich bei meinem Chef versuchen; ich
würde auf der Stelle hinausfliegen. Wer weiß übrigens, ob das nicht
sehr gut für mich wäre. Wenn ich mich nicht wegen meiner Eltern
zurückhielte, ich hätte längst gekündigt, ich wäre vor den Chef
10 hingetreten und hätte ihm meine Meinung von Grund des Herzens
aus gesagt. Vom Pult hätte er fallen müssen. Es ist auch eine sonderbare Art, sich auf das Pult zu setzen und von der Höhe herab mit
dem Angestellten zu reden, der überdies wegen der Schwerhörigkeit
des Chefs ganz nahe herantreten muß. Nun, die Hoffnung ist noch
15 nicht gänzlich aufgegeben; habe ich einmal das Geld beisammen,
um die Schuld der Eltern an ihn abzuzahlen – es dürfte noch fünf

bis sechs Jahre dauern –, mache ich die Sache unbedingt . . .
Vorläufig allerdings muß ich aufstehen, denn mein Zug fährt um
fünf."

FRANZ KAFKA (1883–1924), Die Verwandlung

1 Um wieviel Uhr mußte der Reisende aufstehen?
2 Warum muß der Mensch seinen Schlaf haben?
3 Warum mußte der Reisende im Laufe des Tages ins Gasthaus
  zurückgehen?
4 Warum beneidete er die anderen Reisenden?
5 Warum wagte er nicht später aufzustehen?
6 Warum hatte er nicht längst gekündigt?
7 Was möchte der Reisende tun?
8 Was tat sein Chef, wenn man mit ihm redete?
9 Warum mußte man ganz nahe an ihn herantreten?
10 Wie lange würde der Reisende noch für seinen Chef arbeiten
   müssen?

24 Schwacher Vorsatz

Dann hatte er den Wecker gerichtet und geschlafen, so tief und tot,
wie man schläft, wenn man niemals wieder erwachen möchte. Und
nun war der Montag da, und es war sechs Uhr, und er hatte für
keine Stunde gearbeitet!

5   Er richtete sich auf und entzündete die Kerze auf dem Nacht-
tische. Da aber in der eiskalten Luft seine Arme und Schultern
heftig zu frieren begannen, ließ er sich rasch wieder zurücksinken
und zog die Decke über sich.

Die Zeiger wiesen auf zehn Minuten nach sechs Uhr . . . Ach, es
10 war sinnlos, nun aufzustehen und zu arbeiten, es war zuviel, es gab
beinahe für jede Stunde etwas zu lernen, es lohnte nicht, damit
anzufangen, und der Zeitpunkt, den er sich festgesetzt, war sowieso[1]
überschritten . . . War es denn so sicher, wie es ihm gestern erschie-
nen war, daß er heute sowohl im Lateinischen wie in der Chemie an
15 die Reihe kommen würde? Es war anzunehmen, ja, nach mensch-
licher Voraussicht war es wahrscheinlich. Aber es war doch nicht
unbedingt sicher, nicht ganz und gar zweifellos! Es kamen doch
Abweichungen von der Regel vor! Was bewirkte nicht manchmal

----

[1] sowieso: ohnedies, auf alle Fälle

der Zufall, du lieber Gott! . . . Und während er sich mit diesen
20 trügerischen Erwägungen beschäftigte, verschwammen seine Gedanken ineinander, und er entschlief[1] aufs neue.

THOMAS MANN (1875–1955), Buddenbrooks

1 Warum hatte der Junge den Wecker gerichtet?
2 Warum machte er Licht an?
3 Warum zog er die Decke über sich?
4 Wann hatte er aufstehen wollen?
5 Was hätte der Junge am Sonntag tun sollen?
6 Warum lohnte es jetzt nicht zu arbeiten?
7 Was hoffte der Junge?
8 Warum war es nicht unbedingt sicher, daß er an die Reihe kommen
 würde?
9 Woher wissen Sie, daß der Junge noch müde war?
10 Hatte der Junge Angst vor seinen Lehrern?

Zum Fortsetzen (Umriß, S. 228)

25 Die Wand hat Ohren

Es kann für einen Gastwirt immer wichtig sein, was seine Gäste
miteinander sprechen. So war in dem Haus auch eine Einrichtung[2],
durch die unser Wirt in bequemer Lage die beiden belauschen
konnte, als sie die Kleider ablegten, um ins Bett zu gehen, bei
5 welcher Gelegenheit, wie er aus Erfahrung wußte, häufig der
Tageslauf besprochen wird und Entschlüsse für den folgenden Tag
gefaßt werden.

„Morgen werde ich sie wiedersehen", sagte Don Enrique, indem
er seine Hosen auszog und an einen Nagel hängte. „Wird sie mich
10 erkennen? Und wenn sie mich erkennt, wird dann der Groll[3] auf
den Mörder ihres Gatten[4] übermächtig sein?"

Der Wirt spitzte die Ohren.

Gil gähnte. „Der Kaninchenpfeffer[5] war gut. Etwas schärfer
hätte er sein können. Er muß den Gaumen[6] brennen."

15 An der Wand hing eine Laute. Don Enrique nahm sie, setzte sich

---

[1] entschlafen: einschlafen   [2] die Einrichtung: *contrivance*
[3] der Groll: *resentment*   [4] der Gatte: der Mann
[5] der Kaninchenpfeffer: *jugged rabbit*   [6] der Gaumen: *palate*

im Hemd, mit nackten Beinen, auf den Bettrand und schlug ein paar Töne an. Sie war verstimmt, und er schraubte.

„Ich wette meinen Kopf, daß Donna Elena Euer Gnaden nicht erkennen", sagte Gil.

20 Der Wirt wußte genug. Leise zog er sich aus seinem Versteck, huschte mit nackten Füßen die Treppe hinunter und rief seiner Frau zu: „Schnell den Sonntagsanzug, die guten Schuhe! Ich muß gleich aufs Schloß." Seine Frau fragte erregt, er antwortete: „Bekümmere du dich um deine Töpfe, ich muß aufs Schloß, 25 schnell!"

PAUL ERNST (1866–1933), *Ein Familienbild von Goya*

1 Wie befriedigte der Gastwirt seine Neugierde?
2 Woher wissen Sie, daß er seine Gäste oft belauscht hatte?
3 Was wollte Don Enrique am folgenden Tage machen?
4 Was hatte Don Enrique getan?
5 Warum spitzte der Wirt die Ohren?
6 Warum gähnte Gil?
7 Was ist eine Laute?
8 Warum mußte Don Enrique schrauben?
9 Wo war das Schlafzimmer der Gäste?
10 Warum wollte der Wirt sich schön anziehen?
11 Wo wohnte Donna Elena?

Zum Fortsetzen (Umriß, S. 228)

(B) Passages for Translation, Comprehension or Reproduction

26 Der Mißerfolg

Mit unbeschreiblichem Zorn ging Eduard nach Hause. Er trat wütend ein, warf alle Türen heftig hinter sich zu und eilte durch die großen Zimmer nach einem kleinen Hinterstübchen, wo in der Dämmerung der alte Eulenböck bei einem Glase starken Weines auf 5 ihn wartete. „Hier!" schrie Eduard, „du alter Halunke, ist dein Bild wieder."

„Schade", sagte der alte Maler, indem er sich ein neues Glas einschenkte. „Der Alte hat also von dem Kauf nichts wissen wollen?"

„Du Halunke!" schrie Eduard, indem er das Bild heftig hinwarf; 10 „und um deinetwillen bin ich auch zum Halunken geworden! O wie schäme ich mich vor mir selber, daß ich aus Liebe zu dir eine solche Lüge sagte!"

„Ist keine Lüge, lieber Junge", sagte der Maler, indem er das Bild auswickelte, „ist ein so echter[1] Salvator Rosa[2], wie ich nur noch 15 je einen gemalt habe."

nach JOHANN LUDWIG TIECK (1773–1853), *Die Gemälde*

1 Warum warf Eduard alle Türen heftig hinter sich zu?
2 Was tat Eulenböck in dem kleinen Hinterstübchen?
3 Warum konnte Eduard den alten Eulenböck nicht deutlich sehen?
4 Was ist ein Halunke?
5 Was hatte Eduard zu tun versucht?
6 Warum hatte „der Alte" nichts vom Kauf wissen wollen?
7 Warum schämte sich Eduard vor sich selbst?
8 Hatte er Eulenböck gern?
9 Wie verdiente Eulenböck sein Brot?
10 Was für Bilder malte Eulenböck?

Zum Nacherzählen (Umriß, S. 281)

27 Irrtum der Räuber

Die Räuber überfielen vor einigen Tagen in der Gegend von Albano ein Landhaus, in der Hoffnung, den reichen Besitzer desselben zu erhaschen. Statt dessen fanden sie aber einen armen Maler, den jener bei sich hatte, und nahmen ihn aus Verwechslung mit. Drei 5 Tage schleppten sie ihn mit sich, wobei sie ihm oft mit Dolch und Flinte drohten, wenn er einen Versuch machte, zu entfliehen oder um Hilfe zu rufen. Endlich entdeckte sich der Irrtum. Der junge Mensch, ein Schweizer, der sich etwas auf die Artillerie verstand, hatte inzwischen dadurch ihre Gunst gewonnen, daß er ihnen 10 manches von seiner Feuerwerkskunst[3] mitteilte und durch Zeich-

---

[1] echt: *genuine*   [2] Salvator Rosa: italienischer Maler des 17. Jahrhunderts
[3] die Feuerwerkskunst: *pyrotechnics*; (*here*) *knowledge of gunnery*

nungen versinnlichte[1]. Die Räuber hörten ihm mit großem Vergnügen zu und meinten, wenn sie nur erst einmal Kanonen hätten, dann sollte es ganz anders hergehen. Endlich ließen sie ihn los, indem sie ihn einluden, sie zu besuchen, wenn er wollte.

FRANZ GRILLPARZER (1791–1872),
Tagebuch auf der Reise nach Italien

1 Warum überfielen die Räuber ein Landhaus?
2 Wen glaubten sie erhascht zu haben?
3 Wie kam es, daß der arme Maler im Landhaus war?
4 Was ist ein Maler?
5 Warum drohten die Räuber dem Maler mit Dolch und Flinte?
6 Wo wurde der Maler geboren?
7 Auf welche Weise gewann der Maler die Gunst der Räuber?
8 Was würden die Räuber machen, wenn sie Kanonen hätten?
9 Warum ließen sie den Maler los?
10 Was sollte der Maler tun?

Zum Nacherzählen (Umriß, S. 281)

28 Bestrafte Unachtsamkeit

Eines Tages war ich vor Sonnenaufgang aufgebrochen und nach einer noch nie eingeschlagenen Richtung hingegangen, weil der Löwe tags vorher sich auf der entgegengesetzten Seite herumgetrieben und einen vergeblichen Raubversuch gemacht hatte. Es
5 war totenstill überall und kein lebendes Wesen zu erspähen. Da stieß ich an den Rand einer Schlucht[2]. Es floß ein kühler, frischer Bach auf ihrem Grunde. Ich wünschte, aus dem Bach zu trinken; ich legte mein Gewehr auf den Boden und kletterte eiligst in die Schlucht hinunter, wo ich mich zur Erde warf, aus dem Bach trank
10 und mein Gesicht benetzte. Da hörte ich ganz nah den Löwen ein kurzes Gebrüll ausstoßen, daß der Boden zitterte. Wie besessen sprang ich auf und schwang mich den Abhang hinauf, blieb aber

---

[1] versinnlichen: *illustrate*   [2] die Schlucht: tiefes, enges Tal

wie angenagelt oben stehen, als ich sah, daß das große Tier, kaum
zehn Schritte von mir, eben bei meinem Gewehr angekommen war.

nach GOTTFRIED KELLER (1819–90), *Pankraz der Schmoller*

1 Woher wissen Sie, daß Pankraz die Gegend nicht kannte?
2 Was ist ein Löwe?
3 War es am Tage vorher dem Löwen gelungen, etwas zu rauben?
4 Was konnte Pankraz hören?
5 Was sah er in der Schlucht?
6 Warum legte er sein Gewehr auf den Boden?
7 Warum benetzte er sein Gesicht?
8 Warum war er erschrocken, als er den Löwen brüllen hörte?
9 Warum schwang er sich den Abhang hinauf?
10 Wie weit war der Löwe von ihm?

Zum Nacherzählen (Umriß, S. 281)

29 Unrechter Augenblick

Einige Tage darauf hatte Direktor Meier ihn und seine Frau
eingeladen. Als Helmold gerade den Frack anziehen wollte, kam
Grete hereingestürzt, ganz unglückliche Augen in dem kreideweißen
Gesicht, die linke Hand auf dem Herzen und ein großes Schrift-
5 stück in der anderen. „Nanu?" rief er, „was ist denn los?" Sie hielt
ihm das Papier hin, setzte sich auf das Bett und fing hellauf zu
weinen an. „Lieber Helmcke[1]", schluchzte sie, „um Gotteswillen,
da, lies, ich habe, denke dir, wir haben, von Ohm[2] Mette haben wir
fünfhunderttausend Mark geerbt." Kaum hatte sie das gesagt, so fiel
10 sie in Ohnmacht.

„Verdammter Blödsinn", knurrte ihr Mann; „mußte der Esel
von Anwalt[3] das auch jetzt gerade schicken!" Er klingelte nach dem
Mädchen und brachte mit ihr zusammen seine Frau zu Bett. Sie
erwachte bald wieder, sagte aber, ihr sei so schlecht, daß sie ihn
15 nicht begleiten könne.

HERMANN LÖNS (1866–1914), *Das zweite Gesicht*

[1] Helmcke: Kosename für Helmold   [2] der Ohm: der Onkel
[3] der Anwalt: *lawyer*

1 Warum wollte Helmold den Frack anziehen?
2 Wann kam Grete hereingestürzt?
3 Wer war Grete?
4 Was hielt sie in der rechten Hand?
5 Übersetzen Sie: was ist denn los?
6 Warum weinte Grete?
7 Warum war Helmold nicht mit dem Anwalt zufrieden?
8 Warum klingelte er nach dem Mädchen?
9 Blieb Grete lange in Ohnmacht?
10 Warum konnte Grete Helmold nicht begleiten?

Zum Nacherzählen (Umriß, S. 281)

30 Der störrische Esel

Also nach Tische, mehr als heiter gestimmt, machten wir uns zu
Esel auf den Weg, um bei einbrechender Nacht die Spitze des
Vesuvs zu erreichen. Mein Tier war das trägste von allen, und nur
schwer gelang es mir, es durch Stockschläge in Trott zu bringen,
5 wo es denn nun aber auch allen andern vorauslief. In der Nähe der
Einsiedlerwohnung[1] kommt uns eine Kavalkade von einigen
verschleierten Damen mit Begleitung entgegen. Aus der Livree der
Bedienten merkte ich, daß es die Kaiserin von Österreich sei. Ich
suchte nun vor allem meinen dahinstürmenden Esel zum Stehen
10 oder wenigstens aus der Mitte des Weges zu bringen, welches
letztere mir aber nur so gelang, daß er sich neben den Weg mit dem
Kopf nach außen stellte, so daß die hohe Frau an unsern beider-
seitigen Rücken vorüberreiten mußte, und ich nur den Hut abziehen,
sie aber nicht sehen konnte.

FRANZ GRILLPARZER (1791–1872), *Selbstbiographie*

1 Was hatte Grillparzer heiter gestimmt?
2 Was ist ein Esel?
3 Drücken Sie anders aus: bei einbrechender Nacht.
4 Wohin wollte man gehen?

[1] der Einsiedler: *hermit*

5 Warum mußte Grillparzer seinen Esel schlagen?
6 Von wem wurden die Damen begleitet?
7 Woran erkannte Grillparzer, daß die Kaiserin von Österreich ihm
  entgegenkam?
8 Warum wollte er den Esel aus der Mitte des Weges bringen?
9 Wie stellte sich der Esel?
10 Was tut man, wenn man eine Dame grüßen will?

Zum Nacherzählen (Umriß, S. 281)

31 Das Theater brennt

Diese Nacht, bald nach zwölf Uhr, wurden wir durch Feuerlärm
geweckt; man rief, es brenne im Theater. Ich warf mich sogleich in
meine Kleider und eilte an Ort und Stelle. Die allgemeine Bestürzung war groß. Das Feuer schien im Parterre ausgebrochen zu sein,
5 hatte bald die Bühne ergriffen, und so dauerte es nicht lange, bis die
Flamme überall zum Dache herausschlug. Das Gebäude war nach
und nach ganz mit Spritzen[1] umstellt, die eine Unmasse von Wasser
in die Glut gossen. Allein es war alles ohne Erfolg. Ein wenig
seitwärts, so nahe die Glut es erlaubte, stand ein Mann im Mantel
10 und Militärmütze, in der ruhigsten Fassung eine Zigarre rauchend.
Er schien beim ersten Anblick ein müßiger Zuschauer zu sein;
allein er war es nicht. Personen gingen von ihm aus, denen er mit
wenigen Worten Befehle erteilte, die sogleich vollzogen wurden. Es
war der Großherzog Karl August.

JOHANN PETER ECKERMANN (1792–1854), *Gespräche mit Goethe*

1 Was war los?
2 Warum warf Eckermann sich in die Kleider?
3 Wo war das Feuer ausgebrochen?
4 Warum war das Gebäude mit Spritzen umstellt?
5 Was ist eine Bühne?
6 Gelang es den Leuten, das Feuer zu löschen?
7 Was tat der Mann im Mantel?
8 Warum schien der Mann im Mantel ein müßiger Zuschauer zu
  sein?

[1] die Spritze: *fire-engine*

9 Woher wußte Eckermann, daß dieser Mann kein müßiger Zuschauer war?

10 Warum gehorchten ihm die Leute?

Zum Nacherzählen (Umriß, S. 281)

32 Die Prophezeiung

Ich war eines Abends eben mit Angelina im Garten an dem eisernen Gitter, durch das man auf die Straße hinaussah. Da kam eine alte Zigeunerin am Gitter vorbei und verlangte, als sie uns drinnen erblickte, auf die gewöhnliche ungestüme[1] Art uns zu prophezeien.
5 Ich streckte sogleich meine Hand hinaus. Sie las lange Zeit darin. Inzwischen ritt ein junger Mensch, der ein Reisender schien, draußen die Straße vorbei und grüßte uns höflich. Die Zigeunerin sah erstaunt mich, Angelina und den vorüberziehenden Fremden wechselseitig[2] an, endlich sagte sie, auf uns und ihn deutend:
10 „Eines von euch dreien wird den anderen ermorden." – Ich blickte dem Reiter scharf nach, er sah sich noch einmal um, und ich erkannte erschrocken und zornig sogleich das Gesicht desselben unbekannten Knaben wieder, der uns bei unserem Auszug aus der Heimat so verhöhnt hatte. – Die Zigeunerin war unterdessen verschwunden,
15 Angelina furchtsam fortgelaufen, und ich blieb allein in dem großen, dämmernden Garten.

JOSEPH VON EICHENDORFF (1778–1857), *Ahnung und Gegenwart*

1 Was ist eine Zigeunerin?
2 Warum streckte der Sprecher seine Hand hinaus?
3 Was tat die Zigeunerin mit der Hand?
4 Warum sah ihn die Zigeunerin erstaunt an?
5 Wie alt war der Reiter?
6 Wo hatte der Sprecher den Reiter früher gesehen?
7 War der Reiter immer so höflich gewesen wie heute?
8 Blieb die Zigeunerin dort stehen?
9 Warum war Angelina fortgelaufen?
10 Woher wissen Sie, daß die Sonne untergegangen war?

Zum Nacherzählen (Umriß, S. 282)

[1] ungestüm: *impetuous*   [2] wechselseitig: *alternately*

33 Die freundliche Alte

Die Alte griff erstaunt aber unerschrocken nach ihrer Öllampe. Das Flämmchen mit der Hand gegen den Luftzug deckend, näherte sie sich der Fensteröffnung. Als sie das kluge, junge Gesicht erblickte, wurden ihre scharfen grauen Augen freundlich, und sie sagte: „Ihr 5 seid wohl auch ein Prädikant[1]?" – „Ein Stück davon!" antwortete Waser. „Laßt mich ein, Mütterchen."

Die Alte nickte ihm zu, den Finger auf den Mund legend, und verschwand. Jetzt knarrte ein niedriges Pförtchen[2] neben dem Ziegenstalle, Waser kletterte hinunter und wurde von der Alten, die 10 seine Hand ergriff, über ein paar dunkle Stufen hinauf in die Küche gezogen.

„Ein warmes Kämmerchen findet sich wohl – das meinige!" sagte sie, auf eine Leitertreppe zeigend, die zu einer Falltür in der Decke führte. „Ich habe die ganze Nacht am Feuer zu tun – die 15 Herrschaften drüben setzen sich eben erst zu Tische. Haltet Euch droben still, Ihr seid dort sicher, und einen Geistlichen werd' ich auch nicht verhungern lassen."

nach CONRAD FERDINAND MEYER (1825–98), *Jürg Jenatsch*

1 Was hatte die Alte in Erstaunen gesetzt?
2 Warum deckte sie das Flämmchen mit der Hand?
3 Warum wurde die Alte freundlich?
4 Was wollte Waser?
5 Warum legte die Alte den Finger auf den Mund?
6 Wo hatte Waser gestanden?
7 Wo sollte er die Nacht zubringen?
8 Wie kam man ins Kämmerchen der Alten?
9 Warum brauchte die Alte selber kein Bett?
10 Woher wissen Sie, daß Waser etwas zu essen bekam?

Zum Nacherzählen (Umriß, S. 282)
Zum Fortsetzen (Umriß, S. 228)

[1] der Prädikant: *preacher*   [2] das Pförtchen: kleine Tür

34 Der unehrliche Müller

Ein anderer Nachbar, ein Müller, hat Chlodwig seine Mühle verkauft. Die Hälfte des Kaufpreises war sogleich zu zahlen; und ein Jahr, nachdem der Verkäufer seine Mühle geräumt haben würde, sollte der Rest gezahlt werden. Der Müller macht aber keine
5 Miene zu gehen. Man sagt, er wolle bleiben, die Hälfte des Kaufpreises einstecken und bleiben. Ein Fehler im Kontrakt soll ihm dies möglich machen.

Die Sache kommt Chlodwig zu Ohren; er sieht nach – richtig! Der Kontrakt hat einen Fehler.
10 Sogleich läßt er anspannen, fährt zu dem Müller hinüber und sagt ihm: „Ich höre, du willst Nutzen ziehen aus dem Fehler im Kontrakt. Das glaube ich nicht. Brauchen Männer wie du und ich geschriebene Worte? So habe ich dir auch gleich mitgebracht, was ich dir erst ein Jahr nach deinem Auszug zu zahlen schuldig bin. Ich weiß, du wirst gehen, weil es so ausgemacht wurde."

Und er legt ihm das Geld auf den Tisch; er verlangt nicht einmal einen Schuldschein.

Der verblüffte Müller bringt kein Wort hervor, aber er packt zusammen und geht am nächsten Tage seiner Wege.

nach MARIE VON EBNER-ESCHENBACH (1830–1916), *Chlodwig*

1 Was für ein Mann war der Müller?
2 Was sollte sogleich gezahlt werden?
3 Drücken Sie anders aus: Der Müller machte keine Miene zu gehen.
4 Wie war es möglich, daß der Müller in der Mühle bleiben konnte?
5 Was hatte Chlodwig erfahren?
6 Woher wissen Sie, daß Chlodwig Pferde hatte?
7 Was für Männer brauchen keine geschriebenen Worte?
8 Wieviel Geld hatte Chlodwig mitgebracht?
9 Was war ausgemacht worden?
10 Warum verlangte Chlodwig nicht einmal einen Schuldschein?
11 Warum brachte der Müller kein Wort hervor?

Zum Nacherzählen (Umriß, S. 282)

35 Der arme Fährgast

Als er die Fähre erreichte, lag eben das Boot bereit, und derselbe Fährmann, welcher einst den jungen Samana[1] über den Fluß gesetzt hatte, stand im Boot. Siddhartha erkannte ihn wieder, auch er war stark gealtert.

5 „Willst du mich übersetzen?" fragte er.

Der Fährmann, erstaunt, einen so vornehmen Mann allein und zu Fuße wandern zu sehen, nahm ihn ins Boot und stieß ab.

„Ein schönes Leben hast du dir erwählt", sprach der Gast. „Schön muß es sein, jeden Tag an diesem Wasser zu leben und auf 10 ihm zu fahren."

Lächelnd wiegte sich der Ruderer: „Es ist schön, Herr, es ist, wie du sagst. Aber ist nicht jedes Leben, ist nicht jede Arbeit schön?"

„Es mag wohl sein. Dich aber beneide ich um die deine."

„Ach, du möchtest bald die Lust an ihr verlieren. Das ist nichts 15 für Leute in feinen Kleidern."

Siddhartha lachte. „Schon einmal bin ich heute um meiner Kleider willen betrachtet worden, mit Mißtrauen betrachtet. Willst du nicht, Fährmann, diese Kleider, die mir lästig sind, von mir annehmen? Denn du mußt wissen, ich habe kein Geld, dir einen 20 Fährlohn zu zahlen."

HERMANN HESSE (1877–1962), *Siddhartha*

1 Was fand Siddhartha, als er an die Fähre kam?
2 Was ist eine Fähre?
3 Woher wissen Sie, daß Siddhartha früher dort gewesen war?
4 Auf welche Weise war der Fährmann verändert?
5 Was wollte Siddhartha?
6 Warum war der Fährmann erstaunt?
7 Woher wissen Sie, daß der Fährmann mit seiner Arbeit zufrieden war?
8 Warum beneidete Siddhartha den Fährmann?
9 Warum möchte er bald die Lust an dieser Arbeit verlieren?
10 Warum hatte man Siddhartha mit Mißtrauen betrachtet?
11 Womit wollte Siddhartha seinen Fährlohn zahlen?

Zum Nacherzählen (Umriß, S. 282)

1 der Samana: *Indian ascetic*

36 Der Ringkauf

Erst als der letzte Käufer an der Kasse stand, kam Jürgen aus seiner Ecke hervor, reichte die Fische über den Ladentisch und fragte so leise, daß der Kaufmann sich vorbeugen mußte, ob er dafür ein buntes Tuch und einen Ring haben könnte, einen schmalen, viel-
5 leicht mit einem roten Stein, wie man ihn so auf den Dörfern trage.

Der Kaufmann, seine Verwunderung gewandt verbergend, rechnete mit halb geschlossenen Augen schnell nach und sagte dann, daß es natürlich gehe. Nur einen goldenen Ehering, den könne man natürlich nicht dafür haben. Aber ein „Ringlein", ja, das würde
10 gehen.

Ein solches Ringlein würde genügen, meinte Jürgen.

Er suchte lange und sorgfältig mit seinen vom Wasser ein wenig gekrümmten Fingern, legte ein rotes Tuch zur Seite und behielt nach einer Weile einen der schmalen Ringe in seiner hohlen Hand, der
15 aus einem roten gläsernen Stein ein schwaches und unechtes Leuchten aussandte. Er knüpfte ihn, der wie ein Kinderring in seiner Hand aussah, in ein Taschentuch, fragte, ob er noch etwas schuldig sei, bedankte sich und ging mit niedergeschlagenen Augen zur Tür, die Mütze in der Hand.
20 „Viel Glück!" sagte der Inhaber und lächelte wohlwollend.

ERNST WIECHERT (1887–1950), *Die Magd des Jürgen Doskocil*

1 Warum wollte Jürgen zuletzt an die Reihe kommen?
2 Was für einen Beruf hatte Jürgen?
3 Warum mußte der Kaufmann sich vorbeugen?
4 Was wollte Jürgen für die Fische haben?
5 Warum war der Kaufmann erstaunt?
6 Warum konnte Jürgen keinen goldenen Ring haben?
7 Was für Hände hatte Jürgen?
8 Wie lange dauerte es, bis Jürgen fand, was er wollte?
9 Wie sah der Ring aus?
10 Warum wünschte ihm der Kaufmann viel Glück?

Zum Nacherzählen (Umriß, S. 282)

37 Hilfe in der Not

In der Eingebung eines Moments winke ich ihm. Stumm tritt er
näher. Ich reiße die Knöpfe des Kleides auf, nehme das Paket mit
den achtzig Scheinen heraus und gebe es ihm in die Hand. „Fünf
Menschenleben sind in deiner Hand", sage ich zu ihm, „jetzt
5 mache, was du willst." Ohne mit der Wimper zu zucken, steckt er
das Paket in die Rocktasche und verschwindet. Die andern kommen
gleich darauf in mein Zimmer. Wie drüben wird alles um und um
gewühlt, Wäsche, Kleider, Schuhe, jede Ritze, jede Schublade
untersucht. Dann bleibt das Weib allein bei mir, ich muß mich
10 entkleiden. Auch das ging vorüber, und sie entfernt sich. Eine
Viertelstunde danach erscheint der rothaarige Soldat im Zimmer,
horcht eine Sekunde, zieht das unversehrte Rubelpaket[1] aus der
Tasche und überreicht es mir schweigend. Ich stammle ein paar
Worte; ich frage, was ich für ihn tun könne; ihm Geld anzubieten
15 hatte etwas Unsinniges, da er mir ja achtzigtausend Rubel schenkte.
Er schüttelt den Kopf und sagt: „Machen Sie sich keine Gedanken
darüber. Es ist leider so, daß wir in Blut und Sünde stecken bis an
den Hals. Vielleicht läßt mir Gott jetzt ein weniges nach." Damit
geht er.

JAKOB WASSERMANN (1873–1934), *Golowin*

1 Woher wissen Sie, daß die Frau an diesen Ausweg nicht schon
 gedacht hatte?
2 Warum kam der Soldat zu der Frau?
3 Was hatte die Frau in ihrem Kleid versteckt?
4 Was tat der Soldat mit dem Geld?
5 Warum kamen die andern in das Zimmer der Frau?
6 Was suchten sie?
7 Warum mußte die Frau sich entkleiden?
8 Hatte der Soldat Geld aus dem Paket genommen?
9 Woher wissen Sie, daß die Frau dankbar war?
10 Was war der Wert jedes Scheins?
11 Warum hatte der Soldat die Frau nicht verraten?

Zum Nacherzählen (Umriß, S. 283)

[1] der Rubel: *rouble (Russian coin)*

38 Die alte Frau

„Was fehlt dieser alten Frau?" fragte ich einen der Anwesenden;
da kamen Antworten von allen Seiten: „Sie kommt sechs Meilen
Weges vom Lande, sie kann nicht weiter, sie weiß nicht Bescheid in
der Stadt und kann nicht hinfinden."

5 „Ich wollte sie führen", sagte einer, „aber es ist ein weiter Weg,
und ich habe meinen Hausschlüssel nicht bei mir. Auch würde sie
das Haus nicht kennen, wo sie hinwill." – „Aber hier kann die Frau
nicht liegenbleiben", sagte ein Neuhinzugetretener. „Sie will
aber", antwortete der erste; „ich habe es ihr längst gesagt, ich wolle
10 sie nach Hause bringen, doch sie redet ganz verwirrt, ja sie muß
wohl betrunken sein." – „Ich glaube, sie ist blödsinnig. Aber hier
kann sie doch in keinem Falle bleiben", wiederholte jener, „die
Nacht ist kühl und lang."

Während all dieses Geredes war die Alte, gerade als ob sie taub
15 und blind sei, ganz ungestört mit ihrer Zubereitung fertig geworden,
und da der letzte abermals sagte: „Hier kann sie doch nicht bleiben",
erwiderte sie, mit einer wunderlich tiefen und ernsten Stimme:

„Warum soll ich nicht hier bleiben? Ist dies nicht ein herzogliches Haus? Ich bin achtundachtzig Jahre alt, und der Herzog
20 wird mich gewiß nicht von seiner Schwelle treiben."

CLEMENS BRENTANO (1778–1842),
Geschichte vom braven Kasperl und schönen Annerl

1 Was ist ein Anwesender?
2 Wo wohnte die Frau?
3 Drücken Sie anders aus: sie weiß nicht Bescheid in der Stadt.
4 Warum konnte einer der Anwesenden sie nicht führen?
5 Was tat die Frau?
6 Warum glaubte einer, daß die Frau betrunken sei?
7 Warum konnte die Frau nicht da bleiben?
8 Was kann man nicht tun, wenn man taub ist?
9 Wie alt war die Frau?
10 Warum glaubte die Frau, dort bleiben zu dürfen?

Zum Nacherzählen (Umriß, S. 283)

39 Törichte Nachbarn

Es war eben Topfmarkt gewesen, und man hatte nicht allein die
Küche für die nächste Zeit mit solchen Waren versorgt, sondern
auch uns Kindern dasselbe Geschirr im kleinen eingekauft. An
einem schönen Nachmittag, da alles ruhig im Hause war, spielte ich
5 mit meinen Schüsseln und Töpfen, und da das langweilig wurde,
warf ich ein Geschirr auf die Straße und freute mich, daß es so
lustig zerbrach. Meine kleinen Nachbarn, welche sahen, wie ich
mich daran freute, riefen: „Noch mehr!" Ich warf sofort einen
Topf und, da man immer wieder „Noch mehr!" rief, nach und nach
10 alle Schüsselchen, Tellerchen und Kännchen auf die Straße.
Meine Nachbarn fuhren fort, ihren Beifall zu zeigen, und ich war
sehr froh, ihnen Vergnügen zu machen. Mein Vorrat aber war zu
Ende, und sie riefen immer: „Noch mehr!" Ich eilte daher in die
Küche und holte die irdenen Teller, welche nun freilich im Zer-
15 brechen ein noch lustigeres Schauspiel gaben; und so lief ich hin und
wieder und warf einen Teller nach dem andern auf die Straße. Erst
später erschien jemand, der das Spiel hinderte. Das Unglück war
geschehen, und man hatte für so viel zerbrochenes Geschirr wenigstens eine lustige Geschichte, die besonders meine Nachbarn immer
20 wieder gern erzählten.

nach JOHANN WOLFGANG VON GOETHE (1749–1832),
Dichtung und Wahrheit

1 Was hatte man auf dem Topfmarkt gekauft?
2 Woher wissen Sie, daß Goethe damals ganz klein war?
3 Warum warf Goethe ein Geschirr auf die Straße?
4 Woher wissen Sie, daß das Spiel den kleinen Nachbarn gefiel?
5 Woher wissen Sie, daß das Geschirr nicht aus Holz war?
6 Warum eilte der junge Goethe in die Küche?
7 Warum gaben die Teller im Zerbrechen ein noch lustigeres
   Schauspiel?
8 Wann nahm das Spiel ein Ende?
9 Hatte der junge Goethe alle Teller usw. auf die Straße geworfen?
10 Woher wissen Sie, daß die Geschichte einen großen Eindruck auf
   die Nachbarn machte?

Zum Nacherzählen (Umriß, S. 283)

40 Der Überfall

Er mochte ungefähr eine Stunde so gesessen haben, als der große Hund unten im Hofe ein paarmal bellte. Bald darauf kam es ihm vor, als hörte er draußen mehrere Stimmen. Er horchte hinaus, aber alles war wieder still. Eine Unruhe bemächtigte sich seiner, er
5 stand vom Fenster auf, untersuchte seine geladenen Pistolen und legte seinen Säbel auf den Tisch. In diesem Augenblick ging auch die Tür auf, und mehrere wilde Männer traten herein. Sie blieben erschrocken stehen, da sie den Grafen wach fanden. Er erkannte sogleich die fürchterlichen Gesichter aus dem Waldwirtshaus und
10 seinen Hauswirt, den langen Müller, mitten unter ihnen. Dieser faßte sich zuerst und drückte unversehens eine Pistole nach ihm ab. Die Kugel prallte neben seinem Kopf an die Mauer. „Falsch gezielt, Hund", schrie der Graf außer sich vor Zorn und schoß den Kerl durchs Hirn. Darauf ergriff er seinen Säbel, stürzte sich in den
15 Haufen hinein und warf die Räuber rechts und links die Treppe hinunter. Mitten in dem Kampf glaubte er das schöne Müllermädchen wiederzusehen. Sie hatte selber ein Schwert in der Hand, mit dem sie sich zwischen die Verräter warf, um den Grafen zu verteidigen. Unten an der Treppe endlich, da alles, was noch laufen
20 konnte, die Flucht ergriffen hatte, sank er, von vielen Wunden und Blutverlust ermattet, ohne Bewußtsein nieder.

nach JOSEPH VON EICHENDORFF (1778–1857),
Ahnung und Gegenwart

1 Was hörte der Graf, nachdem er eine Stunde gesessen hatte?
2 Wo saß er?
3 Warum untersuchte er seine Pistolen?
4 Wann ging die Tür auf?
5 Was hatten die Männer nicht erwartet?
6 Was wollten die Männer tun?
7 Was tat der Führer der Bande?
8 Warum wurde der Graf außer sich vor Zorn?
9 Wohin trieb er die Räuber?
10 Kämpfte der Graf allein gegen die Bande?
11 Warum sank er ohne Bewußtsein nieder?

Zum Nacherzählen (Umriß, S. 283)

(C) Longer Passages for Translation or Reproduction

41 Freundlicher Rat

„Helene hat jetzt eine Kuhlausche[1] Sonatine geübt und spielt sie wirklich niedlich, Helene, streich mal deine Haare glatt!" sagte die Schwiegertochter.

„So, das ist recht!" nickte der Professor beifällig, „die mußt du
5 uns gelegentlich mal vorspielen."

„Ach ja, das wäre reizend!" stimmte Frau Mathilde mechanisch bei, die gerade daran dachte, daß die Antwort, die ihr die Köchin heute in der Küche gab, wenn man sie richtig auffasse, eigentlich eine Unverschämtheit gewesen war!

10 „Sie geniert[2] sich nur immer so!" sagte die Schwiegertochter wieder.

„Ach, das ist nichts als bloßes Getue!" bemerkte ihr Mann, – „im Grunde produziert[3] sich jeder gern! Wenn ich sie zum Beispiel jetzt auffordern würde, – heimlich wäre sie beglückt!"

15 Alle sahen lächelnd auf das Kind.

„Nun?" fragte Frau Mathilde, „wie wäre es?" Der Vater warf ihr einen aufmunternden Blick zu.

„Also, zier[4] dich doch nicht so lange!" meinte die Mutter ungeduldig.

20 Helene schüttelte den Kopf, blutübergossen. „Nun wird sie auch noch rot!" rief der Vater ärgerlich, – „du magst nicht, wenn wir dich um etwas bitten? Sieh einer mal an[5]! Was soll denn der Herr Professor von dir denken?"

Die Aufforderungen wurden immer dringlicher, immer gereizter,
25 etwas, an das zwei Minuten zuvor noch niemand gedacht hatte, war auf einmal Hauptsache geworden, in den Mittelpunkt gerückt.

„Also w i l l s t du nun, oder willst du n i c h t?" Sie sah, in ihrer Angst, wie um Hilfe suchend auf den Professor, der bis dahin anscheinend unbeteiligt in seinem Sessel gesessen hatte. Seine Augen
30 glänzten plötzlich animiert: „Mein liebes Kind", sagte er mit freund-

---

[1] Kuhlau: deutscher Komponist   [2] sich genieren: *be bashful*
[3] sich produzieren: *show off*   [4] sich zieren: *make a fuss*
[5] Sieh einer mal an!: *Gracious me!*

licher Stimme, „an deiner Stelle würde ich nun ganz artig zum
Klavier gehen und es dann mit aller Kraft zusammenschlagen!"

FRIEDRICH HUCH (1873–1913), Der Gast

Zum Nacherzählen (Umriß, S. 283)

42 Das Testament

Es ist höchst unangenehm, wenn ein Mann so plötzlich von hinnen
gerufen[1] wird, daß er für die, welche zunächst um ihn sind, nicht
testamentlich sorgen konnte, und das geschieht oft; denn solche
Leute machen nicht gern ein Testament, sie hoffen noch lange zu
5 leben.

Aber auch da wußten sich einmal schlaue Leute wohl zu helfen.
Sie schleppten den Gestorbenen in eine Rumpelkammer[2], und in
das noch nicht erkaltete Bett legten sie einen treuen Knecht,
setzten ihm die Nachtmütze des Gestorbenen auf und liefen nach
10 Schreiber und Zeugen. Schreiber und Zeugen setzten sich an den
Tisch am Fenster, rüsteten[3] das Schreibzeug und probierten, ob
guter Wein in den weißen Kannen sei. Unterdessen ächzt und
stöhnt es im dunkeln Hintergrunde hinter dem dicken Vorhang, und
eine schwache Stimme fragt, ob der Schreiber nicht bald fertig sei –
15 es gehe nicht mehr lange mit ihm. Der Schreiber nimmt hastig das
Glas vom Munde und dagegen die Feder und läßt diese flüchtig
übers Papier gleiten, aber immer halblinks schauend, wo das Glas
steht.

Da diktiert leise und hustend die Stimme hinter dem Vorhange
20 das Testament, und der Schreiber schreibt, und freudig hören die
Anwesenden, wie sie Erben würden von vielem Gut und Geld.
Aber blasser Schrecken fährt über ihre Gesichter, als die Stimme
spricht: „Meinem Knecht aber, der mir so viele Jahre treu gedient
hat, vermache ich 8 000 Pfund." Der Schalk im Bette hatte sich
25 selbst nicht vergessen und bestimmte sich seinen Lohn für die gut
gespielte Rolle.

Er war aber noch bescheiden; er hätte sich gut zum Haupterben
machen können, und was hätten die anderen sagen können?

nach JEREMIAS GOTTHELF (1797–1854), Das Testament

Zum Nacherzählen (Umriß, S. 283)

[1] von hinnen gerufen werden: sterben
[2] die Rumpelkammer: *lumber-room*   [3] rüsten: bereit machen

43 Erfüllter Wunsch

Wir standen eines Abends ziemlich mutlos vor einer Seitentür des Theaters, als eben der Faust gegeben wurde. Wir hatten gehört, daß man Doktor Faust, den wir genugsam kannten, nebst dem Teufel und allen seinen Herrlichkeiten sehen würde, fanden aber
5 heute alle Hindernisse unübersteiglich, welche auf unsern gewohnten Schlupfwegen[1] sich entgegenstellten. So hörten wir betrübt die Klänge der Ouvertüre, welche von den vornehmen Liebhabern der Stadt aufgeführt wurde, und zerbrachen uns die Köpfe über einem noch möglichen Eindringen. Es war ein dunkler Herbstabend, und
10 es regnete kühl und anhaltend. Es fror mich, und ich dachte ans Nachhausegehen, zumal sich die Mutter über das abendliche Umhertreiben beklagt hatte. Da öffnete sich die dunkle Tür, ein dienstbarer Geist[2] sprang heraus und rief: ,,Heda, ihr Buben! Drei oder vier von euch mögen hereinkommen, die sollen einmal mit-
15 spielen!'' Auf dieses Zauberwort drängten sich sogleich die Stärksten in das Haus; denn dies war ein Fall, wo ein jeder nur an sich selbst denken durfte. Er wies sie aber zurück, indem er sie für zu groß und dick erklärte und mich, der ich ohne sonderliche Hoffnungen im Hintergrunde stand, heranrief und sagte: ,,Der da ist recht, der
20 wird eine gute Meerkatze sein!'' Dazu ergriff er noch zwei andere Jungen, schloß die Tür hinter uns und marschierte an unserer Spitze nach einem kleinen Saale, welcher als Garderobe[3] diente. Dort hatten wir nicht Zeit, die aufgehäuften Gewänder, Waffen und Rüstungen[4] zu betrachten; denn wir wurden schnell unserer Kleider
25 entledigt und in abenteuerliche Pelze gesteckt, welche vom Kopf bis zum Fuß eine Hülle[5] bildeten. Das Meerkatzengesicht konnte wie eine Kapuze[6] zurückgeschlagen werden, und als wir solchergestalt verwandelt dastanden, die langen Schwänze in der Hand haltend, lächelten wir ganz vergnügt und beglückwünschten uns nun erst.

GOTTFRIED KELLER (1819–90), *Der grüne Heinrich*

Zum Nacherzählen (Umriß, S. 284)

[1] der Schlupfweg: *secret way*
[2] ein dienstbarer Geist: *a ministering angel*
[3] die Garderobe: *dressing-room*   [4] die Rüstung: *suit of armour*
[5] die Hülle: *covering, garment*   [6] die Kapuze: *cowl*

44 Die Bettlerin

Draußen vor dem Portale stand noch immer die Bettlerin. Wie vor einer Stunde starrten die Augen in die Höhe, die Hand war noch ebenso fordernd ausgestreckt, und auch die Lippen verharrten in ihrem Gemurmel. Fest waren wir entschlossen, ihr diesmal nichts
5 zu geben und stracks[1] vorüber auf ein Gasthaus loszugehen, fühlten uns aber doch aufgehalten, da wir die völlige Leere der Vorhalle wahrnahmen. Die einzigen waren wir nun, denen sich die schrecklich magere, lederfarbene Hand entgegenstreckte, und dies hatte etwas Zwingendes: verdrießlich zogen wir abermals unsere Geldbeutel;
10 aber keinerlei kleine Münze war da mehr zu finden. Ja, beim Zusammenzählen des übrigen kam es heraus, daß wir in der lustigen Nacht über unsere Verhältnisse gelebt hatten: jedem fehlte ein weniges an der Summe, die ihm zur Heimreise nötig war, auch wenn wir auf das Mittagessen verzichteten. Zwar handelte sich's nur um
15 Pfennige, und wir wußten wohl einige Bekannte, die uns aushelfen konnten, doch ergab eine genauere Überlegung, daß keiner von ihnen sich mehr in der Stadt befand; auch meine Pflegeeltern waren am Abend vorher mit Line[2] in die Ferien gefahren.

In der Erregtheit mußten wir unsere Beratungen etwas laut
20 geführt haben, hielten vermutlich auch die alte Kirchenbettlerin für ebenso taub, wie sie blind war, und erschraken fast, als sie sich eintönig und freundlich vernehmen ließ:

„Kinder, Kinder, so arm, so arm, – könnt nicht heimgehen zu Vater und Mutter – geht nicht vorüber, geht nicht vorüber, kommt
25 her zu mir —"

Damit griff sie in eine Tasche und brachte die tiefgehöhlte Hand, gefüllt mit Geldstücken, wieder ans Licht. Wir sahen einander wortlos an; aber Hugo erfaßte als erster die Lage: „Wenn Sie erlauben, Frau Mutter, wir sind wirklich in Verlegenheit", sagte er
30 höflich. Unter sehr viel Kupfer fanden sich auch mehrere Nickelmünzen, sogar etwas Silber.

„Fischt euch nur heraus, was euch abgeht[3]!"

HANS CAROSSA (1878–1956), *Verwandlung einer Jugend* (Insel Verlag)

Zum Nacherzählen (Umriß, S. 284)

[1] stracks: geradeaus, ohne Umweg   [2] Line: Abkürzung für Karoline
[3] abgehen: *be missing, short of*

45 Der listige Kaufmann

Ein französischer Kaufmann segelte mit einem Schiff voll großen
Reichtums aus dem Morgenland heim und dachte schon mit
Freuden daran, wie er jetzt bald ein eignes Schlößlein am Meer
bauen und ruhig leben und alle Abende dreierlei Fische zu Abend
5 speisen wollte. Paff, geschah ein Schuß. Ein algierisches Raubschiff
war in der Nähe, wollte uns gefangennehmen und geraden Wegs
nach Algier führen in die Sklaverei. Denn hat man zwischen Wasser
und Himmel gute Gelegenheit, Luftschlösser zu bauen, so hat man
auch gute Gelegenheit zu stehlen. So denken die algierischen
10 Seeräuber auch. Hat das Wasser keine Balken[1], so hat's auch keine
Galgen. Zum Glück hatte der Kaufmann einen Ragusaner[2] auf dem
Schiff, der schon einmal in algierischer Gefangenschaft gewesen war
und ihre Sprache und ihre Prügel aus dem Fundament verstand. Zu
dem sagte der Kaufmann: ,,Nicolo, hast du Lust, noch einmal
15 algierisch zu werden? Folge mir, was ich dir sage, so kannst du dich
erretten und uns." Also verbargen wir uns alle im Schiff, daß kein
Mensch zu sehen war, nur der Ragusaner stellte sich oben auf das
Verdeck. Als nun die Seeräuber mit ihren blinkenden Säbeln schon
nahe waren und riefen, die Christenhunde sollten sich ergeben, fing
20 der Ragusaner mit kläglicher Stimme auf algierisch an: ,,Wir sind
alle an der Pest gestorben, bis auf die Kranken, die noch auf ihr
Ende warten, und ich. Um Gottes willen, rettet mich!" Dem
Algierer Seekapitän, als er hörte, daß er so nah an einem Schiff voll
Pest sei, kam's grün und gelb vor die Augen[3]. In der größten Ge-
25 schwindigkeit hielt er das Schnupftuch[4] vor die Nase, hatte aber keins,
sondern den Ärmel; und lenkte sein Schiff hinter den Wind. ,,Gott
helfe dir!" sagte er. ,,Aber geh zum Henker mit deiner Pest! Ich
will dir eine Flasche voll Kräuteressig[5] reichen." Darauf ließ er ihm
eine Flasche voll Kräuteressig reichen an einer langen Stange[6] und
30 segelte so schnell als möglich linksum. Also kamen wir glücklich aus
der Gefahr, und der Kaufmann baute hernach in der Gegend von

---

[1] das Wasser hat keine Balken: *the sea is not planked over* (*prov.*)
[2] der Ragusaner: Einwohner von Ragusa in Dalmatien
[3] es einem grün und gelb vor die Augen kommen: *feel giddy*
[4] das Schnupftuch: das Taschentuch
[5] der Kräuteressig: *vinegar made from herbs*   [6] die Stange: langer Stock

Marseille das Schlößlein und stellte den Ragusaner als Haushofmeister an auf lebenslang.

nach JOHANN PETER HEBEL (1760–1826)

Zum Nacherzählen (Umriß, S. 284)

46 Der Unglücksfall

Jetzt fuhr ein Wagen mit einer ziemlich lärmenden Gesellschaft ein:
Vater, Mutter, drei Kinder, eine Bonne[1].
„Deutsche Familie", sagte Geronimo leise zu Carlo.
Der Vater gab jedem der Kinder ein Geldstück, und jedes durfte
5 das seine in den Hut des Bettlers werfen. Geronimo neigte jedesmal
den Kopf zum Dank. Der älteste Knabe sah dem Blinden mit
ängstlicher Neugier ins Gesicht. Carlo betrachtete den Knaben. Er
mußte, wie immer beim Anblick solcher Kinder, daran denken, daß
Geronimo gerade so alt gewesen war, als das Unglück geschah, durch
10 das er das Augenlicht verloren hatte. Denn er erinnerte sich jenes
Tages auch heute noch, nach beinahe zwanzig Jahren, mit voll-
kommener Deutlichkeit. Noch heute klang ihm der grelle Kinderschrei ins Ohr, mit dem der kleine Geronimo auf den Rasen
hingesunken war, noch heute sah er die Sonne auf der weißen
15 Gartenmauer spielen und hörte die Sonntagsglocken wieder, die
gerade in jenem Augenblick getönt hatten. Er hatte wie oftmals mit
dem Bolzen[2] nach der Esche an der Mauer geschossen, und als er
den Schrei hörte, dachte er gleich, daß er den kleinen Bruder
verletzt haben mußte, der eben vorbeigelaufen war. Er ließ das
20 Blasrohr[3] aus den Händen gleiten, sprang durchs Fenster in den
Garten und stürzte zu dem kleinen Bruder hin, der auf dem Grase
lag, die Hand vors Gesicht geschlagen, und jammerte. Über die
rechte Wange und den Hals floß ihm Blut herunter. In derselben
Minute kam der Vater vom Felde heim, durch die kleine Gartentür,
25 und nun knieten beide ratlos neben dem jammernden Kinde.

[1] die Bonne: das Kindermädchen   [2] der Bolzen: *bolt, dart*
[3] das Blasrohr: *air-gun*

Nachbarn eilten herbei; die alte Vanetti war die erste, der es gelang, dem Kleinen die Hände vom Gesicht zu entfernen. Dann kam auch der Schmied, bei dem Carlo damals in der Lehre war und der sich ein bißchen aufs Kurieren verstand; und der sah gleich, daß das
30 rechte Auge verloren war. Der Arzt, der abends aus Poschiavo kam, konnte auch nicht mehr helfen. Ja, er deutete schon die Gefahr an, in der das andere Auge schwebte. Und er behielt recht. Ein Jahr später war die Welt für Geronimo in Nacht versunken.

ARTHUR SCHNITZLER (1862–1931),
Der blinde Geronimo und sein Bruder

Zum Nacherzählen (Umriß, S. 284)

47 Sonderbarer Rechtsfall in England

Man weiß, daß in England jeder Angeklagte zwölf Geschworene von seinem Stand zu Richtern hat, deren Ausspruch einstimmig sein muß und die, damit die Entscheidung sich nicht zu sehr in die Länge verziehe[1], ohne Essen und Trinken so lange eingeschlossen
5 bleiben, bis sie eines Sinnes[2] sind. Zwei Edelmänner, die einige Meilen von London lebten, hatten in Gegenwart von Zeugen einen sehr lebhaften Streit miteinander; der eine drohte dem andern und setzte hinzu, daß, ehe vierundzwanzig Stunden vergingen, ihn sein Betragen reuen solle. Gegen Abend wurde dieser Edelmann
10 erschossen gefunden; der Verdacht fiel natürlich auf den, der die Drohungen gegen ihn ausgestoßen hatte. Man brachte ihn zu gefänglicher Haft[3], das Gericht wurde gehalten, es fanden sich noch mehrere Beweise und elf Geschworene verdammten ihn zum Tode; allein der zwölfte bestand hartnäckig darauf, nicht einzuwilligen,
15 weil er ihn für unschuldig hielte.

Seine Kollegen baten ihn, Gründe anzuführen,[4] warum er dies glaubte; allein er ließ sich nicht darauf ein[5] und beharrte bei seiner Meinung. Es war schon spät in der Nacht, und der Hunger plagte

[1] sich in die Länge verziehen: *drag on*
[2] eines Sinnes sein: einer Meinung sein
[3] zu gefänglicher Haft: ins Gefängnis   [4] anführen: *cite, give*
[5] sich nicht darauf einlassen: *refuse to discuss the matter*

die Richter heftig; einer stand endlich auf und meinte, daß es
20 besser sei, einen Schuldigen loszusprechen, als elf Unschuldige
verhungern zu lassen; man fertigte also die Begnadigung aus[1],
führte aber auch zugleich die Umstände an, die das Gericht dazu
gezwungen hätten. Das ganze Publikum war wider den einzigen
Starrkopf: die Sache kam sogar vor den König, der ihn zu sprechen
25 verlangte; der Edelmann erschien, und nachdem er sich vom
Könige das Wort hatte geben lassen, daß seine Aufrichtigkeit nicht
von nachteiligen Folgen für ihn sein sollte, so erzählte er dem
Monarchen, daß, als er im Dunkeln von der Jagd gekommen und
sein Gewehr losgeschossen, es unglücklicherweise diesen Edelmann,
30 der hinter einem Busche gestanden, getötet habe. „Da ich", fuhr er
fort, „weder Zeugen meiner Tat, noch meiner Unschuld hatte, so
beschloß ich, Stillschweigen zu behalten; aber als ich hörte, daß man
einen Unschuldigen anklagte, so wandte ich alles an, um einer von
den Geschworenen zu werden, fest entschlossen, eher zu verhungern,
35 als den Angeklagten umkommen zu lassen." Der König hielt sein
Wort, und der Edelmann bekam seine Begnadigung.

HEINRICH VON KLEIST (1777–1811)

Zum Nacherzählen (Umriß, S. 284)

48 Die Kur des Vaters

Die Mutter hatte Zeiten der Furcht, wo sie sich freiwillig Entbehrungen[2] und harte Arbeiten auferlegte, um gewissen Unglücksfällen
zuvorzukommen. Dann gab sie mir Legenden zu lesen und leitete
mich ebenfalls zum Entsagen an. Wie mir jedoch alles zum Unmaß
5 geriet[3], so tat ich auch in diesen Dingen der Meisterin bald übergenug, verschenkte Spielsachen, Vesperbrot[4] und Stiefel, ahmte die
Haltung der Armen nach, ging demütig und barfüßig umher und
versetzte mir mit spitzen Oleanderblättern Stiche in die Wangen.
   Da beschloß der Vater eine kräftige Kur und nahm mich in

[1] ausfertigen: *draw up*
[2] die Entbehrung: *privation, self-denial*
[3] alles geriet mir zum Unmaß: *I did everything to excess*
[4] das Vesperbrot: *bread and butter (eaten at tea-time)*

10 seiner Kutsche zu einem Bauern mit, dem vor kurzem die Dreschmaschine einen Arm schwer geschunden hatte. Vorsichtig löste er
die Verbandschichten ab, und als ich beim Anblick der breiten
Wundfläche zusammenzuckte, erörterte[1] er voll Ruhe, während er
mit Schere und Pinzette brandig-schwärzliche[2] Gewebsfetzen
15 wegnahm, das Ganze sei nicht so schlimm, wie es jetzt aussehe, man
brauche nur mehrere Streifchen frischer gesunder Haut aufzulegen
und zu befestigen, so werde diese anwachsen, sich ausbreiten und
der Arm wieder tüchtig werden.

„Ich habe es dem Bauern schon gesagt", fuhr er gleichmütig fort,
20 „daß du gern für andere ein Opfer bringst, – nun zeig, daß dir
damit Ernst ist! Deine Haut ist jung und fein; ein paar Flecken
genügen, sie werden anwurzeln wie Moos."

Ich glaubte, er mache Spaß; aber schon ging er mit blitzendem
Skalpell auf mich zu. Mitten im Schreck mich fassend, zog ich
25 mein Röckchen aus, krempelte den Ärmel hinauf[3] und sah dabei zu
dem Verwundeten hin; mir war, als müsse dieser gegen des Vaters
Beginnen Einspruch erheben[4]. Der Mann aber hatte die Augen
geschlossen, um nichts bekümmert als um sein eigenes Leiden. Und
bereits wirkte das Messerchen; mein Arm blutete an mehreren
30 Stellen, ich sah Hautläppchen[5] eingerollt an der Schneide haften und
verfolgte nun genau, wie sie behutsam auf den wunden Arm des
Bauern übertragen wurden.

„Noch einmal! Es tut kein bißchen weh!" sagte ich triumphierend,
worauf der Vater gelassen den Eingriff wiederholte und mir dann
35 eilig einen Verband darauf anlegte.

Einige Wochen vertaumelte[6] ich in eitler Lust über das herrliche
Abenteuer und erzählte es jedem, der mir begegnete, bis meine
kleinen Wunden geheilt waren und die Borken abfielen; da war ich
auf einmal nüchtern, vermied auch künftig die Gebärden der
40 Armen und die Spitzen des Oleanders.

HANS CAROSSA (1878–1956), *Eine Kindheit* (Insel Verlag)

Zum Nacherzählen (Umriß, S. 285)

---

[1] erörtern: *discuss, give details to show*
[2] brandig: *gangrenous* [3] hinaufkrempeln: *roll up*
[4] Einspruch erheben: *raise objections* [5] das Hautläppchen: *shred of skin*
[6] vertaumeln: *spend in a whirl of excitement*

49 Der wilde Ritt

So war er acht Jahre alt geworden. Als er wieder einmal statt zu lernen sein Roß tummelte[1] und weitab vom väterlichen Schloß durch Wälder und Felder streifte, kam er an eine ihm unbekannte Wiese, auf der eine große Rinderherde weidete. Ein Hirt war nicht
5 zu sehen; das Vieh hatte sich zum Teil tief in den Waldrand hinein zerstreut und fraß dort das junge Grün der niedrigen Bäume ab.

Während der junge Ritter noch hielt und das ihm bisher unbekannte Tal betrachtete, stürmte plötzlich aus den Gruppen der weidenden Rinder ein mächtiger, schnaubender Stier hervor. Jäher
10 Schrecken erfaßte den Jungen. Das wütende Tier jagte mit gesenktem Kopfe über die Wiese heran, daß der feuchte Grasboden dumpf vom Aufschlag der Hufe erbebte. Der Knabe war wie gelähmt – da bäumte sich sein Pferd auch schon hochauf, sprang seitwärts, daß er die Bügel verlor und sich kaum im Sattel halten konnte; dann
15 jagte es wie rasend den Waldrand entlang. Der wilde Ritt endete damit, daß der Reiter aus dem Sattel flog, mit dem Kopfe gegen einen Baumstumpf geschleudert wurde und bewußtlos liegenblieb.

Es war kein angenehmer Abend für die Umgebung des Fürsten, als der besinnungslose kleine Kerl von Bauern ins Schloß gebracht
20 worden war. Der Fürst wechselte zwischen fassungslosem Schmerz und Wutausbrüchen. Dann umarmte er den alten Leibarzt, weil der Hoffnung gab, daß der Gestürzte am Leben bleiben würde.

Er blieb auch am Leben, aber sein Geist schien ausgelöscht und versiegt[2]. Er nahm zwar nach einigen Tagen Nahrung zu sich; doch,
25 wenn er seine Augen öffnete, war sein Blick stier[3], und die Augäpfel schienen sich absichtslos in ihren Höhlen zu bewegen. Auch sprach er nichts.

Das dauerte schon viele Tage so, und immer noch gab der Arzt Hoffnung, daß der Geist wiederkehren werde. Nach drei, vier
30 Wochen wurden seine tröstenden Reden aber seltener, und nach sechs Wochen sagte er dem Fürsten, daß nicht mehr auf eine Wiederherstellung zu rechnen sei. Der Junge werde möglicherweise am Leben bleiben, aber wohl immer toten oder siechen[4] Geistes sein.

---

[1] taumeln: *give exercise to*
[3] stier: starr, leblos
[2] versiegt: vertrocknet
[4] siech: kränklich, langdauernd krank

35   Der Fürst, der vielleicht im stillen selbst schon alle Hoffnung
aufgegeben hatte, nahm das ruhiger auf, als der Arzt erwartet hatte.
Er ging von da ab nicht mehr so oft zu dem Kranken, der nie seine
Anwesenheit bemerkte; er trank noch mehr als früher und war noch
härter zu seinen Untergebenen.

WILHELM VON SCHOLZ (1874–1969), *Eine Wiedergeburt*

Zum Nacherzählen (Umriß, S. 285)

50 Das Kreuzverhör

In meinem Stübchen schien Sonne. Ich sah nach meinen Raupenkästen[1], die ich gestern vernachlässigt hatte, fand ein paar neue
Puppen[2], gab den Pflanzen frisches Wasser.

Da ging die Tür.

5   Ich achtete nicht gleich darauf. Nach einer Minute wurde die
Stille mir sonderbar; ich drehte mich um. Da stand mein Vater. Er
war blaß und sah gequält aus. Der Gruß blieb mir im Halse stecken.
Ich sah: er wußte! Er war da. Das Gericht begann. Nichts war gut
geworden, nichts abgebüßt[3], nichts vergessen! Die Sonne wurde
10 bleich, und der Sonntagmorgen sank welk dahin.

Aus allen Himmeln gerissen starrte ich dem Vater entgegen. Ich
haßte ihn, warum war er nicht gestern gekommen? Jetzt war ich
auf nichts vorbereitet, hatte nichts bereit, nicht einmal Reue und
Schuldgefühl. – Und wozu brauchte er oben in seiner Kommode
15 Feigen zu haben?

Er ging zu meinem Bücherschrank, griff hinter die Bücher und
zog einige Feigen hervor. Es waren wenige mehr da. Dazu sah er
mich an, mit stummer, peinlicher Frage. Ich konnte nichts sagen.
Leid und Trotz würgten mich.

20   „Was ist denn?" brachte ich dann heraus.

„Woher hast du diese Feigen?" fragte er, mit einer beherrschten,
leisen Stimme, die mir bitter verhaßt war.

---

[1] die Raupe: *caterpillar*   [2] die Puppe: *chrysalis*
[3] abbüßen: genügend Strafe leiden

Ich begann sofort zu reden. Zu lügen. Ich erzählte, daß ich die Feigen bei einem Konditor gekauft hätte, es sei ein ganzer Kranz
25 gewesen. Woher das Geld dazu kam? Das Geld kam aus einer Sparkasse, die ich gemeinsam mit einem Freunde hatte. Da hatten wir beide alles kleine Geld hineingetan, das wir je und je bekamen. Übrigens – hier war die Kasse. Ich holte die Schachtel mit dem Schlitz[1] hervor. Jetzt war bloß noch ein Zehner[2] darin, eben weil wir
30 gestern die Feigen gekauft hatten.

Mein Vater hörte zu, mit einem stillen, beherrschten Gesicht, dem ich nichts glaubte.

„Wieviel haben denn die Feigen gekostet?" fragte er mit der zu leisen Stimme.

35 „Eine Mark und sechzig."

„Und wo hast du sie gekauft?"

„Beim Konditor."

„Bei welchem?"

„Bei Haager."

40 Es gab eine Pause. Ich hielt die Geldschachtel noch in frierenden Fingern. Alles an mir war kalt und fror.

Und nun fragte er, mit einer Drohung in der Stimme: „Ist das wahr?"

Ich redete wieder rasch. Ja, natürlich war es wahr, und mein
45 Freund Weber war im Laden gewesen, ich hatte ihn nur begleitet. Das Geld hatte hauptsächlich ihm, dem Weber, gehört, von mir war nur wenig dabei.

„Nimm deine Mütze", sagte mein Vater, „wir wollen miteinander zum Konditor Haager gehen. Er wird ja wissen, ob es wahr ist."

HERMANN HESSE (1877–1962), *Kinderseele*

Zum Nacherzählen (Umriß, S. 285)
Zum Fortsetzen (Umriß, S. 229)

[1] der Schlitz: schmale Öffnung, durch welche das Geld gesteckt wird
[2] der Zehner: das Zehnpfennigstück

Outlines of Passages for Reproduction

26 (S. 254) Der Mißerfolg

Eduard sehr zornig – eilt zum Hinterstübchen – der alte Eulenböck – „Halunke!" – Eulenböck antwortet ruhig – Eduard wirft das Bild hin – schämt sich – Lüge – „echter Salvator Rose".

27 (S. 255) Irrtum der Räuber

Räuber – Landhaus – Besitzer abwesend – Maler wird mitgenommen – Irrtum entdeckt sich – Maler macht sich beliebt – Artilleriekunst – hätten Räuber doch Kanonen! – Maler losgelassen – Einladung.

28 (S. 256) Bestrafte Unachtsamkeit

Früher Aufbruch – noch nie eingeschlagene Richtung – Löwe auf der entgegengesetzten Seite – Raubversuch – totenstill – Schlucht – Bach – durstig – Gewehr hingelegt – hinuntergeklettert – Löwe stößt Gebrüll aus – den Abhang hinauf – wie angenagelt stehen bleiben – Löwe beim Gewehr.

29 (S. 257) Unrechter Augenblick

Einladung von Direktor Meier – Helmold zieht sich um – Grete kommt – Brief von Anwalt – Grete weint – Helmold soll Brief lesen – Onkel gestorben – 500 000 Mark hinterlassen – Ohnmacht – Dienstmädchen kommt – Grete zu Bett gebracht – kann ihren Mann nicht begleiten.

30 (S. 258) Der störrische Esel

Heiter, warum? – zu Esel – Vesuv – träges Tier – Stockschläge – laufen – Einsiedlerwohnung – Kavalkade – Livree – Kaiserin – dahinstürmender Esel – zum Stehen bringen – Kopf nach außen – Rücken – Hut abziehen.

31 (S. 259) Das Theater brennt

Mitternacht – Feuerlärm – Theater – sich anziehen – eilen – Parterre, Bühne, Dach – Gebäude mit Spritzen umstellt – Wasser –

erfolglos – Mann in ruhiger Fassung – müßiger Zuschauer? – erteilt Befehle – Großherzog Karl August.

32 (S. 260) Die Prophezeiung

Abend – Garten – Angelina und ich – Gitter – Zigeunerin – will prophezeien – junger Mensch – grüßt – Zigeunerin ist erstaunt – wer ermordet wen? – Reiter sieht sich um – wird erkannt – hatte uns verhöhnt – Zigeunerin verschwindet – Angelina fort – ich allein.

33 (S. 261) Die freundliche Alte

Alte – Öllampe – Fensteröffnung – wird freundlich, warum? – Prädikant – Alte verschwindet – Pförtchen knarrt – Waser klettert hinunter – Stufen – Küche – Kämmerchen – Leitertreppe – Falltür – Alte bereitet Essen – Waser in Sicherheit – still – soll nicht verhungern.

34 (S. 262) Der unehrliche Müller

Chlodwigs Nachbar – verkauft Mühle – Hälfte des Preises sofort zu zahlen – Müller soll Rest ein Jahr nach seinem Auszug bekommen – Fehler im Kontrakt – Müller bleibt – Chlodwig erfährt davon – Gespräch mit Müller – Chlodwig gibt Müller den Rest – Müller zieht fort.

35 (S. 263) Der arme Fahrgast

Fähre – derselbe Fährmann – älter – erstaunt, warum? – stößt ab – Gespräch – Fährmann führt schönes Leben – Fährmann zufrieden – Siddhartha unzufrieden – will Fährmann werden – unpassende Arbeit, warum? – lästige Kleider – kein Geld – Fährlohn.

36 (S. 264) Ringkauf

Jürgen – Ecke – Ladentisch – Fische – will Ring und Tuch dafür haben – Kaufmann rechnet nach – Ringlein – Jürgen sucht lange – gekrümmte Finger, warum? – Tuch – Ring mit rotem Stein – knüpft ihn in Taschentuch – noch etwas schuldig? – bedankt sich – geht hinaus – viel Glück!

37 (S. 265) Hilfe in der Not

Plötzliche Eingebung – Frau winkt – gibt Soldaten Geld – Soldat verschwindet – alles gründlich untersucht – Weib allein mit Frau – muß sich entkleiden – nichts gefunden – Viertelstunde später – Soldat überreicht ihr Paket – unversehrt – Frau möchte ihn belohnen – Soldat will nichts von ihr – hofft auf etwas von Gott – geht.

38 (S. 266) Die alte Frau

Alte Frau – krank? – viele Anwesende – viele Antworten – Frau kommt vom Lande – weiß nicht, wo sie hinwill – redet verwirrt – liegt – schon spät – kümmert sich nicht um das Gerede – macht Zubereitungen – warum nicht hierbleiben? – herzogliches Haus – 88 Jahre alt.

39 (S. 267) Törichte Nachbarn

Topfmarkt – Geschirr gekauft – Spielzeug – der junge Goethe allein im Hause – wirft ein Geschirr auf die Straße – kleine Nachbarn rufen: „Noch mehr!" – Vorrat zu Ende – Küche – ein Teller nach dem andern – jemand kommt – Spiel zu Ende – Geschichte von Nachbarn immer wieder erzählt.

40 (S. 268) Der Überfall

Graf fürchtet einen Angriff – geht nicht zu Bett – hört etwas – unruhig – untersucht Waffen – Tür geht auf – Leute aus dem Waldwirtshaus – versuchen ihn zu töten – Graf verteidigt sich – wirft Räuber die Treppe hinunter – Hilfe – verwundet – verliert Bewußtsein.

41 (S. 269) Freundlicher Rat

Familie im Wohnzimmer – Unterhaltung – die kleine Helene – Sonatine – Professor will sie spielen hören – Frau Mathilde auch – Helene verlegen – von allen Verwandten aufgefordert – errötet – schüttelt Kopf – was wird der Professor von ihr denken? – Helene sieht auf ihn – sein Rat.

42 (S. 270) Das Testament

Mann stirbt ohne Testament – List der Verwandten – Gestorbener weggeschafft – Knecht des Gestorbenen – Schreiber und Zeugen –

Knecht diktiert Testament – vermacht sich 8 000 Pfund – Schreck der Verwandten – Bescheidenheit des Knechts.

43 (S. 271) Erfüllter Wunsch

Jungen mutlos – Theater – „Faust" – unmöglich ins Theater zu kommen – Stück fängt an – Heinrich will nach Hause – Tür öffnet sich – einige Jungen sollen mitspielen – die Starken drängen sich vor – Heinrich ohne Hoffnung – nur die Kleinen – Heinrich darf mitspielen – Jungen in Meerkatzen verwandelt – freuen sich.

44 (S. 272) Die Bettlerin

Bettlerin – Portal – Jungen wollen ihr nichts geben – die einzigen – fühlen sich aufgehalten – Geldbeutel – haben nicht einmal genug Geld, um nach Hause zu fahren – keine Bekannten dort – sprechen laut – Bettlerin bietet ihnen Geld an – wortlos – Angebot angenommen.

45 (S. 273) Der listige Kaufmann

Französischer Kaufmann – Morgenland – Schiff voll großem Reichtum – algierische Seeräuber – Gefahr der Sklaverei – Ragusaner – versteht algierische Sprache – glücklicher Einfall – Pest – Seeräuber kriegen Angst – Kaufmann kommt glücklich nach Hause – Ragusaner als Haushofmeister angestellt.

46 (S. 274) Der Unglücksfall

Wagen – deutsche Familie – Kinder geben Bettler Geld – Erinnerungen – vor zwanzig Jahren – Bolzen – Schrei – das rechte Auge verletzt – Vater, Nachbarn, Schmied – das rechte Auge verloren – Arzt – das linke Auge in Gefahr – Blindheit.

47 (S. 275) Sonderbarer Rechtsfall in England

Geschworene – einstimmig – Streit – Drohung – einer der Edelmänner erschossen gefunden – anderer verhaftet – von elf Geschworenen zum Tode verdammt – von dem zwölften für unschuldig gehalten – beharrt bei seiner Meinung – Geschworene hungrig – lossprechen – zwölfter Geschworener erscheint vor dem König – Erklärung – Begnadigung.

48 (S. 276) Die Kur des Vaters

Entbehrungen der Mutter – Nachahmung des Jungen – Übertreibung – Kur – verwundeter Bauer – Opfer von Jungen verlangt –
erschrocken – faßt sich – Haut auf die Wunde übertragen – Junge
sehr stolz – Borken fallen ab – Junge auf einmal nüchtern.

49 (S. 278) Der wilde Ritt

Junger Ritter – Pferd – Kuhherde – Wiese – kein Hirt – Stier –
Junge hat Angst – dahinstürmen – Junge aus dem Sattel geschleudert – Kopf verletzt – bewußtlos – ins Schloß gebracht – Schmerz
und Wut des Fürsten – Leibarzt – Hoffnung – nach sechs Wochen –
geisteskrank – Fürst trinkt noch mehr.

50 (S. 279) Das Kreuzverhör

Junge mit Raupenkästen beschäftigt – Tür geht auf – sonderbare
Stille – Junge bemerkt Vater – Vater blaß – Junge erschrocken –
nicht vorbereitet – Bücherschrank – Feigen – woher? – Erklärung
des Jungen – Sparkasse – glaubt ihm der Vater? – Junge lügt weiter –
Vater geht mit ihm fort – warum?

Section Six

German Verse for Translation or for Exercises in Comprehension

Johann Wilhelm Ludwig Gleim (1719–1803)

1 DER GREIS UND DER TOD

Ein Greis von achtundachtzig Jahren,
Ein armer, abgelebter Greis
Mit wenigen schneeweißen Haaren
Kam aus dem Walde, trug
5 Auf seinem krummen Rücken
Ein Bündel Reis.

Ach Gott, der arme Greis!
Er mußte wohl sehr oft sich bücken,
Eh' er's zusammenlas?
10 Er hatte keinen Sohn, sonst hätte der's getan.

Und weil vor Mattigkeit er nun nicht weiter kann,
So setzt er ab, und als er nun da saß
Bei seinem Bündel und bedachte,
Wie viel Beschwerde, Müh und Not
15 Das Bündel Reis ihm machte,
Wie viel sein bißchen täglich Brot,
Da seufzt er lebenssatt und weint und ruft den Tod.

„Befreie mich", spricht er, „von aller meiner Not
Und bringe mich zur Ruh!"

20 Der Tod kommt an, geht auf den Rufer zu.
„Was willst du?" fragt er, „du,
Daß du mich hergerufen hast?
Du trägst auch eine schwere Last!"
„Ach lieber Tod", versetzt darauf
25 Der arme Greis, „hilf sie mir auf!"

1 Wie alt war der Mann?
2 Wo war er gewesen?
3 Warum hatte er sich oft gebückt?
4 Warum konnte er nicht weitergehen?
5 Wo legte er sein Bündel hin?
6 Woraus bestand das Bündel?
7 Warum seufzte der Mann?
8 Wann weint man gewöhnlich?
9 Erklären Sie: „Bringe mich zur Ruh!"
10 Wie sollte der Tod dem Manne helfen?

1 What is the meaning of *ein abgelebter Greis*?
2 How does the man earn his living?
3 What do you know about his family?
4 What is the meaning of *zusammenlas*?
5 Why does the man sit down?
6 What does he do immediately before he sits down?
7 Describe his thoughts while he is sitting.
8 Why does Death come to him?
9 Why does he change his mind?
10 What does he ask Death to do?

Gottfried August Bürger (1747–94)

2 DIE SCHATZGRÄBER

Ein Winzer[1], der am Tode lag,
Rief seine Kinder an und sprach:
„In unserm Weinberg liegt ein Schatz,
Grabt nur danach!" – „An welchem Platz?"
5 Schrie alles laut den Vater an.
„Grabt nur!" – O weh! da starb der Mann.

Kaum war der Alte beigeschafft[2],
So grub man nach aus Leibeskraft.
Mit Hacke[3], Karst[4] und Spaten ward
10 Der Weinberg um und um gescharrt[5].

[1] der Winzer: der Weinbauer
[2] beischaffen: begraben
[3] die Hacke: *pick-axe*
[4] der Karst: *mattock*
[5] scharren: kratzen, graben

Da war kein Kloß¹, der ruhig blieb;
Man warf die Erde gar durchs Sieb
Und zog die Harken² kreuz und quer
Nach jedem Steinchen hin und her.
15 Allein da ward kein Schatz verspürt,
Und jeder hielt sich angeführt³.

Doch kaum erschien das nächste Jahr,
So nahm man mit Erstaunen wahr⁴,
Daß jede Rebe dreifach trug.
20 Da wurden erst die Söhne klug
Und gruben nun jahrein, jahraus
Des Schatzes immer mehr heraus.

1 In welchen Ländern gibt es Weinberge?
2 Warum rief der Winzer seine Kinder zu sich?
3 Was riet er seinen Kindern?
4 Was wollten die Kinder wissen?
5 Warum sagte es ihnen der Vater nicht?
6 Mit welchen Werkzeugen arbeiteten die Söhne?
7 Warum arbeiteten sie so fleißig?
8 Warum hielt sich jeder für betrogen?
9 Was setzte die Söhne in Erstaunen?
10 Wie wurden sie reich?

1 Why did the father summon his children?
2 What was the father and what did he leave his children?
3 Why didn't he specify where the treasure was?
4 How does the poet indicate that the sons were very anxious to know
where it was?
5 How does the poet indicate that no time was wasted?

¹ der Kloß: Erdklumpen, Stück Erde   ² die Harke: *rake*
³ anführen: falsch führen, betrügen   ⁴ wahrnehmen: merken

6 Explain the expression: *aus Leibeskräften.*
7 What actually did the sons do to find the treasure?
8 What was the result of their labours? (ll. 15–16)
9 When did the sons realise what their father had meant?
10 What lesson did they learn from their experience?

Ludwig Heinrich Christoph Hölty (1748–76)

3 MAILIED

Die Schwalbe fliegt, der Kuckuck ruft
In warmer, blauer Maienluft;
Die gelb und weißen Blumen wehn
Wie Gold und Silber auf den Höhn;
5 Es schwimmet Tal und Busch und Hain
Im Meer von goldnem Sonnenschein.

4 AUFTRAG
Fragment

Ihr Freunde, hänget, wann ich gestorben bin,
Die kleine Harfe hinter dem Altar auf,
    Wo an der Wand die Totenkränze
        Manches verstorbenen Mädchens schimmern.

5 Der Küster zeigt dann freundlich dem Reisenden
Die kleine Harfe, rauscht mit dem roten Band,
    Das, an der Harfe festgeschlungen,
        Unter den goldenen Saiten flattert.

5 DIE KNABENZEIT

Wie glücklich, wem das Knabenkleid
    Noch um die Schultern fliegt,
Wem lächelnde Zufriedenheit
    Den jungen Busen wiegt.

5 Der Kreisel¹ und das Steckenpferd²,
   Auf dem er herrisch sitzt,
   Das hölzerne Husarenschwert
   Belustigen ihn itzt³.

   Den Ball, des Knaben Busenfreund,
10 Der durch die Lüfte rollt,
   Sobald der Blumenmond⁴ erscheint,
   Vertauscht er nicht um Gold.

   Nie malt der Harm⁵, die Pest der Welt,
   Sein blühendes Gesicht,
15 Als wenn sein Ball ins Wasser fällt,
   Als wenn sein Schwert zerbricht.

   Er hüpfet oft, vom Schweiße naß,
   Den halben Sommertag,
   Im Garten, durch das bunte Gras,
20 Den Schmetterlingen nach.

   So spielt er, bis das Mittagsbrot
   Ihn in die Stube winkt.
   Und tändelt⁶, bis das Abendbrot
   Durch Silberwolken blinkt.

25 Vergnügen hüpft um ihn herum,
   Wenn Morpheus⁷ Mohn⁸ verstreut,
   Er tanzet in Elysium⁹,
   Beglückte Knabenzeit!

1 Wer ist glücklich – und warum?
2 Was für Spielzeug hat der Knabe?
3 Wann spielt er mit dem Ball?

¹ der Kreisel: *top*   ² das Steckenpferd: Stock mit hölzernem Pferdekopf
³ itzt: jetzt   ⁴ der Mond: der Monat   ⁵ der Harm: das Leid
⁶ tändeln: die Zeit müßig (*idly*) verbringen
⁷ Morpheus: der Gott des Schlafes und der Träume
⁸ der Mohn: *poppy*   ⁹ das Elysium: Inseln der Seligen, Paradies

4 Warum vertauscht er ihn nicht um Gold?
5 Wann wird der Knabe traurig?
6 Was versucht er zu fangen?
7 Woher wissen Sie, daß ihm dabei heiß wird?
8 Was unterbricht sein Spiel?
9 Was macht er am Nachmittag?
10 Wovon träumt er in der Nacht?

1 What is, according to the poet, a boy's dominant feeling?
2 What things please a boy?
3 What is the meaning of the expression: *herrisch sitzen*?
4 What happens when one of the boy's toys breaks?
5 How is a boy different from an adult? (ll. 13–16)
6 What is the boy's occupation on summer mornings?
7 Explain: *Das Mittagsbrot winkt ihn in die Stube.*
8 Describe the sunset.
9 What sort of dreams does a boy have?
10 How old do you think the boy in the poem is – and why?

Johann Wolfgang von Goethe (1749–1832)

6 WANDRERS NACHTLIED

Über allen Gipfeln
Ist Ruh,
In allen Wipfeln
Spürest du
5 Kaum einen Hauch;
Die Vögelein schweigen im Walde.
Warte nur, balde
Ruhest du auch.

7 MEERES STILLE

Tiefe Stille herrscht im Wasser,
Ohne Regung ruht das Meer,
Und bekümmert sieht der Schiffer
Glatte Fläche rings umher.

5 Keine Luft von keiner Seite!
Todesstille fürchterlich!
In der ungeheuern Weite
Reget keine Welle sich.

8 GLÜCKLICHE FAHRT

Die Nebel zerreißen,
Der Himmel ist helle,
Und Äolus[1] löset
Das ängstliche Band.
5 Es säuseln die Winde,
Es rührt sich der Schiffer.
Geschwinde! Geschwinde!
Es teilt sich die Welle,
Es naht sich die Ferne;
10 Schon seh' ich das Land!

9 DIE WANDELNDE GLOCKE

Es war ein Kind, das wollte nie
Zur Kirche sich bequemen[2],
Und Sonntags fand es stets ein Wie,
Den Weg ins Feld zu nehmen.

5 Die Mutter sprach: „Die Glocke tönt,
Und so ist dir's befohlen,
Und hast du dich nicht hingewöhnt,
Sie kommt und wird dich holen."

Das Kind, es denkt: die Glocke hängt
10 Da droben auf dem Stuhle[3].
Schon hat's den Weg ins Feld gelenkt,
Als lief' es aus der Schule.

Die Glocke, Glocke tönt nicht mehr,
Die Mutter hat gefackelt[4].
15 Doch welch ein Schrecken! Hinterher
Die Glocke kommt gewackelt.

[1] Äolus: Windgott (*Æolus*)   [2] sich bequemen: *submit to going*
[3] der Stuhl (=Glockenstuhl): wo die Glocke aufgehängt ist   [4] fackeln: *fib*

Sie wackelt schnell, man glaubt es kaum;
Das arme Kind im Schrecken,
Es läuft, es kommt als wie im Traum;
20 Die Glocke wird es decken.

Doch nimmt es richtig seinen Husch[1],
Und mit gewandter Schnelle
Eilt es durch Anger[2], Feld und Busch
Zur Kirche, zur Kapelle.

25 Und jeden Sonn- und Feiertag
Gedenkt es an den Schaden,
Läßt durch den ersten Glockenschlag
Nicht in Person sich laden[3].

1 Was für ein Kind war es?
2 Warum nahm das Kind den Weg ins Feld?
3 Womit drohte ihm die Mutter?
4 Warum glaubte das Kind nicht an die Drohungen seiner Mutter?
5 Wie zeigte es, daß es nicht daran glaubte?
6 Warum erschrak das Kind plötzlich?
7 Was würde nach der Meinung des Kindes die Glocke machen?
8 Was mußte das Kind tun, um zur Kirche zu kommen?
9 Wann läuten die Kirchenglocken?
10 Was wollte das Kind in Zukunft vermeiden?

1 Describe the child.
2 What had the child to do to avoid unpleasant consequences?
3 Where was the bell?
4 What made the child believe that his mother had fibbed?
5 What made him change his mind?
6 Why did he run?
7 What route did the child take?

---

1 seinen Husch nehmen: zu laufen beginnen   2 der Anger: die Wiese
3 laden: holen

8 What does the child now remember when he hears the bell ringing?
9 What does the child want to prevent happening?
10 What sort of a poem would you call this?

Johann Christoph Friedrich von Schiller (1759–1805)

10 JÄGERLIEDCHEN

Mit dem Pfeil, dem Bogen
Durch Gebirg und Tal
Kommt der Schütz gezogen
Früh am Morgenstrahl.

5 Wie im Reich der Lüfte
König ist der Weih[1],
Durch Gebirg und Klüfte
Herrscht der Schütze frei.

Ihm gehört das Weite,
10 Was sein Pfeil erreicht,
Das ist seine Beute,
Was da kreucht[2] und fleucht[3].

1 In whose praise is this song written?
2 What is the man armed with?
3 What is a man armed with such weapons called (*Schütze*)?
4 Through what sort of country is he going?
5 At what time of the day is he to be seen?
6 What is the kite described as being?
7 What has the man in common with the bird?
8 What belongs to him?
9 Explain the last two lines.
10 Suggest an alternative title for the poem.

[1] der Weih: *kite (bird)*   [2] kreucht: kriecht   [3] fleucht: fliegt

Friedrich Hölderlin (1770–1843)

11 ABBITTE

Heilig Wesen! gestört hab' ich die goldene
 Götterruhe dir oft, und der geheimeren,
  Tiefern Schmerzen des Lebens
   Hast du manche gelernt von mir.

5 O vergiß es, vergib! gleich dem Gewölke dort
 Vor dem friedlichen Mond, geh' ich dahin, und du
  Ruhst und glänzest in deiner
   Schöne[1] wieder, du süßes Licht!

Novalis (Friedrich von Hardenberg) (1772–1801)

12 MARIA

Ich sehe dich in tausend Bildern,
Maria, lieblich ausgedrückt,
Doch keins von allen kann dich schildern,
Wie meine Seele dich erblickt.

Ich weiß nur, daß der Welt Getümmel
Seitdem mir wie ein Traum verweht,
Und ein unnennbar süßer Himmel
Mir ewig im Gemüte steht.

Clemens Brentano (1778–1842)

13 WIEGENLIED

Singet leise, leise, leise
Singt ein flüsternd Wiegenlied,
Von dem Monde lernt die Weise
Der so still am Himmel zieht.

[1] die Schöne: die Schönheit

5 Singt ein Lied so süß gelinde,
Wie die Quellen auf den Kieseln[1],
Wie die Bienen um die Linde
Summen, murmeln, flüstern, rieseln.

Joseph von Eichendorff (1788–1857)

14 WANDERSPRUCH

Der Wandrer, von der Heimat weit,
Wenn rings die Gründe schweigen,
Der Schiffer in Meeres Einsamkeit,
Wenn die Stern' aus den Fluten steigen:

5 Die beide schauern und lesen
In stiller Nacht,
Was sie nicht gedacht,
Da es noch fröhlicher Tag gewesen.

15 DER PILGER

Man setzt uns auf die Schwelle,
Wir wissen nicht, woher?
Da glüht der Morgen helle,
Hinaus verlangt[2] uns sehr.
5 Der Erde Klang und Bilder,
Tiefblaue Frühlingslust,
Verlockend wild und wilder,
Bewegen da die Brust.
Bald wird es rings so schwüle,
10 Die Welt eratmet kaum,
Berg', Schloß und Wälder kühle
Stehn lautlos wie im Traum,
Und ein geheimes Grausen[3]
Beschleichet[4] unsern Sinn:
15 Wir sehnen uns nach Hause
Und wissen nicht, wohin?

[1] der Kiesel: kleiner Stein   [2] uns verlangt: wir sehnen uns
[3] das Grausen: lähmende Furcht, große Angst
[4] Beschleicht: ergreift unmerklich

1 Wer ist der Pilger?
2 Erklären Sie: „Man setzt uns auf die Schwelle".
3 Warum wollen wir hinausgehen?
4 Zu welcher Tageszeit wollen wir hinaus?
5 Was bietet uns die Erde an?
6 Zu welcher Tageszeit wird es schwüle?
7 Warum stehen Berge, Schloß und Wälder lautlos?
8 Warum beschleicht unsern Sinn ein geheimes Grausen?
9 Wohin wollen wir gehen?
10 Wo sind wir zu Hause?

1 Where are we put?
2 What don't we know?
3 Why do we want to go out?
4 What has the earth to offer us?
5 What effect do things of this earth have on us?
6 What happens soon afterwards?
7 What can the world do only with difficulty?
8 What sort of feeling comes over us?
9 Why does this feeling come over us?
10 Why is this poem entitled: *Der Pilger*?

Franz Grillparzer (1791–1872)

16 DER FISCHER

Hier sitz' ich mit lässigen Händen
In still behaglicher Ruh',
Und schaue den spielenden Fischlein
Im glitzernden Wasser zu.

5 Sie jagen und gehen und kommen;
Doch werf' ich die Angel aus,
Flugs sind sie von dannen geschwommen
Und leer kehr' ich abends nach Haus.

Versucht' ich's und trübte das Wasser,
10 Vielleicht geläng' es eh';
   Doch müßt' ich dann auch verzichten,
   Sie spielen zu sehen im See.

1 What are the fisherman's hands doing?
2 How is the fisherman spending his time?
3 What are the fish doing?
4 Why doesn't the fisherman cast his line?
5 How could he catch fish?
6 Why does he prefer not to try?
7 What does he in fact take home after his day's fishing?
8 Suggest an alternative title to the poem.

Heinrich Heine (1797–1856)

17 EIN FICHTENBAUM STEHT EINSAM

   Ein Fichtenbaum steht einsam
   Im Norden auf kahler Höh.
   Ihn schläfert[1]; mit weißer Decke
   Umhüllen ihn Eis und Schnee.

5 Er träumt von einer Palme,
   Die, fern im Morgenland,
   Einsam und schweigend trauert
   Auf brennender Felsenwand.

18 MEIN HERZ, MEIN HERZ IST TRAURIG

   Mein Herz, mein Herz ist traurig,
   Doch lustig leuchtet der Mai;
   Ich stehe, gelehnt an der Linde,
   Hoch auf der alten Bastei[2].

[1] ihn schläfert: er ist schläfrig, er will schlafen
[2] die Bastei: die Bastion

5 Da drunten fließt der blaue
Stadtgraben in stiller Ruh;
Ein Knabe fährt im Kahne,
Und angelt und pfeift dazu.

Jenseits erheben sich freundlich,
10 In winziger, bunter Gestalt,
Lusthäuser, und Gärten, und Menschen,
Und Ochsen, und Wiesen, und Wald.

Die Mägde bleichen Wäsche,
Und springen im Gras herum:
15 Das Mühlrad stäubt Diamanten,
Ich höre ein fernes Gesumm.

Am alten grauen Turme
Ein Schilderhäuschen steht;
Ein rotgeröckter Bursche
20 Dort auf und nieder geht.

Er spielt mit seiner Flinte,
Die funkelt im Sonnenrot,
Er präsentiert und schultert –
Ich wollt, er schösse mich tot.

1 Wie ist dem Dichter zumute?
2 Wo ist er?
3 Wo fährt der Knabe?
4 Was versucht er zu fangen?
5 Woher wissen Sie, daß die Menschen jenseits des Stadtgrabens weit
  entfernt sind?
6 Warum springen die Mägde im Gras herum?
7 Warum trägt der Bursch einen roten Rock?
8 Warum geht er auf und nieder?
9 Was hat der Bursch in der Hand?
10 Was will der Dichter, daß er damit machen soll?

1 What contrast is conveyed in the first two lines?
2 Where is the poet?
3 What is the boy doing?
4 What can the poet see in the distance?
5 What are the maids doing?
6 How is the poet aware of the fact that there is a mill-wheel working?
7 Where is the man walking up and down?
8 What is he playing with?
9 What does he do with it?
10 What would the poet like him to do with it?

Nikolaus Lenau (1802–50)

19 SCHILFLIED

Trübe wirds, die Wolken jagen,
Und der Regen niederbricht,
Und die lauten Winde klagen:
„Teich, wo ist dein Sternenlicht?"

5 Suchen den erloschnen Schimmer
Tief im aufgewühlten See.
Deine Liebe lächelt nimmer
Nieder in mein tiefes Weh!

20 ABENDLIED

Stille wirds im Walde; die lieben kleinen
Sänger prüfen schaukelnd den Ast, der durch die
Nacht dem neuen Fluge sie trägt, den neuen
    Liedern entgegen.

5 Bald versinkt die Sonne; des Waldes Riesen
Heben höher sich in die Lüfte, um noch
Mit des Abends flüchtigen Rosen sich ihr
    Haupt zu bekränzen.

Schon verstummt die Matte[1]; den satten Rindern[2]
10 Selten nur enthallt[3] das Geglock[4] am Halse,
Und es pflückt der wählende Zahn nur lässig
    Dunklere Gräser.

Und dort blickt der schuldlose Hirt der Sonne
Sinnend nach; dem Sinnenden jetzt entfallen
15 Flöt und Stab, es falten die Hände sich zum
    Stillen Gebete.

1 Warum wird es still im Walde?
2 Was sind die lieben kleinen Sänger?
3 Warum prüfen sie den Ast?
4 Was werden sie am nächsten Tage machen?
5 Was sind des Waldes Riesen?
6 Warum sind die Rosen flüchtig?
7 Was hört man, wenn die Rinder sich bewegen?
8 Wer hütet die Rinder?
9 Was hatte er in den Händen?
10 Was macht er mit den Händen?

1 What sign of approaching evening is mentioned in the first line?
2 How do the birds choose where they will sleep?
3 What sort of a sunset is it?
4 What effect has the sunset on the forest?
5 What shows that the cattle are not very active?
6 What have they round their necks?
7 How do you know that they aren't very hungry?
8 In what sort of mood is the herdsman?
9 What has he in his hands?
10 What does he do with his hands?

[1] die Matte: die Wiese   [2] die Rinder (pl.): das Vieh
[3] enthallen: tönen von   [4] das Geglock: die Glocken (pl.)

Eduard Mörike (1804–75)

21 SEPTEMBERMORGEN

Im Nebel ruhet noch die Welt,
Noch träumen Wald und Wiesen:
Bald siehst du, wenn der Schleier fällt,
Den blauen Himmel unverstellt,
5 Herbstkräftig die gedämpfte Welt
In warmem Golde fließen.

22 DENK ES, O SEELE!

Ein Tännlein grünet wo,
Wer weiß, im Walde,
Ein Rosenstrauch, wer sagt,
In welchem Garten?
5 Sie sind erlesen[1] schon,
Denk es, o Seele,
Auf deinem Grab zu wurzeln
Und zu wachsen.

Zwei schwarze Rößlein weiden
10 Auf der Wiese,
Sie kehren heim zur Stadt
In muntern Sprüngen.
Sie werden schrittweis gehn
Mit deiner Leiche;
15 Vielleicht, vielleicht noch eh
An ihren Hufen
Das Eisen los wird,
Das ich blitzen sehe!

1 Whom is the poet addressing?
2 What tree is mentioned in the poem?
3 For what purpose has it been chosen?
4 What other thing is to serve the same purpose?

[1] erlesen: gewählt

5 Why are the animals in the meadow particularly suited to the function they will perform later?

6 What are they doing in the meadow?

7 In what sort of mood do they come back to the town?

8 How will they walk later, and why?

9 How does the poet indicate that this change might come about soon?

10 Suggest an alternative title for the poem.

Friedrich Hebbel (1813–63)

23 HERBSTBILD

Dies ist ein Herbsttag, wie ich keinen sah!
Die Luft ist still, als atmete man kaum,
Und dennoch fallen raschelnd, fern und nah,
Die schönsten Früchte ab von jedem Baum.

5 O stört sie nicht, die Feier der Natur!
Dies ist die Lese[1], die sie selber hält;
Denn heute löst sich von den Zweigen nur,
Was vor dem milden Strahl der Sonne fällt.

Theodor Storm (1817–88)

24 WEIHNACHTSABEND

Die fremde Stadt durchschritt ich sorgenvoll,
Der Kinder denkend, die ich ließ zu Haus.
Weihnachten war's; durch alle Gassen scholl
Der Kinderjubel und des Markts Gebraus.[2]

5 Und wie der Menschenstrom mich fortgespült,
Drang mir ein heiser Stimmlein in das Ohr:
„Kauft, lieber Herr!" Ein magres Händchen hielt
Feilbietend[3] mir ein ärmlich Spielzeug vor.

[1] die Lese: die Ernte
[2] das Gebraus: der Lärm
[3] feilbieten: zum Kauf anbieten

Ich schrak empor; und beim Laternenschein
10 Sah ich ein bleiches Kinderangesicht;
Wes Alters¹ und Geschlechts es mochte sein,
Erkannt' ich im Vorübertreiben nicht.

Nur von dem Treppenstein, darauf es saß,
Noch immer hört' ich, mühsam wie es schien:
15 „Kauft, lieber Herr!" den Ruf ohn' Unterlaß²;
Doch hat wohl keiner ihm Gehör verliehn³.

Und ich? – War's Ungeschick, war es die Scham,
Am Weg zu handeln mit dem Bettelkind?
Eh' meine Hand zu meiner Börse kam,
20 Verscholl⁴ das Stimmlein hinter mir im Wind.

Doch als ich endlich war mit mir allein,
Erfaßte mich die Angst im Herzen so,
Als säß' mein eigen Kind auf jenem Stein
Und schrie nach Brot, indessen ich entfloh.

1 Wo befand sich der Dichter?
2 Warum machte er sich sorgenvolle Gedanken?
3 Was hörte er plötzlich?
4 Woher wissen Sie, daß das Kind arm war?
5 Wo saß das Kind?
6 Wie sah es aus?
7 Was wollte das Kind verkaufen?
8 Warum blieb der Dichter nicht stehen?
9 Was war geschehen, als er seine Börse herausnehmen wollte?
10 Warum tat es dem Dichter leid, daß er nicht stehengeblieben war?

1 In what sort of a mood was the poet?
2 Why were children rejoicing?
3 In what sort of a voice did the child speak?

¹ wes Alters: welchen Alters
² ohn' Unterlaß: ununterbrochen, ohne aufzuhören
³ ihm Gehör verleihen: ihm zuhören
⁴ verschallen: nicht mehr zu hören sein

4 What did the child want to sell him?
5 Was the child a boy or girl?
6 Where was the child sitting?
7 What success did the child have?
8 Why did the poet not stop and buy from the child?
9 Why did the child's voice not carry far?
10 Why did fear suddenly seize the poet?

Gottfried Keller (1819–90)

25 IN DER TRAUER

Ein Meister bin ich worden[1],
Zu weben Gram und Leid;
Ich webe Tag' und Nächte
Am schwarzen Trauerkleid.

5 Ich schlepp' es auf die Straße
Mühselig und bestaubt;
Ich trag' von spitzen Dornen
Ein Kränzlein auf dem Haupt.

Die Sonne steht am Himmel,
10 Sie sieht es und sie lacht:
Was geht da für ein Zwerglein
In einer Königstracht?

Ich lege Kron' und Mantel
Beschämt am Wege hin
15 Und muß nun ohne Trauer
Und ohne Freuden ziehn!

1 Of what craft has the poet become a master?
2 What has he been spending a long time making?
3 What does he do with it when it is made?
4 What does he wear on his head?
5 What does the sun do?

[1] worden: geworden

6 What does the sun call him?
7 What does the sun find incongruous about him?
8 What effect has the sun's remark on him?
9 Why is he worse off than before?
10 Suggest an alternative title for the poem.

Theodor Fontane (1819–98)

26 MITTAG

Am Waldessaume träumt die Föhre,
Am Himmel weiße Wölkchen nur;
Es ist so still, daß ich sie h ö r e,
Die tiefe Stille der Natur.

5   Rings Sonnenschein auf Wies' und Wegen,
Die Wipfel stumm, kein Lüftchen wach,
Und doch, es klingt, als ström ein Regen
Leis tönend auf das Blätterdach.

Hermann Lingg (1820–1905)

27 ROTKEHLCHEN

Schwalben waren schon lang
Fort und auf der Reise,
Nur ein Rotkehlchen sang
Lieblich und leise
5   Unter dem Dach
Eines Hauses, das, halbzerstört,
Allmählich zusammenbrach.
Es wurde von niemand gehört
Und dennoch sang es. Das Moos
10 Wuchs auf der Schwelle,
Die Steine bröckelten los,
Des Abendlichtes Helle
Schlief in den Zimmern allein,

Die Stürme gingen aus und ein
15 In dem großen verödeten Gang,
Aber das Rotkehlchen sang.
Lust und Freude war entflohn,
Alles war aus,
Es wußte nichts davon,
20 Es sang im öden, verfallenden Haus
Mit einem eignen lieblichen Ton.

1 Was ist ein Rotkehlchen?
2 Warum waren die Schwalben schon lange fort?
3 Wie war das Haus?
4 Wer hörte das Rotkehlchen singen?
5 Was bedeutet es, wenn Moos auf einer Schwelle wächst?
6 Wie waren die Mauern des Hauses?
7 Wer betrat das Haus?
8 Was für Möbel waren in dem Gang?
9 Warum war Lust und Freude entflohen?
10 Was wußte das Rotkehlchen nicht?

1 What season of the year was it?
2 Which birds had already gone?
3 What bird was left singing?
4 Where was it singing?
5 How was it singing?
6 Who heard it sing?
7 Where was the moss growing?
8 What was happening to the house?
9 Who lived in the house?
10 What was the bird ignorant of?

Hermann Allmers (1821–1902)

28 FELDEINSAMKEIT

Ich ruhe still im hohen, grünen Gras
Und sende lange meinen Blick nach oben,

Von Grillen¹ rings umschwirrt ohn' Unterlaß,
Von Himmelsbläue wundersam umwoben.

5 Und schöne weiße Wolken ziehn dahin
Durchs tiefe Blau, wie schöne stille Träume; –
Mir ist, als ob ich längst gestorben bin
Und ziehe selig mit durch ew'ge Räume.

Ferdinand von Saar (1833–1906)

29 HERBST

Der du die Wälder färbst,
Sonniger, milder Herbst,
Schöner als Rosenblühn
Dünkt² mir dein sanftes Glühn.

5 Nimmermehr Sturm und Drang,
Nimmermehr Sehnsuchtsklang;
Leise nur atmest du
Tiefer Erfüllung Ruh'.

Aber vernehmbar auch
10 Klaget ein scheuer Hauch,
Der durch die Blätter weht,
Daß es zur Erde geht.

Detlev von Liliencron (1844–1909)

30 AUS DER KINDERZEIT

In alten Briefen saß ich heut vergraben,
Als einer plötzlich in die Hand mir fiel,
Auf dem die Jahresziffer mich erschreckte,
So lange war es her, so lange schon.

¹ die Grille: *cricket* (*insect*)
² dünkt mir: scheint mir

5 Die Schrift stand groß und klein und glatt und kraus
Und reichlich untermischt mit Tintenklecksen:
„Mein lieber Fritz, die Bäume sind nun kahl,
Wir spielen nicht mehr Räuber und Soldat,
Türk[1] hat das rechte Vorderbein gebrochen,
10 Und Tante Hannchen[2] hat noch immer Zahnweh,
Papa ist auf die Hühnerjagd gegangen.
Ich weiß nichts mehr. Mir geht es gut.
Schreib bald und bleibe recht gesund.
Dein Freund und Vetter Siegesmund."–

15 „Die Bäume sind nun kahl", das herbe Wort
Ließ mich die Briefe still zusammenlegen,
Gab Hut und Handschuh mir und Rock und Stock
Und drängte mich hinaus in meine Heide.

1 Wie beschäftigte sich der Dichter?
2 Warum erschrak er plötzlich?
3 Wer hatte den Brief geschrieben?
4 An wen hatte er ihn geschrieben?
5 Woran erkennen Sie, daß der Schreiber jung gewesen sein muß?
6 Zu welcher Jahreszeit hatte er den Brief geschrieben?
7 Wer war Türk?
8 Was wollte der Schreiber des Briefes von seinem Freund?
9 Warum legte der Dichter die Briefe zusammen?
10 Was machte er, bevor er ausging?

1 How was the poet spending his time?
2 What was it that startled him?
3 Why did it startle him?
4 How was the letter written?
5 How do you know what season of the year it was when the letter was
written?
6 What had Türk done?
7 What did the boy's aunt suffer from?
8 What was his father doing?
9 Who was Siegesmund?
10 What did the poet do before going out?

[1] Türk: Name des Hundes   [2] Hannchen: Abkürzung von Johanna

Richard Dehmel (1863–1920)

31 MANCHE NACHT

Wenn die Felder sich verdunkeln,
fühl ich, wird mein Auge heller;
schon versucht ein Stern zu funkeln,
und die Grillen wispern schneller.

5 Jeder Laut wird bilderreicher,
das Gewohnte sonderbarer,
hinterm Wald der Himmel bleicher,
jeder Wipfel hebt sich klarer.

Und du merkst es nicht im Schreiten,
10 wie das Licht verhundertfältigt
sich entringt[1] den Dunkelheiten.
Plötzlich stehst du überwältigt.

Ricarda Huch (1864–1947)

32 FRIEDEN

Aus dem Dreißigjährigen Kriege

Von dem Turme im Dorfe klingt
Ein süßes Geläute;
Man sinnt, was es deute,
Daß die Glocke im Sturme nicht schwingt.
5 Mich dünkt[2], so hört' ich's als Kind;
Dann kamen die Jahre der Schande;
Nun trägt's in die Weite der Wind,
Daß Frieden im Lande.

Wo mein Vaterhaus fest einst stand,
10 Wächst wuchernde Heide;
Ich pflück', eh ich scheide,
Einen Zweig mir mit zitternder Hand.

[1] sich entringen: hervorkommen   [2] mich dünkt: mir scheint

Das ist von der Väter Gut
Mein einziges Erbe;
15 Nichts bleibt, wo mein Haupt sich ruht,
Bis einsam ich sterbe.

Meine Kinder verwehte der Krieg;
Wer bringt sie mir wieder?
Beim Klange der Lieder
20 Feiern Fürsten und Herren den Sieg.
Sie freuen sich beim Friedensschmaus[1],
Die müß'gen Soldaten fluchen, –
Ich ziehe am Stabe hinaus,
Mein Vaterland suchen.

1 Warum nennt die Dichterin das Geläute süß?
2 Wann hatte sie es vorher gehört?
3 Was war in der Zwischenzeit geschehen?
4 Warum wächst Heide dort, wo ihr Vaterhaus einst stand?
5 Warum zittert ihre Hand?
6 Was hat sie vom Vater geerbt?
7 Warum muß sie einsam sterben?
8 Warum freuen sich die Fürsten?
9 Warum fluchen die Soldaten?
10 Warum muß die Dichterin ihr Vaterland suchen?

1 What tidings do the bells bring?
2 When had the poet last heard such ringing?
3 What had the ringing of the bells meant for many years?
4 What does the wind do?
5 What has happened to the estate of the poet's father?
6 What does she inherit from her father?
7 What has happened to her children?
8 What are the princes doing?
9 In what sort of mood are the soldiers, and why?
10 What would the poet like to do before she dies?

[1] der Schmaus: das Festessen

Stefan George (1868–1933)

33 JAHRESTAG

O schwester nimm den krug aus grauem thon[1].
Begleite mich! denn du vergassest nicht
Was wir in frommer wiederholung pflegten.
Heut sind es sieben sommer dass wirs hörten
5 Als wir am brunnen schöpfend uns besprachen:
Uns starb am selben tag der bräutigam.
Wir wollen an der quelle wo zwei pappeln
Mit einer fichte in den wiesen stehn
Im krug aus grauem thone wasser holen.

Hugo von Hofmannsthal (1874–1929)

34 DIE BEIDEN

Sie trug den Becher in der Hand
– Ihr Kinn und Mund glich seinem Rand –,
So leicht und sicher war ihr Gang,
Kein Tropfen aus dem Becher sprang.

5 So leicht und fest war seine Hand:
Er ritt auf einem jungen Pferde,
Und mit nachlässiger Gebärde
Erzwang er, daß es zitternd stand.

Jedoch, wenn er aus ihrer Hand
10 Den leichten Becher nehmen sollte,
So war es beiden allzu schwer:
Denn beide bebten sie so sehr,
Daß keine Hand die andre fand
Und dunkler Wein am Boden rollte.

Gedichte (Insel-Bücherei)

1 What had the girl in her hand?
2 What comparison does the poet make in the second line?
3 How did the girl walk?
4 Where was the man?
5 What did he do? (l. 8)

[1] der T(h)on: *clay, earthenware*

6 How did he do it?
7 Why did they both tremble?
8 What was the effect of their trembling?
9 What fell to the ground?
10 Suggest an alternative title for the poem.

Richard Schaukal (1874–1943)

35 DER ALTE GÄRTNER

In seinem Rosengarten
Der alte Gärtner geht.
Er hat nichts zu erwarten,
Er fühlt, es ist schon spät.

5 Mit seinen harten Händen
Hilft er dem jungen Trieb.
Er weiß, er wird bald enden,
Doch annoch[1] hat er's lieb.

Ausgewählte Gedichte (Insel Verlag)

Rainer Maria Rilke (1875–1926)

36 HERBSTTAG

Herr: es ist Zeit. Der Sommer war sehr groß.
Leg deinen Schatten auf die Sonnenuhren,
und auf den Fluren laß die Winde los.

Befiehl den letzten Früchten voll zu sein;
5 gieb ihnen noch zwei südlichere Tage,
dränge sie zur Vollendung hin und jage
die letzte Süße in den schweren Wein.

Wer jetzt kein Haus hat, baut sich keines mehr.
Wer jetzt allein ist, wird es lange bleiben,
10 wird wachen, lesen, lange Briefe schreiben
und wird in den Alleen hin und her
unruhig wandern, wenn die Blätter treiben.

Sämtliche Werke (Insel Verlag)

[1] annoch: noch

Der König ist sechzehn Jahre alt.
Sechzehn Jahre und schon der Staat.
Er schaut, wie aus einem Hinterhalt,
vorbei an den Greisen vom Rat

5 in den Saal hinein und irgendwohin
und fühlt vielleicht nur dies:
an dem schmalen langen harten Kinn
die kalte Kette vom Vlies.

Das Todesurteil vor ihm bleibt
10 lang ohne Namenszug.
Und sie denken: wie er sich quält.

Sie wüßten, kennten sie ihn genug,
daß er nur langsam bis siebzig zählt,
eh er es unterschreibt.

Sämtliche Werke (Insel Verlag)

1 What sort of a king is the boy?
2 Where might he have been, judging by the way he is looking?
3 What sort of men compose his council?
4 What is the king looking at?
5 What does he perhaps feel?
6 What sort of chin has he?
7 What has he in front of him?
8 What does it lack?
9 What do they think he is doing?
10 What is he in fact doing?

38 DIE ERBLINDENDE

Sie saß so wie die anderen beim Tee.
Mir war zuerst, als ob sie ihre Tasse
ein wenig anders als die andern fasse.
Sie lächelte einmal. Es tat fast weh.

5 Und als man schließlich sich erhob und sprach
und langsam und wie es der Zufall brachte
durch viele Zimmer ging (man sprach und lachte)
da sah ich sie. Sie ging den andern nach,

verhalten, so wie eine, welche gleich
10 wird singen müssen und vor vielen Leuten;
auf ihren hellen Augen, die sich freuten,
war Licht von außen wie auf einem Teich.

Sie folgte langsam und sie brauchte lang,
als wäre etwas noch nicht überstiegen;
15 und doch: als ob, nach einem Übergang,
sie nicht mehr gehen würde, sondern fliegen.

Sämtliche Werke (Insel Verlag)

1 What time of day was it?
2 What did the poet first find strange about the woman?
3 What was the effect of her smile?
4 What did the people do after getting up from their seats?
5 Where was the woman?
6 What did she seem to the poet about to do?
7 What were her eyes doing?
8 How were they lit up?
9 What reason does the poet first suggest for her slow movements?
(l. 14)
10 How does he subsequently modify his suggested reason?

Max Herrmann-Neiße (1886–1941)

39 EIN DEUTSCHER DICHTER BIN ICH EINST GEWESEN...

Ein deutscher Dichter bin ich einst gewesen,
die Heimat klang in meiner Melodie,
ihr Leben war in meinem Lied zu lesen,
das mit ihr welkte und mit ihr gedieh.

5 Die Heimat hat mir Treue nicht gehalten,
sie gab sich ganz den bösen Trieben hin,
so kann ich nur ihr Traumbild noch gestalten,
der ich ihr trotzdem treu geblieben bin.

In ferner Fremde mal ich ihre Züge

10 zärtlich gedenkend mir mit Worten nah,
die Abendgiebel und die Schwalbenflüge
und alles Glück, was einst mir dort geschah.

Doch hier wird niemand meine Verse lesen,
ist nichts, was meiner Seele Sprache spricht;
15 ein deutscher Dichter bin ich einst gewesen,
jetzt ist mein Leben Spuk wie mein Gedicht.

1 What could once be read in the poet's songs?
2 How was his poetry linked up with his native land?
3 What had his own country not done?
4 What had it given itself up to?
5 What can the poet now alone do? (l. 7)
6 What does he do while abroad? (l. 9)
7 What things does he recall?
8 Why does writing poetry now give him no real satisfaction?
9 To what does he compare his poetry and his life?
10 Suggest an alternative title for the poem.

Franz Werfel (1890–1945)

40 ELTERNLIED

Kinder laufen fort.
Langher kanns noch garnicht sein,
Kamen sie zur Tür herein,
Saßen zwistiglich vereint
5 Alle um den Tisch.

Kinder laufen fort.
Und es ist schon lange her.
Schlechtes Zeugnis kommt nicht mehr.
Stunden Ärgers, Stunden schwer:
10 Scharlach, Diphtherie!

Kinder laufen fort.
Söhne hangen Weibern an.
Töchter haben ihren Mann.
Briefe kommen, dann und wann,
15 Nur auf einen Sprung.

Kinder laufen fort.
Etwas nehmen sie doch mit.
Wir sind ärmer, sie sind quitt.
Und die Uhr geht Schritt für Schritt
20 Um den leeren Tisch.

1 Where used the children to be not so long ago?
2 How did they behave there?
3 What used the parents to receive long ago?
4 What other worries did they have?
5 What has happened to the children since?
6 What do the parents receive now?
7 How often do they receive them?
8 Explain the expression: *auf einen Sprung kommen.*
9 In what way are the parents poorer?
10 Suggest an alternative title for the poem.

Vocabulary

German–English

NOTES: 1. The plural ending -(e)n of feminine nouns (19(c)) is not indicated.
2. Compounds whose constituent parts are already listed are omitted.
3. Only those meanings are given that the words have in the text.
4. Figures refer to the paragraphs of Section One.

ab: von da —, from then on
die Abbitte, apology
ab-büßen, atone for
ab-drucken, print (off)
ab-drücken, fire
der Abend (-e), evening
das Abendessen (-), supper
abendlich, evening
das Abendrot, sunset
das Abenteuer (-), adventure
abenteuerlich, exciting, romantic
aber, but
abermals, once again
***ab-fahren (ä, u, a),** drive off, leave
***ab-fallen (ä, ie, a),** fall off
ab-fressen (i, a, e), browse on
abgelebt, senile
der Abhang (¨e), slope
ab-holen, fetch
die Abkürzung, abbreviation
ab-lassen (ä, ie, a), send off
ab-legen, take off
ab-lehnen, decline
ab-lösen, take off
ab-machen, decide upon, arrange to have
der Abschied (-e), leave; **beim —,** on leaving
ab-schneiden (i, i), cut off
abseits, to one side
ab-setzen, set down
die Absicht, intention
absichtslos, vacantly
***ab-steigen (ie, ie),** dismount
***ab-stoßen (ö, ie, o),** push off

ab-warten, wait for (the end of)
die Abweichung, deviation
abwesend, absent
ab-zahlen, discharge
ab-ziehen (o, o), take off, raise
ach, oh
achten (auf), pay heed (to)
ächzen, groan
der Affe (-n, -n), ape, monkey
die Ahnung, foreboding
der Akzent (-e), accent
Algier, Algiers; **-er** (adj.), from Algiers
algierisch, Algerian
all, all; **-e,** everybody; **-es,** everything, everybody; **vor -em,** above all
die Allee, avenue
allein, but; only, alone
allerdings, it is true
allerlei, all kinds of
allgemein, general
allmählich, gradually
allzuschwer, all too heavy
als, as, when; **— wie,** as though
also, thus, so; now then
alt, old
der Altar (¨e), altar
der Alte (see 34), old man
die Alte (see 34), old woman
das Alter (-), old age
***altern,** grow old
von alters her, from time immemorial
das Amt (¨er), office

sich amüsieren, amuse oneself
an, on, at, to
an-bieten (o, o), offer
der Anblick (-e), sight; beim
    ersten —, at first sight
der Anbruch (der Nacht), (night-)
    fall
    ander-, other
    anders (als), differently
    (from)
    an-deuten, hint at
der Anfang (ᵘe), beginning
    an-fangen (ä, i, a), begin
    an-führen, cite, give; hoax
    angeblich, by repute
das Angebot (-e), offer
der Angeklagte (see 34), defend-
    ant
die Angel, fishing-rod
    angeln, fish
die Angelrute, fishing-rod
    angenagelt, nailed, rooted (to
    the spot)
    angenehm, pleasant
der Anger (-), meadow
das Angesicht (-er), face
der Angestellte (see 34), employee
    angezogen, dressed
der Angriff (-e), attack
die Angst (ᵘe), fear, terror; —
    haben, be afraid
    ängstlich, anxious, fearful
    an-halten (ä, ie, a), check,
    stop
    anhaltend, continually
    an-hangen(ä,i,a), be attached
    to, cling to
    animiert, animatedly
der Anker (-), anchor
    an-klagen, accuse
*an-kommen (a, o), arrive
der Ankömmling (-e), (new) ar-
    rival
    an-legen, put on
    an-leiten, lead, train
    an-machen, put on; light
    an-nehmen (i, a, o), suppose;
    accept
    an-rufen (ie, u), summon;
    ring up

anscheinend, apparently
an-schlagen (ä, u, a), strike up
an-schreien (ie, ie), shout to
an-sehen (ie, a, e), look at;
    sieh einer mal an! well, I
    never!
ansichtig *werden (i, u, o)
    (G), catch sight of
an-spannen lassen, order
    carriage to be got ready
an-starren, stare at
an-stellen, appoint
die Anstrengung, effort
    Anton, Anthony
die Antwort, answer
    antworten, answer
*an-wachsen (ä, u, a), grow
    on to
an-wenden (a, a), employ,
    (means)
der Anwesende (see 34), by-
    stander, person present
die Anwesenheit, presence
*an-wurzeln, take root
an-ziehen (o, o), put on;
    sich —, dress (intr.)
der Anzug (ᵘe), suit
der Appetit, appetite
die Arbeit, work, task
    arbeiten, to work
    arbeitslos, out of work
der Ärger, vexation
    ärgerlich, angrily
    arm, poor
der Arm (-e), arm
der Ärmel (-), sleeve
die Armen (pl.), the poor
    ärmlich, wretched
die Armseligkeit, wretchedness
    artig, good, like a good child
der Artikel (-), article
der Arzt (ᵘe), doctor
der Ast (ᵘe), bough
der Atem, breath
    atemlos, breathless
    atmen, breathe
    auch, also, too, even; — nicht,
    nor
    auf, on, up, at, to; — und ab
    (nieder), up and down

auf-atmen, draw a deep breath (of relief)
auf-blicken, look up
*auf-brausen, seethe, surge
auf-erlegen, impose
auf-fassen, understand
auf-fordern, invite
die Aufforderung, demand, invitation
auf-führen, perform
auf-geben (i, a, e), give up
*auf-gehen (i, a), open (*intr.*)
aufgeregt, excited
auf-halten (ä, ie, a), check
auf-häufen, pile up
auf-heben (o, o), pick up
auf-helfen (i, a, o), help up (with)
auf-hören, stop
auf-legen, lay on
auf-muntern, encourage
auf-nehmen (i, a, o), take, raise
die Aufregung, excitement
auf-reißen (i, i), tear open
sich auf-richten, sit up
die Aufrichtigkeit, frankness
der Aufschlag (¨e), impact; tramp
auf-schlagen (ä, u, a), pitch (tent)
auf-sehen (ie, a, e), look up
auf-setzen, put on
der Aufstand (¨e), revolt
*auf-stehen (a, a), get up
das Aufstehen, rising
auf-suchen, seek out
der Auftrag (¨e), commission, order
*auf-wachen, wake up (*intr.*)
auf-wecken, wake (*tr.*)
auf-wühlen, stir up, lash up
der Augapfel (¨), pupil (eye)
das Auge (-n), eye
der Augenblick (-e), moment
das Augenlicht, sight
der Augenzeuge (-n, -n), eyewitness
August, Augustus
aus, from, over, made of; — und ein, in and out

*aus-brechen (i, a, o), burst out, break out
sich aus-breiten, spread
aus-drücken, express
das Ausfahren, rowing out
der Ausflug (¨e), excursion
aus-fragen, interrogate
aus-füllen, fill
der Ausgang (¨e), exit
ausgebreitet, outstretched
*aus-gehen (i, a), go out
aus-halten (ä, ie, a), endure
aus-löschen, extinguish
aus-machen, arrange
aus-packen, unpack
aus-richten, execute
die Aussage, statement
aus-sehen (ie, a, e), look
außen: nach —, outwards; von —, from outside/without
aus-senden (a, a), emit
außer (sich), beside (o.s.)
der Ausspruch (¨e), verdict
*aus-steigen (ie, ie), get out
aus-stoßen (ö, ie, o), emit, utter
sich aus-strecken, stretch (o.s.)
der Ausweg (-e), way out
aus-werfen (i, a, o), cast
aus-wickeln, unwrap
aus-ziehen (o, o), take off
der Auszug (¨e), departure
das Auto (-s), car
das Automobil (-e), car

der Bach (¨e), stream
die Backsteinfüllung, brickwork
der Bahnsteig (-e), platform
bald, soon; — ... —, now ... now
der Balken (-), beam
der Ball (¨e), ball
das Band (-e), bond
das Band (¨er), ribbon
die Bande, gang, band
die Bank (¨e), bench
barfüßig, barefooted
die Barke, barque

die **Bastei**, bastion
bauen, build
der **Bauer** (-s/n, -n), peasant, farmer
der **Baum** (ⁿe), tree
baumeln, dangle
sich **bäumen**, rear up
der **Baumstumpf** (ⁿe), tree stump
beben, quake, tremble
der **Becher** (-), goblet, wine-glass
sich **bedanken**, say thank you
bedenken (a, a), reflect
der **Bediente** (*see 34*), footman
die **Bedingung**, condition; **unter dieser —**, on this condition
befallen, covered
der **Befehl** (-e), order
befehlen (ie, a, o), order
befestigen, fasten
sich **befinden** (a, u), be (in a place); feel
befreien, free
befreundet, friendly
befriedigen, satisfy
*****begegnen** (D), meet
beginnen (a, o), begin
begleiten, accompany, go with
die **Begleitung**, attendants
beglücken, make happy
beglückwünschen, congratulate
die **Begnadigung**, pardon
Begriff: im —* sein, be on the point of
die **Begrüßung**, welcome
behaglich, snug, comfortable, easeful
behalten (ä, ie, a), keep, hold; **recht —**, prove to be right
beharren (bei), stick (to)
beherrscht, controlled
behutsam, carefully
bei, by, to, with, at, on
beide, the two, both
beiderseitig, both
der **Beifall** (ⁿe), approval
beifällig, approvingly
das **Bein** (-e), leg
beinahe, almost
beisammen, together

bei-schaffen, bury
das **Beispiel** (-e), example; **zum —**, for example
bei-stimmen, agree, chime in
bekannt, familiar
der **Bekannte** (*see 34*), acquaintance
die **Bekanntschaft**, acquaintanceship
sich **beklagen** (**über**), complain (of)
die **Bekleidung**, clothing
(*) **bekommen** (a, o), get, obtain; suit
bekränzen, garland
sich **bekümmern** (um), mind, concern oneself (about)
bekümmert, anxiously
belauschen, overhear
belegt: -e Brote, sandwiches
beleidigen, offend, insult
beleuchten, light, illuminate
beliebt, popular
bellen, bark
belustigen, amuse
sich **bemächtigen** (G), take possession of, seize
bemerken, notice, remark
bemoost, moss-covered
beneiden, envy
benetzen, wet, moisten
bequem, convenient, comfortable
die **Beratung**, consultation
bereit, ready
bereiten, make
bereits, already
der **Berg** (-e), mountain, hill
der **Bergarbeiter** (-), miner
der **Berg-mann** (-leute), miner
das **Bergmärchen** (-), mining tale
das **Bergstädtchen** (-), little mining town
das **Bergwerk** (-e), mine
berichten, report
der **Beruf** (-e), calling, profession
sich **bechäftigen**, occupy o.s.
beschämt, ashamed
Bescheid wissen (u, u), know one's way (whereabouts)
bescheiden, modest

die **Bescheidenheit,** modesty
beschleichen (i, i), steal over
beschließen (o, o), decide (on)
beschreiben (ie, ie), describe
die **Beschreibung,** description
die **Beschwerde,** hardship, difficulty
sich **beschweren (über),** complain (of)
besessen, possessed, mad
besinnungslos, unconscious
der **Besitzer (-),** owner
besonders, especially
besprechen (i, a, o), discuss; **sich —,** talk to one another
besser, better
bestaubt, covered with dust
bestehen (a, a), exist; **— auf** (D), insist on; **—aus,** consist of
besteigen (ie, ie), get (on)
bestellen, order
bestimmen, allot
bestrafen, punish
die **Bestürzung,** dismay
der **Besuch (-e),** visit
besuchen, visit
beten, pray
betrachten, look at
das **Betragen,** behaviour
betreten (i, a, e), enter
betroffen, taken aback, smitten
betrübt, disappointed(ly)
betrügen (o, o), deceive
betrunken, drunk
das **Bett (-(e)s, -en),** bed
das **Bettelkind (-er),** beggar-child
der **Bettler (-),** beggar
die **Bettlerin (-nen),** beggar-woman
die **Beute,** booty
bevor, before
bevor-stehen (a, a), be imminent
sich **bewegen,** move, stir
die **Bewegung,** movement
der **Beweis (-e),** proof
beweisen, (ie, ie), prove
bewirken, effect, bring about
bewundern, admire

bewußtlos, unconscious
das **Bewußtsein,** awareness, consciousness
bezahlen, pay
die **Biene,** bee
das **Bild (-er),** picture, scene
bilden, form
das **Bilderbuch (¨er),** picture-book
das **Bildwerk,** illustrations
billig, cheap
binden (a, u), bind
bis, until; **— dahin,** hitherto; **— auf,** except
bisher, hitherto
ein **bißchen,** a bit
bitten (a, e), (um), ask (for)
bitter, bitterly
blaß, pale
das **Blatt (¨er),** leaf
das **Blätterdach (¨er),** leafy canopy
blau, blue
das **Blau,** blue
die **Bläue,** blueness
*****bleiben (ie, ie),** remain
bleich, pale
bleichen, bleach, whiten
der **Blick (-e),** glance
blicken, look
blind, blind
die **Blindheit,** blindness
blinken, flash, gleam
blitzen, flash
der **Blödsinn,** nonsense
blödsinnig, silly, imbecile
bloß, mere
blühen, bloom
die **Blume,** flower
der **Blumenmond,** May
das **Blut,** blood
blutdürstig, bloodthirstily
bluten, bleed
blutübergossen, blushing all over
der **Boden (¨),** ground, floor, soil; attic
der **Bogen (¨),** bow
die **Bonne,** nursemaid
das **Boot (-e),** boat

der Bord, board (ship)
die Borke, scab
die Börse, purse
böse, evil, angry
der Brand (-̈e), fire
braten (ä, ie, a), roast
brauchen, need, take
bräunen, tan
der Bräutigam (-e), betrothed
brav, good, worthy
(*) brechen (i, a, o), break
breit, wide
breitschult(e)rig, broad-
shouldered
brennen (a, a), burn, scorch
der Brief (-e), letter
der Briefträger (-), postman
bringen (a, a), bring, put,
take
das Brot (-e), bread, loaf; living
der Bruder (-̈), brother
brüllen, roar
brummen, mutter
der Brunnen (-), well, spring
die Brust (-̈e), breast, heart
der Bube (-n, -n), lad
das Buch (-̈er), book
der Bücherschrank (-̈e), book-
case
die Büchse, gun
der Büchsenmacher (-), gun-
smith
sich bücken, bend down
der Bügel (-), stirrup
die Bühne, stage
das Bündel (-), bundle
bunt, bright-coloured
der Bürger (-), citizen
das Bürgergeschlecht (-er), pa-
trician family
der Bursch (-en, -en), youth
der Busch (-̈e), bush
der Busen (-), bosom, heart
die Butter, butter
das Butterbrot (-e), (slice of) bread
and butter

der Chef (-s), chief, boss
die Chemie, chemistry

Chlodwig, Lewis
der Christenhund (-e), Christian
dog

da, when, as; here, there, then
dabei, with it; in doing so
das Dach (-̈er), roof
die Dachkammer, attic room
dadurch, thereby
dafür, for them
dagegen, in exchange for it
daher, so, consequently
*daher-traben, canter along
dahin, away, along
*dahin-stürmen, dash along
dahinter, behind them
damals, at that time
die Dame, lady
damit, with it, with those
words; so that
dämmern, grow dark/dusk
die Dämmerung, half-light, dusk
danach, afterwards
daneben, near them
der Dank, thanks
dankbar, grateful
dann, then; **— und wann,**
occasionally
dannen: von —, away
darauf, on it, on which; later,
afterwards
darin, in it
darüber, of it; **— her,** on top
of them
darunter, among them
das, that, those
daß, (so) that
das Datum (Daten), date
dauern, last, take
davon, of it; away
*davon-rennen (a, a), run
away
dazu, for that, to (do) that;
while doing so; in addition
die Decke, blanket; ceiling; mantle
decken, shield, cover
deinetwegen, because of you
deinetwillen: um —, because of you

demütig, humbly
demütigen, humiliate
denken, (a, a), think
denn, for; then; *see 124(b)*
dennoch, yet, nevertheless
der, who
dergleichen, such, of the kind
derselbe, the same; he
deuten (auf), point (to), indicate
deutlich, clearly
die **Deutlichkeit,** clarity, distinctness
deutsch, German
Deutschland (*n.*), Germany
der **Diamant (-en, -en),** diamond
dicht, close, thick
der **Dichter (-),** poet
die **Dichterin (-nen),** poetess
die **Dichtung,** poetry
dick, thick, fat
dienen (D), serve; **— zu,** serve as
der **Diener (-),** servant
dies, this, these
dieser, this
diesmal, this time
diktieren, dictate
das **Ding (-e),** thing
die **Diphtherie,** diphtheria
der **Direktor (-s, -en),** director
doch, yet, however, still; anyhow; *see 124(c)*
der **Doktor (-s, -en),** doctor
der **Dolch (-e),** dagger
das **Dorf (∹er),** village
der **Dorfbewohner (-),** village-inhabitant
der **Dorn (-s, -en),** thorn
dort, there
der **Drang,** stress
drängen, drive; **sich —,** crowd
draußen, outside
dreierlei, three kinds of
dreifach, threefold
dreißigjährig, thirty years'
die **Dreschmaschine,** threshing-machine
dringen (a, u), force one's way
dringlich, pressing

drinnen, inside
droben, upstairs, up there
drohen (D), threaten
die **Drohung,** threat
drüben, over there
drucken, print
drunten, down below
dumm, stupid
dumpf, muffled
dunkel, dark
das **Dunkel,** dark; **im — (n),** in the dark
die **Dunkelheit,** darkness
dünken: dünkt mir, mich dünkt, it seems to me
durch, through
das **Durcheinander,** disorder; **wirres —,** confusion, chaos
durchschreiten (i, i), traverse
durchweichen, soak, drench
durchzogen, criss-crossed
dürfen (*see 109*), be allowed to

eben, just; precisely
ebenfalls, likewise
ebenso, just as
die **Ecke,** corner
edel, noble, precious
der **Edelmann (∹er),** nobleman
Eduard, Edward
eh', ehe, before; sooner
ehemals, formerly
eher, rather
der **Ehering (-e),** wedding-ring
ei, why!
die **Eiche,** oak
eifrig, earnestly
eigen, own, peculiar
eigentlich, strictly speaking
eilen, hurry
eilig, hastily
eiligst, as fast as possible
einander, one another
ein-biegen (o, o), turn (*intr.*)
ein-brechen (i, a, o), fall (of night)
das **Eindringen,** forcible entry
der **Eindruck (∹e),** impression
ein-fahren (ä, u, a), arrive

die **Einfahrt,** sailing into (harbour)

der **Einfall** (ᐨe), idea

    ***ein-fallen (ä, ie, a),** occur

    einfältig, simple-minded

der **Einfluß** (ᐨ(ss)e), influence

der **Eingang** (ᐨe), entrance

    eingebaut, built-in

die **Eingebung,** inspiration

    eingerollt, rolled up

    ein-gestehen (a, a), confess

    ein-graben (ä, u, a), engrave

der **Eingriff (-e),** incision

    einige, some, a few

    ein-kaufen, purchase

    ein-laden (ä, u, a), invite

die **Einladung,** invitation

    ein-lassen (ä, ie a), let in

    einmal, once; **auf —,** all at
    once; **nicht —,** not even

    einsam, lonely, in solitude

die **Einsamkeit,** solitude

    ein-schenken, pour out

    ***ein-schlafen (ä, ie, a),** fall
    asleep

    ein-schlagen (ä, u, a), take
    (path)

    ein-schließen (o, o), lock in/up

    ein-sperren, lock in/up

    einst, once, formerly

    ein-stecken, pocket

    ***ein-steigen,** get on, get in,
    board

sich **ein-stellen,** appear, arise

    ein-stimmen, join (in)

    einstimmig, unanimous

    einstöckig, one-storeyed

    ***ein-stürzen,** cave in, collapse

    eintönig, monotonously

    ***ein-treten (i, a, e),** come in,
    enter

    ein-willigen, acquiesce, con-
    sent

der **Einwohner (-),** inhabitant

die **Einzelheit,** detail

    ***ein-ziehen (o, o),** come in

    einzig, only

    das **Eis,** ice

    das **Eisen(-),** iron; hoof

    eiskalt, icy cold

die **Eltern** (*pl.*), parents

der **Empfang** (ᐨe): **in — nehmen,**
    receive, take

die **Empfindung,** perception,
    realisation

    ***empor-schrecken (i, a, o),**
    start up, be startled

    ***empor-steigen (ie, ie),** rise

    empört, indignant

das **Ende (-s, -n),** end; **zu —**
    ***gehen,** come to an end;
    zu — *sein, be over, at an
    end; **ein — nehmen,** come
    to an end

    enden, end; die

    endlich, at last

    eng, small

    England (*n.*), England

der **Engländer (-),** Englishman

    englisch, English

    entdecken, discover; **sich —,**
    be discovered

    ***entfallen (ä, ie, a),** fall from

    entfalten, unfold

    entfernen, remove; **sich —,**
    go away

die **Entfernung,** distance

    ***entfliehen (o, o),** escape, flee,
    run away

die **Entführung,** abduction

    entgegen, towards

    entgegengesetzt, opposite

sich **entgegen-stellen,** confront

    ***enthallen (D),** sound from

sich **entkleiden,** undress (*intr.*)

    entlang, along

    entledigen, deprive, rid

sich **entringen (a, u),** struggle to
    free o.s. from, escape

    entsagen (D), renounce, forgo

die **Entscheidung,** decision

    ***entschlafen (ä, ie, a),** fall
    asleep

    entschlossen, resolved

der **Entschluß** (ᐨ(ss)e), decision

sich **entschuldigen (bei),** apolo-
    gise (to)

die **Entschuldigung,** excuse; **um**
    — bitten, beg pardon

der **Entschuldigungsbrief (-e),**
    letter of apology

*entspringen (a, u), escape
entzünden, light
eratmen, pant, breathe with
difficulty
der Erbe (-n, -n), heir
das Erbe (Erbschaften), inherit-
ance
*erbeben, start, tremble, shake
erben, inherit
erbittert, embittered
erblicken, catch sight of
die Erblindende (*see 34*), woman
going blind
das Erdbeben (-), earthquake
die Erde, soil, ground, earth
sich ereignen, occur
erfahren (ä, u, a), learn
die Erfahrung, experience
erfassen, seize; size up
der Erfolg (-e), success
erfolglos, unsuccessful
*erfrieren (o, o), freeze to
death
erfüllen, fulfil
die Erfüllung, fulfilment
ergeben (i, a, e), show; **sich
—,** surrender
ergreifen (i, i), seize
erhaschen, seize
sich erheben (o, o), rise, get up
sich erinnern, remember
die Erinnerung, memory
*erkalten, grow cold
erkennen (a, a) (an) (D), recognise (by); realise, make out
die Erkenntnis (-(ss)e), knowledge, awareness, realisation
das Erkennungszeichen (-), dis-
tinguishing sign
erklären, declare; explain
die Erklärung, explanation
sich erkundigen (nach), inquire
(about)
erlangen, obtain
erlauben, allow
erlesen, selected
*erlöschen (i, o, o), go out,
be extinguished
*ermatten, become ex-
hausted

ermorden, murder
sich ernähren, support o.s.
ernst, grave
der Ernst: es ist mir —, I mean it
seriously
die Ernte, harvest
erregt, excited(ly)
die Erregtheit, excitement
erreichen, reach
sich erretten, save o.s.
*erröten, blush
das Erröten, blushing
*erscheinen (ie, ie), appear
erschossen, shot dead
*erschrecken (i, a, o), be
startled, be frightened
erschrecken, frighten, startle
erschreckt, terrified
erschrocken, terrified, struck
with horror
erspähen, descry
erst, only, not until; first
das Erstaunen, astonishment; **in
— setzen,** astonish
erstaunt, astonished, surprised
erstens, in the first place
ertappen, catch
erteilen, give (orders)
*erwachen, wake up (*intr.*)
die Erwägung, reflection
erwählen, choose
erwarten, expect
erwidern, reply
erzählen, tell
erzwingen (a, u), force
die Esche (-n), ash
der Esel (-), donkey
essen (i, a, e), eat
das Essen, food
das Eßzimmer (-), dining-room
etwas, something, anything;
some; somewhat; **noch —,**
anything more
ewig, eternally

die Fähre, ferry
(*) fahren (ä, u, a), go, pass;
travel; drive
die Fahrkarte, ticket

der Fährlohn (-e), fare
der Fährmann (-er), ferryman
das Fahrrad (-er), bicycle
die Fahrt, voyage, journey, progress
der Fall (-e), case
*fallen (ä, ie, a), fall
die Falltür, trap-door
falsch, wrong, poor (shot)
sich falten, fold
die Familie, family
fangen (ä, i, a), catch
das Fangseil (-e), lasso
die Farbe, colour
färben, colour
der Fasan (-s, -e/en), pheasant
fassen, take, catch hold of, seize, make (decisions); sich —, pull o.s. together
die Fassung, composure
fassungslos, uncontrolled
fast, almost
die Feder, pen
fehlen, be short of
der Fehler (-), mistake
die Feier, festival
feiern, celebrate
der Feiertag (-e), holiday
die Feige, fig.
feilbietend, (offering) for sale
feilen, file
fein, fine
das Feld (-er), field
der Feldweg (-e), footpath
der Felsen (-), rock
die Felsenwand (-e), precipice
das Fenster (-), window
die Fensterscheibe, window-pane
die Ferien (pl.), holidays
fern, distant; afar, far away
die Ferne, distance
fertig, ready; — *werden mit, finish
das Fest (-e), party
fest, fixed, tight, fast, firm(ly)
das Festessen (-), banquet
fest-setzen, fix
feucht, damp
das Feuer (-), fire
der Feuerlärm, fire-alarm

der Feuerruf, cry 'Fire'
die Fichte, spruce (fir)
der Fichtenbaum (-e), spruce
der Film (-e), film
finden (a, u), find; sich —, be
der Finger (-), finger
finster, dark
die Finsternis (-se), darkness
der Fisch (-e), fish
fischen, fish
der Fischer (-), fisherman
das Fischlein (-), little fish
die Fläche, surface
das Flämmchen (-), little flame
die Flamme, flame
die Flasche, bottle
(*) flattern, flutter
das Fleckchen (-), little patch
das Fleisch, meat
fleißig, industrious
(*) fliegen (o, o), fly
*fließen (o, o), flow
die Flinte, gun
die Flöte, flute
fluchen, curse
die Flucht, flight; die — ergreifen, take to one's heels
flüchtig, quickly, fleeting
der Flug (-e), flight
der Flügel (-), wing
flugs, at once
die Flur, field
der Fluß (-(ss)e), river
flüstern, whisper
die Flut, water, waves, tide
die Föhre, Scotch fir
die Folge, consequence
(*) folgen, follow; obey
folgend, following
fordernd, demandingly
der Förster (-), gamekeeper
fort, (gone) away
fort-fahren (ä, u, a), continue
fortgesetzt, incessantly, continuously
sich fort-machen, go away
fort-reißen (i, i), drag away
das Fortsetzen: zum —, for continuation

fort-spülen, wash away
*fort-ziehen (o, o), move (away)
der Frack (¨e), tail-coat
fragen, ask
fragend, questioningly
Frankreich (*n***.),** France
französisch, French
die Frau, wife, woman
das Freie, the open
freilich, to be sure
freiwillig, voluntarily
fremd, strange, foreign, alien, other people's
die Fremde (*see 34***),** stranger
die Fremde, foreign land
die Freude, joy
freudig, with joy
sich freuen, be pleased, rejoice, enjoy o.s.; **— an(D),** take pleasure in; **— auf,** look forward to
der Freund (-e), friend
die Freundin (-nen), friend
freundlich, kindly, friendly, affably
die Freundschaft, friendship
der Friede (-ns, -n), peace
friedfertig, peaceably
friedlich, peaceful(ly)
Friedrich, Frederick
(*) frieren (o, o), freeze; **es friert mich,** I am freezing
frisch, fresh
froh, glad
fröhlich, blithesome
fromm, pious
die Frucht (¨e), fruit
früh, early
früher, former
der Frühling (-e), spring
das Frühstück (-e), breakfast
frühstücken, breakfast
frühzeitig, early
(sich) fühlen, feel
führen, lead, take, conduct
füllen, fill
das Fundament (-e), foundation; **aus dem —,** thoroughly
funkeln, flash, sparkle, twinkle

für, for; **was — ein,** what sort of
die Furcht, fear
furchtbar, terrible
fürchterlich, terrible, dread
furchtsam, timid(ly)
der Fürst (-en, -en), prince
der Fuß (¨e), foot; **zu —,** on foot
der Fußboden (¨), floor

gähnen, yawn
der Galgen (-), gallows
der Gang (¨e), errand; corridor; carriage
ganz, whole; quite
das Ganze (*see 34***),** the whole thing
gänzlich, entire(ly)
gar, very, even; **— nicht,** not at all
der Garten (¨), garden
der Gärtner (-), gardener
die Gasse, narrow street, lane
der Gast (¨e), guest
das Gasthaus (¨er), hotel, inn
der Gastwirt (-e), landlord
der Gatte (-n, -n), husband
das Gebälk, beams
die Gebärde, gesture
das Gebäude (-), building
geben (i, a, e), give, perform; **es gibt,** there is/are, exist(s)
das Gebet (-e), prayer
gebieterisch, imperious
das Gebirg(e) (-(e)), mountains
das Gebirgswasser (-), water from mountains, mountain stream
geboren, born
geborsten, riven
das Gebraus, roar, din
das Gebrüll, roar(ing)
gebückt, bent, bowed
der Geburtstag (-e), birthday
gedämpft, muffled
der Gedanke (-ns, -n), thought; **sich -n über etwas machen,** worry about something
*gedeihen (ie, ie), thrive

329

gedenken (a, a) (G or an + A), recall, remember, think

das Gedicht (-e), poem

die Gefahr, danger

gefallen (ä, ie, a) (D), please

gefangen-nehmen (i, a, o), take prisoner

die Gefangenschaft, captivity

das Gefängnis (⁒(ss)e), (im)-prison (-ment)

das Gefühl (-e), feeling

gegen, against, towards

die Gegend, neighbourhood, district

gegenüber, opposite

die Gegenwart, presence

das Geglock, bells

geheim, secret

*__gehen (i, a),__ go, walk, succeed; **es geht ihm gut,** he is well; **es geht nicht lange mit ihm,** he hasn't much longer to live

gehöhlt, hollowed

das Gehör, hearing; **einem — verleihen (ie, ie),** listen to somebody

gehorchen (D), obey

gehören (D), belong

der Geist (-er), mind

geisteskrank, insane

der Geistliche (see 34), clergyman

gelähmt, paralysed

gelassen, calmly

das Geläute (-), ringing

gelb, yellow

das Geld (-er), money, price

der Geldbeutel (-), purse

das Geldstück (-e), coin

die Gelegenheit, occasion, opportunity

gelegentlich, (at) some time

der Gelehrte (see 34), man of learning

gelinde, gentle

*__gelingen (a, u),__ succeed

das Gemälde (-), painting

gemeinsam, in common

das Gemurmel, murmur

die Gemüsesuppe, vegetable soup

das Gemüt (-er), heart, soul

genau, close(ly), exactly

genug, enough

genügen, be sufficient

genugsam, well enough

das Gepäck, luggage

der Gepäckträger (-), porter

gerade, just

das Geräusch (-e), noise

das Gerede, talk

gereizt, irritated

das Gericht (-e), law-court; trial; **— halten (ä, ie, a),** try a case

gern, willingly

*__geschehen (ie, a, e),__ happen; go off

die Geschichte, tale, story

geschickt, skilful

das Geschirr (-e), (piece of) crockery

das Geschlecht (-er), sex

geschwind, swiftly

die Geschwindigkeit, speed

der Geschworene (see 34), juryman

die Gesellschaft, company, party

gesenkt, lowered

das Gesicht (-er), face, sight

das Gespenst (-er), ghost

das Gespräch (-e), conversation

die Gestalt, figure, form, shape

gestalten, give shape to

das Gestammel, stammering

gestatten (D), permit

gestern, yesterday

gestikulieren, gesticulate

der Gestorbene (see 34), dead man

das Gesumm(e), hum

gesund, healthy, well

das Getue, pretence

das Getümmel (-), bustle, turmoil

das Gewand (⁒er), garment

gewandt, nimble, skilful(ly)

der Gewebsfetzen (-), shred of tissue

das Gewehr (-e), gun

gewinnen (a, o), win, gain

gewiß, certain(ly)

gewissermaßen, to some extent

das Gewitter (-), storm

sich gewöhnen (an) (A), get used (to)

die Gewohnheit, habit

gewöhnlich, usual(ly)

gewohnt, accustomed

das Gewölke, (mass of) clouds

der Giebel (-), gable

gießen (o, o), pour

der Gipfel (-), mountain-top

das Gitter (-), railing

glänzen, shine, be resplendent

glänzend, brilliant

das Glas (¨er), glass

gläsern, glass (*adj.*)

glatt, smooth, regular

glauben, believe, think, trust

gleich, immediately; **— einmal,** at the same time

gleichen (i, i), resemble

gleichfalls, likewise

gleichgültig, indifferently

gleichmütig, calmly

*gleiten (i, i), slip, glide

glitzern, glisten

die Glocke, bell

der Glockenschlag (¨e), peal of bells

der Glockenstuhl (¨e), bell-cage

das Glück, happiness, luck; **zum —,** fortunately

*glücken, succeed

glücklich, happy, fortunate, safe and sound, harmlessly

glühen, glow

die Glut, flame

die Gnade, grace; **Euer -n,** Your Grace

das Gold, gold

golden, golden

der Gott, God; **— sei Dank,** thank Heavens; **um -es willen,** for Heaven's sake, I beg you

das Grab (¨er), grave

graben (ä, u, a) (nach), dig (for)

der Graben (¨), moat

der Graf (-en, -en), count

die Gräfin (-nen), countess

der Gram, grief

die Grammatik, grammar

das Gras (¨er), grass

grau, grey

das Grausen, awe

greifen (i, i), seize, put one's hand (into)

der Greis (-e), old man

grell, shrill

Grete, Maggie

die Grille, cricket

groß, big, great, tall

der Großherzog (¨e), grand-duke

die Großmutter (¨), grandmother

grün, green

das Grün, green leaves

der Grund (¨e), reason; (valley-) bottom; **im -e,** at bottom; **aus diesem -e,** for this reason

der Grundbesitzer (-), landowner

grünen, burst into leaf

die Gruppe, group

grüßen, greet

die Gunst, favour

gut, good, very much; **— *werden,** turn out well

das Gut (¨er), property, estate

das Haar (-e), hair

das Haben (-), credit

der Hafen (¨), harbour

die Hafenstadt (¨e), port

haften, stick

der Hain (-e), grove

halb, half

halblinks, half left

die Hälfte, half

der Hals (¨e), neck

halt, stop!

halten (ä, ie, a), hold, keep, celebrate, stop; **— für,** consider to be; **sich —,** keep o.s.

die Haltung, bearing, deportment

der Halunke (-n, -n), scoundrel

hämmern, hammer

die Hand (¨e), hand; **bei der —,**
at hand
das Händchen (-), little hand
handeln, bargain; **sich —**
um, be a matter of
der Handkoffer (-), suitcase
die Handtasche, handbag
das Handwerk (-e), trade
hängen, hang (*tr.*)
hängen (i, a), hang (*intr.*)
Hannchen, Janet
der Harem (-s), harem
die Harfe, harp
der Harm, sorrow
hart, hard, severe
hartnäckig, obstinately
hassen, hate
häßlich, ugly
die Hast, haste
hastig, hastily
der Hauch, breath (of air)
der Haufen (-), crowd, heap
häufig, often
das Haupt (¨er), head; (in compounds) chief
das Hauptgewerbe (-), chief trade
die Hauptsache, chief thing
hauptsächlich, chiefly
das Haus (¨er), house; **nach**
Hause, home
die Hausfrau, lady of the house;
(house-)wife
der Haushofmeister (-), steward,
major-domo
der Hauswirt (-e), landlord
die Haut (¨e), skin
sich heben (o, o), rise, stand out
heda, hoy! hi!
das Heer (-e), army
das Heft (-e), exercise book
heftig, violent(ly), vehement-
(ly), severe(ly)
die Heide, heath, heather
heil, unscathed, whole
das Heil, salvation
(*)heilen, heal (*intr.*)
heilig, holy
heim, home
das Heim (-e), home
die Heimat, home

heimisch, native
die Heimkehr, return home
heimlich, secretly
Heinrich, Henry
heiser, hoarse
heiß, hot
heißen (ie, ei), be called; **es**
hieß, it was rumoured
heiter, cheerful
helfen (i, a, o) (D), help; **sich**
—, find way out of difficulty
hell, bright, clear
hellauf: **— weinen,** burst out
crying
die Helle, brightness
das Hemd (-(e)s, -en), shirt
der Henker (-), hangman; **geh'**
zum —!, go to the devil
her, hither, here
herab, down
heran, up (to)
heran-rufen (ie, u)(*tr.*), call
over to
herauf, up
*herauf-ziehen (o, o), gather
(*intr.*)
heraus, out
heraus-bringen (a, a), manage to say
die Herausforderung, challenge
*heraus-schlagen (ä, u, a),
leap up to, burst through
herb, bitter
herbei, along
herbei-rufen (ie, u), call
der Herbst, autumn
herbstkräftig, with autumnal
vigour
die Herde, herd
herein, in
der Hergang, proceedings,
what happens
*her-gehen (i, a), happen, be
carried on
hernach, afterwards
der Herr (-n, -en), gentleman,
lord; **lieber —,** sir
her-richten, prepare
herrisch, imperiously
herrlich, splendid

die **Herrlichkeit**, splendour
die **Herrschaften** (*pl.*), gentlemen; **die alten** —, the grown-ups
herrschen, reign
her-sagen, say, recite
herum, round, about; **um es** —, round it
sich **herum-treiben** (ie, ie), rove about
herunter, down
hervor, out; *see* *43(a)ii*, *note*
hervor-bringen (a, a), utter
das **Herz** (ens, -en), heart
der **Herzog** (–e), duke
herzoglich, ducal
heute, today
hier, here
die **Hilfe**, help; **zu** — **nehmen**, make use of
der **Himmel** (-), sky, heaven; **aus allen -n gerissen**, brought back to earth with a jolt
hin, thither, down; — **und her**, to and fro; — **und wieder**, back and forth
hinab, down
hinauf, up
hinaus, out
hinaus-fliegen (o, o), be sacked
hinaus-treten (i, a, e), emerge
hindern, stop
das **Hindernis** (-(ss)e), obstacle
hin-drängen, urge, drive
hinein, in
hin-finden (a, u), find one's way
sich **hin-geben** (i, a, e), abandon o.s. to
sich **hin-gewöhnen**, get accustomed to going
hinken, limp
hinnen: von —, from hence
hinter, behind
der **Hintergrund**, background
der **Hinterhalt**, ambush
hinterher, along behind

hinterlassen (ä, ie, a), bequeath
das **Hinterstübchen** (-), little backroom
hinüber, across
hinunter, down
hin-wollen (*see 109*), want to get to
hinzu-fügen, add
hinzu-setzen, add
das **Hirn** (-e), brain
der **Hirt** (-en, -en), herdsman
hoch, high, exalted
hochauf, high up
höchst, most
der **Höchststand**, highest level
der **Hof** (–e), yard
hoffen (**auf**) (A), hope (for)
die **Hoffnung**, hope
hoffnungslos, hopeless
höflich, polite(ly)
die **Höhe**, hill, eminence; **in die** —, up
hohl, hollowed; **die -e Hand**, hollow (palm) of the hand
die **Höhle**, cavity
holen, fetch, haul
das **Holz** (–er), wood
hölzern, wooden
horchen, listen
hören, hear
die **Hornbrille**, horn-rimmed spectacles
die **Hosen** (*pl.*), trousers
das **Hotel** (-s), hotel
der **Huf** (-e), hoof
der **Hufschlag**, sound of horses' hoofs
die **Hühnerjagd**, partridge-shooting
der **Hund** (-e), dog
der **Hunger**, hunger
hungrig, hungry
hüpfen, hop
der **Husar** (-en, -en), hussar
der **Husch: seinen** — **nehmen**, make a sudden dash
der **Hut** (–e), hat
hüten, tend, watch
das **Hüttchen** (-), little hut

immer, always; — **wieder,**
  again and again
in, in(to)
indem, while, (by) -ing
indes, and yet, but; whilst
indessen, whilst; however
der **Inhaber** (-), proprietor
der **Inhalt,** contents
inmitten, amidst
inne-halten (ä, ie, a), stop
das **Insekt** (-(e)s, -en), insect
interessant, interesting
inzwischen, meanwhile
irden, earthen
irgendein, some
irgendwohin, anywhere
der **Irrtum** (¨er), mistake
Italien (n.), Italy
der **Italiener** (-), Italian
italienisch, Italian
itzt, now

ja, yes; see *124(e)*
die **Jagd,** hunt, chase
(*) **jagen,** gallop, scurry; drive
der **Jäger** (-), huntsman
jäh, sudden
das **Jahr** (-e), year
  jahrein, jahraus, year after
  year
der **Jahrestag** (-e), anniversary
die **Jahreszeit,** season (of year)
die **Jahresziffer,** date
das **Jahrhundert** (-e), century
jammern, wail, cry
je, ever; — **und** —, from time
  to time
jeder, every
jedermann, everybody
jedesmal, each time
jedoch, however
jemand, somebody
jener, that, the former
jenseits, on the other side
jetzt, now
Johanna, Joan
Johannes, John
der **Jubel,** joyous shouts
die **Jugend,** youth

jung, young
der **Junge** (-n, -n), lad
Jürg(en), George

der **Kaffee,** coffee
kahl, bare, bleak
der **Kahn** (¨e), boat
die **Kaiserin** (-nen), Empress
kalt, cold
der **Kamerad** (-en, -en), comrade
der **Kamin** (-e), fireplace
die **Kammer,** room
das **Kämmerchen** (-), little room
der **Kampf** (¨e), struggle
kämpfen, fight
das **Kännchen** (-), little jug
die **Kanone,** cannon
die **Kapelle,** chapel
das **Kapital** (-ien), capital, loan
der **Kapitän** (-e), captain
Karl, Charles
Karoline, Caroline
die **Karte,** map; ticket
die **Kasse,** cash-box, money-box
der **Kasten** (¨), box
der **Kauf** (¨e), purchase
kaufen, buy
der **Käufer** (-), purchaser
der **Kauf-mann** (-leute), shop-
  keeper, merchant
kaum, hardly, scarcely; — **ein**
  wenig, scarcely at all
die **Kavalkade,** cavalcade
keck, impudently
***kehren,** return
kein, no
keinerlei, of no kind
kennen (a, a), know; —**ler-**
  nen, get to know
der **Kerl** (-e), fellow, chap
die **Kerze,** candle
die **Kette,** chain
der **Kiesel** (-), pebble
das **Kind** (-er), child
das **Kindermädchen** (-), child's
  nurse
der **Kinderring** (-e), child's ring
der **Kinderschrei** (-e), child's
  scream

die **Kinderzeit**, childhood
das **Kinn** (-e), chin
die **Kirche**, church
die **Klage**, legal action
  klagen, lament, complain of
  kläglich, doleful
der **Klang** (ːe), sound
  klar, limpid, clear
das **Klassenzimmer** (-), form-room
das **Klavier** (-e), piano
das **Kleid** (-er), dress; (*pl.*), clothes
  klein, small, little; **im -en**, in miniature
(*) **klettern**, scramble, clamber
  klingeln (**nach**), ring (for)
  klingen (a, u), sound, resound
die **Klippe**, cliff
der **Kloß** (ːe), clod
  klug, clever, wise
  klüglich, shrewdly
der **Knabe** (-n, -n), boy, lad
die **Knabenzeit**, boyhood
  knarren, creak
der **Knecht** (-e), man-servant
das **Knie** (-), knee
  knien, kneel
der **Knöchel** (-), ankle
der **Knochen** (-), bone
der **Knopf** (ːe), button
  knüpfen, tie
  knurren, growl, grumble
das **Kochen**: **zum — bringen**, bring to the boil
die **Köchin** (-nen), cook
der **Koffer** (—), suitcase
die **Kohle**, coal
der **Kollege** (-n, -n), colleague
  komisch, comical
***kommen** (a, o), come, get
die **Kommode**, chest of drawers
der **Komponist** (-en, -en), composer
der **Konditor** (-s, -en), confectioner
  konfiszieren, confiscate
der **König** (-e), king
  königlich, royal
die **Königstracht**, royal robes
  können (*see 109*), can, be able

die **Konservenbüchse**, tin, can
der **Konsul** (-s, -n), consul
das **Kontor** (-e), counting house, office
der **Kontrakt** (-e), contract
der **Kopf** (ːe), head
der **Korb** (ːe), basket
der **Körper** (-), body
der **Korridor** (-e), corridor
der **Kosename** (-ns, -n), pet name
  kosten, cost
die **Kraft** (ːe), might, strength
  kräftig, energetic
der **Kramladen** (ː), small shop
  krank, ill
der **Kranke** (*see 34*), sick man, patient
das **Krankenhaus** (ːer), hospital
der **Kranz** (ːe), ring, wreath
das **Kränzlein** (-), little wreath
  kraus, irregular
  kreideweiß, white as a sheet
der **Kreisel** (-), top
  kreuz: — und quer, in all directions
das **Kreuzverhör** (-e), cross-examination
***kriechen** (o, o), creep
der **Krieg** (-e), war
  kriegen, get; **Angst —**, become frightened
das **Kristall**, crystal, (cut-)glass
  kristallen, crystal (*adj.*)
die **Kron(e)**, crown
der **Krug** (ːe), jug
  krumm, crooked, bowed
  krümmen, make crooked, double up
die **Küche**, kitchen
der **Kuchen** (-), cake
der **Kuckuck** (-e), cuckoo
die **Kugel**, bullet
die **Kuh** (ːe), cow
  kühl, cool
  kündigen, give notice
  künftig, in future
die **Kunst** (ːe), art
das **Kupfer**, copper
die **Kur**, cure
  kurieren, to cure

kurz, short(ly); vor -em, a
   short while before
kürzlich, recently
der Kuß (ː(ss)e), kiss
die Küste, coast
die Küstenwache, coastguard
der Küster (-), sexton
die Kutsche, carriage
der Kutscher (-), coachman

lächeln, smile
lachen, laugh
laden (ä, u, a), load; summon
der Laden (ː), shop
der Ladentisch (-e), counter
die Lage, situation, position
das Lager (-), couch, bed
die Lagerstätte, resting-place
die Lampe, lamp
das Land (ːer), land, country
*landen, land
das Landhaus (ːer), country-
   house
die Landung, landing
lang, long
lang(e), (a) long (time); —
   her, long ago
die Langeweile, boredom
langsam, slow(ly)
der Langschläfer (-), lazy-bones
längst, for a long time
langweilig, boring
lärmend, noisy
lassen (ä, ie, a), let, leave;
   laß doch! don't; see 109(b)
   vii
lässig, idle, idly
die Last, burden
lästig, burdensome, irksome
das Lateinische (see 34) Latin
die Laterne, lamp
der Laternenschein, lamplight
die Latte, lath
das Laub, foliage
der Lauf (ːe), course
*laufen (äu, ie, au), run
lauschen (D), listen
der Laut (-e), sound
laut, loud

die Laute, lute
läuten, ring
lautlos, mute
leben, live
das Leben (-), life; am —, alive
   lebenslang: auf —, for life
die Lebensmittel (pl.), provision:
lebenssatt, weary of life
lebhaft, lively
lecken, lick
lederfarben, leather-coloured,
   buff
leer, empty
die Leere, emptiness
legen, put; sich —, lie down
die Legende, legend
lehnen, lean
die Lehre: bei einem in der —
   *sein, be apprenticed to
   someone
lehren, teach
der Lehrer (-), teacher
der Leib (-er), body
der Leibarzt (ːe), family doctor
die Leibeskraft: aus —, aus ːen,
   as loud (hard) as possible
die Leiche, corpse
leicht, easy; light
leid: es tut mir —, I am
   sorry
das Leid, sorrow
das Leiden (-), suffering
leider, unfortunately
leidlich, passable, fairly good
die Leine, line
die Leinwand, linen
leise, faint, noiseless, quiet(ly)
leiten, build
die Leiter, ladder; -treppe, ladder
lenken, steer
lernen, learn
die Lese, gathering (of fruit)
lesen (ie, a, e), read
letzt-, last; -eres, latter
leuchten, shine, sparkle
das Leuchten, sparkle
die Leute (pl.), people
das Licht (-er), (candle-)light
   lieb, dear; — haben, love
die Liebe, love

der **Liebhaber** (-), amateur
lieblich, charming
das **Lieblingsinstrument** (-e), favourite instrument
das **Lied** (-er), song
das **Liedchen** (-), little song
liefern, deliver
liegen (a, e), lie
die **Linde**, lime
der **Lindenbaum** (⸚e), lime
link-, left; **-s**, on the left; **nach -s**, to the left
linksum, left about!
die **Lippe**, lip
Lissabon, Lisbon
listig, cunning, wily
die **Livree**, livery
das **Loch** (⸚er), hole
der **Lohn** (⸚e), reward
lohnen: es lohnt, it is worth while
das **Los** (-e), lottery prize
los: was ist —? what's the matter?
***los-bröckeln**, crumble away
löschen, extinguish
lösen, loosen; **sich —**, become detached, break off
***los-gehen** (i, a) (**auf**) (A), go straight up (to)
los-lassen (ä, ie, a), let go, let loose
los-schießen (o, o), fire
los-sprechen (i, a, o), acquit
***los-werden** (i, u, o), come off
die **Lotterie**, lottery
der **Löwe** (-n, -n), lion
die **Luft** (⸚e), air, breeze; (*pl.*) sky
das **Lüftchen** (-), little breeze
lüften, raise
das **Luftschloß** (⸚(ss)er), castle in the air
der **Luftzug** (⸚e), draught
die **Lüge**, lie
lügen (o, o), lie
die **Luke**, dormer-window
die **Lust** (⸚e) (**an**) (D), pleasure (in), delight; **— haben**, feel inclined

das **Lusthaus** (⸚er), country-seat
lustig, amusing; merry, merrily

machen, make, cause
mächtig, powerful, heavy
das **Mädchen** (-), girl, maid, servant-girl
die **Magd** (⸚e), maid
mager, thin, emaciated
die **Mahlzeit**, meal
das **Mal** (-e), time, occasion
malen, paint
der **Maler** (-), painter
manch, many (a); **-es**, much; **-erlei**, various kinds of
manchmal, sometimes
der **Mangel** (**an**) (D), lack of
der **Mann** (⸚er), man, husband
der **Mantel** (⸚), cloak
das **Mäntelchen** (-), little cloak
Margret, Margaret
die **Mark**, mark (coin)
der **Markt** (⸚e), market
***marschieren**, march
die **Maske**, mask
Mathilde, Mathilda
der **Matrose** (-n, -n), sailor
die **Matte**, (alpine) meadow
die **Mattigkeit**, weariness
die **Mauer**, wall
mechanisch, mechanically
das **Meer** (-e), sea
die **Meeresstille**, calm at sea
die **Meerkatze**, (long-tailed) monkey
mehr, more
mehrere, several
die **Meile**, mile
meinen, be of opinion, say
die **Meinung**, opinion
meist-, most
der **Meister** (-), master (of craft)
die **Meisterin** (-nen), mistress
(sich) **melden**, announce (oneself)
die **Melodie**, melody
die **Menge**, quantity, crowd, numbers
der **Mensch** (-en, -en), person, man; (*pl.*) people

das **Menschenleben** (-), human life

menschlich, human

merken, notice, realise

merkwürdig, remarkable, strangely

das **Messerchen** (-), little knife

die **Miene:** — **machen**, show signs (of)

mild, mild

die **Militärmütze**, military cap

die **Minute**, minute

das **Mißbehagen**, discomfort

der **Mißerfolg** (-e), failure

das **Mißtrauen**, mistrust

mit, with; with them

mit-bringen (a, a), bring with one

miteinander, together, with one another

mit-nehmen (i, a, o), take with one

mit-spielen, take part (in play)

der **Mittag** (-e), noon

das **Mittagbrot** (-e), dinner, lunch

das **Mittagessen** (-), dinner, lunch

die **Mitte**, middle

mit-teilen, tell, communicate

der **Mittelpunkt** (-e), centre

mitten (in/unter), in the midst (of)

mittendrin, right in the middle of it

die **Mitternacht** (⁻e), midnight

das **Möbel** (-), (piece of) furniture

mögen (*see 109*), may, like

möglich, possible; **-erweise**, possibly

die **Mole**, mole

der **Moment** (-e), moment

der **Monarch** (-en, -en), monarch

der **Monat** (-e), month

der **Mond** (-e), moon; month (*poet.*)

der **Mondschein**, moonlight

das **Moos** (-e), moss

der **Mörder** (-), murderer

morgen, tomorrow

der **Morgen** (-), morning; **am —**, in the morning

die **Morgenandacht**, morning prayers

die **Morgendämmerung**, dawn

das **Morgenland**, east, orient

müde, tired

die **Mühe**, trouble

die **Mühle**, mill

mühsam, with difficulty

mühselig, weary

der **Müller** (-), miller

der **Mund** (⁻er), mouth, lips

munter, awake, sprightly, frolicsome

die **Münze**, (small) change

murmeln, murmur

die **Muschel**, mussel

die **Musik**, music

müssen (*see 109*), must, have to

müßig, idle

mutlos, dejected(ly)

die **Mutter** (⁻), mother

das **Mütterchen** (-), granny

die **Mütze**, cap

nach, after, towards, according to; — **und** —, gradually

nach-ahmen, imitate

die **Nachahmung**, imitation

der **Nachbar** (-s/n, -n), neighbour

nach-blicken (D), follow with one's glance(s)

nachdem, after (*conj.*)

das **Nacherzählen: zum** —, for reproduction

nach-holen, pull up

nach-lassen (ä, ie, a), remit, forgive

nachlässig, careless

*****nach-laufen**, (äu, ie, au) (D), run after

der **Nachmittag** (-e), afternoon

nachmittags, in the afternoon

nach-rechnen, work out (a sum)

die **Nachricht**, news

nach-rufen (ie, u) (D), call after

nach-sehen (ie, a, e) (D),
follow with one's eyes; examine

nächst-, nearest, next

die **Nacht** (⸚e), night, blackness;
diese —, last night

der **Nachteil** (-e), disadvantage

nachteilig, prejudicial

der **Nachttisch** (-e), bedside table

nackt, bare

der **Nagel** (⸚), nail

nah, near, near by

die **Nähe,** vicinity

sich **nahen** (D), approach

sich **nähern** (D), approach

die **Nahrung,** food

der **Namenszug** (⸚e), signature

nanu! hullo! good gracious!

der **Narr** (-en, -en), fool

naß, wet

die **Nation,** nation

die **Natur,** nature

natürlich, of course, naturally

der **Nebel** (-), mist

neben, near

nebenbei, casually

nebst, together with

nehmen (i, a, o), take; **zu
sich —,** eat

neigen, bow

nein, no

nennen (a, a), name, call,
deem

neu, new; **aufs -e, von -em,**
again

die **Neugierde,** curiosity

der **Neuhinzugetretene** (*see 34*),
newcomer

neumodisch, new-fangled

nicht, not

die **Nichte,** niece

nichts, nothing

das **Nichtstun,** idleness

die **Nickelmünze,** nickel coin

nicken, nod

nie, never; **-mals,** never

nieder, down

***nieder-brechen** (i, a, o)
beat down (*intr.*)

niedergeschlagen, downcast

niedlich, prettily

niedrig, low

niemand, nobody

nimmer, never; **-mehr,** never
again

noch, still, even; **— einmal,**
once again; **— immer,** still;
— nicht, not yet; **— nie,**
never before; **nur —,** only
... left

der **Norden,** north

der **Nordost,** north-east wind

die **Not** (⸚e), distress, trouble,
misery

nötig, necessary

notwendig, necessary

nüchtern, sober

nun, now, well; **— erst,** now
really

nur, only just

der **Nutzen,** use; **— ziehen,** turn
to advantage

ob, whether, if

oben, upstairs, at the top; **nach
—,** up

obgleich, although

der **Ochse** (-n, -n), ox

öde, deserted, desolate

offen, open

sich **öffnen,** open (*intr.*)

die **Öffnung,** opening, aperture

oft, often; **-mals,** often

der **Ohm** (-e), uncle

ohne, without

die **Ohnmacht,** faint

das **Ohr** (-en), ear

das **Oleanderblatt** (⸚er), oleander-
leaf

die **Öllampe,** oil-lamp

der **Onkel** (-), uncle

das **Opfer** (-), sacrifice; **ein —
bringen,** make a sacrifice

ordentlich, downright

der **Ort** (-e), place

Ostern (*see 22*), Easter

Österreich (*n.*), Austria

die **Ouvertüre,** overture

ein paar, a few, one or two; **ein
-mal,** once or twice
paff! bang!
das Paket (-e), packet
der Palast (ᵈe), palace
die Palme, palm
der Papa (-s), daddy
das Papier (-e), paper
die Pappel, poplar
das Parterre (-s), pit
der Passagier (-e), passenger
die Pause, pause
peinlich, distressing
der Pelz (-e), fur
das Pergament (-e), parchment
die Person, person
die Pest, plague
das Pfarrhaus (ᵈer), vicarage
pfeifen (i, i), whistle
der Pfeil (-e), arrow
der Pfennig (-e) (*see 50*)**,** pfennig
die Pflanze, plant
die Pflegeeltern (*pl.*)**,** foster-
parents
pflegen, tend, perform (duty);
be wont to
pflücken, pluck
das Pförtchen (-), little gate (door)
das Pfund (-e) (*see 50*)**,** pound
der Pilger (-), pilgrim
die Pinzette, pincette
die Pistole, pistol
plagen, torment
der Plan (ᵈe), plan
planen, plan
der Platz (ᵈe), square, place, seat
plaudern, chat
plötzlich, sudden(ly)
die Polizei, police
das Portal (-e), porch
prächtig, splendid
präsentieren, present arms
der Preis (-e), price
prellen, rebound
probieren, try
der Professor (-s, -en), professor
prophezeien, prophesy
die Prophezeiung, prophecy
prüfen, test
der Prügel (-), cudgel

prügeln, thrash
das Publikum, public
der Pudel (-), poodle
das Pult (-e), desk

(sich) quälen, distress, torture (o.s.)
der Quartiermeister (-), quarter-
master
die Quelle, spring, source
quitt: —*sein, be quits (even)

die Rache, revenge
das Rad (ᵈer), wheel, bicycle
die Rakete, rocket
die Raketenbatterie, rocket bat-
tery
der Rand (ᵈer), edge, brim
rasch, quickly
rascheln, rustle
der Rasen (-), lawn, grass
rasend, mad
der Rat, counsel, advice
raten (ä, ie, a), advise
ratlos, not knowing what to do
der Raub, prey
der Räuber (-), brigand
das Räuberdram-a (-en), 'blood
and thunder' drama
das Raubschiff (-e), corsair,
pirate ship
der Rauch, smoke
rauchen, smoke
der Raum (ᵈe), room, space
räumen, vacate
rauschen, rustle
die Rebe, vine
rechnen (auf) (A), reckon (on)
die Rechnung, bill
das Recht (-e), right, rightness
recht, right; **-s,** on the right
der Rechtsfall (ᵈe), case, trial
die Rede, talk, remark; **— stehen,**
answer for
reden, talk
die Regel, rule
der Regen, rain, downpour
sich regen, budge
regnen, rain

die **Regung,** movement, stir
reich, rich
das **Reich (-e),** realm
reichen, hand
reichlich, copiously
der **Reichtum (⸚er),** riches
die **Reihe,** row; **an die — *kommen,** be one's turn
reinigen, clean
das **Reis (-er),** twig(s)
die **Reise,** journey, way
die **Reisedecke,** travelling rug
der **Reisegefährte (-n, -n),** fellow-
traveller
der **Reisemantel (⸚),** travelling-
cloak
der **Reisende** (*see 34*), traveller
(*) **reiten (i, i),** ride
der **Reiter (-),** horseman
reizend, charming
die **Reling,** ship's railing
der **Rest (-e),** remainder
(sich) **retten,** rescue, save (o.s.)
der **Rettungsapparat (-e),** life-
saving apparatus
das **Rettungsboot (-e),** life-boat
der **Rettungsring (-e),** life-belt
die **Reue,** remorse
reuen, regret; **es reut mich,**
I regret it
richten, condemn, criticise; set
der **Richter (-),** judge
richtig, true, right(ly), properly, regular
die **Richtung,** direction
der **Riese (-n, -n),** giant
rieseln, ripple, purl
die **Rinder** (*pl.*), cattle
der **Ring (-e),** ring
das **Ringlein (-),** little ring
rings (-umher), round (about)
der **Ritt (-e),** ride
der **Ritter (-),** knight
die **Ritze,** crack
der **Rock (⸚e),** coat, tunic
das **Röckchen (-),** little jacket
die **Rocktasche,** coat-pocket
die **Rolle,** part
(*) **rollen,** roll
die **Rose,** rose

der **Rosenstrauch (⸚er),** rose-bush
das **Roß (-(ss)e),** horse
das **Rößlein (-),** little horse
rot, red
rotgeröckt, red-coated
rothaarig, red-haired
das **Rotkehlchen (-),** red-breast,
robin
der **Rücken (-),** back
(*) **rücken,** move
die **Rückfahrt,** return journey
der **Rucksack (⸚e),** rucksack
der **Ruderer (-),** oarsman
der **Ruf (-e),** cry
rufen (ie, u), call out, exclaim,
summon
der **Rufer (-),** summoner
die **Ruhe,** calm, rest, peace
(sich) **ruhen,** rest
ruhig, calm, undisturbed
quiet(ly)
sich **rühren,** stir, bestir oneself
rührend, moving
die **Ruine,** ruin
rund um, all round
der **Ruß,** soot
rüsten, make ready

der **Saal** (*pl.* **Säle**), hall, room
der **Säbel (-),** sabre, sword
die **Sache,** thing, matter, affair
sagen, say
die **Saite,** string (of instrument)
sammeln, collect
sanft, gentle
der **Sänger (-),** songster
satt, replete
der **Sattel (⸚),** saddle
der **Satz (⸚e),** sentence
sauber, clean
der **Saum (⸚e),** edge
säuseln, sough, whisper
der **Schacht (⸚e),** shaft (of mine)
die **Schachtel,** box
schade, pity
der **Schaden (⸚),** trouble, mischief
der **Schadenersatz,** damages
der **Schalk (-e** *or* **⸚e),** rogue
schallen, resound

die **Scham,** shame
sich **schämen,** be ashamed
die **Schande,** shame
scharf, sharp, hot
der **Scharlach,** scarlet fever
scharren, scratch, dig
der **Schatten (-),** shadow
der **Schatz (ꞈe),** treasure
der **Schatzgräber (-),** treasure-
seeker
schauen, look
schauern, shudder
schaukeln, sway
das **Schauspiel (-e),** spectacle
der **Schauspieler (-),** actor
die **Schauspielerin (-nen),** actress
*****scheiden (ie, ie),** leave (*intr.*)
der **Schein (-e),** note
scheinbar, seemingly
scheinen (ie, ie), seem; shine
*****scheitern,** run aground
schenken, give (as present)
die **Schere,** scissors
scheu, shy
die **Scheune,** barn
die **Schicht,** layer
schicken, send
schießen (o, o), shoot
das **Schiff (-e),** ship
der **Schiffer (-),** boatman, skipper
das **Schilderhäuschen (-),** sentry-
box
schildern, depict
das **Schilf,** reed(s)
der **Schimmer (-),** lustre, sparkle
schinden (u, u), rub off skin
der **Schlaf,** sleep
schlafen (ä, ie, a), sleep
schläfern: es schläfert ihn,
he is drowsy
die **Schlafkammer,** bedroom
schlaflos, sleepless
der **Schlafrock (ꞈe),** dressing-
gown
das **Schlafzimmer (-),** bedroom
schlagen (ä, u, a), press,
strike
schlau, cunning
schlecht, wretched, bad; **mir
ist —,** I feel unwell

der **Schleier (-),** veil
schleifen (i, i), polish, grind
schleppen, drag
schleudern, fling
schließen (o, o), shut; **— aus,**
conclude from
schließlich, finally
schlimm, bad
schlingen (a, u), twine round
der **Schlitz (-e),** slit
das **Schloß (ꞈ(ss)er),** castle, palace,
mansion
das **Schlößlein (-),** little castle
die **Schlucht,** ravine
schluchzen, sob
der **Schlüssel (-),** key
schmähend, abusive
die **Schmähung,** abuse
schmal, narrow, thin
der **Schmaus (ꞈe),** banquet
der **Schmied (-e),** smith
der **Schmerz (-es, -en),** grief,
sorrow, pain
der **Schmetterling (-e),** butterfly
der **Schmoller (-),** sulky person
schnauben, snort
die **Schnauze,** mouth
der **Schnee,** snow
der **Schneeball (ꞈe),** snowball
die **Schneeballschlacht,** snowball fight
die **Schneide,** cutting-edge
schneiden (i, i), cut
schneien, snow
schnell, quickly
die **Schnelle,** speed
das **Schnupftuch (ꞈer),** handkerchief
die **Schokolade,** chocolate
schon, already; *see 124(g)*
schön, beautiful, fine
die **Schönheit,** beauty
schöpfen, draw (water)
der **Schornstein (-e),** chimney
schrauben, screw (up)
der **Schreck (-e),** terror
der **Schrecken (-),** panic, terror
schrecklich, terribly
der **Schrei (-e),** scream
schreiben (ie, ie), write

der **Schreiber** (-), clerk, writer
das **Schreibzeug,** writing material
schreien (ie, ie), exclaim, shout; — **nach,** clamour for
***schreiten (i, i),** stride along
die **Schrift,** writing
der **Schriftsteller** (-), writer, author
das **Schriftstück (-e),** document
der **Schritt (-e),** step, stride, yard; — **für —,** step by step
schrittweis(e), step by step
die **Schublade,** drawer
der **Schuh (-e),** shoe
die **Schularbeit,** homework
die **Schuld,** debt
schuldig, guilty; — ***sein,** owe
der **Schuldige** (*see 34*), guilty man
schuldlos, innocent
der **Schuldschein (-e),** I.O.U.
die **Schule,** school
der **Schüler** (-), schoolboy
der **Schulkamerad (-en, -en),** school-mate
die **Schulter,** shoulder
schultern, shoulder arms
der **Schuppen** (-), shed
der **Schuß** (⸚(ss)e), shot
die **Schüssel,** dish
das **Schüsselchen** (-), little dish
schütteln, shake
der **Schutz,** protection
der **Schütz(e), (-n, -n),** archer
der **Schutz-mann (-leute),** police-man
schwach, weak, faint
die **Schwalbe,** swallow
schwanken, rock
der **Schwanz** (⸚e), tail
***schwärmen,** swarm
schwarz, black
die **Schwärze,** printer's ink
schwärzlich, blackish
schwatzen, chatter
schweben, hang, be (*e.g.* in danger)
schweigen (ie, ie), say nothing, grow still, be hushed
schweigend, without saying a word

der **Schweiß,** sweat
der **Schweizer** (-), Swiss
die **Schwelle,** threshold
schwer, heavy, anxious, badly, with difficulty
das **Schwert (-er),** sword
die **Schwester,** sister
die **Schwiegertochter** (⸚), daughter-in-law
(*) **schwimmen (a, o),** bathe
sich **schwingen (a, u),** swing o.s.
schwören (u/o, o), swear, vow
schwül(e), oppressive, sultry
der **See (-s, -n),** lake
die **See,** sea
die **Seele,** soul
der **Seeräuber** (-), pirate
(*)**segeln,** sail
sehen (ie, a, e), see, look; — **auf,** look at; — **nach,** attend to
sich **sehnen (nach),** long (for)
die **Sehnsucht,** yearning
sehr, very much
sei: — . . ., —, whether . . . or
das **Seil (-e),** rope
die **Seinen** (*pl.*), his family, people
seitdem, since then
die **Seite,** side; **zur —,** to one side
seitwärts, to one side
die **Sekunde,** second
selber, oneself, herself
die **Selbstbiographie,** autobiography
selig, (a) blest (spirit)
selten, rare
seltsam, strange
die **Seltsamkeit,** strange thing
der **Sessel** (-), armchair
setzen, set; ferry; **sich —,** sit down
seufzen, sigh
sicher, certain, assured
die **Sicherheit,** security
sichtbar, visible
das **Sieb (-e),** sieve
siech, infirm
der **Sieg (-e),** victory
das **Silber,** silver

der Silvester, New Year's Eve
die Silversternacht, New Year's
    Eve
    singen (a, u), sing
    *sinken (a, u), sink
der Sinn (-e), mind, sense; eines
    -es *sein, be unanimous
    sinnen (a, o), reflect, think
    sinnend, pensive(ly)
    sinnlos, senseless
der Sitz (-e), seat
    sitzen (a, e), sit; *-bleiben,
    not get one's remove
das Skalpell (-e), scalpel
die Sklaverei, slavery
    so, really, so
    sobald, as soon as
    soeben, just
    sofort, immediately
    sogar, even
    sogleich, immediately
der Sohn (ꞋꞋe), son
    solch, such; -ergestalt, in
    such guise
der Soldat (-en, -en), soldier
das Soll, debit
    sollen (see 109), ought, shall
der Sommer (-), summer
die Sonatine, sonatina
    sonderbar, odd, strange(ly)
    sonderlich, special
    sondern, but
die Sonne, sun
der Sonnenaufgang (ꞋꞋe), sun-
    rise
das Sonnenrot, fiery sun
der Sonnenschein, sunshine
die Sonnenuhr, sun-dial
    sonnig, sunny
    sonst, or else, otherwise
    sorgen für, look after, provide
    for
    sorgenvoll, troubled
    sorgfältig, carefully
    soweit, as far as
    sowie, as well as
    sowieso, anyhow
    sowohl: — . . . wie, both . . .
    and
die Sparkasse, savings-box

der Spaß (ꞋꞋe), amusement;
    machen, amuse; joke
    spät, late
der Spaten (-), spade
    *spazieren, stroll
der Spaziergang (ꞋꞋe), stroll
    speien (ie, ie), spew forth
    speisen, eat
die Sperre, barrier
der Spiegel (-), mirror
das Spiel (-e), game
    spielen, play, sport
die Spielsache, toy
das Spielzeug, toy(s)
der Spirituskocher (-), primus
    stove
    spitz, sharp(-pointed), prickly
die Spitze, top; head; sharp point
    spitzen, prick up (ears)
die Sprache, language
    sprachlos, speechless
    sprechen (i, a, o), speak, say
der Sprecher (-), speaker
    *springen (a, u), jump, leap
die Springflut, spring-tide
die Spritze, fire-engine
der Spruch (ꞋꞋe), saying, motto
der Sprung (ꞋꞋe), caper, gambol;
    auf einen —, for a short
    visit
der Spuk (-e), ghost
    spüren, feel
der Staat (-(e)s, -en), state
der Stab (ꞋꞋe), stick, staff
die Stadt (ꞋꞋe), town, city
    stammeln, stammer
der Stand (ꞋꞋe), profession, rank
die Stange, pole
    stark, strong; very much
    starren, stare
der Starrkopf (ꞋꞋe), stubborn man
    statt, instead of
    stäuben, scatter (showers of)
    stecken, put; be; stick
das Steckenpferd (-e), hobby-
    horse
    stehen (a, a), stand, be;
    *-bleiben, stop, stand still
das Stehen: zum — bringen,
    bring to a halt

stehlen (ie, a, o), steal
*steigen (ie, ie), climb, rise
sich steigern, increase
die Steile, steepness
der Stein (-e), stone
das Steinchen (-), pebble
die Stelle, spot, place
stellen, put; sich —, go and
stand
*sterben (i, a, o), die
der Stern (-e), star
stets, always
der Stich (-e), prick; im -e lassen,
leave in the lurch
der Stiefel (-), boot
stier, vacant
der Stier (-e), bull
still, still, silent; im -en,
secretly
die Stille, stillness, calm
das Stillschweigen, silence; —
behalten, hold one's peace
die Stimme, voice
das Stimmlein (-), little voice
der Stock (⁀e), stick
der Stockschlag (⁀e), blow with a
stick
das Stockwerk (-e), floor, storey
stöhnen, moan
stolz, proud(ly)
der Stolz, pride
stören, disturb
störrisch, stubborn
*stoßen (ö, ie, o), come up
against
stottern, stammer
stracks, straight
die Strafe, punishment
der Strahl (-s, -en), ray; stream
der Strand, shore
die Straße, street, road
strecken, stretch
streichen (i, i): glatt —,
smooth down
das Streichholz (⁀er), match
das Streifchen (-), little strip
*streifen, range
der Streifen (-), strip
der Streit (-igkeiten), quarrel
das Stroh, straw

der Strom (⁀e), stream
*strömen, stream
das Stübchen (-), little room
die Stube, room
das Stück (-e), piece, bit
studieren, study
die Stufe, step
der Stuhl (⁀e), chair
stumm, silent(ly)
die Stunde, hour, lesson
der Sturm (⁀e), storm, gale; im
-e schwingen, sound the
alarm (of bells)
stürmisch, stormy
(*) stürzen, dash; fling violently
sich —, fling oneself
suchen, look for, try, seek
südlich, southern
die Summe, sum
summen, buzz, hum
die Sünde, sin
süß, sweet
die Süße, sweetness
die Szene, scene

der Tag (-e), day
das Tagebuch (⁀er), diary
der Tagesanbruch, daybreak
der Tageslauf, day's doings
täglich, daily
tags vorher, the day before
das Tal (⁀er), valley
tändeln, dally
das Tännlein (-), fir sapling
die Tante, aunt
tanzen, dance
die Tasche, pocket
das Taschentuch (⁀er), handkerchief
die Tasse, cup
die Tat, deed
tätig, active
taub, deaf
der Taugenichts (-e), ne'er-do-
well
der Tee, tea
der Teich (-e), pond
der Teil (-e), part; zum —, partly
sich teilen, divide

teil-nehmen (i, a, o) (an), take part (in)
der Teller (-), plate
das Tellerchen (-), little plate
der Teppich (-e), carpet
das Testament (-e), will
testamentlich, by will
der Teufel (-), devil
das Theater (-), theatre
tief, deep, profound
das Tier (-e), creature, beast
die Tinte, ink
der Tintenklecks (-e), ink-blot
der Tisch (-e), table, meal
die Tochter (⸚), daughter
der Tod, death; **des -es *sein,** be doomed
das Todesurteil (-e), death-sentence
der Ton (⸚e), note, strain
tönen, ring, patter
der Topf (⸚e), pot
der Topfmarkt (⸚e), crockery fair
töricht, foolish
tot, dead, uninhabited
töten, kill
totenbleich, pale as death
der Totenkranz (⸚e), wreath
totenstill, as still as death
träge, sluggish, indolent
tragen (ä, u, a), carry, bear; wear
die Trauer, mourning, sorrow
trauern, mourn
der Traum (⸚e), dream
das Traumbild (-er), phantom
träumen, dream
traurig, sad
(*) treiben (ie, ie), drive, carry on; drift, pass
treppauf, upstairs
die Treppe, (flight of) stairs
der Treppenstein (-e), stone step
*treten (i, a, e), come, go (up to), step
treu, faithful(ly)
die Treue, faith, plighted word
der Trieb (-e), growth; instinct
trinken (a, u), drink
das Trinken, drinking

das Trinkgeld (-er), tip
der Tritt (-e), step
triumphierend, triumphantly
der Trog (⸚e), trough
der Tropfen (-), drop
der Trost, consolation
tröstend, consoling
der Trott (-e), trot
trotz, in spite of it
der Trotz, defiance
trotzdem, in spite of
trotzig, defiant
trübe, overcast
trüben, trouble
trügerisch, delusive
das Tuch (⸚er), cloth, scarf
tüchtig, sound
tun (a, a), make, do; put
die Tür, door
der Turm (⸚e), tower
die Türspalte, chink (of door)

üben, practise
über, over, across, about; — **und —,** all over
überall, everywhere
überbringen (a, a), convey
überdies, besides
der Überfall (⸚e), (surprise) attack, assault
überfallen (ä, ie, a), fall upon, attack
der Übergang (⸚e), transition
übergenug: — tun, more than satisfy
überhaupt, altogether
überholen, overtake
überlaufen (äu, ie, au), run down
die Überlegung, reflection
übermächtig, overpowering
übernachten, spend the night
überreichen, hand over
überschreiben (ie, ie), transcribe
überschreiten (i, i), pass
überschwemmen, flood
übersetzen, translate
über-setzen, ferry across

die **Übersetzung**, translation
übersteigen (ie, ie), surmount
übertragen (ä, u, a), transfer
die **Übertreibung**, exaggeration
überwältigen, overwhelm
überzeugt, convinced
überziehen (o, o), cover
das **übrige**, the remainder
übrigens, anyhow, besides
das **Ufer** (-), bank
die **Uhr**, clock, o'clock
um, at, round, about; in order to; — **und** —, thoroughly
umarmen, embrace
sich **um-drehen**, turn round
umfassen, put one's arms round
umgeben (i, a, e), surround
die **Umgebung**, persons around one
****um-gehen** (i, a), haunt
umher, about
****umher-rennen** (a, a), run about
umhüllen, wrap, enshroud
****um-kehren**, turn back
****um-kommen** (a, o), perish
****um-legen**, put on (cloak)
der **Umriß** (-(ss)e), outline
umschwirren, buzz round
sich **um-sehen** (ie, a, e), look round
umsonst, in vain
der **Umstand** (-̈e), circumstance
umstellen, surround
der **Umweg** (-e), detour
umwoben, woven round
sich **um-ziehen** (o, o), change (clothes)
die **Unachtsamkeit**, inattention
unangenehm, unpleasant(ly)
unbedeckt, bare
unbedingt, without fail, absolutely
unbekannt, unknown
unbekleidet, unshod
unbequem, uncomfortable
unbeschreiblich, indescribable

unbeteiligt, disinterested
unbeweglich, motionless
unbezahlt, unpaid
und, and
unecht, sham
unehrlich, dishonest
unerschrocken, fearless(ly)
unerträglich, unbearable
der **Unfall** (-̈e), accident
unfehlbar, unfailingly
die **Ungeduld**, impatience
ungeduldig, impatient(ly)
ungefähr, about
ungeheuer, frightful, vast
das **Ungeschick**, awkwardness
ungestört, untroubled
ungewarnt, without warning
das **Unglück**, calamity, accident
unglücklich, unhappy; **-erweise**, unfortunately
der **Unglücksfall** (-̈e), accident, mishap
das **Unheil**, calamity, disaster
die **Universität**, university
die **Unmasse**, enormous mass
unmerklich, imperceptibly
unmöglich, impossible
unnennbar, inexpressible
die **Unordnung**, confusion
unpassend, unsuitable
unrecht, wrong
das **Unrecht**, wrongness
die **Unruhe**, (feeling of) disquiet
unruhig, restless(ly)
die **Unschuld**, innocence
unschuldig, innocent
der **Unschuldige** (*see 34*), innocent man
unsicher, unsafe
unsinnig, absurd
unten, down below; **nach** —, down
unter, under, among; (*adj.*) lower
unterbrechen (i, a, o), interrupt
unterdessen, meanwhile
der **Untergebene** (*see 34*), subordinate

*unter-gehen (i, a), set (of sun)

die Unterhaltung, conversation

das Unterholz, underwood

der Unterlaß: ohne —, without intermission

untermischen, intermingle

die Unterredung, conversation

unterschreiben (ie, ie), sign

untersuchen, examine, search

unterwegs, on the way, out

unübersteiglich, unsurmountable

unverletzt, undamaged

die Unverschämtheit, brazen-faced insolence

unversehens, unexpectedly

unversehrt, intact

unverstellt, undisguised

unzufrieden, dissatisfied

urbar, cultivated

urplötzlich, quite suddenly

der Vater (⸚), father

das Vaterhaus, father's house, home

das Vaterland, mother-country, fatherland

väterlich, father's

Venedig, Venice

verändert, altered, changed

der Verband (⸚e), bandage

sich verbergen (i, a, o), conceal, hide oneself

verbieten (o, o), forbid

verblüfft, dumbfounded

verbreiten, spread

verbringen (a, a), spend

verbunden, connected

der Verdacht, suspicion

verdächtig, suspicious

verdammen, condemn

verdammt, cursed

verdauen, digest

das Verdeck (-e), deck

verdienen, earn

verdrießlich, annoyed

sich verdunkeln, grow dark

vereint, united

verfallen, dilapidated

verfallend, decaying

verfolgen, follow

vergeben (i, a, e), forgive

vergeblich, vain

*vergehen (i, a), pass (*intr.*)

vergessen (i, a, e), forget

*verglühen, fade, die away

das Vergnügen (-), pleasure

vergnügt, delighted

vergraben, buried

verhaften, arrest

verhalten, restrained

die Verhältnisse (*pl.*), means

verharren, persist

verhaßt, hateful

sich verheiraten, marry

verhöhnen, deride

verhundertfältigt, increased a hundredfold

*verhungern, starve (to death)

sich verirren, lose one's way

verkaufen (um), sell (for)

der Verkäufer (-), seller

verlangen, demand; **uns verlangt,** we yearn

verlassen (ä, ie, a), leave, abandon

sich verlaufen (äu, ie, au), lose one's way

verlegen, embarrassed

die Verlegenheit, dilemma

verletzen, injure, hurt

sich verlieben (in), fall in love (with)

verlieren (o, o), lose

verlocken, entice

der Verlust (-e), loss

vermachen, bequeath

vermehren, increase

vermeiden (ie, ie), avoid

vermögen (cf. mögen, *see 109*), be able to

das Vermögen (-), fortune

vermutlich, presumably

vernachlässigen, neglect

vernehmbar, audible

vernehmen (i, a, o), hear

verödet, desolate

verraten (ä, ie, a), betray

der **Verräter** (-), traitor
der **Vers** (-e), verse
die **Versammlung**, gathering
*__verschallen__ (o, o), die away
__verschenken__, give away
__verschleiert__, veiled
__verschließen__ (o, o), lock
__verschlingen__ (a, u), swallow up, engulf
*__verschwimmen__ (a, o), merge
*__verschwinden__ (a, u), disappear
__versetzen__, give (blow, etc.); — **auf**, reply to
*__versinken__ (a, u), sink
__versorgen__, provide
__verspätet__, delayed, late
__verspüren__, discover
das **Versteck** (-e), hiding-place
__verstecken__, hide
__verstehen__ (a, a), understand, know how to; **sich — auf** (A), be an expert in
__verstimmt__, out of tune
__verstorben__, deceased
__verstreuen__, scatter
*__verstummen__, become hushed
der **Versuch** (-e), attempt
__versuchen__, try
__versunken__, veiled (in)
__vertauschen__ (um), exchange (for)
__verteilen__, distribute
__vertrocknet__, dried up
__verwandeln__, transform
die **Verwandlung**, transformation
der **Verwandte** (*see 34*), relation
die **Verwechslung**, mistake
(*) __verwehen__, scatter; flee
__verwirrt__, muddle-headedly, confused
__verwunden__, wound
__verwundert__, surprised
die **Verwunderung**, surprise
der **Verwundete** (*see 34*), wounded man
__verzichten auf__ (A), go without, renounce, abstain from
__verzieren__, embellish

__verzweifelt__, desperate
die **Verzweiflung**, desperation, despair
der **Vesuv**, Vesuvius
der **Vetter** (-s, -n), cousin
das **Vieh**, cattle
der **Viehstand** (⸚e), cattle-stall
__viel__, much; **-e**, many; **-fache**, many
__vielleicht__, perhaps
die **Viertelstunde**, quarter of an hour
das **Vlies** (-e), fleece
der **Vogel** (⸚), bird
das **Vögelein** (-), little bird
das **Volk** (⸚er), people
__voll__, full (of)
__vollends__, completely
die **Vollendung**, completion
__völlig__, complete
__vollkommen__, perfect
der **Vollmond**, full moon
__vollziehen__ (o, o), carry out
__von__, of, by; — **... her**, coming from
__vor__, in (to the) front of, before, for; ago; — **allem**, above all
*__voraus-laufen__ (äu, ie, au), run on ahead
die **Voraussicht**, probability, calculation
__vorbei__, past
sich __vor-bereiten__, prepare oneself
__vorbereitet__ (**auf**), prepared (for)
sich __vor-beugen__, lean forward
das **Vorderbein** (-e), foreleg
sich __vor-drängen__, press forward
der **Vorfall** (⸚e), incident
die **Vorhalle**, portico
__vor-halten__ (ä, ie, a), hold out (to)
der **Vorhang** (⸚e), curtain
__vorher__, before
__vorig-__, last, previous
*__vor-kommen__ (a, o), seem; occur
__vorläufig__, for the time being
der **Vormittag** (-e), morning

vornehm, aristocratic, distinguished
der Vorrat (⸚e), supply
der Vorsatz (⸚e), intention, resolution
  vorsichtig, careful(ly), cautious(ly)
  vor-spielen, play (*e.g.* music)
die Vortreppe (-n), front steps
  vorüber, past
  *****vorüber-ziehen** (o, o), pass
  *****vorwärts-kommen** (a, o), make progress
  vor-ziehen (o, o), prefer

  wach, awake
  wachen, stay awake
  *****wachsen** (ä, u, a), grow
  *****wackeln,** waddle along
die Waffe, weapon
  wagen, dare
der Wagen (-), carriage
die Wahl, choice
  wählen, choose
  wählend, fastidious
  wahr, true
  während, while, during
die Wahrheit, truth
  wahr-nehmen (i, a, o), perceive
  wahrscheinlich, probably
das Waisenkind (-er), orphan
der Wald (⸚er), wood, forest
die Wand (⸚e), wall
  *****wandeln,** walk, wander
der Wanderer (-), wanderer, pilgrim, wayfarer
  *****wandern,** walk, wander
der Wanderspruch (⸚e), wayside text
die Wanderung, walk, trek
die Wange, cheek
die Ware, wares
  warm, warm
  warnen (vor), warn (of)
die Warnung, warning
  warten (auf), wait (for)
  warum, why
  was, which; what

die Wäsche, underclothes, linen
sich waschen (ä, u, a), wash (*intr.*)
das Wasser (-), water
  weben, weave
  wechseln, alternate
  wecken, wake (*tr.*)
der Wecker (-), alarm(-clock)
  weder: — ... **noch,** neither ... nor
  weg, away; **über etwas —,** beyond
der Weg (-e), path, way, road-(side); **sich auf den — machen,** set out; **seiner -e *gehen,** go away, go one's way
  wegen, because of
  weg-schaffen, take away
  weh! alas!, — **tun,** hurt
das Weh, grief, woe
  wehen, sway, blow
das Weib (-er), woman
  weiden, graze
sich weigern, refuse
  Weihnachten (*see* 22), Christmas
der Weihnachtsabend, Christmas Eve
  weil, because
die Weile, while
der Wein (-e), wine
der Weinberg (-e), vine-yard
  weinen, cry, weep
die Weise, way; melody; **auf diese —,** in this way
  weisen (ie, ie) (auf), point (to)
  weiß, white
  weit, far, long; spacious; — **ab,** far from
die Weite, expanse; **in die —,** far and wide
das Weite, wide open spaces
  weiter, further on
  *****weiter-segeln,** sail on
  welcher, which
  welk, withered, faded
  *****welken,** wither
die Welle, wave
die Welt, world

die Wendeltreppe, winding stairs

sich wenden (a, a), turn

(ein) wenig, (a) little; -e, few

weniger, less

wenigstens, at least

wenn, whenever, if

wer, who

***werden (i, u, o),** become, get

werfen (i, a, o), throw

das Werk (-e), work

die Werkstätte, workshop

das Werkzeug (-e), tool

das Wesen (-), being, creature

wetten, bet, wager

wichtig, important

wider, against

der Widerspruch (∸e), contradiction, contrast

wie, how, like; as; as though; in the same way as

wieder, again

die Wiedergeburt, renaissance

die Wiederherstellung, restoration

wiederholen, repeat

die Wiederholung, repetition

***wieder-kehren,** return

wiegen, lull; **sich —,** sway, move to and fro

das Wiegenlied (-er), lullaby

die Wiese, meadow

wieviel, how many

wild, wild(-looking)

die Wimper, eyelash

der Wind (-e), wind; **hinter dem —,** to leeward

winken, beckon

der Winzer (-), vintner

winzig, tiny

der Wipfel (-), tree-top

wirken, be at work

wirklich, really

wirr, confused

der Wirt (-e), landlord

das Wirtshaus (∸er), inn

wispern, whisper

wissen (see 127), know

wo, where, somewhere

wobei, during which time

woher, where from

wohin, where to

wohl, well, clearly, most probably, to be sure, all right

wohlwollend, benevolently

wohnen, live

die Wohnung, dwelling-house

das Wohnzimmer (-), sitting-room

das Wölkchen (-), little cloud, cloudlet

die Wolke, cloud

wollen (see 109), will, want, intend

worauf, whereupon

woraus, (made) of what

das Wort (-e), word, promise

wortlos, silently

wozu, for what purpose

wuchernd, rank

wühlen, ransack

wund, sore, grazed

die Wunde, wound

wunderlich, strangely

wundersam, wondrously

die Wundfläche, raw surface of wound

der Wunsch (∸e), wish

würdig, dignified

würgen, choke, suffocate

(*) wurzeln, take root

der Wutausbruch (∸e), outburst of rage

wütend, raging

zahlen, pay

zählen, count

der Zahn (∸e), tooth

das Zahnweh, toothache

zärtlich, fondly

der Zauber, magic

zeichnen, draw

die Zeichnung, drawing

zeigen (auf) (A), point (to), show

der Zeiger (-), hand (of clock)

die Zeit, time, period; **für die nächste —,** for some time to come

der Zeitpunkt (-e), hour, time

die **Zeitung,** newspaper
das **Zelt (-e),** tent
das **Zeltlager (-),** camp
zerbrechen (i, a, o), break, smash; **sich den Kopf —,** rack one's brains
(*) **zerreißen (i, i),** be torn asunder; tear to pieces
zerschunden, grazed
zerstören, destroy
sich **zerstreuen,** scatter
der **Zettel (-),** slip of paper
der **Zeuge (-n, -n),** witness
das **Zeugnis (-se),** report
der **Ziegenstall (-̈e),** goat-shed
(*) **ziehen (o, o),** draw, pull (out); pass, float, go; **gezogen *kommen,** come along
das **Ziel (-e),** aim, destination
zielen, aim
ziemlich, fairly, rather
die **Zigarre,** cigar
die **Zigeunerin (-nen),** gipsy-woman
das **Zimmer (-),** room
die **Zither,** zither
zittern, tremble
das **Zittern,** trembling
der **Zorn,** anger
zornig, angrily
zu, to, for, in; too; shut
die **Zubereitung,** preparation
zu-bringen (a, a), spend
zucken, twitch
zu-drücken, shut tight
zuerst, (at) first
der **Zufall (-̈e),** chance
zufrieden, pleased, satisfied
die **Zufriedenheit,** contentment
der **Zug (-̈e),** train, feature
***zu-gehen (i, a) (auf) (A),** go up (to)
der **Zugführer (-),** guard
zugleich, at the same time
zu-greifen (i, i), help oneself
***zugrunde-gehen (i, a),** perish
zu-hören (D), listen (to)
***zu-kommen (a, o) (auf) (A),** come up (to)

die **Zukunft,** future
zuletzt, at last, finally
zumal, especially as
zumute: wie ist ihm —? how does he feel?
zunächst, nearest
die **Zunge,** tongue
zu-nicken (D), nod to
sich **zurecht-finden (a, u),** find one's way about
zurück, back
zurück-geben (i, a, e), return
zurück-schlagen (ä, u, a), throw back
zurück-streifen, roll back
zurück-weisen (ie, ie), reject
zu-rufen (ie, u) (D), call out to
zusammen, together
***zusammen-brechen (i, a, o),** tumble down, collapse
zusammen-legen, put together, fold up
zusammen-lesen (ie, a, e), collect
zusammen-packen, pack up
(*) **zusammen-schlagen (ä, u, a),** shut with a bang; crash against one another
***zusammen-stoßen (ö, ie, o),** collide
***zusammen-zucken,** start, shudder
zu-schauen (D), watch
der **Zuschauer (-),** spectator
zu-schnüren, lace up
zu-sehen (ie, a, e) (D), watch
der **Zustand (-̈e),** condition, state
***zustande-kommen (a, o),** succeed
***zu-steuern (auf) (A),** make one's way to
zuviel, too much
zuvor, before
***zuvor-kommen (a, o),** prevent, avert
zu-werfen (i, a, o), slam; cast
zuwider, contrary to, unfavourable to, against
zwar, it is true

zweifellos, doubtless
der Zweig (-e), branch, twig
das Zwerglein (-), little dwarf
zwingen (a, u), compel
zwingend, compelling

zwischen, between
der Zwischenfall (ˈ-e), incident, scene
die Zwischenzeit, interval
zwistiglich, squabbling

Vocabulary

English–German

NOTES 1. The plural ending -(e)n of feminine nouns (19(c)) is not indicated.
2. Figures refer to the paragraphs of Section One.

able, to be, können, *see 109*
about, *see 123 and 43(b)ii*
  (= **round**), um (A)
above, über (AD)
abroad, Ausland, *n.*; **to go —,** ins
  A. *fahren, s.
to accept, an-nehmen, *s.*
  accident, Unfall (¨e), *m.*
to accompany, begleiten
to accuse, an-klagen
  accused, der Angeklagte (*see 34*)
  acquaintance, der Bekannte (*see 34*)
  across, hinüber
to act, handeln
  actor, Schauspieler (-), *m.*
  actress, Schauspielerin (-nen), *f.*
to add, hinzu-fügen
  address, Adresse, *f.*
  advantage, Vorteil (-e), *m.*
  advice, Rat, *m.*, Ratschlag (¨e), *m.*
to advise, raten (AD), *s.*
  aeroplane, Flugzeug (-e), *n.*
  afraid, to be, fürchten; **— of,**
  Angst (*f.*) haben vor (D)
  after, *see 34*; **— all,** doch
  afternoon, Nachmittag (-e), *m.*
  afterwards, nachher, darauf
  again, wieder
  against, gegen (A)
  age, Alter, *n.*
  ago, vor (D); **a month —,** vor
  einem Monat; **long —,** längst
  air, Luft (¨e), *f.*
  alive, lebendig
  all, all (79), ganz (83(c))
  allowed, to be, dürfen, *see 109*
  almost, fast
  alone, allein
  along, entlang (A)
  already, schon

to alter, ändern
  although, obgleich
  always, immer
  among, unter (AD)
  anger, Zorn, *m.*
  angry, zornig
  animal, Tier (-e), *n.*
  another, noch ein
to answer, antworten
  answer, Antwort, *f.*
  any, etwas (82); **not —,** nichts, kein
  anybody, irgend jemand, jeder
  anyhow, auf alle Fälle, sowieso
  anything, etwas; **not —,** nichts
to appear, *erscheinen, s.
  appetite, Appetit, *m.*
  apple, Apfel (¨), *m.*
  arm, Arm (-e), *m.*
  arrival, Ankunft (¨e), *f.*
to arrive, *an-kommen, s.
  art, Kunst (¨e), *f.*
  as, wie (8); **— old —,** so alt wie;
  — soon —, sobald; **— well —,**
  wie auch
to ask, *see 123*
  ass, Esel (-), *m.*
  astonishment, Erstaunen, *n.*
  at, an (AD), um (A)
  attempt, Versuch (-e), *m.*
  attentive(ly), aufmerksam
  aunt, Tante, *f.*
  Austria, Österreich, *n.*
  autumn, Herbst, *m.*
to awaken (*tr.*), wecken
  away, entfernt; fort; **go —,** *fort-
  gehen, s.; *verreisen
  axe, Axt (¨e), *f.*

  back, zurück; Rücken, *m.*
  bad(ly), schlecht; (**naughty**), böse

bag, Sack (∺e), *m.*; (= **suitcase**), Koffer (-), *m.*
ball, Ball (∺e), *m.*
Baltic, Ostsee, *f.*
bank (= **river-**), Ufer (-), *n.*; (= **money-**), Bank, *f.*
bare, kahl
barrier, Sperre, *f.*
basket, Korb (∺e), *m.*
bath, Bad (∺er), *n.*
bathe: to have a —, baden
bathroom, Badezimmer (-), *n.*
battle, Schlacht, *f.*
to be, *see 123*
beach, Strand (∺e), *m.*
beast, Tier (-e), *n.*
to beat, schlagen, *s.*, klopfen
beautiful, schön; **most —,** wunderschön
because, weil; **— of it,** deswegen
to become, *werden, irr.
bed, Bett (-(e)s, -en), *n.*
bedroom, Schlafzimmer (-), *n.*
beer, Bier (-e), *n.*
before, *see 123*
to begin, beginnen, *s.*, an-fangen, *s.*
beginning, Beginn (-e), *m.*, Anfang (∺e), *m.*
to behave, sich benehmen, *s.*
behind, hinter (AD)
to believe, glauben (D)
bell, Klingel, *f.*; **the — rings,** es klingelt
to belong, gehören (D)
below, unter (AD)
Berne, Bern
beside, neben (AD)
better, besser
beyond, jenseits (G)
bicycle, Fahrrad (∺er), *n.*
big, groß
bill, Rechnung, *f.*
bird, Vogel (∺), *m.*
birthday, Geburtstag (-e). *m.*
bishop, Bischof (∺e), *m.*
to bite, beißen, *s.*
bitter, bitter
black, schwarz
blackboard, Tafel, *f.*
blanket, Decke, *f.*

blow, Schlag (∺e), *m.*
blunt, stumpf
to board, besteigen, *s.*
boat, Boot (-e), *n.*, Schiff (-e), *n.*
to boil, kochen
to book (ticket), lösen
book, Buch (∺er), *n.*
booty, Raub, *m.*
boring, langweilig, lästig
born, geboren
to borrow, sich (D) borgen
both, beide
bottle, Flasche, *f.*
bough, Ast (∺e), *m.*
boy, Junge (-n, -n), *m.*
branch, Zweig (-e), *m.*
bread, Brot (-e), *n.*
to break, brechen, *s.*
breakfast, Frühstück (-e), *n.*
bridge, Brücke, *f.*
bright(ly), hell
to bring, bringen (AD), *irr.*
brother, Bruder (∺), *m.*
brown, braun
to build, bauen
building, Gebäude (-), *n.*
burglar, Einbrecher (-), *m.*
Burgundy, Burgund, *n.*
to burn, brennen, *irr.*
bus, Omnibus (-se), *m.*, Bus (-se)
business, Geschäft (-e), *n.*
but, *see 8*
butter, Butter, *f.*
to buy, kaufen; **(ticket),** lösen
by, an (AD), bis (A), durch (A), von (D); **— -ing,** indem (*see 122(e)*)

cabin, Kajüte, *f.*
café, Café (-s), *n.*
cake, Kuchen (-), *m.*
to call (out), rufen, *s.*; **call out to,** zu-rufen (AD), *s.*; **call upon (to),** auf-fordern
calm(ly), ruhig
can, können, *see 109*
cap, Mütze, *f.*
capital, Hauptstadt (∺e), *f.*
captain, Haupt-mann (-leute), *m.*

355

car, Auto (-s), *n.*, Wagen (-), *m.*;
— **-driver,** Autofahrer (-), *m.*
care, Sorge, *f.*, Pflege, *f.*
carpenter, Zimmer-mann (-leute),
m.
to **carry,** tragen, *s.*
cart, Wagen (-), *m.*
case, Fall (¨e), *m.*; **in any** —, auf
jeden Fall; (= **suitcase**) Koffer
(-), *m.*
castle, Schloß (¨(ss)er), *n.*
cat, Katze, *f.*
catch, *see 123*; — **sight of,** erblicken
cathedral, Dom (-e), *m.*
cautious, vorsichtig
cave, Höhle, *f.*
to **celebrate,** feiern
central heating, Zentralheizung,
f.
centre, Zentrum, *n.*, Mitte, *f.*; —
of the town, Stadtmitte, *f.*
certain(ly), gewiß, sicher
chair, Stuhl (¨e), *m.*
chalk, Kreide, *f.*
to **change,** *see 123*
Charles, Karl
charming, reizend
cheap, billig
cheek, Wange, *f.*
cheese, Käse (-), *m.*
chemist, Apotheker (-), *m.*; —**'s
shop,** Apotheke, *f.*
chicken, Huhn (¨er), *n.*
child, Kind (-er), *n.*
choice, Wahl, *f.*
to **choose,** wählen
church, Kirche, *f.*
cigarette, Zigarette, *f.*
cinema, Kino (-s), *n.*
circle (theatre), Rang (¨e), *m.*
city, Stadt (¨e), *f.*
class, Klasse, *f.*
classroom, Klassenzimmer (-), *n.*
to **clean,** putzen
clean, sauber
clear, klar
clever, klug
to **climb,** *steigen, *s.*
climb, Aufstieg, *m.*

clock, Uhr, *f.*
to **close** (*intr.*), sich schließen, *s.*
close (*adv.*), dicht
clothes, Kleider, *n. pl.*
cloud, Wolke, *f.*
coat, Rock (¨e), *m.*; (**over-**),
Mantel (¨), *m.*
coffee, Kaffee, *m.*
cold, kalt; Kälte, *f.*
to **collect,** sammeln
Cologne, Köln
colour, Farbe, *f.*
to **come,** *kommen, *s.*
comfortable, bequem
companion, Geselle (-n, -n), *m.*,
Kamerad (-en, -en), *m.*
company, Gesellschaft, *f.*; (**military**), Kompagnie, *f.*
comparison, Vergleich (-e), *m.*
compartment, Abteil (-e), *n.*
composer, Komponist (-en, -en),
m.
concert, Konzert (-e), *n.*
to **connect,** verbinden, *s.*
to **conquer,** erobern
consequence, Folge, *f.*
to **console,** trösten
to **contain,** enthalten, *s.*; fassen
to **continue** (*intr.*), fort-fahren
convenient, bequem
conversation, Unterhaltung, *f.*
to **cook,** kochen
cooking, Kochen, *n.*
cool, kühl
corner, Ecke, *f.*; **-seat,** Eckplatz
(¨e), *m.*
to **correct,** verbessern
correct(ly), richtig
to **cost,** kosten
cottage, Häuschen (-), *n.*, Hütte, *f.*
country, Land (¨er), *n.*; **to the** —,
aufs Land; **in the** —, auf dem
Lande
countryman, Lands-mann
(-leute), *m.*
courage, Mut, *m.*
of **course,** natürlich
cousin, Vetter (-s, -n), *m.*
to **cover,** bedecken
cow, Kuh (¨e), *f.*

to cross, *gehen (s.) über (A), *hinüber-gehen, s.

crossing, Überfahrt, f.

crowd, Menge, f.

to cry (= weep), weinen; (= call out), rufen, s.

cup, Tasse, f.

curtain, Vorhang (-̈e), m.

customer, Kunde (-n, -n), m.

to cut, schneiden, s.

to dance, tanzen

danger, Gefahr, f.

dangerous, gefährlich

to dare, wagen

dark, dunkel

darling, Schatz (-̈e), m.

to dash, *stürzen

daughter, Tochter (-̈), f.

day, Tag (-e), m.

dead, tot

dealer, Händler (-), m.

dear, lieb; (= expensive), teuer

death, Tod, m.

December, Dezember, m.

to decide, beschließen, s., sich entschließen

decision, Entschluß (-̈(ss)e), m.

deed, Tat, f.

deep, tief; (of snow), hoch

to defend, verteidigen

to demand, verlangen

departure, Abreise, f.

to describe, beschreiben, s.

to deserve, verdienen

desk, Schreibtisch (-e), m.; (= school-), Pult (-e), n.; Tisch

to destroy, zerstören

to die, *sterben, s.

difference, Unterschied (-e), m.

different, anders

difficult, schwer, schwierig

difficulty, Schwierigkeit, f.

to dig, graben, s.; — over, umgraben, s. (sep.)

diligent(ly), fleißig

dining-room, Eßzimmer (-), n.

dinner, Mittagessen (-), n.

direction, Richtung, f.; in the —

of, in der Richtung nach (D)

dirty, schmutzig

to disappear, *verschwinden, s.

to discover, entdecken

discovery, Entdeckung, f.

disease, Krankheit, f.

to dismiss, entlassen, s.

distance, Ferne, f.

distant, entfernt

to distinguish, unterscheiden, s.

district, Gegend, f.

to do, tun, s.

doctor, Arzt (-̈e), m.

dog, Hund (-e), m.

door, Tür, f.

down, nieder; (= off), ab; up and —, auf und ab

to draw, zeichnen

drawer, Schublade, f.

drawing, Zeichnung, f.

to dress, kleiden; sich an-ziehen, s.

dress (woman's), Kleid (-er), n.; (= costume), Tracht, f.

to drink, trinken, s.

drinking, Trinken, s.

to drive (intr.), *fahren, s.; (tr.) (car), fahren, s.; (animals), treiben, s.

to dry, trocknen

due: to be — to, sollen, see 109

duke, Herzog (-̈e), m.

dull, langweilig

dust, Staub, m.

dwarf, Zwerg (-e), m.

each, jeder; 2 marks —, 2 Mark das Stück

early, früh

to earn, verdienen

Easter, Ostern (see 22)

easy, leicht

to eat, essen, s.

eating, Essen (-), n.

edge, Rand (-̈er), m.

Edward, Eduard

effect, Wirkung, f.

egg, Ei (-er), n.

either: not —, auch nicht

elderly, älter

357

to elect, wählen
Elizabeth, Elisabeth
embrace, umarmen
emperor, Kaiser (-), *m.*
employee, der Angestellte *(see 34)*
empty, leer
end, Ende (-n), *n.*; (= **destination**), Ziel (-e), *n.*
enemy, Feind (-e), *m.*
engineer, Ingenieur (-e), *m.*
England, England, *n.*
English, englisch
Englishman, Engländer (-), *m.*
Englishwoman, Engländerin (-nen), *f.*
to enjoy (o.s.), *see 123*
enough, genug
entire(ly), ganz
envelope, Umschlag (¨e), *m.*
error, Irrtum (¨er), *m.*
especially, besonders
essay, Aufsatz (¨e), *m.*
estate, Gut (¨er), *n.*
even, *see 123*
evening, Abend (-e), *m.*; **this —,** heute abend
event, Ereignis (-se), *n.*
ever, je
every, jeder
everybody, jeder, jedermann, alle
everything, alles
everywhere, überall
exact(ly), genau
exam(ination), Prüfung, *f.*, Examen (- *or* Examina), *n.*
to examine, untersuchen
example, Beispiel (-e), *n.*
except (for), außer (D)
excited, aufgeregt
excursion, Ausflug (¨e), *m.*
exercise, Aufgabe, *f.*
to expect, erwarten
to explain, erklären (AD)
eye, Auge (-s, -n), *n.*

face, Gesicht (-er), *n.*
in fact, in der Tat
fairly, ziemlich
faithful(ly), treu

to fall, *fallen, s.*; **— asleep,** *einschlafen, s.*
false, falsch
familiar, bekannt
family, Familie, *f.*
famous, berühmt
far, weit
farm, Bauernhof (¨e), *m.*
farmer, Bauer (-s/n, -n), *m.*
fast, schnell; **as — as he could,** so schnell er konnte
fat, dick, fett
father, Vater (¨), *m.*
fear, Furcht, *f.*
to feel, *see 123*
fellow, Kerl (-e), *m.*
fence, Zaun (¨e), *m.*
fête, Fest (-e), *n.*
few, (nur) wenige
field, Feld (-er), *n.*
to fight, kämpfen
fight, Kampf (¨e), *m.*
to fill, füllen
film, Film (-e), *m.*
finally, endlich
to find, finden, *s.*; **— out** (= **discover**), entdecken; (= **learn**), erfahren, *s.*
fine, schön
to finish, *see 123*
finished, fertig
fir(-tree), Tanne, *f.*
fire, Feuer (-), *n.*
firm(ly), fest
first *(adj.),* erst-; *(adv.),* zuerst; **at —,** zuerst
fish, Fisch (-e), *m.*
flat, Wohnung, *f.*
floor, (Fuß-)boden (¨), *m.*
to flow, *fließen, s.*
flower, Blume, *f.*
to fly, (*)fliegen, *s.*
fly, Fliege, *f.*
to follow, *folgen (D)
followers, Gefolge, *n.*
following, folgend
fond: to be — of, gern haben
food, Essen (-), *n.*
fool, Narr (-en, -en), *m.*
foot, Fuß (¨e), *m.*; **on —,** zu Fuß

for (*prep.*), für (A); (*conj.*), denn
to force, zwingen, *s.*
foreign, ausländisch
foreigner, Ausländer (-), *m.*
forest, Wald (⁀er), *m.*
to forget, vergessen, *s.*
fork, Gabel, *f.*
fortnight, vierzehn Tage
fortunately, glücklicherweise
fountain-pen, Füller (-), *m.*
France, Frankreich, *n.*
Fred, Fritz
Frederick, Friedrich
free(ly), frei
to freeze, (*)frieren, *s.*
French, französisch
fresh, frisch
Friday, Freitag (-e), *m.*
friend, Freund (-e), *m.*
friendly, freundlich
to frighten, erschrecken
frightened, to be, *erschrecken, *s.*
from, von (D); aus (D)
in front of, vor (AD)
frontier, Grenze, *f.*
fruit, Obst, *n.*, Frucht (⁀e), *f.*
to fulfil, erfüllen
full, voll
funny, komisch, amüsant
future, Zukunft, *f.*

game, Spiel (-e), *n.*
garden, Garten (⁀), *m.*
gate, Tor (-e), *n.*
to gather, sammeln
gathering, Versammlung, *f.*
gentleman, Herr (-n, -en), *m.*
George, Georg
German (*adj.*), deutsch; (*noun*),
    der Deutsche (*see 34*)
Germany, Deuschland, *n.*
to get, *see 123*
girl, Mädchen (-), *n.*
to give, geben, *s.*
glacier, Gletscher (-), *m.*
glad, froh
glass, Glas (⁀er), *n.*
to go, *see 123*
gold, Gold, *n.*

good, gut
goodbye, auf Wiedersehen
goods, Waren, *f. pl.*
grandfather, Großvater, (⁀), *m.*
grandmother, Großmutter (⁀), *f.*
grandparents, Großeltern, *pl.*
grateful, dankbar
grave(ly), ernst
great, groß
greatly, sehr
green, grün
to greet, grüßen
greeting, Gruß(⁀e), *m.*
grieved at, betrübt über (A)
ground, Erde, *f.*, Boden (⁀), *m.*
grow, *wachsen, *s.*
guard, Garde, *f.*
to guess, raten, *s.*; vermuten
guest, Gast (⁀e), *m.*
gun, Gewehr (-e), *n.*

half (*adj.*), halb; (*noun*) Hälfte, *f.*
half-circle, Halbkreis (-e), *m.*
hall, Saal (Säle), *m.*
hand, Hand (⁀e), *f.*
handkerchief, Taschentuch (⁀er),
    n.
to hang (*intr.*), hängen, *s.*
Hanover, Hannover
Hansel, Hänsel
to happen, *geschehen (D), *s.*
happiness, Glück, *n.*
happy, glücklich
harbour, Hafen (⁀), *m.*
hard (= difficult), schwer,
    schwierig; (*adv.*) fleißig
hardly, kaum
harm, Leid, *n.*
harvest, Ernte, *f.*
hat, Hut (⁀e), *m.*
to hate, hassen
to have, haben; — on, an-haben;
    — to, müssen, *see 109*
head, Kopf (⁀e), *m.*
headache, Kopfschmerzen, *m. pl.*
health, Gesundheit, *f.*
to hear, hören
heart, Herz (-ens, -en), *n.*; by —,
    auswendig

heartily, herzlich
heaven, Himmel (-), *m.*
heavy, schwer
hedge (thorn-), Dornenhecke, *f.*
to help, helfen (D), *s.*
help, Hilfe, *f.*
here, hier, *see 43(a)i*
hero, Held (-en, -en), *m.*
to hesitate, zögern
to hew, hauen, *s.*
to hide (*tr.*), verstecken; (*intr.*), sich verstecken
high, hoch
hill, Hügel (-), *m.*, Berg (-e), *m.*
to hire, mieten
hitherto, bisher
to hold, halten, *s.*
hole, Loch (¨er), *n.*
holiday (= leave), Urlaub, *m.*; **three days'** —, drei Tage Urlaub
holidays, Ferien, *pl.*
home (*adv.*), nach Hause; **at** —, zu Hause
homework, Schularbeit, *f.*
honest, ehrlich
honour, Ehre, *f.*
to hope, hoffen
hope, Hoffnung, *f.*
horse, Pferd (-e), *n.*
horseman, Reiter (-), *m.*
hot, heiß
hotel, Hotel (-s), *n.*
hour, Stunde, *f.*
house, Haus (¨er), *n.*
how, wie
human, menschlich
hungry, hungrig; **to be —,** Hunger haben
huntsman, Jäger (-), *m.*
to hurry, *eilen; — back,* *zurück-eilen
to hurt, verletzen
husband, Mann (¨er), *m.*
hut, Hütte, *f.*

ice, Eis, *n.*
ice-cold, eiskalt
if, *see 8*
ill, krank

to imagine, sich (D) vor-stellen
immediately, sofort
important, bedeutend, wichtig
impossible, unmöglich
impostor, Betrüger (-) *m.*
imprisonment, Gefängnis, *n.*
in (*prep.*), in (AD); (*adv.*), ein, herein (*see 43(a)*)
inconvenient, unbequem
indeed, in der Tat
indoors, im Hause
inhabitant, Einwohner (-), *m.*
ink, Tinte, *f.*
inn, Wirtshaus (¨er), *n.*
inner, inner-
inside, darin, drinnen
instance: for —, zum Beispiel
instead, (an)statt (G)
to intend, die Absicht haben
intention, Absicht, *f.*
interesting, interessant
to interrupt, unterbrechen, *s.*
to introduce, vor-stellen (AD)
invisible, unsichtbar
invitation, Einladung, *f.*
to invite, ein-laden, *s.*
island, Insel, *f.*
Italian, italienisch
Italy, Italien, *n.*

jacket, Jacke, *f.*
January, Januar, *m.*
job, Stelle, *f.*
John, Johann(es)
Joseph, Josef
journey, Reise, *f.*
joy, Freude, *f.*
judge, Richter (—), *m.*
July, Juli, *m.*
to jump, *springen, *s.*
June, Juni, *m.*
just, *see 123*

to keep, *see 123*
key, Schlüssel (-), *m.*
to kill, töten
killing, Töten, *n.*
kilometre, Kilometer (-), *m.*

kind, lieb
king, König (-e), *m.*
to kiss, küssen
kitchen, Küche, *f.*
to kneel, knien
knife, Messer (-), *n.*
to knit, stricken
to knock, schlagen, *s.*, klopfen (*see* 73); — over, um-werfen, *s.*
to know, *see 123*

lady, Dame, *f.*
lake, See (-s, -n), *m.*
lamp, Lampe, *f.*
language, Sprache, *f.*
large, groß
last, letzt-; at —, endlich, zuletzt
late, *see 123*
to laugh, lachen
law, Gesetz (-e), *n.*
to lay (table), decken
lazy, faul
to lead, führen
to learn, *see 123*
at least, wenigstens
leather, Leder, *n.*
to leave, *see 123*
leg, Bein (-e), *n.*
to lend, leihen (AD), *s.*
to let (= allow), lassen, *s.*; (= hire out), vermieten
letter-box, Briefkasten (ᛦ), *m.*
library, Bibliothek, *f.*
to lie, *see 123*; (= tell lies), lügen, *s.*
Liège, Lüttich
life, Leben (-), *n.*
to lift, heben, *s.*
to light, an-zünden
light (= not dark), hell; (= not heavy), leicht; Licht (-er), *n.*
to like, *see 123*
like, wie
line, Zeile, *f.*
liner, Dampfer (-), *m.*
to listen, zu-hören (D)
litre, Liter (-), *n. or m.*
little, klein; (= not much), wenig
to live, leben; wohnen

loaf, Brot (-e), *n.*
to lock, zu-schließen, *s.*
long (*adj.*), lang; (*adv.*), lange; a — time, lange; all day —, den ganzen Tag; — ago, längst
no longer, nicht mehr
to look, *see 123*
loom, Webstuhl (ᛦe), *m.*
lord, Edel-mann (-leute *or* -männer), *m.*
to lose, verlieren, *s.*; (*see 123*)
lot, Menge, *f.*; a — of, viel
loud, laut
to love, lieben
lovely, schön
loyal, treu
luggage, Gepäck, *n.*
lunch, Mittagessen (-), *n.*

magnificent, herrlich
maid, Mädchen (-), *n.*
main road, Hauptstraße, *f.*
main station, Hauptbahnhof (ᛦe), *m.*
to maintain, behaupten
to make, machen; lassen, *s.* (*see 109(b)vii*)
man, Mann (ᛦer), *m.*
to manage, *gelingen, *s.* (*see 105(b)*)
many, viele
March, März, *m.*
Margaret, Margarete
mark, Mark (-), *f.*
marvellous, wunderbar
Mary, Marie
master, *see 123*
to matter: it does not—, es schadet nichts
May, Mai, *m.*
meadow, Wiese, *f.*
meal, Mahlzeit, *f.*
meaning, Bedeutung, *f.*
meanwhile, unterdessen
medicine, Medizin, *f.*
to meet, treffen, *s.*, *begegnen (D); (at station), ab-holen
merchant, Kauf-mann (-leute), *m.*
merely, nur
merry, fröhlich

361

midday, Mittag (-e), *m.*
middle, Mitte, *f.*
mile, Meile, *f.*
milk, Milch, *f.*
minister, Minister (-), *m.*
minute, Minute, *f.*
mirror, Spiegel (-), *m.*
to miss, verpassen
mist, Nebel (-), *m.*
mistake, Fehler (-), *m.*
modern, modern
moment, Augenblick (-e), *m.*; **at that —,** in diesem Augenblick
money, Geld (-er), *n.*
month, Monat (-e), *m.*
mood, Stimmung, *f.*
moon, Mond (-e), *m.*
more, mehr
morning, Morgen; **this —,** heute morgen
mother, Mutter (¨), *f.*
mountain, Berg (-e), *m.*
mouse, Maus (¨e), *f.*
mouth, Mund (¨er), *m.*
to move (*intr.*), sich bewegen; (= **change abode**), *um-ziehen, s.; — **away,** *fort-ziehen, s.
Mr, Herr (-n, -en), *m.*
Mrs, Frau, *f.*
much, viel, sehr, sehr viel
music, Musik, *f.*
must, müssen, *see 109*

name, Name (-ns, -n), *m.*
narrow, eng, schmal
national, national; — **dress,** Nationaltracht, *f.*
near, nah, in der Nähe (G *or* von)
nearest, nächst-
nearly, fast
neck, Hals (¨e), *m.*
to need, brauchen
neighbour, Nachbar (-s/n, -n), *m.*; Nachbarin (-nen), *f.*
neither; — ... **nor,** weder ... noch
nephew, Neffe (-n, -n), *m.*
never, nie
nevertheless, doch

new, neu
news, Nachrichten, *f. pl.*
newspaper, Zeitung, *f.*
next, nächst-
nice(ly), schön
night, Nacht (¨e), *f.*; **last —,** gestern abend
no, nein; kein
noble, edel
noise, Lärm, *m.*, Geräusch (-e), *n.*
nonsense, Unsinn, *m.*
noon, Mittag, *m.*
north, Norden, *m.*; **-east,** Nordosten, *m.*; — **Sea,** Nordsee, *f.*
nose, Nase, *f.*
not, nicht; **—a,** kein; **—any more,** nicht mehr; **— at all,** gar nicht
note (bank-), Schein (-e), *m.*; **hundred-mark —,** Hundertmarkschein; (= **letter**), Schreiben (-), *n.*
to notice, bemerken
novel, Roman (-e), *m.*
now, jetzt; **by —,** schon; **— and then,** ab und zu
nowadays, heutzutage
nowhere, nirgends
number, *see 123*

oak (tree), Eiche, *f.*
to obey, gehorchen (D)
object, Gegenstand (¨e), *m.*
off, ab
to offer, an-bieten (AD), *s.*
office, Büro (-s), *n.*; (= **position**), Amt (¨er), *n.*
official, der Beamte (*see 34*)
often, oft
old, alt; — **man,** der Alte (*see 34*)
once, einmal; **at —,** sofort
only, *see 123*
to open (*tr.*), öffnen, auf-machen; (*intr.*), sich öffnen
open(ly), offen; **in the —,** im Freien
opinion, Meinung, *f.*
opportunity, Gelegenheit, *f.*
opposite, gegenüber (D)
to order, *see 123*

order, *see 123*
other, ander-; the — day, neulich
otherwise, sonst
out, aus, heraus, hinaus; — of,
   aus (D)
outside, draußen
to overtake, ein-holen
own, eigen

to pack, packen
page, Seite, *f.*
painter, Maler (-), *m.*
pale, blaß
paper, Papier (-e), *n.*; (= newspaper), Zeitung, *f.*; — basket,
   Papierkorb (ᵁe), *m.*
parcel, Paket (-e), *n.*
parents, Eltern, *pl.*
part, Teil (-e), *m.*
particularly, besonders
to pass, *vorüber-gehen, *s.*
passenger, der Reisende (*see 34*)
past, vorbei, vorüber
patient, der Kranke (*see 34*)
pattern, Muster (-), *n.*
to pay, zahlen (AD)
peace, Friede (-ns), *m.*
peasant, Bauer (-s/n, -n)
peculiar, sonderbar, komisch
pen, Feder, *f.*
pencil, Bleistift (-e), *m.*
people, Leute, *pl.*; (= one) man;
   (= nation), Volk (ᵁer), *n.*
perhaps, vielleicht
permission, Erlaubnis (-se), *f.*
picture, Bild (-er), *n.*
piece, Stück (-e), *n.*; — of music,
   Musikstück, *n.*
pig, Schwein (-e), *n.*
pipe, Pfeife, *f.*
place, Ort (-e), *m.*, Stelle, *f.*; in
   your —, an Ihrer Stelle
plain, Ebene, *f.*
plan, Plan (ᵁe), *m.*
plate, Teller (-), *m.*
platform, Bahnsteig (-e), *m.*
to play, spielen
play, Schauspiel(-e), *n.*, Stück
   (-e), *n.*

pleasant, angenehm
please, bitte!
pleased, froh
pleasure, Vergnügen (-), *n.*
plenty (of), viel
pocket, Tasche, *f.*
poem, Gedicht (-e), *n.*
poet, Dichter (-), *m.*
point, Punkt (-e), *m.*; to be on
   the — of, im Begriff *sein
pointed, gespitzt
police, Polizei, *f.*
policeman, Polizist (-en, -en),
   m.; Schutz-mann (-leute), *m.*
polite(ly), höflich
poor, arm; — man, der Arme (*see
   34*)
port, Hafen (ᵁ), *m.*
porter, Gepäckträger (-), *m.*
to possess, besitzen, *s.*
possible, möglich
possibility, Möglichkeit, *f.*
postman, Briefträger (-), *m.*
potato, Kartoffel, *f.*
pound, Pfund (-e), *n.*; *see 50*
powder, Pulver (-), *n.*
power, Macht (ᵁe), *f.*; Great —,
   Großmacht, *f.*
powerful, mächtig
to practise, üben
to praise, loben
precious stone, Edelstein (-e), *m.*
to prefer, vor-ziehen, *s.*; *see 122(k)*
to prepare, bereiten
prepared, bereit
to prescribe, verordnen
prescription, Verordnung, *f.*
present, Geschenk (-e), *n.*
president, Präsident (-en, -en), *m.*
to pretend, tun (*s.*), als ob
pretext, Vorwand (ᵁe), *m.*
pretty, hübsch
prick, Stich (-e), *m.*
prince, Fürst (-en, -en), *m.*;
   (= King's son), Prinz (-en,
   -en), *m.*
prison, Gefängnis (-se), *n.*
prisoner, der Gefangene (*see 34*)
prize, Preis (-e), *m.*
probably, wahrscheinlich

problem, Problem (-e), *n.*
progress, Fortschritt (-e), *m.*
to prohibit, verbieten (AD), *s.*
to promise, versprechen (AD), *s.*
proud, stolz
to prove, beweisen, *s.*
punctual(ly), pünktlich
to punish, strafen
pupil, Schüler (-), *m.*; Schülerin (-nen), *f.*
puppy, junger Hund (-e), *m.*
purpose, Zweck (-e), *m.*
to push, schieben, *s.*

quality, Eigenschaft, *f.*
quarter, Viertel (-), *n.*; — **of an hour,** Viertelstunde, *f.*
queen, Königin (-nen), *f.*
question, Frage, *f.*
quick(ly), schnell
quietness, Ruhe, *f.*
quite, ganz

rabbit, Kaninchen (-), *n.*
radio, Radioapparat(-e), *m.*; Radio, *n.*
rack, Netz (-e), *n.*
rail(way), (Eisen)bahn, *f.*
to rain, regnen
rain, Regen (-), *m.*
raincoat, Regenmantel (⸚), *m.*
to raise, höher machen, erhöhen
rare(ly), selten
rather, ziemlich
to reach, reichen; (= get to), erreichen
to read, lesen, *s.*; — **aloud,** vor-lesen (AD)
reading, Lesen, *n.*
ready, fertig; (= **prepared**), bereit
really, wirklich
realm, Reich (-e), *n.*
reason, Grund (⸚e), *m.*; **for this** —, aus diesem Grund
to receive, erhalten, *s.*
to recognise, erkennen, *irr.*
red, rot
to remain, *bleiben, *s.*

to remember, *see 123*
to reply, erwidern
to report, berichten (AD)
to rest, *see 123*
restaurant, Restaurant (-s), *n.*
result, Resultat (-e), *n.*; **as a** — **of,** infolge (G)
to return, *zurück-kehren
Rhine, Rhein, *m.*
rich, reich
rid: to get — **of,** *los-werden, *irr.*
to ride, (*) reiten, *s.*; — **a horse,** auf einem Pferd *reiten; — **nearer to,** näher an (A) *heran-reiten; — **a bicycle,** mit dem Rad *fahren, *s.*
right, to be, recht haben
right(ly), recht, ganz; **to put** —, in Ordnung bringen, *irr.*; **to be all** —, ganz in Ordnung *sein, *irr.*
to ring, klingeln; **the bell rings,** es klingelt; — **up,** an-rufen, *s.*
ripe, reif
to rise, *auf-stehen, *s.*; (**sun**), aufgehen, *s.*
river, Fluß (⸚(ss)e), *m.*
road, Straße, *f.*
robber, Räuber (-), *m.*
rock, Felsen (-), *m.*
roof, Dach (⸚er), *n.*
room, Zimmer (-), *n.*, Raum (⸚e), *m.*
rope, Seil (-e), *n.*
round, um (A)
row, Reihe, *f.*
to rub, reiben, *s.*
rucksack, Rucksack (⸚e), *m.*
to run, *laufen, *s.*; — **over,** überfahren, *s. (insep.)*
running, Laufen, *n.*
to rush, *stürzen
Russia, Rußland, *n.*
Russian, Russe (-n, -n), *m.*

safe, sicher
sail, Segel (-), *n.*
salt, Salz (-e), *n.*
same, derselbe

satisfied, zufrieden
sausage, Wurst (-̈e), f.
to save, retten; (money), sparen
to say, sagen (AD)
scarcely, kaum
school, Schule, f.; at —, in der Schule; to —, zur Schule
Scotland, Schottland, n.
Scotsman, Schotte (-n, -n), m.
Scottish, schottisch
sea, See, f., Meer (-e), n.; at the —side, am Meer; —beast, Seetier (-e), n.
search, Suche, f.; in — of, auf der Suche nach (D)
seat, Platz (-̈e), m.
to see, sehen, s.; — somebody to (= accompany), begleiten
to seem, scheinen, s.
to seize, fassen
seldom, selten
to sell, verkaufen (AD)
to send, schicken (AD)
sentence, Satz (-̈e), m.
serious, ernst
servant, Diener (-), m.; (Dienst-) mädchen (-), n.
to serve, dienen (D)
sesame, Sesam, m.
to set (sun), *unter-gehen, s.; — off, *ab-fahren
set, Apparat (-e), m.
several, mehrere
severe, streng
severity, Strenge, f.
to sew, nähen
shade, Schatten (-), m.
shadow, Schatten (-), m.
shady, schattig
to shake, schütteln
to shine, scheinen, s.
ship, Schiff (-e), n.
shirt, Hemd (-(e)s, -en), n.
shoe, Schuh (-e), m.
shop, Laden (-̈), m.
shore, Ufer (-), n.
short(ly), kurz
to shout, rufen, s.
shout, Ruf (-e), m.
to show, zeigen (AD)

to shriek, schreien, s.
to shut (tr.), schließen, s., zu- machen; (intr.), sich schließen, s.
side, Seite, f.
sight, see 123
sign, Zeichen (-), n.; Spur, f.
silly, dumm
silver, Silber, n.
simple, einfach
since, see 8
to sing, singen, s.
single, einzig
sister, Schwester, f.
to sit, see 123
sitting-room, Wohnzimmer (-), n.
situation, Lage, f.
skin (animal's), Fell (-e), n.
sky, Himmel (-), m.
to sleep, schlafen, s.
sleep, Schlaf, m.
Sleeping Beauty, Dornröschen, n.
slow(ly), langsam
slowness, Langsamkeit, f.
small, klein
to smoke, rauchen
smoking, Rauchen, n.
to snow, schneien
snow, Schnee, m.; -white (adj.), schneeweiß
Snow White, Schneewittchen, n.
so, see 123
sofa, Sofa (-s), n.
soft (= not loud), leise
soldier, Soldat (-en, -en), m.
to solve, lösen
some, einige
somebody, jemand; — else, je- mand anders
something, etwas
sometimes, manchmal
somewhere, irgendwo
son, Sohn (-̈e), m.
song, Lied (-er), n.
soon, bald; as — as, sobald
sore: — throat, Halsschmerzen, m. pl.
sorry, to be, leid tun (D), s.; I am —, es tut mir leid

sort, Art; **that — of thing,** so etwas; **all —s of,** allerlei

soul, Seele, *f.*

to sound, (*) erschallen

sound, Laut (-e), *m.*

South, Süden, *m.*; **— America** Südamerika, *n.*; **— Germany,** Süddeutschland, *n*; **the — of France,** Südfrankreich, *n.*

Spanish, spanisch

to speak, sprechen, *s.*

speaker, Redner (-), *m.*

special, besonder-

spectator, Zuschauer (-), *m.*

speech, Rede, *f.*

to speed, *rasen

to spend, *see 123*

spirit, Geist (-er), *m.*

in spite of, trotz (G); **— the fact that,** trotzdem

spot, Stelle, *f.*

to spread (*intr.*), sich verbreiten

to spring (of river), *entspringen, *s.*

spring, Frühling (-e), *m.*

square, Platz (ːe), *m.*

stable, Stall (ːe), *m.*

stairs, Treppe, *f.*

stamp, Briefmarke, *f.*; **— collection,** Briefmarkensammlung, *f.*

stand, stehen, *s.*; **— out,** abstechen, *s.*

to start, *see 123*

station, Bahnhof (ːe), *m.*

to stay, *bleiben, *s.*

stay, Aufenthalt (-e), *m.*

to steal, stehlen, *s.*

step, Schritt (-e), *m.*

stepmother, Stiefmutter (ː), *f.*

to stick, kleben

stick, Stock (ːe), *m.*

still, *see 123*

stocking, Strumpf (ːe), *m.*

stone, Stein (-e), *m.*; **precious —,** Edelstein (-e), *m.*

to stop, *see 123*

storeroom, Vorratskammer, *f.*

story, Geschichte, *f.*, Erzählung, *f.*

stout, dick

strange, sonderbar, komisch

stranger, der Fremde (*see 34*)

straw, Stroh, *n.*

street, Straße, *f.*

to strike, schlagen, *s.*

string, Schnur (ːe), *f.*

strong(ly), stark

student, Student (-en, -en), *m.*

study, Studierzimmer (-), *n.*

stuff, Zeug (-e), *n.*

stupid, dumm

to succeed, *gelingen (D); **I succeed,** es gelingt mir

success, Erfolg (-e), *m.*

such, solch

sudden(ly), plötzlich

sugar, Zucker, *m.*

suit, Anzug (ːe), *m.*

suitcase, Koffer (-), *m.*

sum, Summe, *f.*

summer, Sommer, *m.*; **— holidays,** Sommerferien, *pl.*

sun, Sonne, *f.*

sunshine, Sonnenschein, *m.*

supper, Abendessen (-), *n.*

to suppose, an-nehmen, *s.*

to surprise, überraschen

surprise, Überraschung, *f.*

surprised, to be, erstaunt *sein (*irr.*) über (A) (= at)

sweet(ly), süß

to swim, (*)schwimmen, *s.*

swim; to have a —, (*)schwimmen, *s.*

Switzerland, Schweiz, *f.*

sword, Schwert (-er), *n.*

sympathy, Mitleid, *n.*

table, Tisch (-e), *m.*

tailor, Schneider (-), *m.*

to take, *see 123*; **— place,** stattfinden, *s.* (*sep.*)

to talk, sprechen, *s.*, reden

tall, hoch, groß

to taste, schmecken (D)

tea, Tee, *m.*; **have —,** Tee trinken, *s.*

to teach, lehren

teacher, Lehrer (-), *m.*; Lehrerin (-nen), *f.*

tear, Träne, *f.*

to tell, sagen (AD); — (a story to), erzählen (AD)

temperature: to have a —, Fieber (n.) haben

tender, Tender (-), m.

tennis, Tennis, n.

tent, Zelt (-e), n.

terrible, schrecklich

Thames, Themse, f.

to thank, danken (D); thank you, danke!

thanks, Dank, m.

that, see 123

theatre, Theater (-), n.

then, see 123

there, da, dort, see 43(a)i

thereupon, darauf

thick, dick

thief, Dieb (-e), m.

thin, dünn

thing, see 123

to think, glauben, denken, irr., see 123

this, dieser

thorn hedge, Dornenhecke, f.

thorough(ly), gründlich

throat: sore —, Halsschmerzen, m. pl.

through, durch (A)

to throw, werfen, s.

to thunder, donnern

Thursday, Donnerstag (-e), m.

thus, so

ticket, Fahrkarte, f.

tidy, ordentlich

to tie, binden, s.

tight, straff

till (conj.), bis; (prep.), bis (A)

time, see 123

tired, müde

to, zu (D), nach (D), an (A), auf (A)

tobacco, Tabak, m.

today, heute

together, zusammen

tomorrow, morgen

too, zu; (= also), auch

top (of the hill), Gipfel (-), m.; at the —, oben

towards, gegen (A)

tower, Turm (¨e), m.

town, Stadt (¨e), f.

trace, Spur, f.

traffic, Verkehr, m.

train, Zug (¨e), m.

tram, die Elektrische, see 34, Straßenbahn, f.

to translate, übersetzen

translation, Übersetzung, f.

to travel, *fahren, s.

traveller, der Reisende (see 34)

travels, Reisen, f. pl.

treasure, Schatz (¨e), m.

to treat, behandeln

tree, Baum (¨e), m.

tributary, Nebenfluß (¨(ss)e), m.

trouble, Mühe, f.

true, wahr

truth, Wahrheit, f.

to try, versuchen

Tuesday, Dienstag, m.

twice, zweimal

ugly, häßlich

umbrella, Regenschirm (-e), m.

uncle, Onkel (-), m.

uncomfortable, unbequem

Underground Railway, Untergrundbahn, f.

to understand, verstehen, s.

to undress (intr.), sich aus-ziehen, s.

unemployed, der Arbeitslose (see 34)

unexpected, unerwartet

unfortunately, leider

unfriendly, unfreundlich

unhappy, unglücklich

unhurt, unverletzt

unknown, unbekannt

unless, wenn . . . nicht

unpleasant, unangenehm

until, bis

untrue, falsch

unusual, ungewöhnlich

up, auf; — and down, auf und ab

upper (circle), zweit-

to use, gebrauchen, benutzen

usual(ly), gewöhnlich
to utter (a shout), aus-stoßen, *s.*

in vain, umsonst
vegetable, Gemüse (-), *n.*
very, sehr
via, über (A)
victory, Sieg (-e), *m.*
view, Blick (-e), *m.*; Aussicht, *f.*
village, Dorf (⸚er), *n.*
virtue, Tugend, *f.*
to visit, besuchen
visit, Besuch (-e), *m.*
visitor, Besucher (-), *m.*
voice, Stimme, *f.*

to wait, warten
waiter, Kellner (-), *m.*
waiting-room, Wartesaal (-säle), *m.*
to wake (*intr.*), *erwachen, *aufwachen (*sep.*)
to walk, *gehen, *s.*, *laufen, *s.*
walk (= **hike**), Wanderung, *f.*; (= **stroll**), Spaziergang (⸚e), *m.*; **an hour's —**, eine Stunde zu laufen
wall, Wand (⸚e), *f.*; (**exterior**), Mauer, *f.*
wallet, Brieftasche, *f.*
to want, wollen, *see 109*
war, Krieg (-e), *m.*
warm(ly), warm
to warn, warnen
to wash (*tr.*), waschen, *s.*; (*intr.*), sich waschen, *s.*
to watch, zu-sehen (D), *s.*
watch, Uhr, *f.*
water, Wasser (-), *n.*
way (= **path**), Weg (-e), *m.*; (= **manner**), Weise; **— one walks**, Gang, *m.*
weak, schwach
to wear, tragen, *s.*
weariness, Müdigkeit, *f.*
weather, Wetter (-), *n.*
to weave, weben
weaver, Weber (-), *m.*
Wednesday, Mittwoch, *m.*

week, Woche, *f.*
to welcome, empfangen, *s.*
well (*adj.*), gesund; (*adv.*), gut
wet, naß
what, was; **— . . . like**, wie
wheel, Rad (⸚er), *n.*
when, wann, wenn, als, *see 8*
whenever, wenn
where, wo, *see 44*
whether, ob
which, der, welcher
while, *see 8*
to whistle, pfeifen, *s.*
white, weiß
who, wer
whole, ganz
why, warum; denn, ja, *see 124*
wide, breit; weit
wife, Frau, *f.*
wild, wild
will, Wille (-ns), *m.*
William, Wilhelm
willing, to be, wollen, *see 109*
willingly, gern
to win, gewinnen, *s.*
window, Fenster (-), *n.*
to wind up, auf-ziehen, *s.*
wine, Wein (-e), *m.*
winter, Winter, *m.*
to wish, wünschen
with, mit (D)
without, ohne (A)
woman, Frau, *f.*
wood (= **material**), Holz (⸚er), *n.*, (= **forest**), Wald (⸚er), *m.*
word (**related**), Wort (-e), *n.*; (**unrelated**), Wort (⸚er), *n.*, Vokabel, *f.*
to work, arbeiten
work, *see 123*
world, Welt, *f.*
wretched, elend
to write, schreiben, *s.*
writer, Schriftsteller (-), *m.*
wrong, to be, unrecht haben

yard (= **measurement**), Meter (-), *n. or m.*; (**court-**), Hof (⸚e), *m.*

year, Jahr (-e), *n.*
yellow, gelb
yes, ja
yesterday, gestern; — afternoon,
  gestern nachmittag

yet: not —, noch nicht
young, jung
youth, Jüngling (-e), *m.*; junger
  Mann

Index to Grammar

(The numbers refer to the paragraphs)